Lecture Notes in Computer Science   8666

Commenced Publication in 1973
Founding and Former Series Editors:
Gerhard Goos, Juris Hartmanis, and Jan van Leeuwen

Editorial Board

David Hutchison
Lancaster University, UK

Takeo Kanade
Carnegie Mellon University, Pittsburgh, PA, USA

Josef Kittler
University of Surrey, Guildford, UK

Jon M. Kleinberg
Cornell University, Ithaca, NY, USA

Alfred Kobsa
University of California, Irvine, CA, USA

Friedemann Mattern
ETH Zurich, Switzerland

John C. Mitchell
Stanford University, CA, USA

Moni Naor
Weizmann Institute of Science, Rehovot, Israel

Oscar Nierstrasz
University of Bern, Switzerland

C. Pandu Rangan
Indian Institute of Technology, Madras, India

Bernhard Steffen
TU Dortmund University, Germany

Demetri Terzopoulos
University of California, Los Angeles, CA, USA

Doug Tygar
University of California, Berkeley, CA, USA

Gerhard Weikum
Max Planck Institute for Informatics, Saarbruecken, Germany

Andrea Bondavalli
Felicita Di Giandomenico (Eds.)

Computer Safety, Reliability, and Security

33rd International Conference, SAFECOMP 2014
Florence, Italy, September 10-12, 2014
Proceedings

 Springer

Volume Editors

Andrea Bondavalli
University of Florence
Department of Mathematics and Informatics
Florence, Italy
E-mail: bondavalli@unifi.it

Felicita Di Giandomenico
ISTI-CNR
Pisa, Italy
E-mail: felicita.digiandomenico@isti.cnr.it

ISSN 0302-9743   e-ISSN 1611-3349
ISBN 978-3-319-10505-5   e-ISBN 978-3-319-10506-2
DOI 10.1007/978-3-319-10506-2
Springer Cham Heidelberg New York Dordrecht London

Library of Congress Control Number: 2014946200

LNCS Sublibrary: SL 2 – Programming and Software Engineering

© Springer International Publishing Switzerland 2014

This work is subject to copyright. All rights are reserved by the Publisher, whether the whole or part of the material is concerned, specifically the rights of translation, reprinting, reuse of illustrations, recitation, broadcasting, reproduction on microfilms or in any other physical way, and transmission or information storage and retrieval, electronic adaptation, computer software, or by similar or dissimilar methodology now known or hereafter developed. Exempted from this legal reservation are brief excerpts in connection with reviews or scholarly analysis or material supplied specifically for the purpose of being entered and executed on a computer system, for exclusive use by the purchaser of the work. Duplication of this publication or parts thereof is permitted only under the provisions of the Copyright Law of the Publisher's location, in ist current version, and permission for use must always be obtained from Springer. Permissions for use may be obtained through RightsLink at the Copyright Clearance Center. Violations are liable to prosecution under the respective Copyright Law.
The use of general descriptive names, registered names, trademarks, service marks, etc. in this publication does not imply, even in the absence of a specific statement, that such names are exempt from the relevant protective laws and regulations and therefore free for general use.
While the advice and information in this book are believed to be true and accurate at the date of publication, neither the authors nor the editors nor the publisher can accept any legal responsibility for any errors or omissions that may be made. The publisher makes no warranty, express or implied, with respect to the material contained herein.

Typesetting: Camera-ready by author, data conversion by Scientific Publishing Services, Chennai, India

Printed on acid-free paper

Springer is part of Springer Science+Business Media (www.springer.com)

Preface

This year we celebrate the 33rd edition of SAFECOMP, a major forum to provide ample opportunity for academic and industrial researchers to exchange insights and experience on emerging methods, approaches and practical solutions in the areas of safety, security and reliability of critical computer applications. Since it was established in 1979 by the European Workshop on Industrial Computer Systems, Technical Committee 7 on Reliability, Safety and Security (EWICS TC7), SAFECOMP has contributed to the progress of the state-of-the-art in dependable application of computers in safety-related and safety-critical systems.

This year SAFECOMP is organized within FLORENCE 2014 a one-week scientific event on the development of safe, secure, dependable and performing systems covering design and assessment both from a quantitative and a formal perspective. Together with SAFECOMP 2014 the other major event is Quantitative Evaluation of SysTems – QEST 2014. Many other satellite events, in addition to the six SAFECOMP workshops, are taking place, such as FORMATS (the International Conference on Formal Modeling and Analysis of Timed Systems), EPEW (the European Workshop on Performance Engineering) and FMICS (the International Workshop on Formal Methods for Industrial Critical Systems).

We are very proud to present this year's SAFECOMP program, which includes 20 research papers and 3 reports on practical experience and tools, out of 85 submissions from 22 countries. Four keynotes given by outstanding representatives from academia (Prof. Henrique Madeira and Prof. Philip Koopman), industry (Mr. Philippe Quere) and EU Research Programs (Mr. Werner Steinhoegl) enrich the program. We are grateful to them for their invaluable contribution in providing additional fuel for fruitful discussion and inspiration for research.

Following the tradition of thoroughness of this conference, all the manuscripts went through a rigorous review process by the 48 members of the Program Committee and a number of external reviewers. Then, final discussion was held at the plenary meeting on May 7th in Pisa, attended by 24 PC members, where the papers appearing in the program were selected.

We would like to express our deep gratitude to the PC members, who contributed their expertise and time from their busy schedules before, during, and after the PC meeting to ensure the quality of the reviewing and shepherding processes. We also greatly appreciate the efforts and expertise of the external reviewers. Of course, we would like to gratefully acknowledge and thank all the authors for their effort in submitting papers!

Several other individuals deserve our gratitude for their help, guidance, visible and invisible work in preparing the conference, among them the EWICS TC7 Chair Francesca Saglietti, the Worskhop Chair Frank Ortmeier, the Industry-Liaison Chair Michael Paulitsch, the Publicity Chair Francesco Flammini, the

Publication Chair Andrea Ceccarelli, the Local Organizing Chair Paolo Lollini and his team (Nicola Nostro, Leonardo Montecchi, Andreia Rossi, Marco Mori, Valentina Bonfiglio) and our Finance Chair Ettore Ricciardi.

Finally, we warmly welcome all the attendees in Florence and wish a very interesting, fruitful, and enjoyable conference!

September 2014   Andrea Bondavalli
                                                        Felicita Di Giandomenico

Organization

EWICS TC7 Chair

Francesca Saglietti   University of Erlangen-Nuremberg, Germany

General Chair

Andrea Bondavalli   University of Florence, Italy

Program Co-Chairs

Andrea Bondavalli   University of Florence, Italy
Felicita Di Giandomenico   ISTI-CNR, Italy

Workshop and Tutorial Chair

Frank Ortmeier   Otto -v.-Guericke-Univ. Magdeburg, Germany

Industry-Liaison Chair

Michael Paulitsch   AIRBUS Group, Germany

Finance Chair

Ettore Ricciardi   ISTI-CNR, Italy

Publication Chair

Andrea Ceccarelli   University of Florence, Italy

Publicity Chair

Francesco Flammini   Ansaldo STS, Italy

Local Organizing Chair

Paolo Lollini   University of Florence, Italy

Program Committee

Stuart Anderson	University of Edinburgh, UK
Friedemann Bitsch	Thales Transportation Systems GmbH, Germany
Robin Bloomfield	ADELARD, UK
Sandro Bologna	Associazione Italiana Esperti in Infrastructure Critiche (AIIC), Italy
Andrea Bondavalli	University of Florence, Italy
Jens Braband	Technische Universität Braunschweig, Germany
Francesco Brancati	Resiltech S.R.L., Italy
Domenico Cotroneo	University of Naples Federico II, Italy
Bojan Cukic	West Virginia University, USA
Salvatore D'Antonio	University of Naples "Parthenope", Italy
Peter Daniel	SELEX ELSAG, UK
Felicita Di Giandomenico	ISTI-CNR, Italy
Kevin R. Driscoll	Honeywell Laboratories, USA
Wolfgang Ehrenberger	Hochschule Fulda - University of Applied Sciences, Germany
Massimo Felici	HP Lab., UK
Francesco Flammini	Ansaldo-STS, Italy
Barbara Gallina	Mälardalen University, Sweden
Janusz Górski	Gdansk University of Technology, Poland
Jérémie Guiochet	LAAS, CNRS, France
Mohamed Kaaniche	LAAS, CNRS, France
Nobuyasu Kanekawa	Hitachi, Japan
Karama Kanoun	LAAS, CNRS, France
Johan Karlsson	Chalmers University, Sweden
John Knight	University of Virginia, USA
Phil Koopman	Carnegie Mellon University, USA
Floor Koornneef	TU Delft, Netherlands
Giuseppe Lami	ISTI-CNR, Italy
Søren Lindskov Hansen	Novonordisk A/S, Denmark
Michael Lyu	University of Hong Kong, Hong Kong
Istvan Majzik	Budapest University of Technology and Economics, Hungary
Fabio Martinelli	IIT-CNR, Italy
Paolo Masci	Queen Mary University, UK
Fatima Mattiello	INPE, Brasil
Silvia Mazzini	Intecs SpA, Italy
Nuno Neves	University of Lisbon, Portugal
Odd Nordland	SINTEF, Norway
Frank Ortmeier	Otto -v.-Guericke-Univ. Magdeburg, Germany
Michael Paulitsch	AIRBUS Group, Germany

Alexander Romanovosky	University of Newcastle, UK
John Rushby	SRI International, USA
Francesca Saglietti	University of Erlangen-Nuremberg, Germany
Christoph Schmitz	Zühlke Engineering AG, Switzerland
Erwin Schoitsch	AIT Austrian Institute of Technology, Austria
Christel Seguin	ONERA, France
Nuno Silva	Critical Software SA, Portugal
Amund Skavhaug	NTNU, Norway
Wilfried Steiner	TTTech, Austria
Mark Sujan	University of Warwick, UK
Elena Troubistsyna	Åbo Akademi University, Finland
Tatsuhiro Tsuchiya	Osaka University, Japan

External Reviewers

Aaron Kane	Leanid Krautsevich
Aikaterini Mitrokotsa	Linas Laibinis
Anatoliy Gorbenko	Linling Sun
András Vörös	Ludovic Pintard
Andre Didier	Malcolm Taylor
Andrea Domenici	Maria Vigliotti
Anna Lanzaro	Mario Fusani
Artsiom Yautsiukhin	Mathilde Machin
Carlo Clarotti	Milda Zizyte
Dan Sheridan	Nicola Nostro
David Powell	Pablo Gutierrez Peon
Davide Iacono	Pierre Bieber
Fanny Dufossé	Robert Buchholz
Fei Xia	Robert Stroud
Felix Hutchison	Roberto Natella
Francesco Fucci	Roberto Pietrantuono
Francesco Santini	Tanja Hebecker
Ilaria Matteucci	Vincenzo Fioriti
Inna Pereverzeva	Wolfgang.D. Ehrenberger
John R. Filleau	Yuliya Prokhorova
Kateryna Netkachova	Zahid Syed
Kevin Mueller	Zoe Andrews

Sponsors

Scientific Sponsors

EWICS TC7

Università degli Studi di
Firenze

Consiglio Nazionale delle Ricerche
(CNR) - Istituto di Scienza e Tecnologie
dell'Informazione (ISTI) "A. Faedo"

ISTITUTO DI SCIENZA E TECNOLOGIE
DELL'INFORMAZIONE "A. FAEDO"

Industrial Sponsors

Technical Co-sponsors

Associazione Italiana Esperti in
Infrastrutture Critiche (AIIC)

Austrian Institute of Technology

European Network of Clubs for
Reliability and Safety of Software

European Research Consortium for
Informatics and Mathematics (ERCIM)

Gesellschaft für Informatik e. V.

International Federation for Information
Processing

Oesterreichische Computer Gesellschaft-
Austrian Computer Society

Quantitative Safety Assessment: Experiments and Field Measurements (Invited Talk)

Henrique Madeira

University of Coimbra, DEI-CISUC
Coimbra, Portugal
`henrique@dei.uc.pt`

The idea of inserting deliberated faults (or errors) in computer systems or computer components to evaluate its behavior in the presence of such faults, or to validate specific fault tolerance mechanisms, is quite intuitive and has been extensively used since the very beginning of the computer industry. There are many variants of this approach, which is generally known as **fault injection**.

Fault injection is often regarded as a testing approach. In fact, a popular utilization of fault injection is to test fault-handling mechanisms, in order to validate them. The idea is simple and obvious: if those mechanisms are supposed to handle faults, then a way to test them is to inject realistic faults and provide such mechanisms with the kind of inputs they are supposed to handle. This is often named **fault removal**, as the aim is to detect the presence of design and/or implementation faults, and then to help to locate and remove them.

But fault injection can also be used to evaluate or to measure the efficiency of specific fault-handling mechanisms (e.g., evaluate the detection coverage and latency of given error detection mechanism), helping quantifying the confidence that can be put on a given component or system, and contributing for the estimation of the number and the consequences of possible faults in the system. This is often named **fault forecasting**.

Fault injection is widely used today by both the industry and the research community but, unfortunately, most of the utilization examples are related to the use of fault injection as a testing approach. In fact, the examples of using fault injection as evaluation or measurement technique are relatively rare and generally not convincing, from a technical perspective (i.e., the relevance and correctness of the evaluation is often questionable).

Many reasons account for this narrow utilization of fault injection techniques but maybe the first one lies in the fact that fault injection tools are not readily available for the industry. Fault injection and experimental dependability evaluation is often regarded as a very expensive approach (indeed, in the ad hoc fashion it is used most of the times is in fact very expensive and time consuming), as the absence of adequate fault injection tools forces the practitioners and researchers to develop their own tools, without taking advantage of decades of progress in the field and quite often repeating the same mistakes others did in the past.

The talk addresses the use of fault injection techniques to assess dependability attributes of components and/or computer systems, with particular focus on the use of fault injection to help on computer safety assessment. The potential use of fault injection techniques in conjunction with traditional methods for safety analyses will be discussed, for both qualitative and quantitative safety assessment methods.

The talk starts with a compact view on the different fault injection approaches and presents in detail the software implemented fault injection techniques that are widely used today, providing examples of the fault injection tools available, including the few commercial tools available in the market. The fundamental issue of the definition of fault models, and the representativeness and coverage of the injected faults, is discussed in detail, as this is an essential element to allow the use of fault injection for the quantitative assessment of the efficiency of fault-handling mechanisms and, consequently, for safety assessment.

Two types of injected faults are particularly relevant. First the injection of software faults, as the problem of residual software faults (i.e., bugs) is, most probably, the main threat for computer-based systems. In fact, the high complexity of the software together with its tight integration with physical systems, the intensive use of third-party software components, and the pressure on the development budgets due to market constraints (including for the safety-critical market segment), lead to residual software defects that escape all the tests and manifest themselves only during operation. The injection of software faults is intended to reproduce realistically similar conditions to the ones observed when a residual software fault is activated in a given software component, with the goal of assessing how the rest of the system copes with the faulty software component.

The second type of faults widely injected is the traditional hardware transient faults. Actually, this kind of faults is quite relevant in safety-critical scenarios, as quite often the environmental conditions are tough and have the potential to induce transient faults in the hardware. Furthermore, the trend in the semiconductor industry to reduce the gate sizes of the integrated circuits, to improve performance and reduced power consumption, makes the newer generation of hardware more susceptible to soft errors. In fact, the decrease in feature sizes and the small operating voltages make the spontaneous bit changes (soft errors) much more frequent. Even considering that the hardware used in safety-critical applications remains some generations behind the most recent hardware versions, the trend of using small smart devices in safety-critical applications, makes the expected increase in the soft error rate a problem for small devices, such as small smart sensors, as the pressure to increased portability by improving the device power consumption will push the use of the most recent hardware versions to safety-critical applications. For all these reasons, the injection of hardware transient faults is one of the major goals in fault injection.

The talk uses examples of real fault injection experiments, in both laboratory conditions and real field environments to illustrate the hurdles and possibilities of using fault injection for the quantitative assessment of computer safety. Whenever possible, the potential use of these examples of fault injection studies in conjunction with traditional methods for safety analyses will be discussed.

Other utilizations of fault injection such as faultload for dependability bench-marking, experimental risk assessment, and computer failure prediction are also presented and illustrated with research examples.

Key Challenges for the Automotive Industry and Renault (Invited Talk)

Philippe Quere

UET Logiciels Embarques Temps Réel- DEA-SFF6
Guyancourt, France
philippe.p.quere@renault.com

The automotive domain will continue to change in the future, for instance cars are becoming more and more connected, ADAS (Advanced Driving Assistance Systems) will more and more help the driver and sometimes take hand on the car, and maybe one day our car will become fully autonomous ! The automotive industry is therefore facing new major technical challenges, with very important safety and security stakes.

The talk will present in five points the challenges in the automotive domain and within Renault more specifically.

At first, a general introduction on the automotive context will recall the key factors driving this industry and business challenges that we are facing.

Some of the differentiating characteristics with other industries will be highlighted in order to allow the understanding of the automotive context.

Then, from this introduction, the focus will be put on Renault and its strategy for his customers. Some orientations that may differ from other car manufacturers will be explained. These orientations influence the research and development efforts for Renault.

Then, the top technical challenges at vehicle level, as seen by Renault will be shown. Some of the actions already on going in order to meet these challenges will be highlighted.

I will then explain more deeply the consequences at the software level, and what are the key areas of interest on Renault's side, and in particular regarding safety and security of the software embedded in the cars.

And as a conclusion, the importance of the link between the industry and the academics will be emphasized. Some figures showing Renault involvement in this domain will be provided.

Software Quality, Dependability and Safety in Embedded Systems (Invited Talk)

Philip Koopman

Carnegie Mellon University,
Pittsburgh, PA, USA
koopman@cmu.edu

We often trust embedded systems with mission-critical functions, and even our own lives. But the designers of such systems (and especially their managers) are often domain experts who have not been formally trained in software development. While many embedded systems work well, in my design reviews I frequently see problems ranging from the subtle to the catastrophic. I have identified commonly occurring technical, process, and quality assurance issues based on my experience performing more than 135 industry design reviews. Common problems include a lack of embedded-specific software engineering skills, software process gaps, and a failure to appreciate that more than just product-level testing is required to create high quality software. Most of these problems cannot simply be fixed by adopting a tool, but rather require a change of culture and perspective in engineering organizations. All too often, the developers and their management simply don't realize they have gotten in over their heads as their product's software has escalated from performing a simple supporting function to providing make-or-break product functionality.

The Toyota Electronic Throttle Control System (ETCS) is a system deployed in almost a decade of vehicle production that exhibits many of the common problems I have seen in design reviews. It has numerous lapses in following good software practices in general, and safety-critical software practices in particular.

Briefly, the ETCS takes inputs from the driver (for example the accelerator pedal position and brake pedal activation), and has complete control over the throttle position as well as fuel and spark. There are practical scenarios in which a fully open throttle can overpower the brakes in Toyota vehicles. This makes the ETCS a safety-critical throttle-by-wire system.

Mishaps involving the Toyota ETCS have resulted in billions of dollars of costs in the US, including an economic loss class action settlement, a criminal cover-up case, and undisclosed settlements in hundreds of individual death and injury cases. Recalls have been issued – but for mechanical issues rather than for software defects. A redacted NASA report has been made public, as well as some transcripts from the one public trial that featured software safety testimony (including testimony by this author). The jury in that one trial found Toyota liable for a fatal crash based on testimony that alleged software defects were responsible. Toyota has denied that software defects have resulted in this or any other mishap.

While the question as to whether software defects caused the hundreds of other loss events involved in lawsuits remains open, the following observations about the ETCS are for practical purposes uncontested: Applying brakes will not necessarily stop the car if the throttle is commanded wide open (whether by floor mat entrapment or a possible software defect). Toyota did not follow an applicable set of safety guidelines (e.g., the MISRA Development Guidelines), and has not made an argument that their development processes are comparably rigorous to any established safety guideline. A significant amount of testing was performed both at the module and vehicle level but, as one would expect, this testing effort pales in comparison to the exposure of a fleet of millions of deployed vehicles. While there are dual redundant analog signals from the accelerator pedal to the ETCS, they both go through the same A/D converter on the same chip. While the ETCS has two CPU chips, they do not form a proper dual path system. While Toyota did have some coding rules, developers did not always follow their own coding rules, and did not have a formalized (written) waiver process. Static analysis of the ETCS software reveals global variables declared with different types, casts that alter values, condition evaluations with side effects, and uninitialized variables. The ETCS main CPU software has approximately 10,000 global variables, most of which could have been declared "local static" or "file static" to reduce their scope – but weren't. Shared global variables are not all declared "volatile," and shared global variables are not always accessed under the protection of interrupt masks. Moreover, NASA identified a specific concurrency hazard situation with the ETCS. Many ETCS software functions are quite long, and modularity is poor in general. There is no mitigation for stack overflow, and NASA did not find it possible to establish a maximum stack depth due to the presence of recursion. The main CPU can be more than 80% loaded, but beyond that NASA found that timing analysis was too difficult to complete due to, for example, the presence of busy-wait loops and indirect recursion. A watchdog timer is used to monitor average CPU load, but is not able to detect some task deaths. Much of the "paperwork" that is typically associated with a rigorous software development process does not seem to exist, including: defect logs, peer review records, comprehensive test plans, recorded test results, and process quality audit records.

Cyber-Physical Systems in Horizon 2020 – Trends in EU research and innovation activities (Invited Talk)

Werner Steinhögl

European Commission, Unit Complex Systems and Advanced Computing,
CONNECT - A3
Brussels, Belgium
Werner.Steinhoegl@ec.europa.eu

Cyber-Physical Systems (CPS) refer to next generation embedded ICT systems that are interconnected and collaborating including through the Internet of Things, and providing citizens and businesses with a wide range of innovative applications and services. These are the ICT systems increasingly embedded in all types of artefacts making "smarter", more intelligent, more energy-efficient and more comfortable our transport systems, cars, factories, hospitals, offices, homes, cities and personal devices. The challenge for Europe is on both reinforcing industrial strengths as well as exploring new markets.

Often endowed with control, monitoring and data gathering functions, CPS need to comply with essential requirements like safety, privacy, security and near-zero power consumption as well as size, usability and adaptability constraints. To maximise impact and return on investment in this field, the following challenges are essential:

- De-verticalising technology solutions with CPS platforms that cut across the barriers between application sectors including mass consumer markets
- Bringing together actors along the value chain from suppliers of components and customised computing systems to system integrators and end users.
- Creating new ICT Platforms for both vertical and core markets from automotive, health, smart buildings and energy to wireless communications and digital consumer products and services.

The goal is to enable every business in Europe, and notable SMEs, to get access to latest CPS technologies, knowledge and skills in order to innovate and generate higher value in its products, processes and services and to compete at a world scale.

Different EU actions are foreseen for this:

- Objectives related to CPS in the "Industrial Leadership" part of Horizon 2020 supporting collaborative research and innovation projects
- In particular, networks of competence centres offering a one stop shop for any business to upgrade their products, processes and services. These should enable the organic development of innovation clusters around these centres and a dynamic environment for business growth in emerging areas such as "smart anything everywhere" and Internet of Things.

– ECSEL, the Joint Technology Initiative in components and systems, strengthens the digital supply chain in Europe and ensures that value creation from the supply industry in Europe is compatible with the size of our economy and provides the technologies needed to drive the whole economy.

Table of Contents

Assurance Cases and Arguments

System Analysis

Security and Trust

Notations/Languages for Safety-Related Aspects

Safety and Security

A Simulated Fault Injection Framework for Time-Triggered Safety-Critical Embedded Systems

Iban Ayestaran[1], Carlos F. Nicolas[1], Jon Perez[1],
Asier Larrucea[1], and Peter Puschner[2]

[1] Embedded Systems Group, IK4-Ikerlan Research Center, Arrasate-Mondragón,
Basque Country (Spain)
{iayestaran,cfnicolas,jmperez,alarrucea}@ikerlan.es
[2] Institut für Technische Informatik, Technische Universität Wien, Wien, Austria
peter@vmars.tuwien.ac.at

Abstract. This paper presents a testing and simulated fault injection framework for time-triggered safety-critical embedded systems. Our approach facilitates the validation of fault-tolerance mechanisms by performing non-intrusive Simulated Fault Injection (SFI) on models of the system at different stages of the development, from the Platform Independent Model (PIM) to the Platform Specific Model (PSM). The SFI enables exercising the intended fault tolerance mechanisms by injecting faults in a simulated model of a system. The main benefit of this work is that it enables an early detection of design flaws in fault-tolerant systems, what reduces the possibility of late discovery of design pitfalls that might require an expensive redesign of the system. We examine the feasibility of the proposed approach in a case study, where SFI is used to assess the fault tolerance mechanisms designed in a simplified railway signaling system.

Keywords: Simulated Fault Injection, Automatic Test Executor, Time-Triggered Systems, Dependable Systems, Safety-Critical Systems, Fault Tolerance.

1 Introduction

Safety-critical embedded systems are dependable systems that could cause loss of life, significant property damages or damages to the environment in case of failure. The selection of appropriate fault-tolerance mechanisms requires a careful analysis of the system through all the design refinement phases using techniques such as Failure Mode and Effect Analysis (FMEA), recommended by the international IEC-61508 safety standard. Typically the safety validation involves fault injection experiments at the final stage of the system development. However, the late fixing of the detected design flaws might require a complete and expensive redesign of the system. Thus, the validation of fault-tolerance mechanisms in the early steps of the development could bring major benefits to

A. Bondavalli and F. Di Giandomenico (Eds.): SAFECOMP 2014, LNCS 8666, pp. 1–16, 2014.
© Springer International Publishing Switzerland 2014

designers. In fact, the IEC-61508 standard recommends fault injection techniques in all steps of the development process of safety-critical systems [21].

Simulated Fault Injection (SFI) is a technique to insert faults in models of systems during their simulation. This technique allows the developers to observe the behavior of the system in the presence of faults, enabling the verification of fault-tolerance mechanisms before assembling a system prototype. The analysis of the results obtained in SFI campaigns can be used to evaluate the effectiveness of the fault tolerance mechanisms, analyze the weaknesses of the system and study possible improvements.

In order to cope with the increasing complexity of embedded systems and to analyze the diverse failures a system might suffer from, the IEC-61508 standard highly recommends the usage of semi-formal methods, like the ones used in Model Driven Development (MDD) approaches such as the Model Driven Architecture (MDA) [17]. According to the MDA, first a purely functional model of the system is created, called Platform Independent Model (PIM). This first separation of the functionality from the hardware (HW) components saves design time and cost during the development process, and eases the early verification of the functionality of the system. Several commercial tools are available to develop functional models, e.g. SCADE Suite [9].

Once the assessment of the PIM is finished, the model is refined into the so-called Platform Specific Model (PSM) by defining a platform model and deploying the functional components of the PIM into it. This enables the introduction of HW-specific errors into the model.

In this context, SystemC [11] is a high-level HW/SW co-design language based on C++ that enables modeling and simulating systems at different levels of abstraction. Therefore, SystemC can be used to design, simulate and verify platform specific models of dependable embedded systems. Nowadays SystemC has become the de-facto standard in HW/SW system development.

Given this situation, the aim of this research work is to provide a modeling and simulation environment for dependable Time-Triggered HW/SW systems based on SystemC. The main contribution of this paper is the presentation of a testing and simulated fault injection framework for the Platform Specific Time-Triggered Model (PS-TTM) approach [2], which enables reproducible non-intrusive SFI at different stages of the development for the early assessment of fault-tolerance mechanisms.

The paper is structured as follows: Section 2 briefly describes previous related work. Section 3 reviews the PS-TTM modeling and simulation platform for dependable time-triggered embedded systems, which is the platform where the testing and fault injection framework has been developed. Section 4 presents the framework for the verification of time-triggered dependable systems by simulated fault injection at different stages of the development, which is evaluated in Section 5 by means of a case study based on a simplified railway signaling system. Section 6 briefly presents the results obtained in the case study and finally Section 7 summarizes the main conclusions of the work.

2   Related Work

According to Avizienis et al. [1], a failure is an event that occurs when the delivered service deviates from correct service. An error is a deviation from the correct service of an external state of the system, and a fault is the cause of an error. In other words, errors are the manifestations of faults whereas failures are the consequence of errors. Therefore, injecting faults into systems is a straightforward technique to verify that such faults do not cause failures in the system, i.e., the system is tolerant to that faults.

Thus, fault injection strategies and techniques have been very widely analyzed [7,27] and several tools have been developed, most of them focusing on VHDL models [12,10,5,19]. However, as previously stated, SystemC is nowadays the de-facto standard in industrial HW/SW system design and simulation. Therefore, fault injection design and simulation in SystemC models has been getting an increasing interest in the latest years [18,24,8,15,23].

Misera et al. [18] adapt fault injection techniques and strategies from VHDL models to SystemC models in order to analyze the limitations and possibilities of the SystemC kernel. They simulate systems including saboteurs and simulator commands, and they extend logic types of SystemC in order to perform a more realistic behavior of logic components. Since the approach is based on strategies used in VHDL models, they focus on logic-level models. In [24] Shafik et al. propose an alternative technique to the one presented in [18], also focusing on logic-level models.

Bolchini et al. go one step further into multiple abstraction level fault injection in [8]. The paper presents a fault injection environment for the ReSP simulation platform [6]. The approach enables injecting faults by using saboteurs and simulator commands, using a novel technique called reflective wrapper. It does not focus on a specific MoC, so simulation is paused and resumed whenever a fault is injected.

In [15] Lu and Radetzki use the Concurrent and Comparative Simulation (CCS) technique to inject faults in SystemC models. This approach makes it possible to perform more than one fault injection experiment in each execution. The developer must use a specific data-type in order to inject faults in variables, and fault libraries are not defined, so the tester must implement the fault models.

Reiter et al. [23] perform error injection in simulated HW models defined using the CHESS modeling language by extending them in order to inject errors. The approach provides a library of different error models, including data-corruption, timing-corruption, halt, and signal-loss. The framework does not rely on a concrete model of computation, and the paper does not describe how timing constraints of the System Under Test (SUT) are guaranteed.

Regarding to fault models and their simulation, the Model-Based Generation of Test-Cases for Embedded Systems (MOGENTES) project [20] specifies a number of HW and SW related fault and failure models and taxonomies. On the other hand, the international ASAM AE HIL [26] standard defines an interface to perform error simulation in Hardware in the Loop testing.

In this context, this paper describes a novel testing and simulated fault injection framework for the verification of time-triggered safety-critical embedded systems at different stages of the development, including PIM and PSM. The framework is integrated in the PS-TTM modeling and simulation platform [2], and includes a time-triggered Automatic Test Executor (ATE) with libraries of fault models in order to assess the robustness of the SUT in the presence of faults without making any modification to the models.

3   The PS-TTM Modeling and Simulation Platform

The Platform Specific Time-Triggered Model (PS-TTM) [2] is a modeling and simulation platform for time-triggered safety-critical embedded systems, based on the Y-chart approach [4,13] and MDA models. The goal of the PS-TTM framework is to give the designer an environment based on SystemC for the development and testing of time-triggered safety-critical embedded systems following the MDA.

In compliance to the MDA, the development of a system in the PS-TTM framework starts with the definition of a functional model, called Platform Independent Model (PIM). Since the approach focuses in time-triggered systems, PIMs rely on the Logical Execution Time (LET) model of computation (MoC) [14]. The LET MoC defines the functionality of systems by specifying a logical duration for each computational job of the system, regardless of its physical duration. This permits the software engineers to communicate more effectively with the control engineers, since the properties of the system are closely aligned with the mathematical model of the control design.

Thus, a LET computation engine called Platform Independent Time-Triggered Model (PI-TTM) has been developed for the simulation of the PIMs [3]. This engine has been built by providing an extension that imposes LET MoC constraints to the E-TTM simulation platform [22].

The design framework includes a library of HW components that can be assembled to generate a model of the target platform. In accordance to the MDA, once the PIM has been validated, it is deployed into the platform description model in order to generate the final PSM. The simulation of PSMs is handled by the E-TTM engine. This gives the designers a higher freedom regarding to the definition of the temporal behavior of their systems, as the restrictions previously imposed by the LET MoC disappear.

This approach eases the modeling and validation of time-triggered systems, since it starts with the design of a purely functional LET-based model and enables a straightforward transformation into a platform specific E-TTM-based model, what guarantees that time-properties are intrinsically preserved in the final implementation when the platform is based on the TTA.

4   Testing and Simulated Fault Injection Framework

The PS-TTM simulation platform has been extended with facilities to perform testing and simulated fault injection experiments. Two are the main aims of this

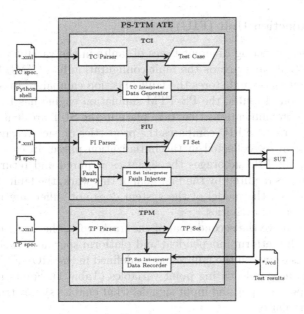

Fig. 1. PS-TTM Automatic Test Executor (ATE)

framework: On one hand, it must enable non-intrusive fault injection, i.e. fault injection activities must not require the designer to modify the model of the system. On the other hand, testing and fault injection must be possible in all stages of the development of the systems, in order to enable an early detection of design flaws.

In order to achieve these goals, this work presents the PS-TTM Automatic Test Executor (ATE) shown in Fig. 1, a time-triggered testing and SFI framework. The PS-TTM ATE is composed by three different modules: The Test Case Interpreter (TCI), the Fault Injection Unit (FIU), and the Test Point Manager (TPM).

4.1 Test Case Interpreter (TCI)

The TCI is the module that enables exercising the desired test-cases. It provides two services:

1. Automatic interpretation of test-cases: The test-case parser reads and stores the test-cases specified in XML files during the initialization phase. During simulation the data-generator feeds the SUT at each time tick with the signals corresponding to the test-case defined.
2. Interactive signal setting: The module provides a set(signal,value) command that permits the testing team to modify the input signals of the SUT during simulation, sending commands via a Python command shell.

4.2   Fault Injection Unit (FIU)

The FIU enables injecting different types of faults in the variables of the SUT. The fault injection parser reads the fault configuration files (XML files) during the initialization phase and stores the fault injection campaign. In order to perform the injection of faults, the PS-TTM simulation engine has been modified so that all the communications that take place in the SUT are sent to the FIU. The fault injector of the FIU compares the properties of each received signal to the fault injection set collected in the initialization phase. In case a fault has to be injected, the FIU sabotages the signal as required and returns it to the SUT. Therefore, as required by the first goal of this work, the faults are injected non-intrusively, i.e., the model of the system does not suffer any modification for the fault injection activities.

In order to achieve the second goal of the framework, the FIU provides fault libraries for both platform independent and platform specific models. The fault library for PIMs draws on the failure modes defined in the MOGENTES project for boolean, integer and floating point variables (Table 1). Faults in PIMs can be injected in both output and input signals, what enables symmetric and asymmetric fault simulation.

Since the PS-TTM approach models the HW components at a high abstraction level, the fault library for PSMs is composed by the effects to which HW-related faults are typically reduced in the literature [23] (Table 2). However, as it is possible to extend the PSM component library with more detailed models of HW components, the fault library may also be extended for fault injection at a lower level of abstraction.

The FIU supports two different fault modes: transient and permanent. Transient faults are temporary misbehaviors, so their configuration requires to specify a duration. Instead, permanent faults only need to specify their trigger time, as these faults are assumed to remain active until the simulation ends.

The selected XML schema for the definition of fault injection campaigns complies with the international ASAM AE HIL standard for hardware-in-the-loop testing. Although the aim of this work is not to perform fault injection at

Table 1. Fault library for platform independent models

	Fault Effect	Name	Config. attributes	Description
Boolean	Invert	B_I	-	Boolean value is inverted
	Stuck At	B_SA	stuck_value	Signal gets stuck at a given value
	Stuck	B_S	-	Signal gets stuck at the actual value
	Stuck If	B_SI	stuck_value, condition	Signal gets stuck if a given condition holds
	Open Circuit	B_OC	-	Wire is disconnected, signal takes an arbitrary value (noise)
	Delay	B_D	delay	Signal is delayed by an amount of time
Integer/Float	Constant	I_C, F_C	constant_value	Signal gets stuck at a given constant value
	Amplification	I_A, F_A	ampl_value	Signal is amplified by fixed value
	Amplification Range	I_AR, F_AR	min_amp_value, max_ampl_value	Signal is amplified by a randomly selected value (between given max. and min. values)
	Drift	I_D, F_D	drift_value	At each time stepc, the signal drifts away from its nominal value by a given value
	Offset	I_O, F_O	offset_value	A given fixed offset is added to the signal
	Offset Range	I_OR, F_OR	min_offset_value, max_offset_value	A randomly selected offset value is added to the signal (between given max. and min. values)
	Stuck	I_S, F_S	-	Signal gets stuck at the actual value
	Random	I_R, F_R	min_value, max_value	Signal takes an arbitrary value (between given max. and min. values)
	Delay	I_D, F_D	delay	Signal is delayed by an amount of time

Table 2. Fault library for platform specific models

Fault Effect	Name	Attributes	Description
Corruption	C	-	The functionality is performed incorrectly. The information provided in the interface is corrupted
No execution	NE	-	The functionality is not executed. No information is provided as a result
Out of time	OoT	Delay	Time bounds of the functionality are not respected. Information is provided later than expected
Babbling	B	Delay	Information in the interface is erroneous both in terms of content and time.

hardware-in-the-loop level, sticking to the standard enables forward reuse of the fault injection campaigns until the final prototyping phase. In order to ease the definition of the fault injection specification, we developed a graphical tool with automatic code generation.

4.3 Test Point Manager (TPM)

The TPM is the module for the observation of internal signals of the SUT. The signals to be observed are specified in an XML file which is read by the test-point parser during the initialization. During simulation the data recorder stores at each time stamp the values of the signals specified on the test point configuration file. At the end of the simulation, the recorded data is saved in a value-change-dump file (*.vcd). The file can be textually and graphically visualized using different tools for the assessment of the system behavior.

5 Case Study

In order to check the testing and simulated fault injection framework described in Section 4, we model a simplified railway signaling system by means of the PS-TTM platform. Following the approach described in the PS-TTM, we first design a PIM and we later refine it into a PSM.

The European Railway Traffic Management System (ERTMS) [25] is an European Union backed initiative for the definition of a unique train signaling standard throughout Europe. The high-speed train on-board European Train Control System (ETCS) is a safety-critical embedded system (SIL-4, Safety Integrity Level) that protects the train by supervising the traveled distance and speed, and activating the emergency brake if the authorized values are exceeded.

The ETCS is composed by several subsystems connected to the central safety processing unit called European Vital Computer (EVC). The EVC contains an on-board odometry system that performs an estimation of the speed and traveled distance based on the measurements provided by a set of sensors, such as wheel speed encoders, accelerometers or Doppler radars, and the Balise Transmission Module (BTM) that gives the exact position as the train passes the eurobalises placed in the railway track. If the estimations exceed the authorized values, the EVC automatically activates an emergency brake.

In this case, we summarize the basic functionality of the EVC system in four main tasks: speed and position estimation, operational mode control, emergency brake control and service brake control.

The speed and position estimation reads the information provided by a set of sensors and the BTM and makes an estimation of the speed and position of the train.

The operational mode control manages the activation of the *Standby* and *Supervision* modes in the emergency and service brake control tasks, depending on the command received from the DMI.

The emergency brake control task implements the safety-critical (SIL-4) functionality of the system. It receives the information about the position and speed estimated by the odometry system, the *Standby* and *Supervision* activation signals from the mode control unit, and the *reset* command from the DMI. When the operational mode control unit sends the *Standby* activation signal the emergency brake is activated. When the system is set to *Supervision* mode, the estimated distance and speed are compared to a pre-defined braking-curve that sets a maximum speed for each point in the track. If the maximum speed is exceeded the emergency brake is activated. The brake is only deactivated if a *reset* command is received from the DMI when the train is stopped.

The service brake control implements the non-safety-critical functionality. It receives the estimated position and speed from the odometry unit, and the mode activation signals from the mode control unit. If the system is in *Standby* mode, the service brake and the warning are deactivated. However, in *Supervision* mode, the warning signal and the service brake are activated when the speed of the train reaches the warning and service brake activation speeds respectively. The maximum speeds are pre-defined in two braking-curves. Both the warning and the service brake are deactivated when the speed of the train falls below the warning activation speed.

5.1   Platform Independent Model

We design the PIM of the system relying on the meta-model described in section 3. As Figure 2 shows, the PIM implementation consists of 5 jobs deployed in 4 DASes. The *DMI*, *odometry* and *mode-control* DASes contain one job each, whereas the *brake-system* DAS executes the *emergency-brake-control* and the *service-brake-control* jobs.

Since the system activates an emergency brake when the values estimated by the odometry system exceed the authorized limits, the odometry algorithm has to provide accurate and reliable measurements. Thus, the algorithm is usually based on a fault-tolerant sensor-fusion approach. In this case, we design the algorithm following one of the approaches described by Malvezzi et al. in [16]. The algorithm estimates the speed of the train and the traveled distance with the information provided by an accelerometer that measures the acceleration of the train and two encoders that measure the speed of a different wheel each.

We design the functions of the SUT in SCADE and we generate the C-code implementation automatically using KCG. Then we integrate the resulting components into the platform independent model of the system for their verification. We also design a simplified model of the environment using SCADE.

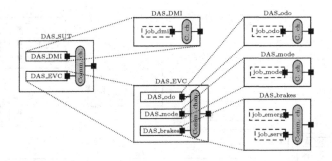

Fig. 2. SUT: Railway signaling system modeled at PIM level

5.2   Platform Specific Model

In this example the platform independent model is deployed into a Triple Module Redundant (TMR) platform, in compliance with the requirements from the international EN-50126 safety standard for railway applications. The TMR system is composed by three main nodes, each of them hosting a replica of the simplified EVC functionality. Each of the nodes is connected to its dedicated sensors and BTM.

Two voters handle the replicated values of the EVC nodes. The voters receive 9 input signals (a warning, service brake and emergency brake from each EVC node) and they compare the replicated values to produce 3 output signals (voted warning, service brake, and emergency brake). In addition to this, two other output signals, the *failure warning* and the *system-failure warning*, are used to inform the driver about the detection of failures in the system. The functionality of the voting system is the following:

- The voting algorithm is based in a *2oo3* design. The voters start in *normal voting mode*. In this situation, if the three replicated input values are equal, the voter remains in *normal voting mode* and forwards the input values to the output value. No failure warning is sent to the DMI.
- If one of the replicated values received by the voter is distinct to the other two, the voter switches to *degraded voting mode*. In that case the voter behaves as a *1oo2* voter, where the inputs coming from the faulty node are no longer taken into account for the voting algorithm. The result of the *1oo2* algorithm is forwarded to the output, and a *failure warning* is sent to the DMI.
- If there is a disagreement between the two active inputs when the voter is in *degraded voting mode*, the voter sends a *system-failure warning* to the DMI to inform about a multiple failure in the system. The voting system is disconnected and the emergency brakes are applied to the train, whereas the service-brake and the warning are deactivated.

Figure 3 shows the platform specific model of the system in the PS-TTM. As the figure shows, the two voters and the DMI are deployed into dedicated

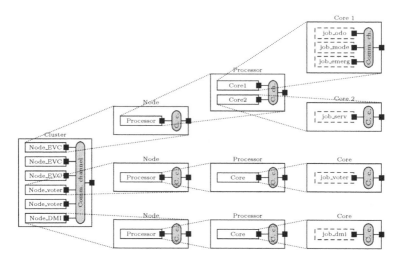

Fig. 3. SUT: Railway signaling system modeled at PSM level

nodes containing a single-core processor, whereas the each EVC node contains a dual-core processor. The first core of the processor is the host for the *odometry, mode-control* and *emergency-brake-system* jobs, whereas the *service-brake system* job is hosted on the second core.

We design the functions with SCADE and we generate C code automatically using the KCG tool. C code for the voters is also automatically generated from SCADE models.

The PS-TTM ATE is connected to the SUT and the environment model again as shown in Fig. 4 in order to assess the fault-tolerance mechanisms introduced in the platform specific model of the system by injecting faults during simulation.

6   Reliability Assessment

This section describes the reliability assessment made to the railway signaling system model described in Section 5. The fault-tolerance provided by the system is evaluated by means of simulated fault injection. To do so, the PS-TTM ATE framework described in Section 4 is connected to the SUT and the environment model as shown in Fig. 4.

This way, the TCI parses the test-cases defined in XML files and feeds the the environment during simulation with the corresponding input signals. The environment model generates the sensor values and sends them to the SUT. The simulation engine sends all the communication signals inside the SUT to the FIU, which modifies their value according to the fault injection campaigns defined by the testing team. The results of the simulations are sent to the TPM, which stores them for their off-line evaluation.

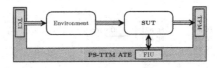

Fig. 4. Composition of the testing and fault injection environment

6.1   Platform Independent Model

As mentioned before, the odometry algorithm should be tolerant to a fault in one of its sensors. Injecting faults at the functional model enables an early assessment of the of the robustness of the algorithm. Therefore, we first simulate the PIM by means of the PI-TTM engine with a pre-defined test-case and we store the results provided by the odometry algorithm. We consider the results of this fault-free simulation the golden behavior of the system. Then, we carry several simulations including the fault injection campaigns shown in Table 3, and we compare their results with the golden behavior.

Table 3. Fault injection campaigns for PIM model

#	Fault Location			Fault		Fault Set			Description
	Job	Entity	Type	Effect	Attributes	Mode	Trig.time(s)	Duration(s)	
1	job_odo	enc_1	input	LC	0	p	130.0	-	Wheel stuck / Encoder broken
2	job_odo	enc_1	input	LS	-	p	180.0	-	Encoder broken (measuring a fix value)
3	job_odo	enc_1	input	LR	0,600	p	80.0	-	Encocer broken (measuring wrong values)
4	job_odo	enc_1	input	LC	600	t	91.0	7.0	Wheel slipping during acceleration
5	job_odo	enc_2	input	LC	0	t	150.0	8.0	Wheel skidding (blocked by brakes)
6	job_odo	$accel$	input	F_A	1.1	p	0.0	-	Accelerometer incorrectly installed
7	job_odo	$accel$	input	F_S	-	p	200.0	-	Accelerometer broken(measuring a fix value)
8	job_odo	$accel$	input	F_R	-2, 2	p	20.0	-	Accelerometer broken(measuring wrong values)
9	job_odo	$accel$	input	F_OR	-0.1, 0.1	t	35.0	50.0	Noise in the signal

Figure 5 shows an extract of the results obtained in the simulation. The results show that odometry algorithm designed for this system provides accurate results in the estimation of the traveled distance even in the presence of faults in the sensors. Overall, the maximum estimation errors occurred during the 8th fault injection campaign, where the maximum error raised up to $3.07m$ from a total of $6044.46m$ (0.05%, at $160.5sec$). The maximum error in percentage took place during the 6th campaign, and reached 4.76%. Anyway, this happened at instant $8.250sec$, where the traveled distance was still very low ($0.21m$ traveled, $0.22m$ measured due to the fault).

Regarding the estimation of the speed, the experiments made by means our fault injection framework show the robustness of the algorithm. In this case we also get the maximum error in the 8th campaign, where at instant $151.75s$ we find a disagreement of $1.350m/s$ respect to the non-faulty simulation ($60.23m/s$, 2.24%) .

All in all, estimation errors made by the algorithm are considered acceptable, since they always fall below the 5% of the traveled distance and speed, and never

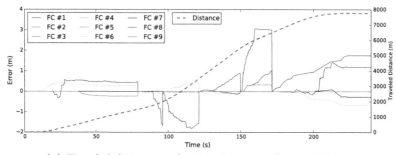

(a) Traveled distance and estimation error due to faults

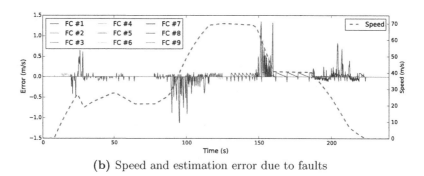

(b) Speed and estimation error due to faults

Fig. 5. Results of the PIM simulation and fault injection

go further than $\pm 5m$ and $\pm 2m/s$. As a conclusion, we state that the algorithm has shown to be specially sensitive to faults in the accelerometer, so future work could focus on the improvement of this fact.

6.2   Platform Specific Model

The PSM of the system introduces redundancy in order to tolerate hardware related faults. A TMR architecture has been chosen in order to guarantee the availability of the system even in the presence of faults. As stated before, the voting algorithm should be able to identify any failure in the replicated nodes. In that case, the voters send a failure warning signal and ignore the results provided by the faulty node. If a second failure is detected in the system, the voters activate the emergency brake and inform about a failure in the system. We set the period of each job to the time-triggered macrotick, i.e., 250 milliseconds. Table 4 shows the fault injection campaigns made to the PSM in order to evaluate the voting algorithm.

During the fault-free simulation, the system activated the warning 4 times, and the service brake once. As expected, the failure and system-failure warnings

Table 4. Fault injection campaigns for PSM model

#	Fault Location	Fault		Fault Set			Description
		Effect	Attributes	Mode	Trig.time(s)	Duration(s)	
1	Node_EVC_A	NE	-	p	85.0	-	Node A stopped working
2	Proc_EVC_B	C	-	p	20.0	-	Processor B provides incorrect results
3	EVC_C_Core1	OoT	0.50	p	120.0	-	Core 1 of a processor C is out of time bounds
4	Node_EVC_A	B	-	t	40.0	25.0	Node A babbling, incorrect results
5	Node_EVC_B, Proc_EVC_C	NE, C	-	p, p	60.0, 150.0	-	Double failure (Node B stops, then processor C incorrect)
6	job_serv_A *serv* output	B_I	-	t	160.0	0.50	Bit-flip in Service. Brake signal sent by node A
7	job_emrg_C *emrg* output	B_OC	-	t	105.0	15.0	Emerg. Brake not received from Node C (noise)

Table 5. Results of fault injection campaigns in the PSM model

#	Fault trigger instant (s)	Fault warning activ. instant (s)	System fault activ. instant (s)
1	85.0	125.25	-
2	20.0	20.25	-
3	120.0	125.25	-
4	40.0	40.25	-
5	60.0, 150.0	79.00	150.25
6	160.0	160.25	-
7	105.0	105.25	-

were not activated. The results obtained for each fault injection campaigns are summarized in Table 5.

As the table shows, all the faults injected in the system during the simulations were detected by the voters. Since we configured all jobs in the system with a period of one macrotick (250ms), *corruption* and *babbling* faults were detected 250ms after their injection in the system, as expected. *Bit-flips* in signals and *open circuits* were also detected in the next macrotick.

However, *no-execution* and *out of time* faults, injected in the 1st, 3rd and 5th fault configurations, took longer to detect. This happened because, due to the state of the system at the moment of the injection, the faults were dormant. In fact, *no-execution* and *out of time* faults do not get active until the value of the signal changes, since they do not cause an alteration of the signal values by themselves.

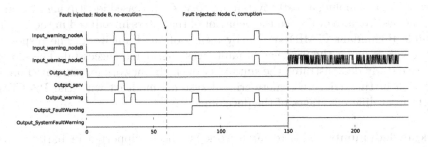

Fig. 6. Results of PSM simulation with fault configuration #5

All in all, the faults were detected as expected. The voters also notified a multiple failure caused by the two faults injected in the system during the 5th simulation. That occurred at instant 150.25s, and also caused the activation of the emergency brakes of the train, as stated by the requirements. Fig. 6 shows an extract of the results of the the 5th simulation. For the sake of simplicity, we omit input signals of emergency and service brakes from the figure.

7   Conclusion

This paper introduced a testing and simulated fault injection framework for time-triggered dependable-systems based on the PS-TTM approach. The environment enables testing and injecting faults at different stages of the design, from platform independent models to platform specific models, what enables an early detection of design flaws in the system.

The Automatic Test Executor (ATE) presented in this paper is composed by three different modules for the design and simulation of test-cases, injection of faults during simulation and storage of simulation results for the evaluation of the behavior of the system under such faults. The ATE is synchronized with the simulation time of the SUT, a way that functional tests and fault injection experiments become reproducible.

The herein presented simulated fault injection technique is non-intrusive, i.e., enables injecting faults in the system models during simulations without the need of performing any modifications to them. This is achieved by monitoring the signals of the SUT and modifying their values if required. The framework provides the user with a library of faults in order to configure the fault injection experiments. The ATE imports these configurations for carrying out the simulations. As the mapping of LET and E-TTM-based models to time-triggered architectures is straightforward, this eventually facilitates the re-usability of tests even on real prototypes, provided that we could build a test harness with equivalent real-world Fault Injection Units (FIUs).

We evaluated our framework in a case study consisting of a railway signaling system. We modeled the system at both PIM and PSM levels, and checked the behavior of the system under different faults by means of the Simulated Fault Injection (SFI) capabilities provided by the framework. Our non-intrusive SFI approach enabled an early assessment of a fault-tolerant odometry algorithm long before assembling a costly system prototype, and eased identifying its main weaknesses. We also evaluated the behavior of the voters introduced in the Triple Module Redundant (TMR) system by means of our framework. The response of the voters under the presence of faults was considered successful. Therefore, the case study demonstrated the suitability of the framework for simulated fault injection in time-triggered safety-critical systems modeled with the PS-TTM platform at different stages of the development.

Acknowledgments. This research work has been supported in part by the European FP7 DREAMS project under grant No. 610640 and the Spanish IN-NPACTO project VALMOD under grant number IPT-2011-1149-370000.

References

1. Avizienis, A., Laprie, J.-C., Randell, B., Landwehr, C.: Basic Concepts and Taxonomy of Dependable and Secure Computing. IEEE Trans. Dependable Secur. Comput. 1(1), 11–33 (2004)
2. Ayestaran, I., Nicolas, C.F., Perez, J., Larrucea, A., Puschner, P.: Modeling and Simulated Fault Injection for Time-Triggered Safety-Critical Embedded Systems. In: IEEE 17th International Symposium on Object/Component/Service-Oriented Real-Time Distributed Computing, ISORC (2014)
3. Ayestaran, I., Nicolas, C.F., Perez, J., Puschner, P.: Modeling Logical Execution Time Based Safety-Critical Embedded Systems in SystemC. In: 3rd Mediterranean Conference on Embedded Computing, MECO (2014)
4. Balarin, F., Chiodo, M., Giusto, P., Hsieh, H., Jurecska, A., Lavagno, L., Passerone, C., Sangiovanni-Vincentelli, A., Sentovich, E., Suzuki, K., Tabbara, B.: Hardware-software co-design of embedded systems: the POLIS approach. Kluwer Academic Publishers (1997)
5. Baraza, J.C., Gracia, J., Blanc, S., Gil, D., Gil, P.J.: Enhancement of Fault Injection Techniques Based on the Modification of VHDL Code. IEEE Transactions on Very Large Scale Integration (VLSI) Systems 16(6), 693–706 (2008)
6. Beltrame, G., Bolchini, C., Fossati, L., Miele, A., Sciuto, D.: ReSP: A non-intrusive Transaction-Level Reflective MPSoC Simulation Platform for Design Space Exploration. In: Asia and South Pacific Design Automation Conference, ASPDAC 2008, pp. 673–678 (2008)
7. Benso, A., Prinetto, P.: Fault Injection Techniques and Tools for Embedded Systems Reliability Evaluation. Kluwer Academic Publishers (2003)
8. Bolchini, C., Miele, A., Sciuto, D.: Fault Models and Injection Strategies in SystemC Specifications. In: 11th EUROMICRO Conference on Digital System Design Architectures, Methods and Tools, DSD 2008, pp. 88–95 (2008)
9. Esterel, A.: SCADE Suite (2014), http://www.esterel-technologies.com/products/scade-suite/
10. Gracia, J., Baraza, J.C., Gil, D., Gil, P.J.: Comparison and Application of different VHDL-Based Fault Injection Techniques. In: Proceedings of the 2001 IEEE International Symposium on Defect and Fault Tolerance in VLSI Systems, pp. 233–241 (2001)
11. IEEE. IEEE Standard SystemC Language Reference Manual (2005)
12. Jenn, E., Arlat, J., Rimen, M., Ohlsson, J., Karlsson, J.: Fault Injection into VHDL Models: The MEFISTO Tool. In: Twenty-Fourth International Symposium on Fault-Tolerant Computing, FTCS-24. Digest of Papers., pp. 66–75 (1994)
13. Kienhuis, B., Deprettere, E., Vissers, K., van der Wolf, P.: An Approach for Quantitative Analysis of Application-Specific Dataflow Architectures. In: Proceedings of the IEEE International Conference on Application-Specific Systems, Architectures and Processors, pp. 338–349 (1997)
14. Kirsch, C.M., Sokolova, A.: The Logical Execution Time Paradigm, ch 5, pp. 103–120. Springer, Heidelberg (2012)
15. Lu, W., Radetzki, M.: Efficient Fault Simulation of SystemC Designs. In: 2011 14th Euromicro Conference on Digital System Design (DSD), pp. 487–494 (2011)
16. Malvezzi, M., Allotta, B., Rinchi, M.: Odometric estimation for automatic train protection and control systems. Vehicle System Dynamics 49(5), 723–739 (2010)
17. Miller, J., Mukerji, J.: MDA Guide Version 1.0.1, 2003/06/12 (2003)

18. Misera, S., Vierhaus, H.T., Sieber, A.: Fault Injection Techniques and their Accelerated Simulation in SystemC. In: 10th Euromicro Conference on Digital System Design Architectures, Methods and Tools, DSD 2007, pp. 587–595 (2007)
19. Moazzeni, S., Poormozaffari, S., Emami, A.: An Optimized Simulation-Based Fault Injection and Test Vector Generation Using VHDL to Calculate Fault Coverage. In: 2009 10th International Workshop on Microprocessor Test and Verification (MTV), pp. 55–60 (2009)
20. MOGENTES. Fault Models. Technical report, MOGENTES, 2009/12/29 (2009)
21. Perez, J., Azkarate-askasua, M., Perez, A.: Codesign and Simulated Fault Injection of Safety-Critical Embedded Systems Using SystemC. In: European Dependable Computing Conference, p. 9 (2010)
22. Perez, J., Nicolas, C.F., Obermaisser, R., Salloum, C.E.: Modeling Time-Triggered Architecture Based Real-Time Systems Using SystemC. In: Kaźmierski, T.J., Morawiec, A. (eds.) Forum on specification & Design Languages (FDL) 2010, vol. 106, pp. 123–141. Springer, Heidelberg (2010)
23. Reiter, S., Pressler, M., Viehl, A., Bringmann, O., Rosenstiel, W.: Reliability assessment of safety-relevant automotive systems in a model-based design flow. In: 2013 18th Asia and South Pacific Design Automation Conference (ASP-DAC), pp. 417–422 (2013)
24. Shafik, R.A., Rosinger, P., Al-Hashimi, B.: SystemC-based Minimum Intrusive Fault Injection Technique with Improved Fault Representation. In: International On-line Test Symposium (IOLTS), p. 6 (2008)
25. Winter, P., Guiot, B., International Union of Railways: Compendium on ERTMS: European Rail Traffic Management System. Eurail Press (2009)
26. ASAM HIL workgroup. ASAM AE HIL Programmers Guide (2009)
27. Ziade, H., Ayoubi, R., Velazco, R.: A Survey on Fault Injection Techniques. The International Arab Journal of Information Technology 1, 16 (2004)

Rapid Fault-Space Exploration
by Evolutionary Pruning

Horst Schirmeier, Christoph Borchert, and Olaf Spinczyk

Technische Universität Dortmund, Computer Science 12
Otto-Hahn-Str. 16, 44221 Dortmund, Germany
{horst.schirmeier,christoph.borchert,olaf.spinczyk}@tu-dortmund.de

Abstract. Recent studies suggest that future microprocessors need low-cost fault-tolerance solutions for reliable operation. Several competing software-implemented error-detection methods have been shown to increase the overall resiliency when applied to critical spots in the system. Fault injection (FI) is a common approach to assess a system's vulnerability to hardware faults. In an FI campaign comprising multiple runs of an application benchmark, each run simulates the impact of a fault in a specific hardware location at a specific point in time. Unfortunately, exhaustive FI campaigns covering all possible fault locations are infeasible even for small target applications. Commonly used sampling techniques, while sufficient to measure overall resilience improvements, lack the level of detail and accuracy needed for the identification of critical spots, such as important variables or program phases. Many faults are sampled out, leaving the developer without any information on the application parts they would have targeted.

We present a methodology and tool implementation that application-specifically reduces experimentation efforts, allows to freely trade the number of FI runs for result accuracy, and provides information on *all* possible fault locations. After training a set of Pareto-optimal heuristics, the experimenting user is enabled to specify a maximum number of FI experiments. A detailed evaluation with a set of benchmarks running on the eCos embedded OS, including MiBench's *automotive* benchmark category, emphasizes the applicability and effectiveness of our approach: For example, when the user chooses to run only 1.5 % of all FI experiments, the average result accuracy is still 99.84 %.

1 Introduction

Recent technology roadmaps [1,2,3] suggest that future hardware designs for embedded systems will exhibit an increasing rate of soft errors, trading reliability for smaller structure sizes, lower supply voltage, and reduced production costs. This trend creates new challenges for embedded software development, which must application-specifically place error detection [4] and recovery mechanisms [5,6,7] (EDM/ERMs) that do not diminish all gains from these new hardware designs. In future embedded software, critical spots in the software stack must be hardened against hardware faults, while the remaining unprotected components economize resource consumption by occasionally tolerating incorrect results.

Architecture-level fault injection (FI) has been the standard analysis technique in the software fault-tolerance community for at least two decades [8,9]. In an FI *campaign*

A. Bondavalli and F. Di Giandomenico (Eds.): SAFECOMP 2014, LNCS 8666, pp. 17–32, 2014.
© Springer International Publishing Switzerland 2014

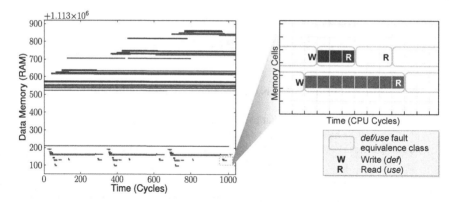

Fig. 1. Fault-space plot (left): Each coordinate in the fault space (RAM × Time) shows the outcome of one *independent* experiment that injects one transient fault at the particular coordinate. Faults that have no effect are shown as *white* points. Timeouts are denoted in *blue*, CPU exceptions in *red*, and SDCs in *black*. The magnified subplot (right) reveals def/use fault equivalence classes (see Sect. 2.1).

comprising many similar runs of an application benchmark, each run simulates the impact of a fault in a specific hardware location (e.g., a single bit in main memory or a CPU register) at a specific point in time during the benchmark's execution (e.g., one µs after the start). Unfortunately, FI campaigns exhaustively covering *all* possible fault locations are infeasible even for small target applications.

Consequently, most studies leveraging FI for dependability analysis purposes resort to *statistically sampling* fault locations [10,11]: A randomized selection of fault locations (usually in the thousands) is used to drive the FI campaign, until statistics predict a "good enough" probability for the overall result distribution to lie within the desired confidence interval. The result is an estimate on the aggregated campaign outcome – i.e., the usual probability breakup that an experiment finishes with the expected output (*no effect*), with a different output (a *silent data corruption*, SDC), that it terminates prematurely with a CPU exception, or that it runs into an endless loop and never terminates (*timeout*).[1] While an estimate on the aggregated results suffices for measuring the resiliency improvement between a benchmark's baseline and an ERM-protected variant, it gives no authoritative insights on critical spots and local phenomena, such as the vulnerability of specific data structures or program phases.

In contrast, the left half of Fig. 1 shows a visual representation of FI campaign results that were collected injecting faults into *all* possible fault locations of a particular benchmark application, requiring enormous computing power using the FAIL* [12] FI framework with an x86 simulator backend. The fault model used for Fig. 1 constitutes uniformly distributed transient bit flips in the main memory. The *fault space* spans all CPU cycles during a benchmark run, and all bits in the address space. Thus, each coordinate in Fig. 1 shows the outcome of one independent FI experiment after injecting a burst bit-flip at a specific point in time (*CPU cycles* axis) and a specific byte in main

---

[1] This result categorization is just a (common) example; depending on the analyzed benchmarks and EDMs/ERMs, the FI campaign designer may choose a more fitting categorization.

memory (*memory address* axis). A large fraction of the injected bit flips is never read by the benchmark. This fact is acknowledged by most of the white areas in Fig. 1. Only injections into memory locations that are read in subsequent CPU cycles can have an effect, indicated by a colored coordinate. With information on the memory locations of program variables, and the phases in time certain system modules are active, the user can draw detailed conclusions on the vulnerability of specific variables and program phases.

In this paper, we describe a *fault-space pruning* methodology that massively reduces the FI campaign runtime *and* keeps information on all possible fault locations in the program. The basic idea stems from a simple insight: If in two FI experiments *the machine state is similar* (or *identical*) at the point in time where the fault is injected, *the experiment result will be similar* (or *identical*), too. The primary contributions of this paper are (1) a detailed description of an effective **application-specific fault-space pruning technique** that **preserves local features** of the application's reaction to faults, (2) a means to **freely trade accuracy for experimentation runtime** without suffering the drawbacks of randomized sampling, and (3) **detailed evaluation results with benchmarks running on the eCos embedded OS [13]**, including the *automotive* category of the MiBench [14] benchmark suite.

In the following, we focus on transient burst bit flips (flipping all eight bits at one address) in main memory to approximate multi-bit flips induced by single-event upsets [15], which are commonly caused by particle strikes. We assume a uniform distribution of faults, meaning that a fault can be triggered independently at any CPU cycle and memory address. We believe, though, that our approach can be easily applied to other fault models, such as single-bit flips or transient faults in CPU registers or caches, and intend to analyze this in future work. The following section revisits related FI and fault-space pruning principles, and points to related work in these areas. Sections 3 and 4 describe the design and implementation of our generic fault-equivalence heuristic, Section 5 presents and discusses evaluation results, and Section 6 summarizes and concludes the paper.

2 Background and Related Work

Recent FI techniques that proceed with more sophistication than randomly sampling locations in the fault space are based on deterministic experiment runs[2] and recorded instruction and memory-access traces. These traces are created during a *"golden run"*, which exercises the target software without injecting faults, and, thus, serves as a reference for the expected program behavior. In the following we describe the most important FI techniques based on trace information, which opens up a wide variety of possibilities to systematically reduce the number of FI experiments.

2.1 Conservative Def/use Analysis

Smith et al. are among the first concisely describing the classical *def/use analysis* technique [16] that was subsequently reinvented several times, e.g., by Benso et al. [17],

---

[2] Note that *deterministic* does not mean that system reactions on external events, such as asynchronous device interrupts, cannot be analyzed. In deterministic benchmark runs, such events are replayed at the exact same point in time during each run.

Berrojo et al. [18], Barbosa et al. [19], and recently by Grinschgl [20]. This method *conservatively* prunes the fault space, i.e., without compromising the result quality in any way. The basic insight is that all fault locations between a *def* (a **W**rite) or *use* (a **R**ead) of data in memory[3], and a subsequent *use*, are equivalent (see the right half of Fig. 1): regardless of when exactly in this time frame a fault is injected there, the earliest point where it will become architecturally visible is when the corrupted data is read. Instead of conducting one experiment for every point within this time frame, it suffices to conduct a *single* experiment (for example at the latest possible time directly before the **R**ead), and assume the same outcome for all remaining coordinates within that *def/use equivalence class* (green frame in Fig. 1). Similarly, all points in time between a **R** or **W** and a subsequent **W** are known to result in *no effect*, as the corrupted data will be overwritten in all cases. The result is a partitioning of the fault space into def/use equivalence classes, some of which a single experiment needs to be conducted for (those ending with a **R**ead), and some with a priori known experiment outcome. Note that even if we conduct only one experiment for a particular def/use equivalence class, the experiment's result contributes to many fault locations in the fault space. For example, in the right half of Fig. 1, the lower equivalence class, which ends with a **R**ead, represents *eight* fault-injection outcomes, and has a greater weight in the outcome distribution than the upper def/use class representing *three* FI outcomes.

2.2   Fault Equivalence Heuristics

Although def/use pruning significantly reduces the number of experiments, the computational efforts for complete fault-space coverage are still far too heavy for most benchmarks. For example, the experiment count for the MiBench benchmark BASICMATH (*small* input data set, x86 build) is reduced from 5.3×10^{13} to 1.8×10^8 – still prohibitively many, even if a single experiment only takes a few seconds.

Only recently, more advanced fault-equivalence pruning techniques appear in literature, leaving the realm of conservative, accuracy-neutral methods. A significant contribution constitutes the RELYZER tool by Hari et al. [21], who describe several heuristics that combine multiple def/use equivalence classes into larger groups. From each group, only *one* representing def/use equivalence class (the *pilot*) gets picked, and the experiment result is assumed to be identical for the remaining group members. Although rather effective, a major deficiency of this approach is the inflexibility regarding the result accuracy (the authors report an average accuracy of 96 % for pilots representing their group) and experiment count tradeoff: If the result accuracy turns out too low, no alternative is offered, and if the experiment count is still too high, the authors suggest sampling from the set of pilots (resulting in the fault-space coverage problems mentioned in Sect. 1). Additionally, the grouping heuristics are based on complex control and data-flow analyses, SPARC platform specifics, and assumptions on the experiment result interpretation: RELYZER only differentiates between *no effect* and *SDC* outcomes, while in many use cases more outcome types, or even quality thresholds on the output [22], become relevant.

---

[3] This technique also works for any other level in the memory hierarchy, e.g., CPU registers or cache memory.

Li and Tan [23] describe similar pruning heuristics in their SMARTINJECTOR tool. They provide a slightly better experiment count reduction than RELYZER, but otherwise share the aforementioned drawbacks, including the single focus on SDCs, and a fixed tradeoff between accuracy (reportedly 94 % on average) and pruning effectivity.

3 A Generic Fault-Equivalence Heuristic

In the following, we outline a generalization – and simplification – of the *fault equivalence* notion coined in the works of Hari et al. [21] and Li & Tan [23], and subsequently derive a generic heuristic that ameliorates the inflexibilities mentioned in Sect. 2.2.

3.1 Fault Similarity, and a Generalization of Fault Equivalence

Instead of using the term "fault-equivalence class" from Hari and Li to denote groupings of multiple def/use equivalence classes, we will use the term *fault-similarity class* in the following to avoid confusion with *def/use equivalence classes* (cf. Sect. 2.1), and to capture the following facts:

Mispredictions May occur: One def/use class (the *pilot*) represents all the other fault-similarity class members. Due to the approximate nature of heuristics, one or more non-pilot members can have a different experiment outcome than the pilot, making the word "equivalence" unwarranted.

Equivalence Is in the Eye of the Beholder: The equivalence of two FI experiment outcomes purely depends on the experimenter's definition. While for one type of FI campaign, any deviation from the golden run is a *failure*, for others a detailed differentiation into several outcome types (cf. Sect. 1) is important. Hence, multiple def/use classes are *similar* only under the chosen evaluation metric.

Although both studies [21,23] invent various complicated analysis techniques to combine multiple def/use equivalence classes into larger groups, the general notion of *fault similarity* can be reduced to a simple insight: If at one point in time during the benchmark run the machine state is *completely identical* to the state at another point in time, conducting two FI experiments that inject a fault (e.g., a single-bit flip) at a specific memory location will yield the same result, no matter whether the fault was injected at the first or the second point in time. For example, if one FI experiment results in an *SDC* that affects the program's output, the very same thing will happen in the other experiment.

Of course, in reality the machine state is never completely identical at two points in time during a program run; even if the benchmark would enter an infinite loop, some parts of the machine (e.g., a wallclock timer) would be in a different state. Nevertheless, over the program's runtime, a *relevant part* of the machine state may be identical at several points in time. To gain a better intuition on what we mean by a relevant part of the machine state, observe the x86 assembler code snippet in Fig. 2 (left-hand side): In a loop, the (integer) elements of an array are added up in the EAX register, keeping the array index (also used for the loop abort condition) in the EDX register. When considering faults in memory only, and applying the def/use pruning method described in Sect. 2.1, the only memory-reading (*use*) instruction is the one in Line 2 (marked with

```
Assembler Source Code
1: loop:
2: # READ!, EAX += array[EDX]
3: addl array(,%edx,4),%eax
4: # increase loop count/index
5: addl $1,%edx
6: # check loop abort condition
7: cmpl $1000,%edx
8: jne loop
```

corresponding execution trace ➡

EIP	Dynamic Instruction	ESP	EBP	EDX	EAX
0x4711	addl array(,%edx,4),%eax	0xffc0	0xffe4	0x0000	0x8403
0x4716	addl $1,%edx	0xffc0	0xffe4	0x0000	0x84d4
0x4718	cmpl $1000,%edx	0xffc0	0xffe4	0x0001	0x84d4
0x471a	jne 0x4711	0xffc0	0xffe4	0x0001	0x84d4
0x4711	addl array(,%edx,4),%eax	0xffc0	0xffe4	0x0001	0x84d4
0x4716	addl $1,%edx	0xffc0	0xffe4	0x0001	0x8591
0x4718	cmpl $1000,%edx	0xffc0	0xffe4	0x0002	0x8591
0x471a	jne 0x4711	0xffc0	0xffe4	0x0002	0x8591
0x4711	addl array(,%edx,4),%eax	0xffc0	0xffe4	0x0002	0x8591
0x4716	addl $1,%edx	0xffc0	0xffe4	0x0002	0x8ce2
0x4718	cmpl $1000,%edx	0xffc0	0xffe4	0x0003	0x8ce2
0x471a	jne 0x4711	0xffc0	0xffe4	0x0003	0x8ce2

Fig. 2. Short x86 assembler snippet (left) adding up the contents of an array: All memory reads in the dynamic execution (right) share a similar machine state, and FI will lead to similar results in all cases (a wrong sum). For simplicity registers carry dummy 16-bit values.

the comment "READ!"). Injecting a fault into the memory location being read from directly before the read will lead to a similar result in all loop iterations: The resulting sum will be calculated faultily. Thus, it would suffice to do a single experiment instead of 1000, and predict the same result outcome for the others.

Now consider the machine state right before each memory read in the dynamic execution (right-hand side, highlighted lines): Among others, the EIP (instruction pointer), ESP and EBP registers are the same in all cases, EDX only differs by its lower-order bits in most consecutive loop iterations, and EAX may (depending on the magnitude of the values in the array) not change too much from one iteration to the next either. A (geometric) *projection function* of the machine-state vector – preserving only the components EIP, ESP, EBP, and the higher-order bits of EDX and EAX – therefore serves very well as a criterion to combine all these def/use equivalence classes into a single group, and to conduct a single experiment instead of one per loop iteration.

3.2 A Flexible Fault-Similarity Heuristic

Our working hypothesis is that a *projection of the machine-state vector* can successfully be used to combine multiple def/use equivalence classes with high result accuracy, depending on the user's requirements. We assume that this projection highly depends on the analyzed program(s) (including the underlying operating system) and their chosen input, the CPU architecture, the compiler, the chosen compiler optimizations, the chosen time discretization, the fault model, and what experiment outcome differentiation the user chooses. A generic fault-similarity heuristic therefore has to adapt to these factors; a detailed analysis of their impact is beyond the scope of this paper, though.

The basic idea behind our heuristic is to find a suitable machine-state projection that can be used to accurately combine def/use classes with "mostly" equivalent FI results. More in detail, we first record a machine-state vector for each *def* and *use* when recording the golden run trace; for efficiency reasons, we do not record the complete machine state, but only the values listed in Tab. 1. Then we determine FI results by running actual experiments for a feasible, randomly chosen subset of all def/use classes, which serve as the *training set* for searching a state-vector projection that accurately groups def/use classes with mostly equivalent experiment outcomes. An optimization algorithm then searches for a projection function that is optimal regarding the specified result accuracy, or the limit on the number of FI experiments, which refers to the number of fault-similarity classes.

These two criteria – *maximum accuracy* and *minimal number of fault-similarity classes* – are contradictory and can be traded for each other. One extremal point (in favor of *accuracy*) uses the identity function as the state-vector projection – hence defines all available machine state as *relevant* for grouping – and combines *no* def/use partition with another: it produces fault-similarity classes with *one* def/use member each, hence conducts an FI experiment for *every* def/use class, and achieves maximum accuracy. The other extremal point combines *all* def/use classes to a single similarity class and only conducts a single experiment, resulting in minimal experimentation effort and maximal result error. Between these extremal points exists a large search space with all possible machine-state vector projections, some of them representing Pareto-optimal solutions that optimally trade experiment effort for accuracy.

3.3 Applying the Similarity Heuristic

After finding a projection function that satisfies the user's requirements regarding accuracy and FI campaign efforts, the user can apply it to the remaining def/use classes with yet unknown outcome: multiple def/use classes with identical values in the projected machine-state vector are grouped into one common fault-similarity class. Speaking in the example from Sect. 3.1, all def/use classes with the same values in EIP, ESP, EBP, and the higher-order bits of EDX and EAX, are assigned the same fault-similarity class. For all fault-similarity classes that do not yet contain at least one member with a known outcome (because an FI experiment was run in the training phase), one pilot def/use class gets picked, and one experiment is run. After this step is completed, all def/use classes (and, thus, every coordinate in the fault space, as depicted in Fig. 1) either directly – by running an FI experiment for them – or indirectly – by looking at the pilot in their fault-similarity class – can be assigned an experiment outcome.

4 Implementation

We implemented a tool set for the outlined fault-space pruning approach in the FAIL* [12] FI experimentation framework, configured to run with the Bochs x86 simulator [24]. Ideally, we would simulate faults in a detailed register transfer and gate-level processor model; however, since simulation of realistic benchmarks on low-level models is extremely slow, this work chooses a fast architecture simulator. We extended the *tracing* plugin of FAIL* with the capability to record the additional machine state listed in Tab. 1 alongside the usual instruction and memory-access trace.

We encode the recorded machine state (Tab. 1) into a single, long bit vector with all state variables concatenated. This *state vector* exists once for every dynamic instruction in the golden run that reads memory. The projection function we want to search for is also encoded as a bit vector (with the same length as the state vector), which we call the *projection vector*. Its bits indicate whether the corresponding bit position in the machine state is **used** (1) or **not used** (0) for comparing the machine state of def/use classes, deciding whether or not to group them into a common fault-similarity class.

Table 1. Information recorded for every dynamic *def* or *use* instruction executed during the golden run of each benchmark.

data_address	Memory address the def/use writes/reads
data_value	Actual value that is written/read
EIP	Instruction pointer of the def/use instruction
dyn_instr	Dynamic instruction count since benchmark start
opcode	Instruction's opcode
EAX, EBX, ECX, EDX, ESI, EDI, ESP, EBP, EFLAGS	Contents of general-purpose registers, stack pointer, CPU flags
*EAX, *EBX, *ECX, *EDX, *ESI, *EDI, *ESP, *EBP	Contents of the machine word the respective register points to (if interpretable as a mapped memory address)
jumphistory	RELYZER [21] style (control-equivalence) bit list indicating whether each of the last 16 and next 16 conditional branches was taken
duration	Temporal duration of the def/use equivalence class (e.g., in CPU cycles)
benchmark_id	An ID uniquely identifying each benchmark

The bitwise AND of an – initially randomly chosen – projection vector and each state vector yields a vector uniquely identifying the similarity class each def/use class belongs to. The example projection function from Sect. 3.1 – preserving only the components EIP, ESP, EBP, and the higher-order bits of EDX and EAX – can directly be encoded by setting the corresponding bits in this vector.

In order to find an *optimal* projection vector, we model the search problem on the training data using the SPEA2 multi-objective evolutionary algorithm [25] (implemented in the PISA library [26]) with the projection vector as the genome, and simple multi-bit mutation and single-point crossover operators [27]. Initially we run a fixed number of 100,000 FI experiments[4] per benchmark to gain training data. Then the genetic algorithm is initialized with a population of randomized projection vectors. In every *generation* of the search algorithm, each individual's (i.e., projection bit vector's) fitness is evaluated by **1.** performing the aforementioned grouping of def/use classes from the training set into similarity classes, **2.** picking the largest[5] def/use class in each similarity class as the pilot and pretending it properly represents the remaining class members, and **3.** measuring the two fitness criteria *accuracy* and the emerging *number of fault-similarity classes* within the training set.

The *accuracy* measures how accurately the pilots *actually* represent the remaining members within their similarity classes. As a misprediction of a large (i.e., many clock cycles wide) def/use class has a greater impact on the outcome quality than a small one (cf. Sect. 2.1), the correctly predicted *area* in the fault space is used for this metric, taking the weights of the def/use classes into account:

$$\text{Accuracy} = \frac{\text{Correctly predicted fault-space area}}{\text{Total fault-space area}}$$

---

[4] This number was arbitrarily chosen for the purpose of this article, but may be selected application-specifically in the future.

[5] Currently the def/use class spanning the most CPU cycles (cf. Sect. 2.1) is chosen as each similarity class's pilot to minimize error when mispredictions occur.

The second fitness criterion is the *number of different similarity classes* emerging from the def-use class grouping step. These two criteria – the number of correctly represented faults, and the number of similarity classes that directly translates into the number of pilots (and, hence, the total number of necessary FI experiments) – are used as the optimization objectives for the SPEA2 algorithm.

5   Evaluation

In the following, we will elaborate on the evaluation setup we used, and subsequently analyze the effectiveness and efficiency of our fault-space pruning heuristic.

5.1   Evaluation Setup and Ground Truth

First, we chose a subset of the benchmark programs that accompany the eCos operating system (namely those we already used in a previous work [5]). The 19 eCos/BASELINE programs are relatively small, and test eCos kernel capabilities, such as synchronization, scheduling, and inter-process communication (refer to [5] for a more detailed description). They are also reasonably similar to each other regarding their fault propagation, which allows us to consider them as a single, combined benchmark for the remainder of this section. A second variant of the 19 programs – eCos/CRC – is hardened against memory faults by error-detection measures (CRC32 codes for all kernel objects [5] and for the stacks of preempted threads [28]), and subsequently executes about three times more dynamic executions (cf. Tab. 2). Additionally, we picked MiBench's [14] *automotive* benchmark category as a set of real-world application benchmarks. The four benchmarks (QSORT, BASICMATH, BITCOUNT, SUSAN, using the *small* input data set) each execute more dynamic instructions than all eCos benchmarks combined and represent a more heavyweight workload for our tooling.

To determine the "ground truth" for our pruning experiments, we ran FI experiments for *all* def/use equivalence classes of our benchmarks, resulting in the total (single-CPU) simulation time shown in the last column of Tab. 2. We limited FI to the first 10^7 dynamic instructions for the MiBench benchmarks to keep our computing time budgets reasonable.

For each benchmark in Tab. 2 we randomly[6] picked 100,000 def/use classes as the training set, and parametrized the genetic algorithm with a population size of 100 individuals, 400 optimization generations, and a mutation probability of 10 %. The values for these parameters were picked from experiences in early evaluation rounds; we will analyze their impact on the approach more in detail in future work.

5.2   Heuristic Training and Test

Fig. 3a shows the training results and fitness values for eCos/BASELINE after $3'40''$ of optimization (on a 32-core Intel Xeon E5-4650): Each point represents an individual (the *machine-state projection vector*; cf. Sect. 3.2), which partitions the training set into

---

[6] Uniform sampling without taking the def/use class size into account.

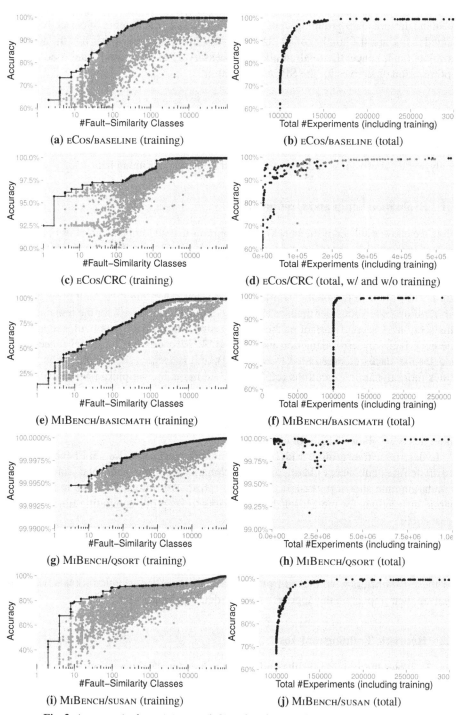

Fig. 3. Accuracy in the training set (left) and in the complete fault space (right).

Table 2. Dynamic instruction counts, simulated CPU cycles, num. of 8-bit burst FI experiments necessary after basic def/use pruning (cf. Sect. 2.1), and FI simulation runtime for all experiments (and the 100,000 experiment training set). For the eCos benchmarks, the total CPU cycles differ from the dynamic instructions due to idle phases; for MiBench, we limited FI to the first 10^7 dynamic instructions.

Benchmark	Dyn. instr.	CPU cycles	# FI exp. after def/use pruning	FI simulation runtime
eCos/BASELINE	1.08×10^7	9.7×10^9	1.48×10^7	4,946 hrs (33.4 hrs)
eCos/CRC	2.73×10^7	9.7×10^9	4.15×10^7	15,035 hrs (36.1 hrs)
MiBench/QSORT	4.20×10^7	4.20×10^7	1.48×10^7 (of 5.49×10^7)	44,139 hrs (297.6 hrs)
MiB/BASICMATH	1.47×10^8	1.47×10^8	1.24×10^7 (of 1.84×10^8)	95,068 hrs (767.8 hrs)
MiB/BITCOUNT	4.08×10^7	4.08×10^7	2.89×10^6 (of 9.15×10^6)	3,621 hrs (124.9 hrs)
MiBench/SUSAN	2.95×10^7	2.95×10^7	1.25×10^7 (of 3.68×10^7)	23,526 hrs (186.9 hrs)

a number of fault-similarity classes (X-axis, logarithmic scale, with possible values from 1 to 100,000). As described in Sect. 4, the accuracy of such a partioning, plotted on the Y-axis, is defined as the percentage of correctly represented fault-space area.

The optimization yields a set of Pareto-optimal solutions (black) the user can choose from to partition the benchmark's *complete* fault space in the next step (cf. Sect. 3.3). Fig. 3b shows the test results when applying all previously determined, Pareto-optimal projection vectors to the complete fault space while reusing all results from the 100,000 training FI experiments: Depending on the partitioning our heuristic creates in the complete fault space, more experiments than the initial training experiments need to be conducted to get a representing pilot for *all* new fault-similarity classes. For a chosen projection, the accuracy drops by a nonlinear factor (in the order of 0.1 % for highly-accurate, up to 20 % for the low-quality solutions) from training to test. For example, a solution with 99.9986 % accuracy in the training set (9,012 fault-similarity classes) requires the user to conduct 99,308 additional FI experiments (totaling in 199,308 including the training set, from a total of 14.8 million, cf. Tab. 2) and reconstructs the complete fault space with 99.2512 % accuracy; a solution with 99.9903 % training set accuracy (2,100 fault-similarity classes) yields 90.4036 % accuracy with 8,243 additional experiments (108,243 total).

In Fig. 4, we apply the latter example solution to the complete eCos/BASELINE fault space, illustrating the advertised local fault-space feature preservation of our heuristic: A close-up of a small area of the fault-space plot of the eCos/BASELINE MUTEX1 benchmark (actually the same excerpt as in Fig. 1) even remains largely intact when after training only 8,243 additional FI experiments (totaling 108,243 including the training set, a mere 0.73 % of all 14.8 million eCos/BASELINE experiments) are conducted.

Subsequently we investigated how well previously trained solutions apply to a new, unknown (yet not completely different) benchmark. As described in the previous section,

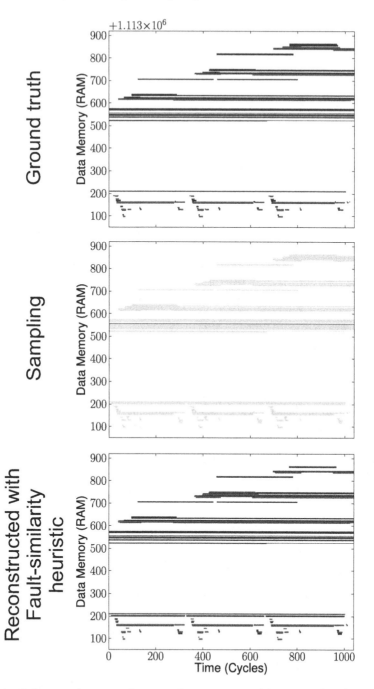

Fig. 4. A tiny fault-space plot excerpt from a stack memory area of the MUTEX1 benchmark (from top to bottom; color coding as in Fig. 1): Ground-truth results (100 % FI experiments), results from sampling 0.73 % of all experiments (gray areas are unknown results, i.e., def/use classes that were not sampled or known a priori), and reconstructed results with also a total of 0.73 % (including training set) of all experiments for the ECOS/BASELINE benchmarks.

the ECos/CRC benchmark comprises the same 19 programs as ECos/BASELINE, yet they are hardened against memory faults, and execute substantially more dynamic instructions. Probably most notably they introduce a new FI experiment outcome type "detected" that signals a successful error detection of an EDM: This outcome type does not exist in ECos/BASELINE, and, thus, cannot have been observed by the training process from Fig. 3a. The black points in Fig. 3d show how well these projection vectors perform for ECos/CRC without any ECos/CRC-specific training. (Hence, there is no initial 100,000 FI experiment penalty for the training set). One interesting observation is that the solutions requiring up to 300,000 FI experiments are partially in the 90–97 % accuracy range, but by far not as close to 100 % as in the ECos/BASELINE plot (Fig. 3b). Nevertheless, previously trained heuristics seem to be reusable even for unknown benchmarks: As our training process only learns how to group def/use classes into fault-similarity classes, but does not try to completely *predict* experiment outcomes without carrying out new FI experiments, it can even deal with previously unseen experiment outcomes, such as "detected" in this case. Fig. 3c and the green points in Fig. 3d show the accuracy results after training specifically for ECos/CRC:[7] The accuracy (and especially the accuracy mapping from training to test) is significantly better than without training (the low-quality left margin vanishes), but at the cost of an initial training phase and more FI experiments depending on the desired accuracy.

Among the remaining Fig. 3e–3j (MIBENCH/BITCOUNT is omitted due to space constraints, but closely resembles the plots for SUSAN), MIBENCH/QSORT displays an extremely high accuracy even for minimal numbers of additional experiments: With 100,012 FI experiments (results from training, plus 12 new fault-similarity classes in the complete fault space) it achieves an accuracy of 99.9902 %. The primary reason for this is that the vast majority (99.9892 %) of experiment outcomes for this benchmark are SDCs (not very astonishing for a benchmark sorting a long list of text strings), which allows to create extremely large fault-similarity classes that yield the same outcome.

5.3 Experiment Outcome Breakup and Comparison with Sampling

As the user is, apart from fault-space details, also interested in the usual experiment outcome breakup (for example, in the BASICMATH benchmark, 34.18 % of all faults result in *no effect*, 19.34 % *SDC*, 31.80 % *CPU exception*, 14.68 % *timeout*), this aggregate should not turn out to be inaccurate either. Fig. 5 shows the root mean squared error (RMSE) of experiment outcome breakups for a selection of benchmarks with the Pareto-optimal heuristics from Fig. 3 applied to their complete fault space (black points and green points with the same meaning as in the previous section): As expected, the fault-space reconstruction accuracy and the outcome breakup RMSE correlate quite well – good local accuracy also yields a good global accuracy.

The plots in Fig. 5 also include the outcome breakup RMSE for FI sampling (with fault expansion [29]; red lines in the figure), a technique commonly used to *only* estimate the breakup without gaining any information on local fault-space details. Interestingly, in some cases sampling yields inferior results – especially for the un-trained

---

[7] ... and reusing some of the ECos/BASELINE projection vectors as the initial population for the optimization algorithm.

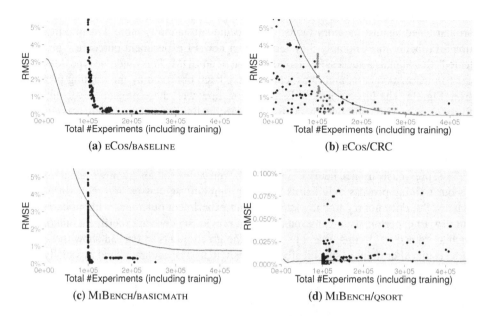

Fig. 5. Comparison to sampling (red line): RMSE of the outcome probability breakup is comparable to, and many cases better than the common sampling approach – which completely lacks information on local fault-space details.

heuristic configurations in the ECos/CRC case (Fig. 5b, black points) as it does not have the experiment-count penalty of a training set. This means our heuristic can compete with sampling, although it yields much more detailed information on the fault space, e.g., for EDM/ERM placement.

6   Conclusions and Future Work

We presented an adaptive, application-specific fault-space pruning technique that preserves local features of the fault space for detailed susceptibility analyses. The approach allows the user to freely trade accuracy for experimentation runtime, choosing a Pareto-optimal heuristic that was trained with a feasible FI experiment subset from the program(s) under analysis. Our results confirm the assumption that a machine-state subset can be successfully used to partition the fault space into fault-similarity classes, allowing to gain insights on local phenomena for EDM/ERM placement with massively reduced experimentation efforts: For example, when the user chooses to run 1.5 % of all FI experiments, the average (weighted by the total number of faults in each benchmark) result accuracy is 99.84 %.[8] In many cases our fault-space pruning technique even outperforms classic sampling techniques, although they do not preserve any fault-space details.

Future work includes a detailed analysis of the various free parameters of our approach, including the impact of different training-set sizes, the genetic algorithm's

---

[8] Except for BITCOUNT, where training yields no solution that only needs 1.5 % experiments. Here, the user can achieve, e.g., 99.84 % accuracy for 4 % of all experiments.

configuration (population size, generation number, and mutation probability), and the chosen genome representation itself. To gain more confidence in the genericity of our approach, we intend to evaluate it on other instruction-set architectures and with other types of benchmark applications. We also plan to analyze different fault models, and consider to completely replace the evolutionary algorithm with a more sophisticated machine-learning algorithm. Beyond this, merging the training phase and the FI campaign into a continuously adapting online training might speed up the dependability assessment process even more.

Acknowledgments. This work was partly supported by the German Research Foundation (DFG) priority program SPP 1500 under grant no. SP 968/5-2. The authors would like to thank Jochen Streicher for lenghty discussions on quality metrics and machine learning, Adrian Böckenkamp, Richard Hellwig and Lars Rademacher for feedback on the core idea of the pruning heuristic, and Daniel Cordes for initial help with the PISA library.

References

1. Borkar, S.Y.: Designing reliable systems from unreliable components: The challenges of transistor variability and degradation. IEEE Micro 25(6), 10–16 (2005)
2. Duranton, M., Yehia, S., de Sutter, B., de Bosschere, K., Cohen, A., Falsafi, B., Gaydadjiev, G., Katevenis, M., Maebe, J., Munk, H., Navarro, N., Ramirez, A., Temam, O., Valero, M.: The HiPEAC vision. Technical report, HiPEAC (2010)
3. Narayanan, V., Xie, Y.: Reliability concerns in embedded system designs. IEEE Comp. 39(1), 118–120 (2006)
4. Hari, S.K.S., Adve, S.V., Naeimi, H.: Low-cost program-level detectors for reducing silent data corruptions. In: 42nd IEEE/IFIP Int. Conf. on Dep. Sys. & Netw., DSN 2012. IEEE (2012)
5. Borchert, C., Schirmeier, H., Spinczyk, O.: Generative software-based memory error detection and correction for operating system data structures. In: 43rd IEEE/IFIP Int. Conf. on Dep. Sys. & Netw., DSN 2013. IEEE (June 2013)
6. Borchert, C., Schirmeier, H., Spinczyk, O.: Protecting the dynamic dispatch in C++ by dependability aspects. In: 1st GI W'shop on SW-Based Methods for Robust Embedded Sys., SOBRES 2012. LNI, pp. 521–535. German Society of Informatics (September 2012)
7. Borchert, C., Schirmeier, H., Spinczyk, O.: Return-address protection in C/C++ code by dependability aspects. In: 2nd GI W'shop on SW-Based Methods for Robust Embedded Sys., SOBRES 2013. LNI. German Society of Informatics (September 2013)
8. Arlat, J., Aguera, M., Amat, L., Crouzet, Y., Fabre, J.C., Laprie, J.C., Martins, E., Powell, D.: Fault injection for dependability validation: A methodology and some applications. IEEE TOSE 16(2), 166–182 (1990)
9. Benso, A., Prinetto, P.: Fault injection techniques and tools for embedded systems reliability evaluation. Frontiers in electronic testing. Kluwer, Boston (2003)
10. Leveugle, R., Calvez, A., Maistri, P., Vanhauwaert, P.: Statistical fault injection: Quantified error and confidence. In: IEEE 2009 Conf. on Design, Autom. & Test in Europe, DATE 2009, pp. 502–506 (2009)
11. Ramachandran, P., Kudva, P., Kellington, J., Schumann, J., Sanda, P.: Statistical fault injection. In: 38th IEEE/IFIP Int. Conf. on Dep. Sys. & Netw., DSN 2008, pp. 122–127. IEEE (2008)

12. Schirmeier, H., Hoffmann, M., Kapitza, R., Lohmann, D., Spinczyk, O.: FAIL*: Towards a versatile fault-injection experiment framework. In: Mühl, G., Richling, J., Herkersdorf, A. (eds.) 25th Int. Conf. on Arch. of Comp. Sys., ARCS 2012, Workshop Proceedings. LNI, vol. 200, pp. 201–210. German Society of Informatics (March 2012)

13. Massa, A.: Embedded Software Development with eCos. Prentice Hall (2002)

14. Guthaus, M.R., Ringenberg, J.S., Ernst, D., Austin, T.M., Mudge, T., Brown, R.B.: MiBench: A free, commercially representative embedded benchmark suite. In: IEEE Int. W'shop. on Workload Characterization (WWC 2001), pp. 3–14. IEEE, Washington, DC (2001)

15. Mukherjee, S.: Architecture Design for Soft Errors. Morgan Kaufmann (2008)

16. Smith, D.T., Johnson, B.W., Profeta III, J.A., Bozzolo, D.G.: A method to determine equivalent fault classes for permanent and transient faults. In: Annual Reliability and Maintainability Symposium, pp. 418–424 (January 1995)

17. Benso, A., Rebaudengo, M., Impagliazzo, L., Marmo, P.: Fault-list collapsing for fault-injection experiments. In: Annual Reliability and Maintainability Symposium (January 1998)

18. Berrojo, L., Gonzalez, I., Corno, F., Reorda, M., Squillero, G., Entrena, L., Lopez, C.: New techniques for speeding-up fault-injection campaigns. In: 2002 Conf. on Design, Autom. & Test in Europe, DATE 2002, pp. 847–852 (2002)

19. Barbosa, R., Vinter, J., Folkesson, P., Karlsson, J.: Assembly-level pre-injection analysis for improving fault injection efficiency. In: Dal Cin, M., Kaâniche, M., Pataricza, A. (eds.) EDCC 2005. LNCS, vol. 3463, pp. 246–262. Springer, Heidelberg (2005)

20. Grinschgl, J., Krieg, A., Steger, C., Weiss, R., Bock, H., Haid, J.: Efficient fault emulation using automatic pre-injection memory access analysis. In: SOC Conference, pp. 277–282 (2012)

21. Hari, S.K.S., Adve, S.V., Naeimi, H., Ramachandran, P.: Relyzer: Exploiting application-level fault equivalence to analyze application resiliency to transient faults. In: 17th Int. Conf. on Arch. Support for Programming Languages and Operating Systems, ASPLOS 2012, pp. 123–134. ACM, New York (2012)

22. Döbel, B., Schirmeier, H., Engel, M.: Investigating the limitations of PVF for realistic program vulnerability assessment. In: 5rd HiPEAC W'shop on Design for Reliability (DFR 2013), Berlin, Germany (January 2013)

23. Li, J., Tan, Q.: SmartInjector: Exploiting intelligent fault injection for SDC rate analysis. In: IEEE Int. Symp. on Defect & Fault Tol. in VLSI & Nanotech. Sys., DFT 2013 (2013)

24. Lawton, K.P.: Bochs: A portable PC emulator for Unix/X. Linux Journal 1996(29es) (1996)

25. Zitzler, E., Laumanns, M., Thiele, L.: SPEA2: Improving the strength pareto evolutionary algorithm for multiobjective optimization. In: Giannakoglou, K.C., Tsahalis, D.T., Périaux, J., Papailiou, K.D., Fogarty, T. (eds.) Evolutionary Methods for Design Optimization and Control with Applications to Industrial Problems, Athens, Greece. International Center for Numerical Methods in Engineering, pp. 95–100 (September 2001)

26. Bleuler, S., Laumanns, M., Thiele, L., Zitzler, E.: PISA — a platform and programming language independent interface for search algorithms. In: Fonseca, C.M., Fleming, P.J., Zitzler, E., Deb, K., Thiele, L. (eds.) EMO 2003. LNCS, vol. 2632, pp. 494–508. Springer, Heidelberg (2003)

27. Mitchell, M.: An Introduction to Genetic Algorithms. MIT Press (1998)

28. Hoffmann, M., Borchert, C., Dietrich, C., Schirmeier, H., Kapitza, R., Spinczyk, O., Lohmann, D.: Effectiveness of fault detection mechanisms in static and dynamic operating system designs. In: 17th IEEE Int. Symp. on OO Real-Time Distrib. Computing, ISORC 2014. IEEE (2014)

29. Smith, D.T., Johnson, B.W., Andrianos, N., Profeta III., J.A.: A variance-reduction technique via fault-expansion for fault-coverage estimation. IEEE TR 46(3), 366–374 (1997)

Safety Validation of Sense and Avoid Algorithms Using Simulation and Evolutionary Search

Xueyi Zou, Rob Alexander, and John McDermid

Department of Computer Science, University of York, UK
{xz972,rob.alexander,john.mcdermid}@york.ac.uk

Abstract. We present a safety validation approach for Sense and Avoid (SAA) algorithms aboard Unmanned Aerial Vehicles (UAVs). We build multi-agent simulations to provide a test arena for UAVs with various SAA algorithms, in order to explore potential conflict situations. The simulation is configured by a series of parameters, which define a huge input space. Evolutionary search is used to explore the input space and to guide the simulation towards challenging situations, thus accelerating the process of finding dangerous faults of SAA algorithms and supporting the safety validation process. We applied our approach to the recently published Selective Velocity Obstacles (SVO) algorithm. In our first experiment, we used both random and evolutionary search to find mid-air collisions where UAVs have perfect sensing ability. We found evolutionary search can find some faults (here, interesting problems with SVO) that random search takes a long time to find. Our second experiment added sensor noise to the model. Random search found similar problems as it did in experiment one, but the evolutionary search found some interesting new problems. The two experiments show that the proposed approach has potential for safety validation of SAA algorithms.

Keywords: Sense and Avoid, Unmanned Aerial Vehicles, safety validation, multi-agent simulation, evolutionary search, Genetic Algorithm.

1   Introduction

Amazon, the world's largest online retailer, announced its "Prime Air" plan in 2013, where Unmanned Aerial Vehicles (UAVs) will be used to deliver goods to customers. However, this is only a fiction now: UAVs are not currently permitted to access civilian airspace in most countries due to safety considerations. One of the safety concerns is the UAV's inability to avoid mid-air collision with other aircraft. To alleviate this concern, UAVs must provide what is referred to as a Sense and Avoid (SAA) capability. In [1], SAA is defined as *"the capability of a UAV to remain well clear from and avoid collisions with other airborne traffic. Sense and Avoid provides the functions of self-separation and collision avoidance to establish an analogous to "see and avoid" required by manned aircraft"*.

As for collision avoidance, a wide variety of approaches have been proposed in the general field of robotics [2-6] that have the potential to be adapted for UAVs.

A. Bondavalli and F. Di Giandomenico (Eds.): SAFECOMP 2014, LNCS 8666, pp. 33–48, 2014.
© Springer International Publishing Switzerland 2014

The safety of these approaches, however, is by no means well understood. Considering the strict safety requirements in the aviation sector, a collision avoidance algorithm cannot be accepted and deployed without rigorous safety validation.

Validation is the process of determining whether a product (e.g. a piece of implemented software or a system) has the desired properties; desired, that is, in hindsight, rather than with reference to a pre-defined specification. Validation is different from verification, which is often conducted at the end of each development stage to determine whether a product of that stage (e.g. specification, computer model, design, and implementation etc.) is consistent with an explicit specification (or reference model). It is entirely possible that a product passes verification but fails validation, for example when the specification has not captured what the user actually wants or needs.

By *safety* validation, we mean the process of determining whether a product will behave safely during operation in terms of protecting itself, the environment it inhabits, and humans. Safety validation is difficult, firstly because users (regulators, operators, bystanders) often cannot provide precise safety requirements for complex, novel systems. Secondly, the operational environment of the product may be too complex to predict the range of possible operational scenarios in advance, which makes it hard to fill in the missing requirements.

For SAA algorithms, the conventional approaches for safety validation are simulation and flight test. Due to the high cost of flight test, it can only be conducted for a very limited time and thus gives limited assurance, although it does have the great advantage of testing real aircraft behaviours. Simulation is more cost-effective and thus can cover a far larger part of the possible operational situations, albeit subject to limitations in the fidelity of the simulation.

In this paper, we present a safety validation approach for SAA algorithms based on multi-agent simulation and evolutionary search. Arnold and Alexander previously presented an approach to testing autonomous robot control software [7], which they claimed to also have potential for validation. They randomly created a diverse range of situations and executed them in the Player/Stage robot simulator to test whether the robot behaved safely. The work presented in this paper is an advancement of [7], specifically in that we use evolutionary search to guide the simulation towards challenging situations. We believe that this has greater potential to reveal safety issues than randomized simulations. Moreover, we test our approach using a promising new collision avoidance algorithm (Selective Velocity Obstacles), rather than the quite simple algorithm (Smoothed Nearness Diagrams) tested in [7].

The paper is organized as follows: in section 2 we identify the challenges for such a safety validation approach, in section 3 we explain our proposed approach, and in section 4 we describe experimental use of our approach to validate the safety of the Selective Velocity Obstacles approach. Section 5 summaries the paper and outlines our future plans.

2   Challenges for an Automated Safety Validation Approach

Ideally, a safety validation approach would reveal all safety issues (dangerous faults) of the validated system (if there are any). It would do so efficiently, and would give confidence regarding the extent to which all the credible faults have been revealed. In this paper we attack only a small piece of the puzzle – given a space of situations and a system under validation, how we can efficiently home in on hazardous situations that we haven't seen before?

As stated in [7], to reveal as many faults as possible, a wide range of diverse test situations should be generated. It is important to favour situations that have a high likelihood of causing dangerous behaviours of the validated system; otherwise, it would be easy for an approach to spend most of its time in generating safe situations, which is computationally inefficient. In this paper, we use evolutionary search to generate test situations with a high collision risk.

A second challenge is "situation coverage" – testing the maximum proportion of potentially dangerous situations that the system could ever encounter [7]. Here, we partially address this using an encounter model of possible situation types to generate a broad distribution of specific situations.

A third challenge is simulation fidelity, in particular whether there are faults in the system that the simulation cannot reveal because they depend on details that are not modelled. In this paper, we explore this issue in a simple way – we run simulations with both infallible sensors and sensors subject to random noise, and look at how the results of the latter simulations are richer (in terms of the range of hazardous situations found).

In section 5, we discuss briefly how we will further address these issues in our future work.

3   Proposed Method

The proposed method is the integration of multi-agent simulation and evolutionary search. We build multi-agent simulations to provide a test arena for UAVs with various SAA algorithms, in order to explore potential conflict situations. The simulation is configured by a series of parameters, which define a huge input space. Evolutionary search is used to explore the input space and to guide the simulation towards challenging situations, thus accelerating the process of finding faults and supporting the safety validation process.

Multi-agent Simulation

We use MASON (See *http://cs.gmu.edu/~eclab/projects/mason/*) as our multi-agent simulation framework. In a typical multi-agent simulation, there are three basic elements: agents, environment, and their interactions. The agents in our simulation are UAVs with various kinds of SAA algorithms. They have attributes, such as maximum and minimum speed, maximum turning rate, etc., and they also have behaviours, such as sensing other UAVs and avoiding them. The environment in our simulation is simplified as a 2-D rectangular horizontal flight area with length and width set according to the range of the "Traffic Advisory (TA)" and "Resolution Advisory (RA)" regions of the TCAS (traffic alert and collision avoidance system). Apart from UAVs, some other entities in the environment are waypoints for navigation, and the start point and destination of each UAV. The interactions between the UAVs are only via the sense and avoid algorithms. We have not modelled any explicit communication between UAVs. The interactions between UAVs and the environment include UAVs following waypoints and generating new waypoints for collision avoidance.

To validate the safety of SAA algorithms, the simulation should simulate different encounters for the SAA algorithm to handle. We developed "encounter generators" that can generate three kinds of encounters, each involving two UAVs: (1) head on encounters, (2) crossing encounters, and (3) tail approach encounters. We refer to one of the UAVs as the "subject" UAV and the other as an intruder. Using any one of the encounter generators, the intruder's start point, velocity vector and destination can be decided on the premise that the subject UAV's start point, velocity vector and destination have been fixed. The three encounters are explained as follows:

1. The head on encounter is where the subject UAV and the intruder approach each other in opposite directions, as illustrated in Fig. 1 (a). The intruder can approach the subject UAV from either the left side or the right side with a certain offset.
2. The crossing encounter is where the subject UAV and the intruder approach each other at an encounter angle ranging from $0°$ (exclusive) to 180^0 (exclusive) from either the left or the right side, as illustrated in Fig. 1 (b). If the encounter angle equals 180^0, it is a head on encounter without offset. If the encounter angle equals $0°$, it is a tail approach encounter without offset, which will be discussed next.
3. The tail approach encounter is where the intruder overtakes or is overtaken by the subject UAV flying on parallel tracks, as illustrated in Fig. 1 (c). The intruder can overtake or be overtaken by the subject UAV from the left side or the right side with a certain offset.

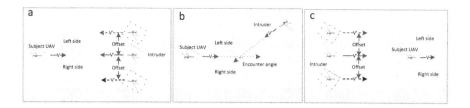

Fig. 1. (a) Head on; (b) Crossing; (c) Tail approach

Some global agents are utilized to monitor the simulation: a "proximity measurer" measures the nearest distance of each UAV to other UAVs in every simulation step and the most dangerous proximity of each UAV to others in a simulation run; an "accident detector" monitors the simulation and logs accidents and removes UAVs disabled by a collision. These global monitoring agents play an important role in guiding the search (which will be described later) towards challenging situations.

As stated above, the simulation is configured by a series of parameters, which can be divided into three categories:

1. parameters for one or more encounters, e.g. the parameter to decide which encounter should be simulated in a simulation run, and the parameters used to generate that encounter;
2. parameters for the subject UAV, e.g. the subject UAV's destination, its maximum and minimum speed, maximum acceleration and turning rate;
3. parameters for the intruders, e.g. the intruder's (or intruders') maximum and minimum speed, maximum acceleration and turning rate.

Evolutionary Search

The evolutionary search part of the approach is implemented by using ECJ (See *http://cs.gmu.edu/~eclab/projects/ecj/*), which is a Java-based evolutionary computation research system. We have experimented with Genetic Algorithms (GA).

To use GA, first, the initial population is set up with n individuals, with each individual's genome representing the settings of the simulation parameters identified above. Then each individual of the population is evaluated by a simulation run and the fitness of that individual can be calculated. According to the fitness, the selection process will (re)sample n individuals from the population, and the selected individuals' genome will be "crossed-over" and mutated. After these genetic operations, the individuals will be used to form the next generation of the population, which will replace the old population. This process goes on until it runs out of time or the ideal individual(s) has been found.

The fitness of an individual is calculated by applying a "fitness function" to it. Defining a good fitness function is a crucial task in GA work, as it will ultimately determine where the search moves towards. In our case, a good fitness function should favour those individuals that embody hazardous situations, while avoiding premature convergence (i.e. avoiding the population becoming very homogenous). Since the main concern of SAA is mid-air collision, we define a fitness function based on the nearest distance between pair of UAVs during each simulation run observed by our "proximity measurer".

Similarities to Existing Approaches

It is noted that our approach shares commonalities with search-based software testing where meta-heuristic search techniques are employed for automatic generation of test data [8]. Whilst none of the results from that work are directly comparable to what we have presented here, we have adapted some of the ideas for our work. In search-based software testing, test data are generated as the input of a piece of code (or software) while in this paper, we use evolutionary search to generate input data (e.g. configuration parameters) for multi-agent simulations. This is because, for SAA algorithms, safety cannot be analysed without consideration of other UAVs and the environment.

Similar approaches have also been used in the ASHiCS (Automating the Search for Hazards in Complex Systems) project [9] and by Alam et al. in [10, 11] to conduct safety analysis of ATM (Air Traffic Management) systems. However, their main concern is to identify the combination of airspace configurations and Air Traffic Controller's actions that can result in a high collision risk. This is different from our work that is to identify safety issues of SAA algorithms.

4   Experiments and Findings

4.1   Case Study Introduction

We confine the experiments to two UAV encounters, where the two UAVs run the same SAA algorithm, though it is possible for our approach to handle multiple UAVs with heterogeneous SAA algorithms. We have tested our proposed approach on the recently published Selective Velocity Obstacles (SVO) [4] algorithm for collision avoidance. We selected SVO because it improves the widely studied Velocity Obstacles [3] approach to accommodate the common right-of-way rules of the air while providing collision avoidance capability. Full details of SVO are provided in [4]; below, we provide a brief summary.

A velocity obstacle is the set of all velocity vectors of an agent (UAV) that will result in a collision with other agents (or obstacles) at some moment in time, assuming that the other agents maintain their current velocity vectors [3]. It follows that if the agent chooses a velocity vector outside its velocity obstacle, then a collision will not occur in a certain time horizon.

SVO is designed for cooperative collision avoidance, where each UAV in an encounter cooperatively avoids each other while obeying the right-of-way rules. The rules are as follows [4, 12]:

1. On a converging encounter, the one on the right has the right-of-way;
2. On a head-on encounter, both aircraft should move to the right side;
3. The one that is about to be overtaken has the right-of-way;
4. Avoidance manoeuvres should not go over, under, or in front of other aircraft that have the right-of-way, except when it is clear.

Here three types of encounters are defined: Converging, Head-on, and Overtaking as illustrated in Fig. 2. Note they are different from the encounters defined by our simulation as illustrated in Fig. 1, which we think will help in revealing faults. SVO defines a way to selectively avoid the other UAV(s) by defining three manoeuvre modes [4], which are

1. **Avoid**, where the host UAV takes an manoeuvre to avoid collision with others;
2. **Maintain**, where the host UAV keeps its current velocity vector;
3. **Restore**, where the collision avoidance system gives back the control to the original controller/pilot.

It is noted that, for a UAV to use the SVO approach, the only information it needs about the others is their current positions, velocity vectors and shapes. It is assumed that each UAV has perfect sensing ability when fitted with ADS-B[1] to enable the cooperative collision avoidance (comments on the capabilities of ADS-B are outside the scope of this paper). In the experiments, we added some dynamic constraints on the UAVs, which were converted from the performance data of Global Hawk given in [6], as shown in Table 1. For SVO, when in the "Avoid" mode, it is desirable for the host UAV to select a new velocity vector outside its velocity obstacle induced by others but still obey the right-of-way rules. However, considering the dynamic constraints, we assume that each UAV can only avoid others by turning right 2.5deg/s. This means that during a simulation run, the magnitude of each UAV's velocity vector keeps constant and only the direction of the velocity vector will change. Another consideration for this is that we follow the policy given in [4] and set the other manoeuvres, such as the "climb and descend" for non-cooperative situations and speed and direction change for conflict resolution[2]. Note that, between simulation runs, the velocity magnitude also varies.

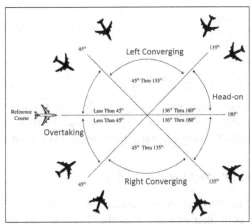

Fig. 2. AV encounter types, adapted from manned air traffic [13]

Table 1. UAV performance limits

Max speed	92.6m/s	Min speed	51.4m/s
Normal speed	77.2m/s	Max turning rate	2.5deg/s

Collision avoidance manoeuvres in some typical encounters are shown in Fig. 3. In the figures in this paper, the subject UAV always starts from the middle of the left side. The points in the diagram were generated by the SVO algorithm to denote the waypoints the host UAV should navigate by – the bigger red points generated from

---

[1] ADSB (Automatic Dependent Surveillance-Broadcast) is a cooperative surveillance technology with which a UAV will send its real time information, such as position and velocity, to its peers via a radio frequency.

[2] Conflict resolution resolves situations where the distance between two UAVs becomes or is forecasted to become less than the minimum desired separation distance. It happens before collision avoidance, so is outside the scope of the SVO algorithm.

Avoid" modes, the smaller orange points from "Maintain" modes, and the black hollow points from "Restore" modes.

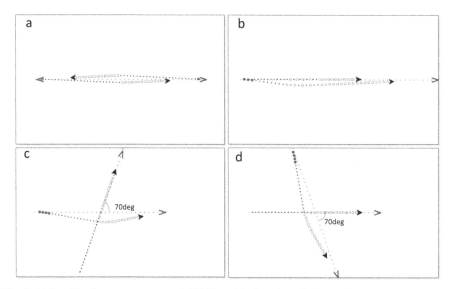

Fig. 3. (a) In a Head-on encounter, each UAV avoids the other; (b) In an Overtaking encounter, the front one has the right-of-way; (c) In a right Converging encounter, the intruder has the right-of-way; (d) In a left Converging encounter, the subject UAV has the right-of-way

4.2   Experiment 1: Perfect Sensing Ability

Experiment 1 was conducted under the assumption that each UAV has perfect sensing ability – they know both their own and the other UAV's real time position and velocity vector.

Experiment 1.1

We first used random search as pre-treatment to find some "obvious" mid-air collisions. We conducted random search 3 times, with 250,000 uniformly distributed sample points (simulation runs) each time. Overall there were 9 mid-air collisions, all of which happened in crossing encounters. Examples and their parameter settings are shown in Table 2.

From Table 2 one pattern can be found – the encounters are all left side crossing (according to Fig. 1) with encounter angles around 46°; and the subject UAV's speed is very high (92.6 is the maximum speed for this kind of UAV) while the intruder's speed is very low (51.4 is the minimum speed for this kind of UAV).

When we scrutinize all these encounters, a typical situation is shown in Fig. 4. The situation is "Left Converging" according to Fig. 2, where the subject UAV has the right-of-way. The intruder made a right turn manoeuvre. But since the subject UAV was at high speed and the intruder was at low speed, the manoeuvre was not enough to avoid a collision.

Table 2. Mid-air collisions and their parameter settings revealed in experiment 1.1

	Subject UAV speed	Is right side	Encounter angle	Intruder speed
Trial 1	92.00	NO	46.15	54.34
Trial 2	90.70	NO	45.18	54.30
	....	....	....	....
Trial 3	89.86	NO	45.27	52.70
	....	....	....	....
	92.60	NO	46.75	55.50
Average	90.98		46.01	54.33

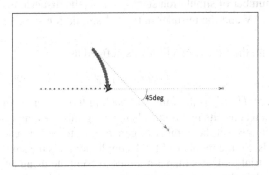

Fig.4. A typical encounter found in experiment 1.1

It is noted that of all the 3*250,000=750,000 random searched points, random search found only 9 "obvious" mid-air collisions. Either there are few obvious collision situations, or random search has difficulty finding more challenging situations.

It was not clear whether or not the "obvious" situations found so far constitute all the possible situations that will result in a mid-air collision for the SVO algorithm. We explored this in experiments 1.2 and 1.3.

Experiment 1.2

Experiment 1.2 was intended to find new, subtler, situations that will result in mid-air collisions other than those found in experiment 1.1 using random search. To this end, if we sampled a point that corresponded to the class of collision situations found in 1.1, it was discarded without ever being simulated. These points were identified based on them satisfying all of the following conditions:

1. It is a left side crossing encounter;
2. The subject UAV's speed minus the intruder's speed is more than 18m/s;
3. The encounter angle is greater than 45°, but it is less than 51.2°.

The numbers above were estimated from the numbers in the "Average" row of Table 2 with some extra margin. Thus we excluded the "obvious" dangerous encounters already identified, ensuring that the search were only looking for "new" problems.

We conducted random search 3 times, with 250,000 sample points each time. Of all the sampled points, we found *no* mid-air collision and thus nothing interesting.

Experiment 1.3

The purpose of experiment 1.3 was the same as experiment 1.2, but evolutionary search was used instead. The point discarding conditions were the same as those in experiment 1.2. Whenever a new individual was created that matched all of the conditions, it was immediately awarded the worst possible fitness value (i.e. 0) without ever being simulated.

In the experiment, since we only considered two UAV encounters, the objective was thus to minimize the average of the minimum distances[3] of each UAV to the other (the minimum distances were actually equal). Formally, it was defined as:

$$minimize Z = \frac{min_{i \in [0,s]}\{X_{jk_i}\} + min_{i \in [0,s]}\{X_{kj_i}\}}{2}$$

where s is the number of simulation steps; X_{jk_i} is the distance to collision between the subject UAV and the intruder in the ith simulation step; and X_{kj_i} is the reverse.

In this experiment, the fitness function was defined as:

$$f(ind) = \frac{1}{1+Z}$$

where the value of $f(ind)$ is the fitness of each individual, and when Z equals 0 this fitness function reaches its maximum, 1, meaning there is a mid-air collision.

In this experiment, we set the number of generations to be 500, each generation with 500 individuals. So the number of total sample points is the same as before. We made 3 trials. Each trial took less than 3 minutes to compute using an ordinary desktop, slightly longer than the previous random searches, which took about 2.5 minutes.

From the log we can see a fast increase in average fitness in the beginning generations as illustrated by the blue curves in Fig. 5. It means over these generations, the average minimum distance between the two UAVs decreased quickly and the evolutionary search was guiding the simulation towards more challenging situations. The figure also shows that the average fitness curves all reached a near-plateau before 100 generations, but their values varied. The third trial got the greatest value.

As shown by the orange curves in Fig. 5. (a) and (b), the first two trials did not find any mid-air collision, but the third trial found many (Fig. 5. (c)). Note that in Fig. 5. (c), the average fitness near-plateaus before the average number of accidents. This is because one accident only happens and is counted when the fitness of that individual is exactly 1 (i.e. the distance between the two UAVs is exactly 0).

When we checked these mid-air collisions found in trial 3, we found that the genomes (parameter settings) were almost the same – the genomes that code for accident scenarios were almost clones of each other. This is because when the GA finds a good individual, it will have a high probability to focus on the individual and make some minute modifications to it. So GA has a strong tendency to converge. But if the initial genomes are not very good, the minute modifications are not enough to find some better individuals and an evolutionary search may fail to find the best individuals in a finite number of generations ("premature convergence" in GA terms), which was what happened in the first two trials. We tried to overcome this by using a much bigger initial population in experiment 2.3, see below.

---

[3] Here, the distance was scaled for simulation visualization purpose. Whenever a collision happened the distance was set to 0.

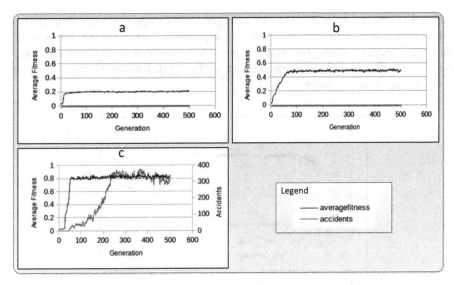

Fig. 5. Average fitness and accidents of each generation in experiment 1.3

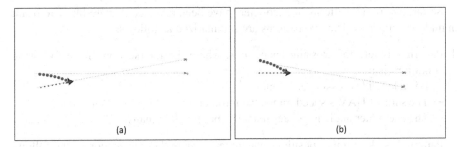

Fig. 6. Typical encounters found in experiment 1.3

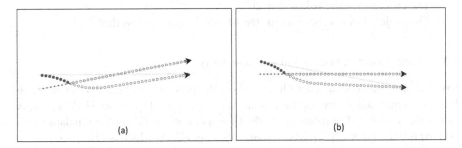

Fig.7. Collisions shown in Fig. 6 can be avoided with a slightly larger turning rate

Two typical encounters that resulted in mid-air collisions are shown in Fig. 6. These encounters are not so interesting, as the initial positions of the two UAVs are too close. But even in such close initial positions conditions, if the UAV's maximum turning rate is a bit greater than 2.5deg/s, say 3deg/s, all the collisions can be avoided, as shown in Fig. 7.

Fig. 8 shows the average fitness of each generation using GA (data from trial 1) and random search (data from trial 1, 2, 3 of experiment 1.2). Since the fitness represents the nearest proximity between the two UAVs during a simulation run, we can conclude that the evolutionary search is more efficient in finding subtler challenging situations than random search.

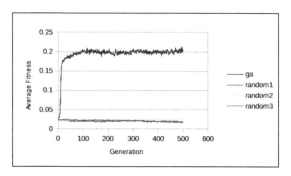

Fig. 8. Average fitness of GA and random searches

So far, two rough patterns of encounters have been revealed that are likely to result in mid-air collisions. The two patterns are summarized as follows:

1. Pattern 1 is left 45° crossing encounters, where the intersection of the following conditions is true:
   — It is a left side crossing encounter;
   — The subject UAV's speed minus the intruder's speed is more than 18m/s;
   — The encounter angle is greater than 45°, but it is less than 51.2°.

2. Pattern 2 is close initial positions encounters, where the intersection of the following conditions is true:
   — The encounter angle is less than 20°;
   — The subject UAV's speed minus the intruder's speed is less than 5m/s.

4.3   Experiment 2: Sensor Value Uncertainty

Experiment 2 was conducted without making the perfect sensing ability assumption. Here we simply add Gaussian noise to the sensing result of the other UAV's position and velocity vector. The mean (μ) of the Gaussian noise is 0, and the standard deviation (σ) is 0.05*{*real value*}. The sensing rate is as TCAS, which is 1Hz.

Experiment 2.1

Again, we first used random search to find "obvious" mid-air collisions. We conducted random search 5 times, with 250,000 sample points each time.

In the first 4 trials, all the collision situations found can either be categorized as pattern 1 or pattern 2, except one. No collision was found in trial 5. The one exception is a left side crossing according to Fig. 1, where even though the subject UAV and the intruder's speeds are very close (i.e. 85.84m/s and 83.04m/s), their encounter angle is larger (28.56°) than that in pattern 2. This exceptional encounter recurred as shown in Fig. 9 (a).

According to SVO, this is an Overtaking encounter, where the speeds of the UAVs are very close. Due to the sensor noise, the intruder sometimes decided its speed was greater than the subject UAV's and took avoidance manoeuvres while in fact it shouldn't have. The result is that the intruder's right turn avoidance manoeuvres cancelled out some of the effect of the subject UAV's and they collide sometime in the future. But if there were no sensor noise, the collision would not have happened as shown in Fig. 9 (b).

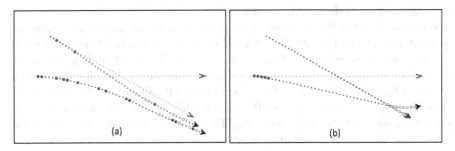

Fig. 9. (a) Trajectory with sensor noise; (b) Trajectory without sensor noise

Again we need to ask whether or not the situations found so far constitute all the possible situations that will result in a mid-air collision under sensor noise. We explored this in experiments 2.2 and 2.3.

Experiment 2.2

Experiment 2.2 tried to find subtler situations that will result in mid-air collisions other than those found in experiment 2.1 using random search. We conducted random search 5 times, with 250,000 sample points each time. Of all the sampled points, we found *no* mid-air collision.

We then checked some of the nearest mid-air approaches and found another situation that may lead to mid-air collision – the intruder approaches the subject UAV from the *right* side with an encounter angle a little greater than 45°; and the intruder has a high speed while the subject UAV has a low speed. This is actually the same as those identified in pattern 1 except the intruder approaches from the right side. It follows that the random search should have found some collisions in this situation as it did in experiment 1.1 considering that we have searched such a huge number of sample points. One explanation for this could be that with the Gaussian noise added, more uncertainty was added and the set of possible paths through the simulation became far larger than before.

Experiment 2.3

Experiment 2.3 tried to find even subtler situations that will result in mid-air collisions other than those found in experiment 2.1 and 2.2 using evolutionary search. To achieve this, we noted that GA has a strong tendency to converge and the existence of some good initial genomes determines whether it can find the "best" individuals in a finite number of generations. (See our earlier comment on this in experiment 1.3). We set the search to run for 50 generations (ten times fewer than before), each generation with 5000 individuals (ten times more than before). The number of total sample points is also the same as experiment 2.1 and 2.2. The fitness function is the same as that of experiment 1.3.

We made 5 trials, of which all but the third trial found mid-air collisions. A typical collision is shown in Fig. 10 (a). This is a little like those identified in pattern 1, except that the encounter angle is a little greater (51.7° for this typical encounter). Due to sensor noise, sometimes the intruder decided to "Maintain" its velocity while in fact it should have made an "Avoid" manoeuvre.

When we observed this encounter without sensor noise, we found the trajectory as shown in Fig. 10 (b). The intruder did avoid the subject UAV, but it could not get to its target due to the maximum turning rate constraint. So it kept circling around the target. This is undesirable and also forms a hazard, because it may cause the UAV to run out of fuel and finally crash. As can be seen from the figure, this happened in the "Restore" stage and it is actually not the responsibility of the collision avoidance system but the autopilot (or other controllers). This problem can be solved by letting the UAV take a Dubins Curve [14] to its target.

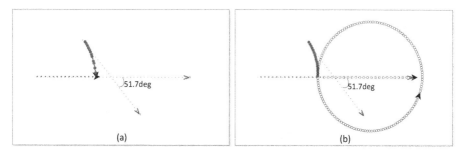

Fig. 10. A typical encounter in experiment 2.3, (a) with sensor noise; (b) without sensor noise

4.4   Findings

Through the experiments, we found the following:

1. Whether with random search or evolutionary search, our multi-agent simulations have the ability to reveal safety issues of a SAA algorithm (SVO). Using the encounters generated by our "encounter generators", SAA algorithms can be tested in different situations;

2. Even though random search can reveal some relatively obvious safety issues, evolutionary search has the ability to guide the simulations towards much subtler challenging situations for SVO to handle. With the combination of the two, the safety validation process has the potential to be accelerated;

3. Some plausible safety issues of SVO have been revealed by our approach – it is dangerous to let low speed UAV avoid high speed UAV in some situations; the $45°$ encounter angle for crossing is a dangerous boundary value for SVO; the SVO algorithm is sensitive to sensor noise on velocity.

5   Conclusions and Future Work

We have described a safety validation approach for SAA algorithms using multi-agent simulation and evolutionary search. Through experiments we have shown that our approach can reveal faults that random simulation takes a long time to find, and thus that our approach may accelerate the safety validation process. In the process, we found some safety issues with the SVO algorithm.

When building simulations, we treat SAA algorithms as black boxes. The information on positions, velocities and shapes of UAVs is provided as input to the algorithm and the next waypoint the host UAV should navigate to is returned as output. Therefore, this approach can be easily used to assess a variety of SAA algorithms as long as they follow that input and output protocol (or can be adapted to do so).

The collision avoidance algorithm analysed in this paper is relatively simple, and thus the fitness function used in this paper is straightforward – only the nearest proximity to the other UAV is considered. In the future, we will study more sophisticated algorithms (e.g. the ACAS X algorithm [5]) and devise risk measurements that accommodate factors beyond simple proximity. We will then base our fitness function on these risk measurements to lead the simulation towards high risk situations.

In the experiments, the GA was not well-tuned and sometimes it would lead to premature convergence to local maxima (or minima). We will explore ways to overcome this in the future by adaptively controlling the crossover and mutation probabilities (e.g. as discussed in [15]).

According to section 2, this work partially addresses the challenge of efficiency and touches on challenges of fidelity and coverage. Our future work will tackle these further, the latter two in particular by creating more complex encounter generators that produce richer situations (including equipment failure and other degraded modes). Also, we will consider multi-body encounter problems and the use of 3D simulations. In this way we hope to contribute to the development of effective SAA algorithms, and to provide a cost-effective approach for validation of this important class of algorithm.

Acknowledgements The first author would like to thank the China Scholarship Council (CSC) for its partial financial support for his PhD study.

References

1. Federal Aviation Administration, U.S. Department of Transportaion: Integration of Civil Unmanned Aircraft Systems (UAS) in the National Airspace System (NAS) Roadmap, 1st edn (2013)

2. Fox, D., Burgard, W., Thrun, S.: The dynamic window approach to collision avoidance. IEEE Robotics & Automation Magazine 4, 23–33 (1997)

3. Fiorini, P., Shiller, Z.: Motion planning in dynamic environments using velocity obstacles. The International Journal of Robotics Research 17, 760–772 (1998)

4. Jenie, Y.I., Van Kampen, E.-J., de Visser, C.C., Chu, Q.P.: Selective Velocity Obstacle Method for Cooperative Autonomous Collision Avoidance System for Unmanned Aerial Vehicles. In: AIAA Guidance, Navigation, and Control (GNC) Conference. American Institute of Aeronautics and Astronautics (2013)

5. Kochenderfer, M.J., Chryssanthacopoulos, J.: Robust airborne collision avoidance through dynamic programming. Massachusetts Institute of Technology, Lincoln Laboratory, Project Report ATC-371 (2011)

6. Temizer, S., Kochenderfer, M.J., Kaelbling, L.P., Lozano-Pérez, T., Kuchar, J.K.: Collision avoidance for unmanned aircraft using Markov decision processes. In: AIAA Guidance, Navigation, and Control Conference. American Institute of Aeronautics and Astronautics (2010)

7. Arnold, J., Alexander, R.: Testing Autonomous Robot Control Software Using Procedural Content Generation. In: Bitsch, F., Guiochet, J., Kaâniche, M. (eds.) SAFECOMP. LNCS, vol. 8153, pp. 33–44. Springer, Heidelberg (2013)

8. McMinn, P.: Search-based software test data generation: A survey. Software Testing, Verification and reliability 14, 105–156 (2004)

9. Clegg, K., Alexander, R.: The discovery and quantification of risk in high dimensional search spaces. In: Proceeding of the Fifteenth Annual Conference Companion on Genetic and Evolutionary Computation Conference Companion, pp. 175–176. ACM (2013)

10. Alam, S., Lokan, C., Abbass, H.: What can make an airspace unsafe? characterizing collision risk using multi-objective optimization. In: IEEE Congress on Evolutionary Computation, CEC, pp. 1–8 (2012)

11. Alam, S., Lokan, C., Aldis, G., Barry, S., Butcher, R., Abbass, H.: Systemic identification of airspace collision risk tipping points using an evolutionary multi-objective scenario-based methodology. Transportation Research Part C: Emerging Technologies 35, 57–84 (2013)

12. Federal Aviation Administration: Federal Aviation Regulations (FAR) Chapter I, subchapter F Air Traffic and General Operating Rules, 91.113 Right-of-way rules: Except water operations (1989)

13. Federal Aviation Administration: JO 7110.65U, Air Traffic Control, Chapter 1: General. In: U.S. Department of Transportation (ed.) (2012)

14. Dubins, L.E.: On curves of minimal length with a constraint on average curvature, and with prescribed initial and terminal positions and tangents. American Journal of Mathematics, 497–516 (1957)

15. Srinivas, M., Patnaik, L.M.: Adaptive probabilities of crossover and mutation in genetic algorithms. IEEE Transactions on Systems, Man and Cybernetics 24, 656–667 (1994)

Debugging with Timed Automata Mutations

Bernhard K. Aichernig[1], Klaus Hörmaier[2], and Florian Lorber[1]

[1] Institute for Software Technology
Graz University of Technology, Austria
{aichernig,florber}@ist.tugraz.at
[2] Infineon Technologies Austria AG. Villach, Austria
klaus.hoermaier-ee@infineon.com

Abstract. Model-based Debugging is an application of Model-based Diagnosis techniques to debugging computer systems. Its basic principle is to compare a model, i.e., a description of the correct behaviour of a system, to the observed behaviour of the system. In this paper we show how this technique can be applied in the context of model-based mutation testing (MBMT) with timed automata. In MBMT we automatically generate a set of test sequences out of a test model. In contrast to general model-based testing, the test cases of MBMT cover a pre-defined set of faults that have been injected into the model (model mutation). Our automatic debugging process is purely black-box. If a test run fails, our tool reports a diagnosis as a set of model mutations. These mutations provide possible explanations why the test case has failed. For reproducing the failure, we also generate a set of minimal test cases leading to the implementation fault. The technique is implemented for Uppaal's timed automata models and is based on a language inclusion check via bounded model checking. It adds debugging capability to our existing test-case generators. A car-alarm system serves as illustrating case study.

Keywords: Timed automata, debugging, model-based mutation debugging, mutation testing, model-based testing, language inclusion, mutation operators.

1 Introduction

Testing and debugging are important tasks of the development process in the automotive industry. Especially for safety related products exhaustive testing/debugging needs to be done to ensure functional safety. This leads to a high effort spent during product development. So what is testing and debugging about? The verification engineer is stimulating the device under test (DUT) with input patterns and is observing the outputs of the DUT simultaneously. If the observed outputs are equal to the expected outputs, everything is fine. But if at least one test case fails (the observed output is not equal to the expected output), the investigation of why the test fails starts. There are two possibilities why a test case can fail. The test case or the test setup could be faulty or the implementation can be incorrect. Especially in larger products where more designers are

A. Bondavalli and F. Di Giandomenico (Eds.): SAFECOMP 2014, LNCS 8666, pp. 49–64, 2014.
© Springer International Publishing Switzerland 2014

working on the DUT, it is important to identify the erroneous part as fast as possible. Therefore the verification engineer has to go through the design and probe outputs / signals / variables related to the faulty test case to judge their correctness. This debugging process is a difficult and time consuming task which is up to now mostly done manually. Within this paper we propose a method for speeding up the debugging process by automation.

Related Work. Model-based software debugging (MBSD) [17,13] is an automated debugging approach with the goal of identifying model components that might be responsible for faulty behavior. MBSD relies on a set of test cases that specify the correct behavior and one or more models that reflect incorrect behavior. Usually the models are divided into a set of components, e.g. the set of code statements. Then the goal of MBSD is to find minimal sets of components (called "diagnoses") that, if assumed to be faulty, explain the fault in the implementation. Several different model notations have already been used for model based debugging [14], using formal textual specifications for the models, usually created automatically from the source code. The most commonly used models are Dependency-based Models, Value-based Models and Abstraction-based Models. Other common approaches rely on satisfiability checking and worst-case analysis of several different models [14].

Model-based testing (MBT) [20] provides techniques to automatically generate test cases from specification models. These test cases are used to check conformance of the DUT to the specification. Most MBT approaches rely on the input/output behaviour of the DUT and do not need any access to its internal structure. They are therefore called "black-box" methods. Usually MBT techniques generate test cases until the test suite meets a predefined coverage criteria (e.g. transition coverage, where the test cases have to reach every transition of the model at least once).

Mutation testing [7,9] provides a way to measure the quality of such a test suite: By introducing small errors into the DUT, a set of faulty implementations, called mutants, is created. A test case that is able to distinguish between the original and a mutant is said to *kill* the mutant. By executing the whole test suite on the mutants, the *killing rate* of the test suite can be calculated, indicating how many of the mutants could be killed. Instead of altering the DUT, one can also mutate the model and check for conformance between the test case and the mutated model, to see whether the test case can kill it.

Model-based mutation testing is a specific type of model-based testing, in which faults are deliberately injected into the specification model. The aim of mutation-based testing techniques is to generate test cases that can detect the injected errors. This means that a generated test case shall fail if it is executed on a (deterministic) system-under-test that implements the faulty model. The power of this testing approach is that it can guarantee the absence of certain specific faults. In practice, it will be combined with standard techniques, e.g. with random test-case generation [1]. Mutation-based testing was studied in [2,18] in the context of UML models, in [6,8] in the context of Simulink models and in

[3,10] in the context of Timed Automata. Model-based mutation testing is also known as specification-based mutation testing.

Contribution. In this paper, we propose a methodology for mutation-based debugging of real-time systems combining model-based debugging, classical mutation testing and model-based mutation testing. Given a faulty DUT and a testcase that fails when executed on it, we can determine a set of model mutants that reflects the implemented fault on model level.

To the best of our knowledge, this approach is novel. The used tool and test case generation procedure have already been published [4,3], yet they were only used for test case generation, whereas in this paper we describe a model-based debugging methodology. In contrary to most previous model-based debugging approaches, our approach does not rely on creating its own model from the faulty implementation, but needs a correct specification model. While using manually designed models is not common practice in standard software engineering, safety critical domains, like automotive or railway domains, use models to comply with their verification standards. If there are any real-time requirements on the DUT, timed automata models grant some important benefits.

Wotawa [22] introduced mutation debugging, using code mutations as possible diagnoses for faulty implementations. Model-based debugging is used to determine possibly faulty components and the mutation algorithm is only executed on these candidates, to speed up the process.

Nica et al. [16] propose a method for combining debugging, testing and mutants to reduce the set of possible fault candidates. Contrary to our work, they use white-box methods: by mutating the faulty code, they try to find mutants behaving correctly, while we mutate the correct model, trying to find mutants that show the same faulty behavior as the implementation.

Within this paper, we also present a framework implementing this method for specifications modeled using a deterministic class of timed automata with inputs and outputs. We already work on the field of mutation testing for quite some time and recently presented our model-based mutation testing tool for timed automata, MoMuT::TA [4,3]. To benefit from the functionalities already available there, this method was integrated into the existing tool. The tool is implemented in Scala (v2.9.1), using the standard Uppaal [12] Timed Automata XML format for specifying the models as well as the test cases. It uses the Satisfiability Modulo Theories (SMT) solver Z3 (v4.0) [15] to compute conformance checks of TA via language inclusion.

Within Section 2, we describe the basic concept of our novel model-based mutation debugging approach. Section 3 illustrates a model of a car alarm system, which is used as a running example during this paper. In Section 4 we define our deterministic Input/Output Timed Automata. In Section 5, we explain model mutation and a set of mutation operators for TA models and describe the linkage between model mutants and corresponding implementation faults. We explain our notion of the timed input/output conformance relation tioco and show the equivalence between language inclusion and tioco conformance in Section 6.

Section 7 describes the experimental results we achieved for the car alarm system case study. In Section 8, we conclude the paper.

2   Model-Based Mutation Debugging

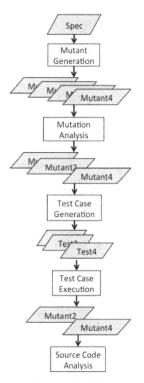

Fig. 1. Workflow

Model-based mutation debugging (MBMT) starts with a common in model-based testing situation: we are given a specification model (assumed to be correct), a faulty implementation and a random test case failing on the implementation. Since many test cases are not minimal, they do not give a lot of feedback on which part of the implementation is faulty.

Via model mutation we can create model mutants representing possible implementation faults. In different filtering steps we can select a small subset of those mutants showing the same faulty behavior as the DUT. These mutants are therefore likely to represent the implemented fault and can be seen as "mutant diagnoses" for the faulty implementation. Since correct timing behavior gains more and more importance in safety critical domains, we decided to use timed automata [5] to model the specification.

Our approach consists of several steps, each of which will be explained in detail in the next sections. The basic concept behind the approach works as illustrated in Figure 1 and is described in the following. The whole procedure is done automatically by our framework. Only the final step, the analysis of the source code, steered by the final mutants, needs to be done manually.

- **Mutant Generation:** First, we create a set of all model mutants our framework supports (Mutant1, Mutant2, Mutant3, Mutant4 in Figure 1). Details on the different supported mutation operators can be found in Section 5.
- **Mutation Analysis:** Next, the random test case can be compared to the mutants. If a mutant shows any faulty behaviour along the path of the test case, the mutant is said to be killed by the test case. The killed mutants are stored for the next step. All mutants that are not killed are disregarded (Mutant3 in Figure 1), because either their mutations did not lie along the path of the initial test case or did not introduce any faults. The mutation analysis is implemented as a language inclusion check of timed traces (see Section 6).
- **Test Case Generation:** Then, we use our model-based mutation testing technique [3,4] for creating minimal test cases (Test1, Test2, Test4) for the selected mutants (Mutant1, Mutant2, Mutant4). The test cases reflect the shortest input/output sequence leading to the faulty output of the mutants.

- **Test Case Execution:** Next, by executing the test cases on the faulty implementation, we can identify the subset of test cases (and their corresponding mutants) that still are able to find the bug. Some of the test cases cover the bug, but contain several unnecessary steps afterwards. By discarding these test cases and their corresponding mutants, an even smaller set of test cases (Test2, Test4) and mutants (Mutant2, Mutant4) can be achieved.
- **Source Code Analysis:** Finally, the remaining subset of mutants consists of those mutants that reflect the behavior of the faulty implementation the best. Each mutant reflects a specific implementation fault at a specific location. By examining these code fragments, the location of the bug can usually be traced easily. We give some detailed examples in Section 7.

3   Running Example

Within this paper, we illustrate our approach with a Car Alarm System (CAS) [2,18]. We developed a timed automata model of the CAS from the requirements:

Arming: The system is armed 20 s after the vehicle is locked and the bonnet, luggage compartment and all doors are closed;

Alarm: The alarm sounds for 30 s if an unauthorized person opens the door, the luggage compartment or the bonnet. The hazard flasher lights flashes for 5 min;

Deactivation: The anti-theft alarm system can be deactivated at any time, even when the alarm is sounding, by unlocking the vehicle from outside.

A correct model is shown in Figure 2(a). Input signals are denoted by question marks, output signals by exclamation marks. In the initial state, the car is *open and unlocked* hence the *close?* and *lock?* signals are enabled. Timing properties are modeled via guards and invariants. After a *close?* and a *lock?* signal, the invariant forbids waiting longer than 20 seconds (modeled via invariant), and the *armedOn?* signal must be triggered after exactly 20 seconds (modeled via guard).

Additionally to the model, we have a Java implementation, a tool to generate random test cases and our model-based mutation test case generation tool MoMuT::TA. Now let us assume a fault in our implementation, skipping the effect of the *unlock?* signal after the alarm went silent. The corresponding model mutant mimicking this implementation fault can be seen in Figure 2(b). Also assume the untimed abstract test case TC_1[1]: *close? - lock? - armedOn! - open? - armedOff! - flashOn! - soundOn! - soundOff! - soundOff!- flashOff! - unlock? - lock? - close? - armedOn!* to return the verdict **fail** after this sequence. Now of course if it was a real random test case, it could be much longer and the trace would not lead straight towards the fail. But already in this simple version, it is hard to trace the exact location of the fault, that could have been introduced anywhere along the path.

---

[1] For presentation purposes, the test case does not include any timing information.

Our method provides mutant diagnoses for the bug that can be created without access to the source code, are simple to understand, illustrated as UPPAAL models and give information about both the possible locations and the possible types of fault.

Example 1. Applying MBMD to the CAS:

- Mutant Generation: we produce the whole set of model mutants. For the CAS the total number of mutants is 296.
- Mutation Analysis: we filter out all mutants that conform to the test case and keep only those that are killed. E.g. all mutations on the *unlock?* signal while the alarm is still active are not within the scope of the test case.
- Test Case Generation: we can produce minimal test cases for each remaining mutant, leading straight to the fault. A mutation of the *armedOn!* signal might for example produce the test case TC_2 *lock? - close? - armedOn!* to make sure that the implementation fault corresponding to this specific mutation would be detected in the implementation.
- Test Case Execution: after executing the new test cases on the faulty implementation, mutants with test cases that cannot reach the implementation fault are filtered out. TC_2 does not reach the fault, therefore it would be filtered out, as well as its corresponding mutant. Only the shortest test cases and their mutants pass this selection step and are presented to the user as the final set of mutant diagnoses.
- Source Code Analysis: For this specific fault, only two of our mutants remain at the end. Both represent implementation faults of the *unlock* signal, deactivating its functionality after the alarm went silent. Both lead to the same faulty implementation statement. Figure 2 (b) shows one of them.

4   Timed Automata with Inputs and Outputs

The time domain that we consider is the set $\mathbb{R}_{\geq 0}$ of non-negative reals. The following definitions are based on definitions we used in previous publications [3,4]. We denote by Σ the finite set of actions, partitioned into two disjoint sets Σ_I and Σ_O of input and output actions, respectively. A *time sequence* is a finite or infinite non-decreasing sequence of non-negative reals. A *timed trace* σ is a finite alternating sequence of actions and time delays of the form $t_1 \cdot a_1 \cdots t_k \cdot a_k$, where for all $i \in [1, k]$, $a_i \in \Sigma$ and $(t_i)_{i \in [1,k]}$ is a time sequence.

Let $\mathcal{C}$ be a finite set of *clock* variables. Clock *valuation* $v(c)$ is a function $v : \mathcal{C} \to \mathbb{R}_{\geq 0}$ assigning a real value to every clock $c \in \mathcal{C}$. We denote by $\mathcal{H}$ the set of all clock valuations and by $\mathbf{0}$ the valuation assigning 0 to every clock in $\mathcal{C}$. Let $v \in \mathcal{H}$ be a valuation and $t \in \mathbb{R}_{\geq 0}$, we then have $v + t$ defined by $(v + t)(c) = v(c) + t$ for all $c \in \mathcal{C}$. For a subset ρ of $\mathcal{C}$, we denote by $v[\rho]$ the valuation such that for every $c \in \rho$, $v[\rho](c) = 0$ and for every $c \in \mathcal{C} \backslash \rho$, $v[\rho](c) = v(c)$. A *clock constraint* φ is a conjunction of predicates over clock variables in $\mathcal{C}$ defined by the grammar

$$\varphi ::= c \circ k \mid \varphi_1 \wedge \varphi_2,$$

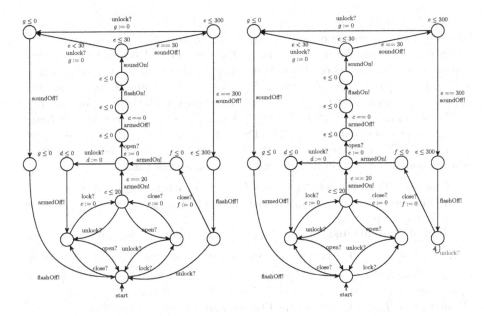

Fig. 2. Car alarm system: correct TAIO specification (a) and a mutant (b)

where $c \in \mathcal{C}$, $k \in \mathbb{R}_{\geq 0}$ and $\circ \in \{<, \leq, =, \geq, >\}$. Given a clock valuation $v \in \mathcal{H}$, we write $v \models \varphi$ when v satisfies the clock constraint φ. We are now ready to formally define *input/output* timed automata (TAIO):

Definition 1. A TAIO[2] A is a tuple $(Q, \hat{q}, \Sigma_I, \Sigma_O, \mathcal{C}, I, \Delta)$, where Q is a finite set of locations, $\hat{q} \in Q$ is the initial location, Σ_I is a finite set of input actions and Σ_O is a finite set of output actions, such that $\Sigma_I \cap \Sigma_O = \emptyset$ and Σ is the set of actions $\Sigma_I \cup \Sigma_O$, $\mathcal{C}$ is a finite set of clock variables, I is a finite set of location invariants, that are conjunctions of constraints of the form $c < d$ or $c \leq d$, where $c \in \mathcal{C}$ and $d \in \mathbb{N}$ and each invariant is bound to its specific location, and Δ is a finite set of transitions of the form (q, a, g, ρ, q'), where

- $q, q' \in Q$ are the source and the target locations;
- $a \in \Sigma$ is the transition action
- g is a guard, a conjunction of constraints of the form $c \circ d$,
  where $\circ \in \{<, \leq, =, \geq, >\}$ and $d \in \mathbb{R}_{\geq 0}$;
- $\rho \subseteq \mathcal{C}$ is a set of clocks to be reset.

We say that a TAIO A is *deterministic* if for all transitions (q, a, g_1, ρ_1, q_1) and (q, a, g_2, ρ_2, q_2) in Δ, $q_1 \neq q_2$ implies that $g_1 \wedge g_2 = \emptyset$. We denote by $\mathcal{A}$ the set of all TAIO and by $\mathrm{Det}(\mathcal{A}) \subset \mathcal{A}$ its deterministic subset. We denote

---

[2] TAIO are similar to UPPAAL TA, which we use to illustrate our examples. One difference is that for simplicity of presentation we do not have *urgent* and *committed* locations. However, these types of locations are just syntactic sugar to make modelling easier, and can be expressed with standard timed automata.

by $\Delta_O \subseteq \Delta$ the set $\{\delta = (q, a, g, \rho, q') \mid \delta \in \Delta$ and $a \in \Sigma_O\}$ of transitions labeled by an output action and by $\Delta_I = \Delta \backslash \Delta_O$ the set of transitions labeled by an input action. We define $|\mathcal{G}|$ to be the number of basic constraints that appear in all the guards of all the transitions in A, i.e. $|\mathcal{G}| = \Sigma_{\delta \in \Delta} |J_g|$, where $\delta = (q, a, g, \rho, q')$ and g is of the form $\bigwedge_{j \in J_g} c_j \circ d_j$. We define $|\mathcal{I}|$ as the number of basic constraints that appear in all the invariants of all the locations in A.

The *semantics* of a TAIO $A = (Q, \hat{q}, \Sigma_I, \Sigma_O, \mathcal{C}, I, \Delta)$ is given by the *timed input/output transition system* (TIOTS) $[[A]] = (S, \hat{s}, \mathbb{R}_{\geq 0}, \Sigma, T)$, where $S = \{(q, v) \in Q \times \mathcal{H} \mid v \models I(q)\}$, $\hat{s} = (\hat{q}, \mathbf{0})$, $T \subseteq S \times (\Sigma \cup \mathbb{R}_{\geq 0}) \times S$ is the transition relation consisting of *discrete* and *timed* transitions such that:

- **Discrete Transitions:** $((q, v), a, (q', v')) \in T$, where $a \in \Sigma$, if there exists a transition (q, a, g, ρ, q') in Δ, such that: (1) $v \models g$; (2) $v' = v[\rho]$ and (3) $v' \models I(q')$; and
- **Timed Transitions:** $((q, v), t, (q, v + t)) \in T$, where $t \in \mathbb{R}_{\geq 0}$, if $v + t \models I(q)$.

A *run* r of a TAIO A is the sequence of alternating timed and discrete transitions of the form $(q_1, v_1) \xrightarrow{t_1} (q_1, v_1 + t_1) \xrightarrow{\delta_1} (q_2, v_2) \xrightarrow{t_2} \cdots$, where $q_1 = \hat{q}$, $v_1 = \mathbf{0}$ and $\delta_i = (q_i, a_i, g_i, \rho_i, q_{i+1})$, inducing the timed trace $\sigma = t_1 \cdot a_1 \cdot t_2 \cdots$. We denote by $L(A)$ the set of timed traces induced by all runs of A.

5   Model Mutation

Mutation of a specification is done by altering the model in a small way, mimicking common implementation errors. In our setting, this is done via 9 different predefined mutation operators, that were already introduced in a previous publication [3]. Each of them represents an individual type of implementation fault, that can occur at multiple parts of the model. We only create first order mutants, which means we only apply one operator at a time to one part of the model at a time. Each operator creates a set of mutants:

1. **Change Action:** changes a single output transition in A by replacing the action labeling the transition by a different output label. This mutation mimics an implementation fault producing incorrect output signals.
2. **Self Loop:** changes a single output transition in A by replacing the target location of the transition by the source location. The intention behind this operator is to mimic an implementation fault that omits the original behavior of a signal.
3. **Change Target:** replaces the target location of a transition in A, by another location in A. This mimics an implementation fault, where signals lead to wrong internal states, e.g. by setting internal state variables to wrong values. Figure 3 (b) gives an example on this kind of mutation.
4. **Change Source:** replaces the source location of a transition in A, by another location in A. A corresponding implementation fault would enable triggering a signal that should be disabled for a certain state. A second corresponding implementation fault is the fact that the signal cannot be triggered in the original state. Figure 3 (c) illustrates this, by changing the transition $q2 : q4$ to $q0 : q4$.

5. **Change Guard**: replaces the guard of a transition in A by replacing every equality/inequality sign appearing in the guard by another one. This expresses implementation faults caused by incorrect enabling conditions. An example is given in in Figure 3 (d), on the transition between $q2$ and $q4$.

6. **Negate Guard**: replaces the guard in a transition in A, by its negation. This covers faults that happened because a programmer forgot to negate an enabling condition.

7. **Change Invariant**: replaces the invariant of a location with another invariant which adds 1 to the right side of an invariant. This mimics an "off by one" fault, allowing to stay in a state longer than intended.

8. **Sink Location**: replaces the target location of a transition in A, by a newly created sink location that models a *don't care location* which accepts all inputs. This expresses program faults leading to a quiescent state where every input is accepted, but ignored. This kind of behavior is experienced in implementation faults leading to internal states outside of the state domain.

9. **Invert Reset**: replaces a transition in A, by another transition with the occurrence of one clock flipped compared to the original set of clocks. This reflects different timing errors, e.g. the incorrect resetting of a timer.

Figure 3 illustrates a sample model and mutants resulting from applying the mutation operators to the model. Formal definition of the above mutation operators and an upper bound of mutants created by each operator can be found in our technical report [4]. There are two major changes compared to the technical report: In order not to get too many mutants representing the same type of implementation fault at the same location, the three mutation operators 1, 2 and 4 are only applied once per transition. Hence instead of creating several *change actions* mutants for the same output transition (one per possible other output action) only one mutant per output transition is created, with the action name changed to a random other output label. All omitted mutants create the same test cases and would only worsen the debugging results. Consequently, we also use only one random target / source location for the *change target / change source* mutation operators.

The second difference is the fact that for the experiments in this paper, all mutants are transformed to be *input-enabled*. Since we assume all implementations to be input-enabled, we tried to keep the mutants as similar as possible. So implementations and mutants accept any undefined input, but do not react to it. We applied angelic completion [20] to the mutants in order to achieve this.

6 Conformance Check

6.1 tioco Conformance

During the debugging process, we need to check conformance two times. To exploit the timing properties of timed automata we use tioco [19], a real time extension of Tretman's input-output conformance ioco [21]. Intuitively, a TAIOA_1 conforms to a second TAIOA_2, if for each trace specified in A_2 the set of possible

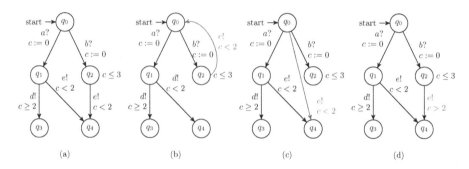

Fig. 3. (a) a sample specification; (b-d) corresponding mutants with (b) a mutated target location; (c) a mutated source location; (d) a mutated guard

outputs of A_1 is a subset of the possible outputs of A_2. Note that the passing of time is seen as an output.

We consider TAIO without silent (τ) transitions, hence all actions are observable. Consequently, we can use a simplified version of the tioco definition from [11]. We need four operators (illustrated in Equation 1) for the definition of the relation.

$$
\begin{aligned}
A \text{ after } \sigma &= \{s \in S \mid \hat{s} \xrightarrow{\sigma} s\} \\
\text{elapse(s)} &= \{t > 0 \mid s \xrightarrow{t}\} \\
\text{out}(s) &= \{a \in \Sigma_O \mid s \xrightarrow{a}\} \cup \text{elapse(s)} \\
\text{out}(S) &= \bigcup_{s \in S} \text{out}(s)
\end{aligned}
\tag{1}
$$

Given a TAIO A and $\sigma \in L(\Sigma)$, A after σ is the set of all states of A that can be reached by the sequence σ. Given a state $s \in S$, elapse(s) is the set of all delays that can elapse from s without A making any action, and out(s) is the set of all output actions or time delays that can occur when the system is at state s, a definition which naturally extends to set of states S.

Definition 2. *The* timed input-output conformance relation, *denoted by tioco, is defined as*

$$A_I \text{ tioco } A_S \text{ iff } \forall \sigma \in L(A_S) : \text{out}(A_I \text{ after } \sigma) \subseteq \text{out}(A_S \text{ after } \sigma)$$

Several theoretical results about the tioco have been published in [11]. One of them states that given two TAIO A_I and A_S, if A_I tioco A_S, then the set of observable traces of A_I is included in the set of observable traces of A_S, while the converse is not true in general. However, if A_S is input-enabled, then the set inclusion between observable traces of A_I and A_S also implies the tioco conformance of A_I to A_S.

In previous work [4,3] we included demonic completion to make A_S input enabled. In this paper we apply a more efficient technique for handling partial models. A pruning of A_I is performed, removing all inputs unspecified by A_S in a certain state. The same results are obtained when checking language inclusion between a demonic completed specification and an mutant, as when checking language inclusion between a specification and a pruned mutant.[3]

The language inclusion is computed via the SMT solver Z3 for a bounded depth, since we are only interested in finite counter examples. Due to space limitations, the detailed SMT formula will not be presented here, but can be found in previous publications [4,3].

6.2   Conformance Checks within Model-Based Mutation Debugging

Conformance checks are needed at two different stages of our method: The first conformance check is done in the *Mutation Analysis* step, between the abstract failing test case and the model mutants. This is possible, because our abstract test cases are timed automata traces in sequential form, that can be seen as partial models of the specification. Since the initial test case only covers a certain part of the specification, a lot of the mutations will be placed at parts that are not reached by the test case. Yet since the test case fails on the faulty implementation, we are only interested in parts of the model covered by the test case. Hence we can disregard each mutant that conforms to the test case.

By applying this conformance check, we already gain a reduced set of mutants, but not yet any further knowledge on which of them correspond to the actual fault. The second conformance check is applied within the *Test Case Generation* step, by our model-based mutation technique [4,3]: for each mutant it generates a specific new test case that leads exactly to the first output discrepancy between specification and mutant. The result is a set of minimal test cases that covers all of the mutations that were covered by the initial test case.

Now while the initial test case covers a lot of different regions of the specification, only one of which is supposed to be faulty, the new test cases contain the direct, minimal way to the mutation they were created for, only covering as little of the specification as possible.

The next step consists in executing the newly generated test cases on the faulty implementation. Only the test cases that cover the implementation fault will fail, hence the other test cases and their corresponding mutants can again be disregarded.

All of the remaining timed automata mutants represent fault models that show the same faulty behavior as the faulty implementation. Each of them was created with the intention of mimicking one or more specific implementation faults, and hence we only need to check the code for a small set of possible implementation errors. Section 7 shows the results of applying this technique to the Car Alarm System.

7   Results

To validate our approach we conducted several experiments on a Java implementation of the Car Alarm System [1]. For experimentation we produced 38 faulty

---

[3] A detailed argument of this is out of scope of the paper. Our experiments give evidence that our technique works.

Table 1. Possible fault models derived by the remaining mutant diagnoses

Model Mutation	Mutated Transitions	Corresponding Implementation Fault
Invert Reset	*lock?*	A wrong clock reset during the *lock?* signal.
Self Loop	*close?/lock?*	The *close?/lock?* signal has no effect.
Sink Location	**close? / lock?**	**The close?/lock? signal leads to a quiescent state.**
Change invariant	-	The *armedOn!* signal is delayed longer than allowed by the specification.
Change source	*close?/lock?*	The *close?/lock?* signal is enabled in a wrong internal state & disabled in the right one.
Change target	*close?/lock?*	The *close?/lock?* signal leads to a wrong internal state.
Negate Guard	*close?/lock?*	The *close?/lock?* signal is disabled.

implementations of this program. The implementation consists of four public methods, *open, close, lock* and *unlock*, and two internal methods, *SetState* and the constructor. Elapse of time is simulated with a *tick* method. The faulty implementations were generated with the mutation tool μJava[4]. Since none of the automatically generated faulty implementations contained any timing errors, we additionally created six of those: we generated two faulty implementations for each of the three signals *armedOn, flashOff* and *soundOff*, one where the signal is delayed and one where the signal is triggered too early.

We applied our method to each of the faulty implementations in a separate experiment: In each experiment, we used the specification model shown in Figure 2, one of the faulty implementations and a random test case of length 50, generated from the model by our tool MoMuT::TA. If the random test case passed on the faulty implementation, new test cases were generated until one failed on it. All experiments used the same model mutants, which were produced from the specification model by our tool chain. The total number of timed automata model mutants for the CAS is 296.

This section is split into three subsections: The first two will show two of the experiments in detail. They represent the two most demonstrative special cases, a mutation that can be reached from the initial state, and a mutation that needs ten preceding signals to be reached. Then in the third subsection, we will give an overview on how good our method performed, presenting the average values of the 44 experiments.

7.1 Experiment 1

The first experiment was started with a random test case of length 50. The mutated code of the faulty implementation is shown in Listing 1.1: The introduced implementation fault (negating the state variable in Line 10) causes the *close?* signal to lead to an incorrect internal state that can never be left. The bug only occurs if *close?* is triggered from the initial state.

By doing the tioco - conformance check between the mutants and the test case, the number of possible mutants was already reduced to 108. Hence, 188 mutants were disregarded either because they were equivalent to the specification, or because the mutation was not covered by the random test case.

---

[4] http://cs.gmu.edu/~{}offutt/mujava/

Listing 1.1. Code mutation of the *close?* signal leading to a wrong internal state, by negating the state variable in the initial state.

```
1   public static final int OpenAndUnlocked = 1;
2   public static final int ClosedAndUnlocked = 2;
3   public static final int OpenAndLocked = 3;
4   public static final int ClosedAndLocked = 4;
5   public static final int SilentAndOpen = 5;
6   ...
7   public void Close() {
8     switch (m_state) {
9       case CarAlarmSystemState.OpenAndUnlocked :
10        SetState(-CarAlarmSystemState.ClosedAndUnlocked);
11        break;
12      ...
```

Executing MoMuT::TA on the remaining mutants took 724 seconds and produced the corresponding set of test cases. A total of 51 out of the 108 test cases were able to kill the faulty implementation. 17 of these test cases are minimal and all of the minimal test cases are identical, consisting of the trace *close? - lock? - armedOn!*. All test cases longer than this trace and their mutants are disregarded.

Observing that all test cases contain the trace *close? - lock? - armedOn!* and none of them contains *lock? - close? - armedOn!* allows two conclusions: The fault is not located at the *armedOn!* signal and it is state dependent. The fault is either located in the *close?* signal, when triggered from the initial state, or in the *lock?* signal, when triggered from the *closed* and *unlocked* state.

Since there is no possible output between the *close?* and the *lock?* signal, the test cases cannot provide more information on the location of the bug.

However, using this information, one can discard all mutants with mutations in the *armedOn!* signal, further reducing the 17 mutants to 11. This is however the first step that requires manual input, while the execution so far can be done automatically. Table 1 presents the implementation faults represented by the remaining mutant diagnoses. The bold row shows the model mutant representing the actual implementation fault, which could easily be found with this information.

7.2   Experiment 2

Part of the second experiment has already been discussed in the introduction, yet here we present the full results. The exact fault is shown in Listing 1.2. The switch condition for the *silent and open* state in the mutated *unlock* signal (Line 3) has been negated and can never evaluate to true, hence the unlock method has no effect after the alarm went silent.

Listing 1.2. Code mutation of the *unlock?* signal. The switch condition cannot evaluate to true, because of the incorrect negation.

```
1   public void Unlock() {
2       switch (m_state) {
3       case -CarAlarmSystemState.SilentAndOpen :
4           SetState(CarAlarmSystemState.OpenAndUnlocked);
5           break;
6       ...
```

Our initial test case was produced randomly with a length of 50 and is able to kill our faulty implementation. The tioco - conformance check between the model mutants and the test case reduced the total amount of mutants to 127, taking 742 seconds. Hence, 169 mutants were disregarded because the test case did not cover any unspecified output on them.

In the next step, we produced the corresponding test cases with our model-based mutation testing technique, obtaining 127 test cases in 68 seconds. Due to the fact that the mutation is not easy to reach, only 2 of the test cases were able to kill the faulty implementation, therefore only two mutant diagnoses remained in the final set. One of them can be seen in Figure 2(b). It was produced with the "self loop" mutation operator, applied to the *unlock?* transition leaving the *silent and open* state. "Self loop" mutations mimic the behavior of implementation faults that disable the functionality of a signal. The second mutant diagnosis remaining was created via the "Negate Guard" mutation operator, disabling the guard of the *unlock?* signal. Both diagnoses are valid explanations for the faulty behavior.

7.3   Average Results

Applying the whole procedure to a faulty implementation took an average of 835 seconds. The final set of mutant diagnoses contained an average of 13 mutants. The reason for this value to be so high is that in black box methods at least one observable has to be reached before a difference in behaviour can be detected. Consequently, the minimal length of a test case for the CAS is three and most implementation faults that lie within these three steps show the same behavior with respect to tioco. Therefore, all model mutations that lie within these steps are seen as possible explanations for the faults. Faults that are harder to reach and therefore usually harder to detect, can be identified far better by our approach.

An average of 14 mutants were selected as diagnoses for the timed faults of the six manually created faulty implementations. Several of these diagnoses contained mutations of the (time dependent) guard of the transition and mutations on the time invariant. This shows that MBMD also supports the debugging of timing faults. Table 2 shows the relation between the faulty implementations and the amount of mutant diagnoses produced by them. The nine faulty implementations that produce 30 possible mutant diagnoses all contain a fault introduced within the first three transitions. The last row shows the average length of the

Table 2. Characteristics of the generated mutant diagnoses and minimal test cases. E.g. for nine of the faulty implementations we produced 30 diagnoses, that could be reached via test cases of length three, while for five of the faulty implementations one diagnosis was enough.

# Faulty implementations	9	1	1	3	1	4	1	2	3	4	2	1	5	2	5	**Avg.**
# Mutant diagnoses	30	29	28	17	16	13	10	9	8	7	6	5	3	2	1	**12.65**
Avg. length of minimal TCs	3	3	3	3	3	3	10	9	8	6.5	4	11	3	13	4.6	**4.95**

minimal test cases per cardinality of the diagnosis set. It highlights the fact that, in general, deeper faults generate fewer possible explanations.

8   Conclusion and Future Work

We proposed a model-based debugging technique, combining debugging and testing and presented a framework implementing the whole technique. We illustrated the approach by applying it to a Car Alarm System to locate automatically introduced faults and presented the first promising results.

The technique can illustrate the type and location of implementation faults at the model level. It returns a set of mutant diagnoses (model mutants) that explain why a given test case failed. For the Car Alarm System, it reduces the number of possible diagnoses from 296 to an average of 13 for each of the faulty implementations. Interestingly, for faults that only occur after long execution traces and are therefor usually harder to locate, the number of diagnoses is below average. The process does not need access to the source code during the first four out of five steps. Hence, it can be started even if the source code is not yet accessible. Experiments showed that timing faults can be identified as accurate as standard faults.

Since the approach is novel, there are still several topics we want to address in future work: in the next step we will refine our mutation operators and elaborate the correspondence between model mutants and implementation faults. We also want to examine the performance of our technique on more complex examples. A very promising point for future improvement would be switching from positive to negative test cases. While negative test cases are too restrictive for our model-based mutation testing approach, this restriction would be very beneficial for debugging. It would allow a more fine-grained matching between faulty implementations and model mutants, consequently reducing the set of mutant diagnoses. We also believe the technique could be combined with other debugging or testing methods. It can detect the location and possible fault type, which can then be investigated in detail by the other testing / debugging methods.

Acknowledgement. The research leading to these results has received funding from the ARTEMIS Joint Undertaking under grant agreements N° 269335 and N° 332830 and from the Austrian Research Promotion Agency (FFG) under grant agreements N° 829817 and N° 838498 for the implementation of the projects MBAT, Combined Model-based Analysis and Testing of Embedded Systems and CRYSTAL, Critical System Engineering Acceleration.

References

1. Aichernig, B.K., Brandl, H., Jöbstl, E., Krenn, W.: Efficient mutation killers in action. In: ICST, pp. 120–129 (2011)
2. Aichernig, B.K., Brandl, H., Jöbstl, E., Krenn, W.: UML in action: A two-layered interpretation for testing. ACM SIGSOFT SEN 36(1), 1–8 (2011)

3. Aichernig, B.K., Lorber, F., Ničković, D.: Time for mutants - model-based mutation testing with timed automata. In: Veanes, M., Viganò, L. (eds.) TAP 2013. LNCS, vol. 7942, pp. 20–38. Springer, Heidelberg (2013)
4. Aichernig, B.K., Lorber, F., Ničković, D.: Model-based mutation testing with timed automata. Technical Report IST-MBT-2013-02, TU Graz (2013), http://www.ist.tugraz.at/aichernig/publications/papers/IST-MBT-2013-02.pdf
5. Alur, R., Dill, D.L.: A theory of timed automata. Theor. Comput. Sci. 126(2), 183–235 (1994)
6. Brillout, A., He, N., Mazzucchi, M., Kroening, D., Purandare, M., Rümmer, P., Weissenbacher, G.: Mutation-based test case generation for Simulink models. In: de Boer, F.S., Bonsangue, M.M., Hallerstede, S., Leuschel, M. (eds.) FMCO 2009. LNCS, vol. 6286, pp. 208–227. Springer, Heidelberg (2010)
7. DeMillo, R.A., Lipton, R.J., Sayward, F.G.: Hints on test data selection: Help for the practicing programmer. Computer 11(4), 34–41 (1978)
8. He, N., Rümmer, P., Kroening, D.: Test-case generation for embedded Simulink via formal concept analysis. In: DAC, pp. 224–229 (2011)
9. Jia, Y., Harman, M.: An analysis and survey of the development of mutation testing. IEEE Transactions on Software Engineering 37(5), 649–678 (2011)
10. Krenn, W., Ničković, D., Tec, L.: Incremental language inclusion checking for networks of timed automata. In: Braberman, V., Fribourg, L. (eds.) FORMATS 2013. LNCS, vol. 8053, pp. 152–167. Springer, Heidelberg (2013)
11. Krichen, M., Tripakis, S.: Conformance testing for real-time systems. Formal Methods in System Design 34(3), 238–304 (2009)
12. Larsen, K.G., Pettersson, P., Yi, W.: Uppaal in a nutshell. STTT 1(1-2), 134–152 (1997)
13. Mayer, W., Stumptner, M.: Model-based debugging - state of the art and future challenges. Electr. Notes Theor. Comput. Sci. 174(4), 61–82 (2007)
14. Mayer, W., Stumptner, M.: Evaluating models for model-based debugging. In: ASE, pp. 128–137. IEEE (2008)
15. de Moura, L., Bjørner, N.S.: Z3: An efficient SMT solver. In: Ramakrishnan, C.R., Rehof, J. (eds.) TACAS 2008. LNCS, vol. 4963, pp. 337–340. Springer, Heidelberg (2008)
16. Nica, M., Nica, S., Wotawa, F.: Does testing help to reduce the number of potentially faulty statements in debugging? In: Bottaci, L., Fraser, G. (eds.) TAIC PART 2010. LNCS, vol. 6303, pp. 88–103. Springer, Heidelberg (2010)
17. Reiter, R.: A theory of diagnosis from first principles. Artif. Intell. 32(1), 57–95 (1987)
18. Schlick, R., Herzner, W., Jöbstl, E.: Fault-based generation of test cases from UML-models: Approach and some experiences. In: Flammini, F., Bologna, S., Vittorini, V. (eds.) SAFECOMP 2011. LNCS, vol. 6894, pp. 270–283. Springer, Heidelberg (2011)
19. Schmaltz, J., Tretmans, J.: On conformance testing for timed systems. In: Cassez, F., Jard, C. (eds.) FORMATS 2008. LNCS, vol. 5215, pp. 250–264. Springer, Heidelberg (2008)
20. Tretmans, J.: Model based testing with labelled transition systems. In: Hierons, R.M., Bowen, J.P., Harman, M. (eds.) FORTEST. LNCS, vol. 4949, pp. 1–38. Springer, Heidelberg (2008)
21. Tretmans, J.: Test generation with inputs, outputs and repetitive quiescence. Software - Concepts and Tools 17(3), 103–120 (1996)
22. Wotawa, F.: On the relationship between model-based debugging and program mutation. Artificial Intelligence 135, 2002 (2001)

Systematic Derivation of Functional Safety Requirements for Automotive Systems

Kristian Beckers[1], Isabelle Côté[2], Thomas Frese[3],
Denis Hatebur[1,2], and Maritta Heisel[1,*]

[1] Universität Duisburg-Essen, Germany, Fakultät für Ingenieurwissenschaften
{kristian.beckers,maritta.heisel}@uni-due.de
[2] Institut für technische Systeme GmbH, Germany
{i.cote,d.hatebur}@itesys.de
[3] Ford Werke GmbH
tfrese@ford.com

Abstract. The released ISO 26262 standard for automotive systems requires breaking down safety goals from the hazard analysis and risk assessment into functional safety requirements in the functional safety concept. It has to be justified that the defined functional safety requirements are suitable to achieve the stated safety goals. In this paper, we present a systematic, structured and model-based method to define functional safety requirements using a given set of safety goals. The rationale for safety goal achievement, the relevant attributes of the functional safety requirements, and their relationships are represented by a UML notation extended with stereotypes. The UML model enables a rigorous validation of several constraints expressed in OCL. We illustrate our method using an example electronic steering column lock system.

1 Introduction

The automotive standard for road vehicles ISO 26262 [1], released in 2011, is seen as an automotive industry standard for developing functional safety systems, because it offers the ability to achieve a consistent functional safety process. Its scope covers electronic and electric (E/E) systems for vehicles with a max gross weight up to 3500 kg. Since ISO 26262 is a risk-based functional safety standard addressing malfunctions, its process involves a hazard analysis to determine the necessary risk reduction to achieve an acceptable level of risk. In [2], we described how to define safety goals with an automotive safety integrity level (ASIL) that describes this necessary risk reduction. According to ISO 26262, the next step is to break down these safety goals into functional safety requirements. It has to be justified that the defined functional safety requirements are suitable to achieve the stated safety goals. Functional safety concepts in practice are currently document-based using text processing and drawing tools such as Microsoft

---

* Part of this work is funded by the German Research Foundation (DFG) under grant number HE3322/4-2 and the EU project Network of Excellence on Engineering Secure Future Internet Software Services and Systems (NESSoS, ICT-2009.1.4 Trustworthy ICT, Grant No. 256980).

A. Bondavalli and F. Di Giandomenico (Eds.): SAFECOMP 2014, LNCS 8666, pp. 65–80, 2014.
© Springer International Publishing Switzerland 2014

Word and Visio. In this paper, we present a systematic, structured and model-based method to define functional safety requirements using a given set of safety goals. The rationale for safety goal achievement, the relevant attributes of the functional safety requirements, and their relationships are represented by using UML notation [3] extended by stereotypes. The UML models enable a rigorous validation of several constraints expressed in the Object Constraint Language (OCL) [4]. Our method is applied to an electronic steering column lock system, serving as illustrative example.

For the break-down of safety goals into functional safety requirements, the ISO 26262 gives no dedicated guidance. It only defines requirements on the content of the documentation. Performing such a break-down is a challenging task because:

- A sound rationale has to be provided.
- Assumptions have to be handled appropriately.
- For the functional safety requirements, the necessary attributes depending on the requirement type have to be defined.
- The functional safety requirements have to be implementable.
- Review activities have to be performed.

In this paper, we propose a structured method based on UML environment models supported by a tool. We assume that an item definition, hazard analysis, risk assessment and safety goals according to ISO 26262 are given (see e.g. [2]). In this paper, we focus on the next step: the creation of a functional safety concept (FSC) in which we show how the functional safety requirements are systematically derived. In the FSC, additionally, requirements may be decomposed in order to lower the ASIL. Furthermore, the functional safety requirements are allocated to elements of a preliminary architecture. These aspects are appropriately described in the ISO 26262 and need no further explanation and improvement and are, therefore, not part of this paper. The contribution of our paper can be summarized as follows:

Rationales are given that show that all safety goals are fulfilled if the requirements are realized, as required by ISO 26262. This will be achieved by using the goal structuring notation with patterns for several solution strategies.

Assumptions are generated based on different sources. It has to be ensured that these assumptions are valid. This is ensured by generating requirements with corresponding descriptions of validation and verification (V&V) activities for them.

Only relevant attributes are described by the developer. This is achieved by classifying the requirements into different categories and by defining, which attributes are required, which are optional, and which should be left out according to the category.

UML profile for **expressing all elements** of a functional safety concept is created in compliance with ISO 26262 making it possible to apply all already mentioned aspects. The profile also provides the basis for validation checks written in OCL.

OCL validation checks concerning consistency and correctness of the functional safety concept are set up. Thus, we provide a **computer-aided technique** to discover errors in the hazard analysis caused by finding inconsistencies or errors in one or more of the UML models.

Functional safety concept document can be generated by the tool, based on the information contained in our UML models. The resulting documentation can then be used for reviewing purposes.

Our paper is organized as follows. The goal structuring notation is introduced in Sect. 2.1. In Sect. 2.2, we give a brief overview of ISO 26262. Our method is presented in Sect. 3. This section also describes our UML profile, which is used to express the functional safety concept. Based on this profile, we define the validation conditions. The tool support is outlined in Sect. 4. We introduce the illustrative example of an electronic steering column lock system as case study in Sect. 5. Section 6 presents related work, while Sect. 7 concludes the paper and gives directions for future work.

2   Background

This section introduces the notation used to derive and justify functional safety requirements (Sect. 2.1. It also provides a short reference to the standard used in this paper (Sect. 2.2).

2.1   Goal Structuring Notation

The Goal Structuring Notation (GSN)[5] - a graphical argumentation notation - explicitly represents the individual elements of any safety argument (goal, strategy, assumption, justification, context, and requirements) and – perhaps more significantly – the relationships that exist between these elements, i.e., how individual requirements are supported by specific strategies, and the assumed context that is defined for the argument.

In the *Functional Safety Concept*, GSN is used to provide an argument for *Functional Safety Requirements* starting from *Safety Goals*, thus also providing the means to check the consistency between Safety Goals and Functional Safety Requirements. In Fig. 1, the GSN elements and their usage for Functional Safety are depicted [6,7]. The "claim" of the argumentation is the *(Safety) Goal* (e.g. SG03). The *Strategy* expresses the rationale how the goal is addressed by subgoals or functional safety requirements (e.g. ESCL-F-S-Req 03). *Sub-Goals* represent an intermediate step between safety goals and functional safety requirements. Relationships between these elements are expressed with *supported by*,

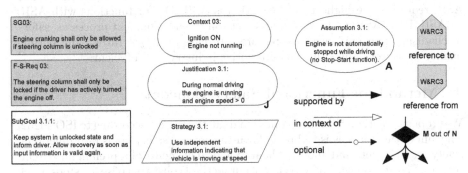

Fig. 1. GSN Notation Overview

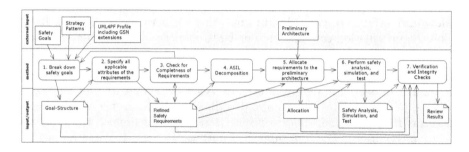

Fig. 2. Method for Functional Safety Concept Creation

optional and alternatives with the element for *M out of N*. For a goal, strategies, subgoals, functional safety requirements, *Context*, *Justifications*, and *Assumptions* can be defined. These relationships are annotated using *in context of*.

Goal structures might reach a size that is hard to fit on a page. To split such a big structure into several smaller ones, we introduced two additional reference elements (see "W&RC3" in Fig. 1).

2.2   ISO 26262

ISO 26262 is a risk-based functional safety standard intended to be applied to safety-related systems that include one or more E/E systems and that are installed in series productions of passenger cars It addresses possible hazards caused by malfunctions of E/E safety-related systems, including the interaction of these systems.

ISO 26262 was derived from the generic functional safety standard ISO/IEC 61508 [8]. It is aligned with the automotive safety life-cycle including specification, design, implementation, integration, verification, validation, configuration, production, operation, service, decommissioning, and management. ISO 26262 provides an automotive-specific risk-based approach for determining risk classes that describe the necessary risk reduction for achieving an acceptable residual risk, called *automotive safety integrity level (ASIL)*.

The possible ASILs are *QM, ASIL A, ASIL B, ASIL C*, and *ASIL D*. The ASIL requiring the highest risk reduction is ASIL D. For functions with ASIL A, ASIL B, or ASIL C, fewer requirements on the development processes, safety mechanisms, and evidences are required. In case of a QM rating, the normal quality measures applied in the automotive industry are sufficient.

3   Method for Functional Safety Concept

We propose a method to create a functional safety concept according to ISO 26262. The aim of the analysis is to break down the generic safety goals into functional safety requirements and allocate them to logical elements of a preliminary architecture. Figure 2 depicts an overview of our method consisting of seven steps. Each step is described in the subsequent paragraphs.

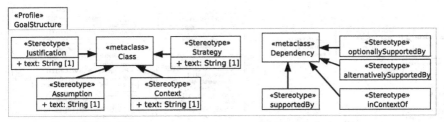

Fig. 3. UML Profile for Goal Structuring Notation Elements

1. Break-down safety goals into functional safety requirements

ISO 26262 requires that the safety goals from the hazard analysis [2] are broken-down into functional safety requirements. This can be documented using the goal structuring notation (see Sect. 2.1). Figure 3 shows the UML profile for the elements of a goal structure. Throughout several projects, it was possible to detect recurring patterns while setting up goal structures. These patterns were transformed into so-called *strategy patterns*. One of these patterns being used in Ford projects, is the *use of independent sources* to obtain certain information, e.g., the vehicle speed and the ignition status can be used for detecting stand-still. Further patterns can be found in [9]. The stereotypes for ($\ll$*SafetyGoal*$\gg$, $\ll$*SubGoal*$\gg$, as well as sub-types of $\ll$*FunctionalSafetyRequirement*$\gg$) including their respective attributes, are shown in Fig. 4. These elements are explained in more detail in Step 2 of our method. The goal structures document the justification that the functional safety requirements are suitable to address the safety goals obtained from the hazard analysis and risk assessment. They include all assumptions necessary to address the respective safety goal. For better readability, the names of the elements in the goal structure (i.e. safety goal, subgoal, strategy, assumption, context, justification, functional safety requirement or its sub-types) are unique. To verify that, the condition 1M01UE[1] has been formulated (see Tab. 4). According to [6] and [7], not all elements can be connected with each other. The relationships between the different elements are realized as follows:

- classes with the stereotypes $\ll$*SafetyGoal*$\gg$, $\ll$*SubGoal*$\gg$, or $\ll$*Strategy*$\gg$ are connected to classes with stereotypes $\ll$*SubGoal*$\gg$, $\ll$*Strategy*$\gg$, or sub-types of $\ll$*FunctionalSafetyRequirement*$\gg$ by dependencies starting from the former and pointing to the latter. This is checked by condition 1M02DG. Furthermore, we check that two strategies are not directly connected to each other (see Tab. 4, 1M03DS).
- $\ll$*Justification*$\gg$, $\ll$*Context*$\gg$, and $\ll$*Assumption*$\gg$ are connected to $\ll$*SafetyGoal*$\gg$, $\ll$*SubGoal*$\gg$, $\ll$*Strategy*$\gg$ or sub-types of $\ll$*Functional-SafetyRequirement*$\gg$ by dependencies starting from the former pointing to the latter. This is verified by condition 1M04DC.[2]

---

[1] The first number refers to the step in the procedure, C is for consistency checks, M is for checks considering correct modeling, G is for generation, the next number is the number of the check within the step, and the last characters are an abbreviation of the description.

[2] In the following, references to validation conditions are given in parentheses.

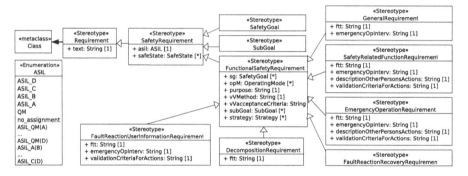

Fig. 4. Elements for Safety Requirements

2. Specify all applicable attributes of the requirements

The requirements developed in Step 1 must to be refined. We support Step 2 with a UML profile that can be used to express the different requirement types. Figure 4 shows the part of our profile that is used to express the different requirement types. A class with the stereotype ≪*Requirement*≫ is used to describe the requirements in general. Safety requirements (≪*SafetyRequirement*≫) are – according to ISO 26262 – special requirements with additional attributes for ASIL and safe states. Safety Goals (≪*SafetyGoal*≫) are top-level safety requirements. A ≪*SubGoal*≫ (not being defined in the ISO 26262) is used in goal structures to structure the argumentation. Functional safety requirements (≪*FunctionalSafetyRequirement*≫) are special safety requirements. They describe the functionalities to achieve the safety goals from a functional perspective without any technical details, such as CAN messages. Each functional safety requirement addresses a set of safety goals (sg), is valid for a given set of operating modes (omM) and should have a purpose (purpose) that may be similar to the strategy or subgoal above. To define functional safety requirements that can be verified, e.g., by testing, the method for verification (vVMethod) and the acceptance criteria (vVAcceptanceCriteria) should be defined. The subgoals or the strategies being supported by the functional safety requirement must be documented. It is important that operating mode, purpose, text, validation and verification method, and acceptance criteria are set for all functional safety requirements (see Tab. 4, 2M01RA). The attributes strategy or subGoal of a ≪*FunctionalSafetyRequirement*≫ can be automatically set based on the information in the goal structure by following the dependencies with the stereotypes ≪*supportedBy*≫, ≪*alternativelySupportedBy*≫ and ≪*optionallySupportedBy*≫ (see Tab. 4, 2M02SG and 2M03SS).

Based on our experience it is helpful to structure the functional safety requirements according to the following categories:

– general requirements,
– safety-related function requirements,
– emergency operation requirements,
– fault reaction: user information requirements,
– fault reaction: recovery requirements, and
– decomposition requirements.

General requirements (≪*GeneralRequirement*≫) could be generic requirements to electronic or electric elements, requirements to elements of other technologies, external measures, or other requirements, e.g., requirements addressing assumptions. For general requirements, it should be possible to define a fault tolerant time (ftt) and the emergency operation interval (emergencyOpInterval). The fault tolerant time defines the period of time between the occurrence of a functional fault and this fault actually becoming dangerous (if it remains undetected). If a safe state cannot be reached by a transition within an acceptable time interval, an emergency operation time interval and a reference to the emergency operation requirement shall be specified. We define general safety requirements for all assumptions to ensure that they are validated or verified. Assumptions are defined

- in the hazard analysis to focus the scope of the analysis to a dedicated vehicle line,
- in the risk assessment on actions of driver or other persons involved to ensure controllability,
- in the rationale for safety goal fulfillment, and
- in the analysis of driver or other persons involved given in the hazard analysis and risk assessment.

Note that it is not necessary to define an ASIL for all general safety requirements, e.g., if they treat external measures or elements of other technologies, no ASIL is required.

We define at least one safety-related function requirement (≪*SafetyRelated-FunctionRequirement*≫) for each safety goal. Safety related-functions include the requirement, the functionality itself, the fault detection requirement and a description of the reaction in case of a detected fault, including transition to a safe state. In addition to the fault tolerant time and the emergency operation interval, a description of actions by the driver or other persons involved (descriptionOfDriverOtherPersonsAction) and validation criteria for these actions (validationCriteriaForActions) can be added. For safety-related function requirements, it is required to specify the ASIL, at least one safe state, and the fault tolerant time (see Tab. 4, 2M04RA).

If an emergency operation interval is specified, we define the corresponding emergency operation requirement (≪*EmergencyOperationRequirement*≫) with the same kind of attributes and conditions as the safety-related function requirement (see Tab. 4, 2M05RA).

If a safe state is entered, usually the driver should be informed. This part of the fault reaction can be defined by user information requirements (≪*FaultReactionUserInformationRequirement*≫). For user information requirements, the fault tolerant time, a description of actions by the driver or other persons involved, and validation criteria for these actions can be added. For user information requirements, it is required to specify at least one safe state, and a description of actions by the driver or other persons involved (see Tab. 4, 2M06RA).

Additionally, the safe state shall be maintained, i.e., the condition for leaving the safe state shall be defined by a fault reaction recovery requirement (≪*FaultReactionRecoveryRequirement*≫). These requirements shall refer to at least one safety goal and the safe state that may be left (see Tab. 4, 2C07RA).

ASIL   decomposition   requirements   ($\ll DecompositionRequirement \gg$)
with fault tolerant time are specified in Step 4. These requirements shall refer to at least one safety goal (see Tab. 4, 2M08RA).

3. Check for completeness of defined requirements

It is important that the functional safety concept is complete. The following
criteria can be used to reach this aim:

- for each safe state at least one safety-related function is defined,
- for each assumption at least one general safety requirement is defined,
- for each safe state emergency operation requirement, user information requirements and recovery requirements are defined if, applicable,
- all relevant operating modes are referred to by requirements, and
- requirements necessary to ensure controllability referring to technical means
  or controls necessary for driver (or other persons involved) actions are identified.

For each safe state, the conditions and the transition to enter this safe state
have to be specified. This is achieved by specifying a safety-related function
requirement. It can be checked automatically that for each safe state at least
one safety-related function requirement is defined (see Tab. 4, 3C01SS) and
that for each assumption at least one general safety requirement is defined (see
Tab. 4, 3C02AS).

For each safe state and strategy/subgoal-combination, emergency operation
requirements, user information requirements, and recovery requirements shall
be defined, if applicable. This can be checked by an engineer. The engineer is
supported by a table containing all references (see Tab. 4, 3G03SS).

It is important to maintain the consistency of the model of the system to be
developed. Therefore, each relevant operating mode shall be referred to by a set of
safety-related function requirements. This must be checked by an engineer. The
engineer is supported by a table containing all references (see Tab. 4, 3G04OR).

The engineer has to check if all requirements necessary to ensure controllability are identified. These requirements may refer to technical means or controls
necessary for the driver (or other persons involved) to perform necessary actions.
To perform this step, the engineer has to check the controllability rationales in
the risk assessment. The engineer is supported by a table containing controllability rationales (see Tab. 4, 3G05CR). Using this table, the engineer documents
appropriate assumptions.

The automated checks mainly cover the consistency of the model. The content
of a requirement (e.g., if the requirement text as such is correct and appropriate)
has to be verified manually by the engineer.

4. ASIL decomposition

To lower the ASIL for certain components, ASIL decomposition (described appropriately in ISO 26262) can be applied. The necessary requirement category
($\ll ASILDecompositionRequirement \gg$) has been defined as part of Step 2. In
this step, the values for this category are set. The decomposed requirements
have a lower ASIL for the technical realization, but the processes have to be established for the original ASIL. This is indicated by providing the original ASIL
in parentheses behind the lowered one, e.g. ASIL A(D) (see Fig. 4).

5. Allocation of Requirements

ISO 26262 requires that the functional safety requirements are allocated to the logical blocks in the preliminary architecture. The allocation supports the next document, in which technical safety requirements are generated for dedicated elements (e.g., electronic control units). The allocation can be performed according to safety capabilities, technical complexity of logical blocks, and to commonality of logical blocks with existing requirements. To document this allocation, our UML profile defines the stereotype ≪LogicalElement≫ for classes and the stereotype ≪allocatedTo≫ for dependencies. The dependencies with the stereotype ≪allocatedTo≫ point from classes with the stereotype with a subtype of ≪FunctionalSafetyRequirement≫ assigned to classes with stereotype ≪LogicalElement≫ (see Tab. 4, 5M01AR).

6. Safety Analysis, Simulation, and Test

ISO 26262 requires to perform safety analysis, simulation, and test. This is beyond the scope of this paper. However, some of the ISO 26262 requirements for this safety analysis are covered by the goal structures set up in Step 1.

7. Verification Review

ISO 26262 requires to perform a verification review of the functional safety concept. This must be performed by a different person who knows the technology of the system-to-be. This is supported by some of the OCL validation constraints in Tab. 4 and the generation of a structured document from the model.

4   Tool Support

We used a tool called UML4PF, developed at the University of Duisburg-Essen, and integrated support for the method to create a functional safety concept as described in Sect. 3. After the developer has drawn some diagram(s) using an EMF-based editor, for example Papyrus UML [10] and applied our stereotypes, UML4PF provides him or her with the following functionality: it checks if the developed model is valid and consistent by using our OCL constraints described in Table 4, it returns the location of invalid parts of the model, and it generates documentation that can be used for (manual) validation and review activities.

Basis for the tool is the Eclipse platform [11] together with its plug-ins EMF [12] and OCL [4]. Our UML profile is conceived as an Eclipse plug-in, extending the EMF meta-model. The OCL constraints are integrated directly into the profile. Thus, it is possible to automatically check the constraints using the validation mechanisms provided by Eclipse.

```
1  Dependency.allInstances() ->select(
2    getAppliedStereotypes().name ->includes('supportedBy') or
3    getAppliedStereotypes().name
          ->includes('alternativelySupportedBy') or
4    getAppliedStereotypes().name ->includes('optionallySupportedBy')
5  ) ->forAll(f |
6    (source.getAppliedStereotypes().name ->includes('SafetyGoal') or
7     source.getAppliedStereotypes().name ->includes('SubGoal') or
8     source.getAppliedStereotypes().name ->includes('Strategy') ) and
9    (target.getAppliedStereotypes().name ->includes('SubGoal') or
10    target.getAppliedStereotypes().name ->includes('Strategy') or
11    target.getAppliedStereotypes().general.name
          ->includes('FunctionalSafetyRequirement')))
```

Listing 1.1. Validation Condition 1M02DG

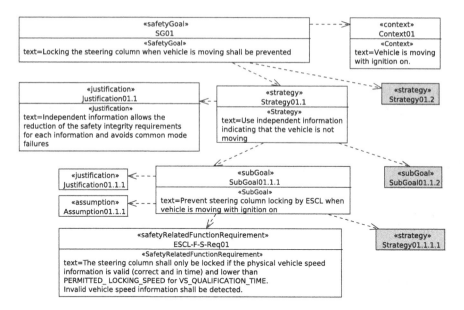

Fig. 5. Goal Structure for SG01 of ESCL

Usually, we consider only one feature at a time in a project. However, it is our believe, that even if all safety related features of a vehicle would be considered in one project, it could be handled by the Eclipse platform running on an appropriate computer.

For example, the OCL expression in Listing 1.1 checks that supporting dependencies connect appropriate elements. To perform the check, it first selects all dependencies (in Line 1) with the either one of the stereotypes ≪supportedBy≫, ≪alternativelySupportedBy≫ or ≪optionallySupportedBy≫ applied (using the EMF keyword getAppliedStereotypes in Lines 2-4). For each of the dependencies matching the stereotypes, it checks if it points from (using the EMF keyword source in Lines 6-8) ≪SafetyGoal≫, ≪SubGoal≫, or ≪Strategy≫ to (using the EMF keyword target in Lines 9-11) ≪SubGoal≫, ≪Strategy≫, or sub-types of ≪FunctionalSafetyRequirement≫ (using the EMF keyword general in Line 11).

The other validation conditions given in Table 4 are implemented in a similar way.

5   Case Study

Our case study is an electronic steering column lock (ESCL) system, which was presented at the "VDA Automotive SYS Conference 2012", June 18/20, 2012, Berlin, Germany and at the VDI Conference "Baden-Baden Spezial 2012", October 10/11, 2012, Baden-Baden, Germany. Item definition, hazard analysis, risk assessment and the safety goals exist. More details on this topic can be found in [2]. We show the applicability of our method by executing the method steps to the ESCL-example.

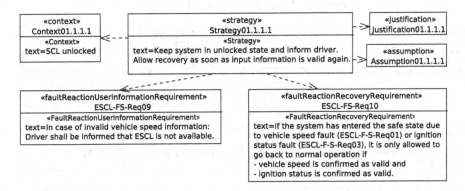

Fig. 6. Goal Structure for Warning and Recovery Concept for SG01 of ESCL

1. Break down safety goals into functional safety requirements

Starting from the safety goals (derivation described in [2]), the goal structures are created. The goal structure in Fig. 5 is created using the pattern "use independent sources" for standstill detection with the appropriate justification (J 01.1) and strategy (S 01.2) to monitor the actuator. Context 01 refers to the situation in which safety is relevant. References to other diagrams are depicted as gray-shaded classes as means to indicate that the diagram is split-up.

Subgoal 01.1.1 and requirement ESCL-F-S-Req01 considering vehicle speed to detect vehicle movement are depicted. Subgoal 01.1.2 considering the ignition status is treated in a different diagram.

Strategy 01.1.1.1 refers to the warning and recovery concept of ESCL-F-S-Req01 and is shown in Fig. 6. In the warning and recovery concept, the context is the safe state that is established by ESCL-F-S-Req01. In the corresponding goal structure given in Fig. 6, a requirement for user information in case of prevented locking and a recovery requirement defining the conditions for entering the normal operation state again, are identified (ESCL-F-S-Req09 and ESCL-F-S-Req10, respectively).

2. Specify all applicable attributes of the requirements

Several requirements have been derived in Step 1. For all of them, it is necessary to specifiy the all relevant attributes. These attributes can be detailed by using a table or to generate such a table. Such a requirement table depicted in Tab. 1. It contains all attributes relevant to ESCL-F-S-Req01.

3. Check for completeness of defined requirements

After defining all attributes of the functional safety concept, it is automatically checked that for each safe state at least one safety-related function is defined and that for each assumption at least one general safety requirement exists by executing Conditions 3C01SS and 3C02AS (see Tab. 4).

To check that for each safe state and strategy/subgoal-combination, all relevant requirement categories have been considered, Tab. 2 was generated automatically (see Tab. 4, 3G03SS) to support the manual completeness check.

An operating mode overview (see Tab. 4, 3G04OR) can be generated from the functional safety concept information. Additionally, a controllability rationale

Table 1. Attributes of ESCL-F-S-Req01

Safety Req-ID[3]	ESCL-F-S-Req01	Strategy/Subgoal	01.1.1
Safety Goal Ref.	SG01, SG02	Operating Modes	Steering column unlocked
ASIL Classification (if applicable)	C (D)	Safe State (if applicable)	ESCL off; Steering column unlocked
Functional Safety Requirement			The steering column shall only be locked if the physical vehicle speed information is valid (correct and in time) and the absolute value is lower than PERMITTED_LOCKING_SPEED for VS_QUALIFICATION_TIME. Invalid vehicle speed information shall be detected. The PERMITTED_LOCKING_SPEED shall be such that locking below this speed is not dangerous. [4]
Purpose			To prevent steering column locking while vehicle is moving at speed and steering is required.
Fault Tolerant Time interval (if applicable)			VS_QUALIFICATION_TIME for vehicle speed faults
Reduced Functionality interval (if applicable)			n/a
Functional Redundancies (e.g. fault tolerance) (if applicable)			No
Description of actions of the driver or other endangered persons (if applicable)			n/a
Validation Criteria for these actions (if applicable)			n/a
V&V method			Set vehicle speed > PERMITTED_LOCKING_SPEED while ignition status = ignition off. Set vehicle speed < PERMITTED_LOCKING_SPEED. Fault insertion of vehicle speed signal.
V&V acceptance criteria			Steering column is not locked until vehicle speed is valid and for VS_QUALIFICATION_TIME below PERMITTED_LOCKING_SPEED.

overview table (see Tab. 4, 3G05CR) can be generated from risk assessment information. Both tables support reviews by engineers.

4. ASIL decomposition

It is possible to lower the ASIL assigned to SG01. The following decomposition of ASIL D was chosen:

- an ASIL C(D) for no locking in case of vehicle speed,
- an ASIL A(D) for no locking if the ignition status shows that ignition is on, and
- the ASIL decomposition requirement with ASIL D that excludes dependencies between vehicle speed and ignition status.

The decomposition is performed according to ISO 26262.

5. Allocation of Requirements

The functional safety requirements are allocated to the elements of the preliminary architecture. This can be done with UML diagrams as depicted in Fig. 7. From these diagrams, an allocation table as depicted in Table 3 can be generated.

7. Verification Review

To support the reviews, the validation conditions listed in Tab. 4 are executed on the complete case study. These validation conditions check the consistency and correctness of the model. That is, we check

- that all necessary attributes are defined and
- the functional safety concept is complete with respect to the safety goals.

[3] Req-ID = name of the class.

[4] The value for VS_QUALIFICATION_TIME is derived in later phases of the Functional Safety Project (e.g. during creation of the Technical Safety Concept).

Table 2. Safe State and Requirement References

Safety Goal reference	Safe State	Strategy (S) or Sub Goal (SG) reference (optional)	Safety Related Functions With this Safe State reference	Reduced Functionality reference (if applicable)	User Information reference	Maintain Safe State / Recovery to Normal Operation reference (if applicable)
SG01	ESCL off; Steering Column unlocked	1.1.1 (SG)	ESCL-F-S-Req01	n/a	ESCL-F-S-Req09	ESCL-F-S-Req10
		1.1.2 (SG)	ESCL-F-S-Req03			
	Steering Column unlocked and further locking prevented	1.2 (S)	ESCL-F-S-Req05	n/a	ESCL-F-S-Req05b	ESCL-F-S-Req05c
	No engine start allowed due to reduced safety integrity	1.2.1 (SG)	ESCL-F-S-Req05a	n/a	ESCL-F-S-Req05b	ESCL-F-S-Req05c

Fig. 7. Allocation of Functional Safety Requirements to Logical Elements

F-S-Req. ID	Req. text	ASIL	Subsystem/ Component							
			KVM	Power Line	K-Line	SCL	ABS	ECM	DIM	Power But.
ESCL-F-S-Req01	...	C (D)	X	X			X			
...										

Table 3. Allocation of Functional Safety Requirements to Logical Elements

6 Related Work

Basir, Denny, and Fischer [9] present goal structures for safety cases in the automotive sector. They do not focus on the technical realization but consider the entire safety process with their documents as entities.

Dittel and Aryus [13] present an overview of V&V activities at Ford Motor Company applied for the lane keeping aid system. This paper also presents elements of the process for functional safety according to ISO 26262, i.e. the analysis activities.

Sinha [14] illustrates an example of a brake-by-wire system for road vehicles including a safety and reliability analysis compliant to ISO 262626. The conclusions derive suggestions for future projects, such as that the system architecture of road vehicles shall support the detection of failures and have the means to still provide desired services until the failures are repaired.

Palin et al. [15] provide guidelines for safety practitioners and researchers to create safety cases compliant to the ISO 26262 standard. The authors propose extensions of the Goal Structuring Notation, patterns, and a number of re-usable safety arguments for creating safety cases. For confidentiality reasons, the authors cannot show example instantiations of their patterns or generic arguments.

Conrad et al. [16] compares software tools that support ISO 26262 certification. The authors identified a list a qualification requirements for selecting ISO 26262 support tools. The publication also contains a report about Conrad et al.'s experience with these tools.

Hillebrand et al. [17] discuss how to develop electric and electronic architectures (EEA) compliant with the ISO 26262 standard. The authors focus on safety requirements during early development phases. Hillenbrand et al. present a method for eliciting safety requirements, and mapping their safety concerns to functions of design artifacts. Previously, Hillebrand et al. [18] proposed a model-based and tool- supported approach for the failure mode and effect analysis (FMEA) of EAAs complaint to ISO 26262. The authors contribute a formalized method for eliciting and analyzing data for a FMEA.

Habli et al. [19] propose a process for model-based assurance for justifying automotive functional safety. They use SysML and GSN as graphical notations. Their goal and ours is similar. We both want to support a method based on ISO 26262 to derive functional safety requirements. In contrast to their work, we use UML, which gives us a broader spectrum of modeling possibilities. Furthermore, we provide tool support for our method and equipped our approach with formal consistency checks on the model. These checks can be automatically checked by our tool. In addition, our way of modeling allows us to trace elements within our models.

Born et al. [20] report on lessons learned from applying a model-based approach for ISO 26262 certification. The authors also discuss the advantages of models instead of text in the ISO 26262 certification process.

7   Conclusions and Future Work

The method presented in this paper has been and currently is applied in several Ford of Europe projects. However, the formal validation conditions and tool support were and are not part of these projects. Both have been developed as contribution of this paper. Still, we are confident that the validation conditions in combination with the tool support ensure at least the same consistency and correctness as the currently used approach, with the benefit of less effort needed. Furthermore, the method is the logical next step to the work presented in [2].

Our contribution has the following main benefits:

- a structured and model-based approach for deriving functional safety concepts for the automotive domain compliant to ISO 26262
- a UML profile to express all required elements for a functional safety concept compliant to ISO 26262
- computer-aided validation of created UML models via executable OCL expressions, e.g., checks for correctness and completeness of the model
- enforcing considering adequate assumptions and safety reasoning by explicitly checking that these are present (by computers) and their soundness (by human experts)

Functional safety concepts in practice are currently document-based using text processing and drawing tools. If the documents are created using a UML tool, the information can be checked for consistency and the document can be created. With our method, a seamless integration into a model-based development process is possible. In the future, we intend to apply our method and tool in different projects. In addition, we plan to focus on technical safety requirements generation and metric derivation.

Table 4. Validation Conditions

Step	ID	Condition
1	1M01UE	Names of the elements in the goal structure (safety goal, subgoal, strategy, assumption, context, justification, functional safety requirement or subtype) are unique.
1	1M02DG	Dependencies with the stereotypes ≪*supportedBy*≫, ≪*alternativelySupportedBy*≫ and ≪*optionallySupportedBy*≫ point from classes with the stereotypes ≪*SafetyGoal*≫, ≪*SubGoal*≫, or ≪*Strategy*≫ to ≪*SubGoal*≫, ≪*Strategy*≫, or subtypes of ≪*FunctionalSafetyRequirement*≫.
1	1M03DS	A dependency between 2 strategies is not allowed.
1	1M04DC	A dependency with the stereotype ≪*inContextOf*≫ point from classes with the stereotypes ≪*SafetyGoal*≫, ≪*SubGoal*≫, or ≪*Strategy*≫ to ≪*Justification*≫, ≪*Context*≫ or ≪*Assumption*≫.
2	2M01RA	For each functional safety requirement and their subtypes: the operating mode is required to be set, the purpose, the text, the validation and verification method, and its acceptance criteria is required not to be empty.
2	2M02SG	If the dependency with stereotypes ≪*supportedBy*≫, ≪*alternativelySupportedBy*≫ or ≪*optionallySupportedBy*≫ point from a class with stereotype ≪*SubGoal*≫ to a class with a stereotype being subtypes of ≪*FunctionalSafetyRequirement*≫, its attribute subGoal points to the source of the dependency.
2	2M03SS	If the dependency with stereotypes ≪*supportedBy*≫, ≪*alternativelySupportedBy*≫ or ≪*optionallySupportedBy*≫ point from a class with stereotype ≪*Strategy*≫ to a class with a stereotype being subtypes of ≪*FunctionalSafetyRequirement*≫, its attribute strategy points to the source of the dependency.
2	2M04RA	For a class with the stereotype ≪*SafetyRelatedFunctionRequirement*≫, ASIL, at least one safe state, and fault tolerant are specified.
2	2M05RA	For a class with the stereotype ≪*EmergencyOperationRequirement*≫, ASIL, at least one safe state is referred to, and fault tolerant time is specified.
2	2M06RA	For a class with the stereotype ≪*FaultReactionUserInformationRequirement*≫, at least one safe state is referred to, and a description of actions by the driver or other persons are specified.
2	2C07RA	For a class with the stereotype ≪*FaultReactionRecoveryRequirement*≫, at least one safety goal and one safe state are referred to.
2	2M08RA	For a class with the stereotype ≪*ASILDecompositionRequirement*≫, at least one safety goal is referred to.
3	3C01SS	Each a state or state machine with the stereotype ≪*SafeState*≫ is referred to by a class with the stereotype ≪*SafetyRelatedFunctionRequirement*≫.
3	3C02AS	From each class with the stereotype ≪*Assumption*≫, a dependency with the stereotype ≪*supportedBy*≫ points to a class with the stereotype ≪*GeneralRequirement*≫.
3	3G03SS	For each class with the stereotype ≪*SafetyRelatedFunctionRequirement*≫, all safe states and the related strategies or subgoals are determined. For each combination of safe state and the related strategy or subgoal, references to emergency operation requirements, user information requirements, and recovery requirements are listed in a table.
3	3G04OR	For each state or state machine, the name of the classes with the stereotype ≪*SafetyRelatedFunctionRequirement*≫ are listed in a table. The line is removed, if all substates are referenced or if the containing state is referenced.
3	3G05CR	The controllability rationales from all assessment together with the addressing safety goals are listed in a table.
5	5M01AR	Dependencies with the stereotype ≪*allocatedTo*≫ points from subtype of ≪*FunctionalSafetyRequirement*≫ to ≪*LogicalElement*≫.

References

1. Int. Organization for Standardization (ISO): Road Vehicles – Functional Safety. ISO 26262 (2011)

2. Beckers, K., Frese, T., Hatebur, D., Heisel, M.: A Structured and Model-Based Hazard Analysis and Risk Assessment Method for Automotive Systems. In: Procs of the 24th IEEE Int. Symposium on Software Reliability Engineering, pp. 238–247. IEEE Computer Society (2013)

3. UML Revision Task Force: OMG Unified Modeling Language: Superstructure. Object Management Group (OMG) (May 2010)

4. UML Revision Task Force: OMG Object Constraint Language: Reference (February 2010)

5. Kelly, T.P.: A Systematic Approach to Safety Case Management. In: Procs. 28th Symp. on Applied Computing, Detroit, Society for Automotive Engineers (2004)

6. Spriggs, J.: GSN - The Goal Structuring Notation: A Structured Approach to Presenting Arguments, 2012th edn. Springer (2012)

7. Goal Structuring Notation Working Group. GSN community standard version 1 (2011)

8. International Organization for Standardization (ISO) and International Electrotechnical Commission (IEC): Functional safety of electrical/electronic/programmable electronic safety-relevant systems. ISO/IEC 61508 (2000)

9. Basir, N., Denney, E., Fischer, B.: Deriving safety cases for hierarchical structure in model-based development. In: Schoitsch, E. (ed.) SAFECOMP 2010. LNCS, vol. 6351, pp. 68–81. Springer, Heidelberg (2010)

10. Atos Origin: Papyrus UML Modelling Tool (February 2011),
    http://www.papyrusuml.org/

11. Eclipse Foundation: Eclipse - An Open Development Platform (2011),
    http://www.eclipse.org/

12. Eclipse Foundation: Eclipse Modeling Framework Project (EMF) (June 2012),
    http://www.eclipse.org/modeling/emf/

13. Dittel, T., Aryus, H.-J.: How to 'survive' a safety case according to ISO 26262. In: Schoitsch, E. (ed.) SAFECOMP 2010. LNCS, vol. 6351, pp. 97–111. Springer, Heidelberg (2010)

14. Sinha, P.: Architectural design and reliability analysis of a fail-operational brake-by-wire system from ISO 26262 perspectives. Reliability Engineering & System Safety, 1349–1359 (2011)

15. Palin, R., Ward, D., Habli, I., Rivett, R.: ISO 26262 safety cases: Compliance and assurance. In: 2011 6th IET Int. Conf. on. System Safety, pp. 1–6 (2011)

16. Conrad, M., Munier, P., Rauch, F.: Qualifying software tools according to ISO 26262. In: Proc. Dagstuhl-Workshop Modellbasierte Entwicklung Eingebetteter Systeme, MBEES 2010 (2010)

17. Hillebrand, J., Reichenpfader, P., Mandic, I., Siegl, H., Peer, C.: Establishing Confidence in the Usage of Software Tools in Context of ISO 26262. In: Flammini, F., Bologna, S., Vittorini, V. (eds.) SAFECOMP 2011. LNCS, vol. 6894, pp. 257–269. Springer, Heidelberg (2011)

18. Hillenbrand, M., Heinz, M., Adler, N., Matheis, J., Müller-Glaser, K.: Failure mode and effect analysis based on electric and electronic architectures of vehicles to support the safety lifecycle ISO/DIS 26262. In: 2010 21st IEEE International Symposium on apid System Prototyping, RSP, pp. 1–7 (June 2010)

19. Habli, I., Ibarra, I., Rivett, R., Kelly, T.: Model-Based Assurance for Justifying Automotive Functional Safety. In: SAE Technical Paper 2010-01-0209 (2010)

20. Born, M., Favaro, J., Kath, O.: Application of ISO DIS 26262 in Practice. In: Procs of the 1st Workshop on Critical Automotive Applications: Robustness & Safety, CARS 2010, pp. 3–6. ACM, New York (2010)

Making Implicit Safety Requirements Explicit
An AUTOSAR Safety Case

Thomas Arts, Michele Dorigatti, and Stefano Tonetta

QuviQ and FBK
thomas.arts@quviq.com,
{mdorigatti,tonettas}@fbk.eu

Abstract. Safety standards demand stringent requirements on embedded systems used in safety-critical applications such as automotive, railways, and aerospace. In the automotive domain, the AUTOSAR software architecture provides some mechanisms to fulfill the ISO26262 requirements. The verification of these mechanisms is a challenging problem and it is not always clear in which context the safety requirements are supposed to be met.

In this paper, we report on a case study developed in the SafeCer project, where we combined contract-based design and model-based testing. A contract-based approach has been used to formalize the safety requirements to detect communication failures. The formal specification shows under which assumptions the AUTOSAR protection mechanism fulfills these requirements. A model-based testing approach has been used to test the software implementing such protection mechanism. The model used for testing has been model checked against the contract specification ensuring that the system-level safety requirements are met.

Keywords: Formal Methods, Contract-Based Design, Testing, AUTOSAR.

1 Introduction

The AUTOSAR standard [1] is a detailed architectural description of software components for the automotive industry. Modern cars contain many different computing units (ECUs) that are connected via several networks. The basic software running on all these units is written by different vendors, but it should be compatible. The AUTOSAR standard is created to "enforce" compatibility. The C software implementing AUTOSAR components is highly configurable and has in general a practically infinite number of possible internal states. Ensuring compatibility is in practice performed by testing and, in the setting of our work, by using Model-Based Testing (MBT): a formal model of the software is instantiated by the same configuration used for the C software. This model instance is then used to automatically generate thousands of random tests. Failing tests indicate a conformance deviation with the model.

Sensors and actuators often handle data for safety-critical applications such as an airbag or a parking brake. They can be located at different physical ECUs so that safety-critical data are communicated over one of the networks. For this reason, the ISO26262 standard [2] prescribes to implement measures to detect communication faults such as loss or corruption of messages. The AUTOSAR standard caters for a common set of these fault models by offering a solution called *End-to-End (E2E) Protection* [3] and is

A. Bondavalli and F. Di Giandomenico (Eds.): SAFECOMP 2014, LNCS 8666, pp. 81–92, 2014.
© Springer International Publishing Switzerland 2014

specified as a library with functions to protect a data item and to check it at the other end of the communication. In short, it adds a counter and identifier to the data, computes a checksum and sends the data and checksum over the bus instead of the raw data. At the other end, the checksum is used to see if the data got corrupted and if not, the data is compared to an earlier value to see if it can be trusted. By addressing a number of fault models once and for all with a library, the AUTOSAR software developers know what they can use when they are faced with specific safety requirements. However, what is achieved by using such libraries is not always clear: by just using the protection mechanism of AUTOSAR, the software developer is not guaranteed to obtain a fault-tolerant system, and it is critical to define the context in which the system is safe and level of tolerance that is guaranteed.

In this paper, we formalized the guarantees of the E2E Protection library components (with the simplest profile $P01$) and the assumptions on the communication failures into the input language of OCRA [4], a tool for Contract-Based Design (CBD) of embedded systems. Given that we have formalized the protection mechanism, we can combine this with system-level safety requirements of a system architecture. In particular, we modeled an airbag that inflates when the sensors send a message that we are in collision, whereas at the same time, the airbag never inflates if no such message arrives from the sensor. The contract-based refinement of the airbag using the AUTOSAR protection mechanism was proved correct with the OCRA support to contract-refinement checking. We finally verified with model checking techniques the contract specification on existing test models of the AUTOSAR library for QuickCheck [5,6], a tool for MBT of software. With QuickCheck, we can automatically generate arbitrary tests for the communication stacks. These tests are clearly enhanced by the formal proof that the test models correctly refine the safety requirements.

The contributions of the paper are manifold. First, we showed how to bridge the gap between system requirements and guarantees on the E2E Protection library. Second, we derived the guarantees on the communication stacks for a concrete example. Third, we showed how the properties of the AUTOSAR library used in the contract-based derivation can be verified on the models used for code testing. Finally, we provided a methodology to integrate CBD and MBT tools.

The paper is structured as follows: in Sec. 2, we give an overview of the AUTOSAR E2E Protection mechanism and the related ISO26262 safety requirements; in Sec. 3, we describe the background tools and techniques, which are CBD, OCRA, MBT, and QuickCheck; in Sec. 4, we present the main part of the paper, including the airbag example, the methodology integrating CBD and MBT, the formalization of the E2E Protection library, the contract-based derivation, and the verification of the code implementation; in Sec. 5 we give an overview of the related work, and finally in Sec. 6, we draw some conclusions.

2   AUTOSAR E2E Protection

2.1   AUTOSAR

AUTOSAR is a software standard for the automotive industry providing the specification of the basic software components, such as several protocol stacks, memory management, communication routing, etc. The AUTOSAR platform offers a variety of components to provide functionality, for example a component for E2E data protection that encodes and decodes a message in a standard way so that corruption or message loss can be detected. Each software component is specified by both a very specific programmer API as well as a behavioral description. The diversity of demands from different hardware platforms and car models are catered for by specifying the configurability of the software. Each component can be configured in many different ways. The actual software that is eventually put in a vehicle is partly generated from a confuguration file and partly statically provided.

The flexibility in configurations makes it difficult to test AUTOSAR software, since a test case typically consists of both a sequence of API calls with expected return values and side-effects as well as a configuration for which the code under test has to be generated. Manually creating test cases is tedious and error prone. Therefore, Quviq has developed a method to generate test cases from a formal model of one or more AUTOSAR components. Given a configuration, test cases, valid and meaningful for that configuration, are generated and executed.

Clearly, the correctness of software applications built on top of the AUTOSAR basic software components requires correctly implemented components and a correct use and configuration of these components. The latter is an engineering challenge due to the difficult in understanding from the set of requirements on software what guarantees the software components offers in a specific configuration and architecture. For example, the E2E Protection library is recommended, among others, as an implementation measure against *message loss during transmission* [3]. Clearly, message may get lost for several reasons and the engineering task is to handle that. Using the E2E protection library may seem the right thing to do, but the engineering challenge is to understand the context of this guarantee. If communication is safety-critical and many messages in a row are lost in few milliseconds, can one then still use the designed solution? What configuration of the E2E Protection library should be used in order to protect against this scenario? These questions are based on the use of the software component by an application outside the AUTOSAR basic software. Without knowledge about this application, such questions are difficult or impossible to answer. This paper shows how one can make the assumption of the application explicit in order to formulate precise guarantees on the E2E Protection library.

2.2 ISO26262 Requirements and E2E Protection

In order to implement effective measures against communication loss the ISO26262 standards prescribe to take into account a series of possible communication faults: loss of peer to peer communication; unintended message repetition due to the same message being unintentionally sent again; message loss during transmission; insertion of messages due to receiver unintentionally receiving an additional message, which is interpreted to have correct source and destination addresses; re-sequencing due to the order of the data being changed during transmission, i.e. the data is not received in the same order as in which it was been sent; message corruption due to one or more data bits in the message being changed during transmission; message delay due to the message being received correctly, but not in time; blocking access to data bus due to a faulty node not adhering to the expected patterns of use and making excessive demands for service, thereby reducing its availability to other nodes, e.g. while wrongly waiting for non existing data; and constant transmission of messages by a faulty node, thereby compromising the operation of the entire bus.

The faults described above are represented in AUTOSAR by the following fault models:

- repetition: a message is received more than once.
- deletion: a message or parts of it have been removed from the communication stream.
- insertion: an additional message or parts of it have been inserted into the communication stream.
- incorrect sequence: the messages of a communication stream are received in an incorrect order.
- corruption: the corruption data of a message or parts of it occurred.
- delay: a message is received too late.
- addressing faults: a message is sent to the wrong destination.

The protection measure provided by the AUTOSAR E2E library consists of using:

1. a counter modulo N ($N = 15$ in Profile 1) which is increased by one at every sent message;
2. a checksum provided by the AUTOSAR CRC library;
3. data ID to verify the identity of each transmitted safety-related data element.

In particular, the repetition, deletion, insertion, and incorrect sequence are addressed by the counter, corruption by the CRC checksum, addressing faults by the data ID. In addition to this, the real-time properties of AUTOSAR in combination with periodically sending messages enable detection of not receiving new data on the bus. Timeouts are therefore represented by either no new data available or by receiving new data with the same counter as the previously received valid data.

3   Background Techniques

3.1   OCRA and CBD

In this paper, we adopt the CBD framework supported by the OCRA tool [4]. In particular, we use a finite-state discrete-time model of the system. Component interfaces are described with Boolean or bounded integer data ports and with events, which are instantaneous triggers of changes (from the formal point of view, they are Boolean labels on the state transitions). An execution trace of the component is therefore a sequence of states, which are assignments to the port variables. The transition from a state to another one can be labeled with an event. Assertions on the execution traces are specified by means of linear-time temporal logic. In particular, we use LTL [7] with past operators and predicates over current and next variables to represent state changes, as informally described in Table 1.

The OCRA input language is a component-based description of the system architecture where every component is associated with one or more contracts. Each contract

Table 1. Overview of the temporal logic used to specify the contracts

Syntax	Informal Description	Example	Example description
$P(V)$	atomic predicate over the port variables V	$m \geq 2$	m is greater or equal to 2
$P(V, V')$	atomic predicate over the current port variables V and their next value after a transition	$c' = c + 1$	c is increased by 1
$\neg \phi$	Boolean negation	$\neg f$	f is false
$\phi_1 \{\wedge, \vee, \rightarrow\} \phi_2$	binary Boolean operators	$m = n \rightarrow c' = c$	if $m = n$ then c is not changed
$\mathbf{G} \, \phi$	ϕ holds in every future state	$\mathbf{G} \, (f \rightarrow \mathbf{G} \, f)$	when f is true, it remains true forever
$\mathbf{F} \, \phi$	ϕ holds in some future state	$\mathbf{G} \, (f \rightarrow \mathbf{F} \, e)$	f is always followed by e
$\mathbf{O} \, \phi$	ϕ holds in some past state	$\mathbf{G} \, (f \rightarrow \mathbf{O} \, e)$	f is always preceded by e
$\mathbf{X} \, \phi$	ϕ holds in the next state	$\mathbf{G} \, (f \rightarrow \mathbf{X} \, e)$	f is always immediately followed by e
$\mathbf{Y} \, \phi$	ϕ holds in the previous state (so, we are not in the initial state)	$\mathbf{G} \, (f \rightarrow \mathbf{Y} \, e)$	f is always immediately preceded by e

consists of an assumption and a guarantee specified as temporal logical formulas. The assumption represents a requirement on the environment of the component. The guarantee represents a requirements for the component implementation to be satisfied when the assumption holds.

When a component S is decomposed into subcomponents, the contract refinement ensures that the guarantee of S is not weakened by the contracts of the subcomponents while its assumption is not strengthened. This is checked independently from the actual implementation of the components and is verified by means of a set of proof obligations in LTL, which are discharged with model checking techniques [8,9].

OCRA allows to associate to a component a behavioral model representing its implementation. The language used for the behavioral model is SMV, the input language of the NuSMV model checker [10]. OCRA checks if the SMV model is a correct implementation of the specified component simply calling NuSMV to verify if the SMV model satisfies the implication $A \rightarrow G$ for every contract $\langle A, G \rangle$ of the component.

3.2 QuickCheck and MBT

QuickCheck is a testing technique and tool originating from the functional programming community [11] where one expresses properties of the software under test in a functional language. QuickCheck then computes test cases that should be satisfied if this property holds for the software. The original stateless and logic properties have been extended by Quviq into conformance properties, where the functional language is used to implement a kind of reference implementation from which test cases are automatically generated [5].

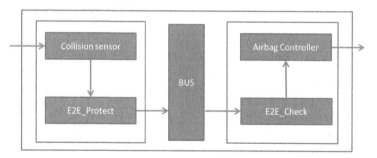

Fig. 1. A simple architecture of an airbag system communicating with a collision sensor

Thus, rather than focusing on individual test cases to encapsulate the behavior of a system, this behavior is specified by properties, expressed in a logical form. The system is then tested by checking whether it has the required properties for randomly generated data, which may be inputs to functions, sequences of API calls, or other representations of test cases. In this way, large software systems, such as the AUTOSAR basic software or Radio Base Station Software, have successfully been tested.

Some versions of QuickCheck can systematically inflate the complete state space of a model. However, the models in general have an infinite or at least practically infinite state space. Therefore, the Quviq QuickCheck version is optimized for random walks through the state space, not for guaranteeing that all paths have been walked through.

4 Making Implicit Safety Requirements Explicit

4.1 The Airbag Example

As an example of usage of the E2E Protection mechanism, we consider a simplified version of an airbag system. An informal picture of the system architecture is shown in Figure 1. In real systems the airbag software is different, but we use this example to show how we handle systems similar to real industrial ones. The formalization of the real E2E library is faithful and the method we present for deriving the constraints of using the E2E library is generally applicable to any similar system.

The Airbag System communicates with a Collision Sensor to know when to trigger the airbag. The communication runs on a bus which may fail. In this example, the Collision Sensor is split into two components: the actual sensor that senses the collision and the E2E Protection which enriches the message with the E2E Protection mechanism before sending it over the bus. Similarly, the Airbag System is split into the actual airbag controller and the software component that checks the message to detect communication failures.

After making a design like this, one wants to reason about it in the presence of the given fault models. In theory, when the world is perfect, as soon as the sensor detects a collision, a message is sent and the airbag inflates. In practice, the sensor may be broken, the bus may experience one of the faults described above and the controller may be disfunctional. In other words, there is no guarantee that this is going to work.

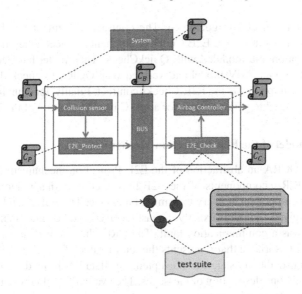

Fig. 2. Integration of CBD and MBT

Since it is important to know whether the sensor is working, it will continuously send messages to the controller. In that way, a broken sensor is detected. We do not want to report sensor failure if only one message is lost and therefore it is important that the E2E Protection detects message deletion.

It is also important to only inflate the airbag if the car is in a real collision. We therefore want to detect data corruption at the same time as that we do not just send a one bit zero and one message, but use over engineering to send a byte with two different bit patterns to distinguish normal and collision situation.

4.2   Integration of CBD and MBT

We propose a methodology that integrates Contract-Based Design (CBD) and Model-Based Testing (MBT). CBD is used at the system level in order to ensure a correct derivation of the properties of the components. In particular, in case of safety-related requirements, it forces to explicitly state the assumptions on the failures that are necessary in order to guarantee the requirements. MBT is used at the code level to ensure the compliance of the code with the model.

The proposed methodology integrates CBD and MBT as depicted in Figure 2: the system architecture is enriched with a contract refinement, which is proved correct with formal methods; the software components are implemented with a state machine and with a concrete program; the state machine is proved to satisfy the component contracts with model checking and is used to generate a test suite for the program.

The airbag system has been formalized with OCRA. Each component is enriched with contracts to specify the assumption and guarantee of the component. The contract of the Bus component include the possibility to have failures (either a message corruption or loss). The system component explicitly specifies the assumptions on such failures in order to ensure its guarantee. The contract refinement has been proved correct. The state machine of the E2E_Check component has been taken from the AU-TOSAR specification and modeled with QuickCheck. This model has been automatically translated into an SMV model and verified with OCRA to check that the state machine correctly implements the E2E_Checks contract. Finally, the QuichCheck state machine has been used to generate tests for a real C implementation of the E2E_Check.

4.3 Formal Model of the E2E Protection Mechanism

We modeled in OCRA an abstraction of the E2E Protection mechanism described in Sec. 2.2. The OCRA components of the E2E have a counter that is incremented by the E2E_Protect component at every transmitted message. The E2E_Check component checks if the received counter is exactly the last received valid counter incremented by one or if there was a communication fault. The CRC checksum is abstracted with a Boolean ValidCRC variable that represents the return value of the CRC Library. Thus, if ValidCRC is false, the message was corrupted. The data IDs instead are not modeled since we have only one destination of messages. The availability of new data on the bus is represented by a Boolean variable.

The interface of the E2E_Check component has therefore the following ports:

- NewDataAvailable: a Boolean input port that represents if there is new data available on the transmission medium;
- ReceivedCounter: a 4-bit input port that represents the value of the counter on a new received message;
- ValidCRC: a Boolean input port that represents if the received message is valid;
- MaxDeltaCounter: a parameter used to define acceptable number of lost messages;
- Status: an output port that defines the status of the received message, which can be: NONEWDATA, WRONG_CRC, INITIAL, REPEATED, OK, OKSOMELOST, WRONG_SEQUENCE;
- LastValidCounter: an output port that stores the counter of the last received message.

The main guarantees of the component are formalized by the following formulas (a complete version of the specification can be found in
https://es.fbk.eu/people/tonetta/tests/safecomp14):

- **G** $(((NewDataAvailable \land ValidCRC \land 1 \leq DeltaCounter \leq MaxDeltaCounter) \land$ **Y O** $(NewDataAvailable \land ValidCRC)) \rightarrow (\mathbf{X}\ status\_ok(Status)))$; in the OCRA syntax this is written as:

```
always (((NewDataAvailable and ValidCRC and
           1<=DeltaCounter and DeltaCounter<=MaxDeltaCounter)
 and previously in the past (NewDataAvailable and ValidCRC))
   implies (then status_ok(Status)));
```

this means that whenever the component receives a new valid message with a valid counter and previously another valid message was received, then the status is set to OK or OKSOMELOST depending on the value of the counter (this is encoded by the macro "status_ok").

- **G** (*status_ok(Status)* → (**Y** ((*NewDataAvailable* ∧ *ValidCRC* ∧ 1 ≤ *DeltaCounter* ≤ *MaxDeltaCounter*) ∧ **Y O** (*NewDataAvailable* ∧ *ValidCRC*)))); in the OCRA syntax this is written as:

```
always (status_ok(Status) implies
  (previously ((NewDataAvailable and ValidCRC and
  DeltaCounter>=1 and DeltaCounter<=MaxDeltaCounter) and
  previously in the past (NewDataAvailable and ValidCRC))));
```

this means that the status is set of OK or OKSOMELOST only if the component just received a valid message with a valid counter and in the past another valid message was already received.

4.4 Contract-Based Refinement of the Airbag Requirements

The top-level requirements of our airbag example are that every collision must be followed by the inflation of the airbag and vice versa, the airbag inflates only after a collision. This is formalized in the LTL formulas **G** (*collision* → **F** *inflate*) and **G** (*inflate* → **O** *collision*). This is accomplished by the five components of the system as follows: the sensor senses the collision and generates a message; the message is enriched with the counter by the E2E_Protect component; the message is transmitted from the sender to receiver by the bus; on the receiver side, the message is checked by the E2E_Check component and then passed to the airbag controller that makes the airbag inflate. Each of these functions is formalized by an LTL formula.

The bus contracts include the fault models of message corruption and deletion. In particular, the bus component receives in input two events, fault_deletion and fault_corruption. Whenever fault_deletion happens, the NewDataAvailable output is set to false. Whenever fault_corruption happens, the ValidCRC output is set to false.

If we do not specify any assumption on the system inputs, the contract refinement fails, confirming that some assumptions are implicit. There are three assumptions that we added in order to obtain a correct refinement:

1. **G** (*fault* → **X** ¬*fault*): we assume that there cannot be two consecutive faults, either corruption or deletion of a message;
2. *MaxDeltaCounter* ≥ 2: we assume that at least one lost message is acceptable and the E2E_Check component will consider the new message valid even if the counter has been increased by 2;
3. **G** (*collision* → **G** *collision*): whenever there is collision, this will be permanent, so that collision messages will be continuously sent to airbag controller.

If we remove one of these assumption, the OCRA tool gives us a counterexample showing an execution trace that violates the top-level contract. Note however that these assumptions are not guaranteed to be the weakest conditions.

4.5 Formal Model and Verification of the E2E Check Implementation

The E2E Check function is informally presented as a state machine description in the AUTOSAR specification. In our case, we took that informal presentation as a start for a

QuickCheck model. This QuickCheck model has a formal semantics and has been used to generate test cases. On turn, these were used to verify a C implementation of the E2E Check function.

The QuickCheck model was also translated into an SMV model. This translation is to a high extent automated. Erlang [12] is a functional language, with single assignment. In a few steps, we transform the program by partially evaluating all occurrences of local variables. The result is a program that only has the input variables present. For technical reasons we rewrite if-statements into case statements and make all case statements into Boolean choices by nesting them. The resulting transformation is a completely equivalent Erlang program. The QuickCheck model uses records to store data in. The input record is processed and a similar output record is returned. For each field in the output record, we backtrace in the source code what conditions should hold to change its value into the value that it can get in the return record. This then results in the SMV next state function for each input variable.

Finally, the SMV model has been model checked with OCRA to verify that it is a correct implementation of the E2E_Check component, in other words that it satisfies the contracts of the component. We can conclude that the Erlang model satisfies such contracts. Moreover, we can be confident that the C implementation satisfies such contracts, since the state space is finite and by collecting the model state space while running a few hundred thousand tests (which takes about an hour), we can show to have covered all model states during testing. We also performed other sanity checks provided by OCRA such as the checking the receptiveness of implementation [4].

4.6   Discussion

In this section, we discuss the results that we achieve giving also a critical overview of the pros and cons of the approach. We start highlighting the importance of the feedback on the requirements that we achieved. Protection mechanisms such as the one implemented in AUTOSAR are fundamental to detect failures and to fulfill the safety requirements prescribed by the safety standards. However, it should be clear that they do not allow to achieve a complete tolerance to failures and that the system requirements are fulfilled only under some assumptions. The contract-based approach allows to formalize a context in which this holds.

These conclusions should also suggest to improve the safety standards accordingly. In fact, requiring that the system is robust to any communication failures in absolute terms is not realizable and pose on the designer an arbitrary choice on the assumptions under which the requirements should be fulfilled. It would be desirable instead that such assumptions are defined by the standard itself.

Another important aspect of the case study is that the E2E_Check component that has been used and verified can be reused in another case study as is. Using it in another system architecture will require to perform a different contract refinement of the top-level contract, but the contracts of the E2E components should not be changed.

The main weakness of the case study is that is a small example and many details are abstracted. This has the advantage that the example is suitable to explain and understand the approach. We focused on the protection mechanism disregarding a more realistic representation of the airbag controller or of the bus. The E2E_Check component is faithfully represented and we also consider a real C implementation of it.

In a contract-based approach the analysis is compositional so that the verification of the contract refinement would remain the same even if we added a full description of the airbag controller. In future work, we plan to model a more complex system involving more components communicating on the same bus. We used only two types of faults, but these were sufficient to elicit the modeled protection mechanisms. Finally, we used a discrete model of time, but this seems acceptable due to the real-time properties of AUTOSAR and the periodic sending of messages via an external scheduling algorithm.

5 Related Work

Contracts have been previously used in the context of safety-critical systems and in particular in relation to standards such as ISO26262. Many of these works focused on processes and methodologies [13,14]. In [15] and [16], example of contracts are elaborated and it is shown that they can be used to reason about safety. The relation between contracts and ISO26262 is made stronger in [17] where contracts are used to structure the safety requirements of the standard.

Our paper differs from previous ones in a number of distinguishing features: first, we take a critical look at the implicit assumptions on safety requirements and use contracts to make such assumption explicit; second, we focus on the usage of concrete tools to support contracts and testing; to the best of our knowledge, it is the first contribution that concretely integrates a tool that supports contracts with a tool for testing in a way that the same model is used by both tools.

Model based testing in combination with fault-injection has been presented in [18] on exactly the same airbag example, but without CBD. Fault injection is a technique to demonstrate that even in the presence of faults, the system behaves in a safe way. This is highly valuable from a testing point of view, but like testing in general, it shows weaknesses rather than that it provides guarantees. In best case one obtains knowledge on what guarantees are not fulfilled.

6 Conclusions and Future Work

In this work, we experimented with a new integration of CBD supported by the OCRA tool and MBT supported by QuickCheck. The goal of the integration is to exploit the contract-based refinement to make explicit the assumptions of the model used for testing. The approach has been applied to the AUTOSAR measures to protect safety-critical communication from communication failures as specified by the ISO26262 standard. The assumption of the AUTOSAR protection mechanism has been formalized with OCRA on an airbag example.

In the future, we want to link the proposed approach to the development and certification process defined in the SafeCer project; we may also integrate both tools in a common design environment, develop further the case study introducing real-time aspects and generalizing the assumption using parametrized properties.

Acknowledgments. We like to thank Hans Svensson from Quviq for writing the Erlang QuickCheck model for the end-to-end protection library. The research leading to these results has received funding from the ARTEMIS JU under grant agreement n° 295373, from National funding, and from the Swedish research foundation Vinnova for its support of the Acsäpt project (ref. 2012-00943).

References

1. AUTOSAR: Software architecture specification, www.autosar.org
2. ISO 26262: Road vehicles Functional safety (2011)
3. AUTOSAR. In: Specification of SW-C End-to-End Communication Protection Library. AUTOSAR consortium (2008-2013)
4. Cimatti, A., Dorigatti, M., Tonetta, S.: OCRA: A tool for checking the refinement of temporal contracts. In: ASE, pp. 702–705 (2013)
5. Arts, T., Hughes, J., Johansson, J., Wiger, U.: Testing telecoms software with Quviq QuickCheck. In: ACM SIGPLAN Workshop on Erlang (2006)
6. Svenningsson, R., Johansson, R., Arts, T., Norell, U.: Formal methods based acceptance testing for AUTOSAR exchangeability. SAE Int. Journal of Passenger Cars Electronic and Electrical Systems 5(1), 209–213 (2012)
7. Pnueli, A.: The Temporal Logic of Programs. In: FOCS, pp. 46–57 (1977)
8. Cimatti, A., Tonetta, S.: A Property-Based Proof System for Contract-Based Design. In: EUROMICRO-SEAA, pp. 21–28 (2012)
9. Cimatti, A., Tonetta, S.: Contracts-refinement proof system for component-based embedded systems. Sci. Comput. Program (to appear)
10. Cimatti, A., Clarke, E., Giunchiglia, E., Giunchiglia, F., Pistore, M., Roveri, M., Sebastiani, R., Tacchella, A.: NuSMV 2: An OpenSource Tool for Symbolic Model Checking. In: Brinksma, E., Larsen, K.G. (eds.) CAV 2002. LNCS, vol. 2404, pp. 359–364. Springer, Heidelberg (2002)
11. Claessen, K., Hughes, J.: QuickCheck: A lightweight tool for random testing of Haskell programs. In: ACM SIGPLAN ICFP, pp. 268–279 (2000)
12. Armstrong, J.: A history of erlang. In: HOPL, pp. 1–26 (2007)
13. Blanquart, J.-P., et al.: Towards Cross-Domains Model-Based Safety Process, Methods and Tools for Critical Embedded Systems: The CESAR Approach. In: Flammini, F., Bologna, S., Vittorini, V. (eds.) SAFECOMP 2011. LNCS, vol. 6894, pp. 57–70. Springer, Heidelberg (2011)
14. Baumgart, A., Reinkemeier, P., Rettberg, A., Stierand, I., Thaden, E., Weber, R.: A Model-Based Design Methodology with Contracts to Enhance the Development Process of Safety-Critical Systems. In: Min, S.L., Pettit, R., Puschner, P., Ungerer, T. (eds.) SEUS 2010. LNCS, vol. 6399, pp. 59–70. Springer, Heidelberg (2010)
15. Damm, W., Josko, B., Peikenkamp, T.: Contract Based ISO CD 26262 Safety Analysis. In: Safety-Critical Systems. In: SAE (2009)
16. Damm, W., Hungar, H., Josko, B., Peikenkamp, T., Stierand, I.: Using contract-based component specifications for virtual integration testing and architecture design. In: DATE, pp. 1023–1028 (2011)
17. Westman, J., Nyberg, M., Törngren, M.: Structuring Safety Requirements in ISO 26262 Using Contract Theory. In: Bitsch, F., Guiochet, J., Kaâniche, M. (eds.) SAFECOMP. LNCS, vol. 8153, pp. 166–177. Springer, Heidelberg (2013)
18. Vedder, B., Arts, T., Vinter, J., Jonsson, M.: Combining fault-injection with property-based testing. In: Proc. of Int. Workshop on Engineering Simulations for Cyber-Physical Systems, ES4CPS 2014, pp. 1–8. ACM, New York (2014)

Securing Vehicle Diagnostics in Repair Shops

Pierre Kleberger and Tomas Olovsson

Department of Computer Science and Engineering
Chalmers University of Technology
SE–412 96 Gothenburg, Sweden
{pierre.kleberger,tomas.olovsson}@chalmers.se

Abstract. Diagnostics over IP (DoIP) is a new ISO standard for transmitting diagnostics messages, such as ISO 14229 Unified Diagnostic Services (UDS), over IP-based networks. The standard specifies the communication architecture needed for diagnostics communication and defines an application layer protocol for exchanging management and diagnostics messages between DoIP-enabled devices. However, DoIP relies on the insecure network protocols used in today's Internet and no additional security was added in the standard to tackle this. Thus, to prevent malicious manipulations of vehicle diagnostics sessions in repair shops, appropriate security mechanisms need to be in place.

In this paper, we analyse possible approaches to find the most suitable security architecture for diagnostics communication in repair shop networks. First, an evaluation of possible approaches is conducted. These are then analysed with respect to a set of security requirements and implementation challenges. Finally, we present the approach that best meets the requirements for a secure diagnostics architecture in repair shops.

Keywords: Vehicle diagnostics, repair shop, security, diagnostics over IP, ISO 13400, ISO 14229, ISO 15764.

1 Introduction

It can be expected that much of the maintenance of tomorrow's vehicles will be performed using wireless communication. A great benefit of such an approach is the reduced maintenance time and the possibility to maintain multiple vehicles at the same time, both leading to increased productivity in future connected repair shops. However, since communications with vehicles so far have been performed within controlled environments using wired connections, security has not yet been widely implemented [1–3]. Therefore, to benefit from wireless communications in tomorrow's connected repair shops and to prevent malicious manipulations of vehicles, appropriate security mechanisms must be in place, both in the vehicles as well as in the other devices used for vehicle diagnostics.

In an aim to enable standardised vehicle diagnostic messages, such as ISO 14229 Unified Diagnostic Services (UDS) [4], to be transmitted over IP-based networks, ISO has recently issued a new standard 13400 Diagnostics over IP (DoIP) protocol [5]. Unfortunately, not much attention was given to security and DoIP lacks

A. Bondavalli and F. Di Giandomenico (Eds.): SAFECOMP 2014, LNCS 8666, pp. 93–108, 2014.
© Springer International Publishing Switzerland 2014

fundamental security mechanisms to ensure data integrity and data authenticity [6]. Well known security protocols exist to provide secure communications for applications, e.g., SSL/TLS, but a complicating factor in DoIP is the use of broadcast functionality to announce the presence of DoIP-enabled devices in Local Area Networks (LANs). Thus, new approaches are needed that supports secure broadcast in LANs.

The introduction of DoIP enables vehicle diagnostics to be performed in repair shops using ordinary network equipment. Unfortunately, this means that vehicle diagnostics also becomes affected by many of the threats and vulnerabilities available in today's Internet. Especially critical becomes the lack of security in fundamental protocols used in LANs, since an attacker can exploit them and gain control of the (diagnostics) traffic as a man-in-the-middle [7]. In this paper, we address secure diagnostics in repair shops and more specifically we try to answer the questions:

– how can *diagnostics messages* be securely transmitted between diagnostics equipment and vehicles, and
– how can the *diagnostics infrastructure* in the repair shop be secured?

Based on the OSI layering model, we present possible approaches to secure these protocols and provide secure communication in the repair shop.

The rest of this paper is organised as follows. In next section, an introduction to DoIP and ISO 14229 is given. Requirements for a secure diagnostics architecture is then defined in Section 3. In Section 4, possible approaches are evaluated to define the security architecture and an analysis of these to best meet the security architecture is presented in Section 5. The paper concludes with related work in Section 6, followed by our conclusion in Section 7.

2 Vehicle Diagnostics

2.1 ISO 13400 — Diagnostics over IP (DoIP)

Diagnostics over IP (DoIP) [5] is a newly approved ISO standard for conducting diagnostics over IP-based networks. The required services from layer 2–4 and 7 (following the OSI layering model) are stated for the diagnostics architecture and an application protocol is defined for exchanging management and diagnostics messages between DoIP-enabled devices. The diagnostics messages themselves are not specified by DoIP as the purpose of the standard only is to transmit these messages over IP-based networks. Instead, the diagnostics messages are described in other standards, such as ISO 14229 Unified Diagnostic Services (UDS) and ISO 27145-3 World-Wide Harmonised On-Board Diagnostics (WWH-OBD) [8]. Figure 1 shows the DoIP stack with encapsulation of ISO 14229 diagnostics messages.

The following scenario exemplifies how a vehicle connects to a DoIP-enabled network [5, 9]:

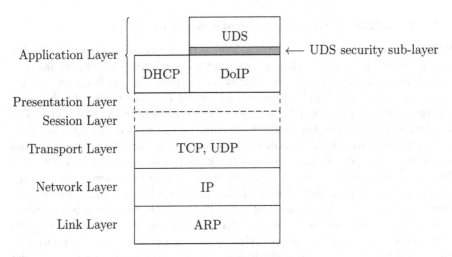

Fig. 1. The DoIP Stack

1. The vehicle establishes a connection to the LAN, either by wire or through a wireless access point (AP).
2. The vehicle requests an IP address by a DHCP request (IPv4) or through auto configuration (IPv6).
3. The vehicle announces its presence in the network by sending **vehicle announcement** messages (in accordance to conformance requirement DoIP-050 [9]) to the LAN. The announcement messages are broadcast to the local network on port 13400/udp and hold the newly configured IP-address together with the vehicle's ID; the <IP, VID>-association.
4. Diagnostics equipment receive the announcement messages and record the mapping of VID and IP-address. The mapping is used by the diagnostics application to present vehicles available in the network for further communication to their operators.

If diagnostics equipment for some reason does not receive the **vehicle announcement** messages, diagnostics equipment may broadcast a **vehicle identification request** message that the vehicle should respond to.

DoIP uses the protocols IP, TCP, and UDP, both in unicast and broadcast. Port 13400 is reserved for exchanging management communication over UDP and to establish diagnostics connections over TCP. Since no attention was made to security, DoIP is vulnerable to common threats available in ordinary IP-based networks, such as spoofing and packet modifications by other parties. Without proper authentication and integrity mechanisms, messages sent by DoIP cannot be trusted. For example, an attacker may impersonate as another vehicle by simply sending a **vehicle announcement** with that vehicle's ID.

2.2   ISO 14229 — Unified Diagnostic Services (UDS)

ISO 14229 [4] defines an application layer protocol for diagnostics of vehicles and provides two services that are relevant to security: SecurityAccess and SecuredDataTransmission. SecurityAccess protects applications in an Electronic Control Unit (ECU) from unauthorised access by means of a challenge response mechanism. First the client sends a seed request to the ECU. The ECU responds with a seed number for which the client is expected to reply with the corresponding "key" to unlock the protected application. SecuredDataTransmission introduces a security sub-layer in the network stack as shown in Figure 1. The sub-layer enables an implementor to add security functionality, however, the current standard does not describe details of which security mechanisms to implement, nor how to negotiate the security association: "The task of the Security sub-layer when performing a diagnostic service in a secured mode is to encrypt data provided by the "Application", to decrypt data provided by the "Application Layer" and to add, check, and remove security specific data elements." [4] In a previous version of the standard, ISO 15764 was referred to for an implementation of the security sub-layer. ISO 15764 [10] describes security mechanisms suitable for the security sub-layer and these mechanisms aim to prevent masquerading, replaying, and eavesdropping of diagnostics messages, as well as non-repudiation and detection of message manipulation. However, references to ISO 15764 as a security sub-layer protocol have been removed in the latest ISO 14229 standard.

The security sub-layer implemented by the SecuredDataTransmission service enables manufacturers to implement end-to-end security (all the way to the ECUs in the vehicle). The sub-layer mandates a request-response approach, where each request must be succeeded by a response, but three message types do not follow this approach and cannot be transmitted using this service. These are ResponseOnEvent, ReadDataByPeriodicIdentifier, and TesterPresent.

3   Requirements for Secure Vehicle Diagnostics

3.1   Threat Model

An attacker is assumed to be able to perform the following operations on all network traffic in the local network: *read, copy, steal, modify, delete, spoof, delay* (a combination of steal and spoof), and *replay* (a combination of copy and spoof) [11]. Furthermore, we assume that encryption algorithms are secure and cannot be broken.

We assume that an attacker cannot perform a Denial-of-Service (DoS) attack by network overloading or jamming wireless communication. Protection mechanisms to prevent such attacks are complicated, if not impossible, and are in this context considered to be out of scope.

3.2   Digital Certificates

All vehicles and diagnostics equipment are assumed to have digital certificates installed, used to authenticate the device. These certificates have been issued by a common Certificate Authority (CA), which is acknowledged by the automotive company.

3.3 Security Requirements

The following security requirements *must* be fulfilled on transmissions of *all diagnostics messages*:

- **Data Integrity.** To prevent malicious manipulation of vehicles, unauthorised modification of diagnostics messages must be detectable.
- **Data Authenticity.** To prevent unauthorised manipulation of vehicles, the source of diagnostics messages must be possible to verify.
- **Data Freshness.** To prevent replay of old diagnostics messages, protection from replay attacks must exist.
- **Data Confidentiality.** To protect ECU firmware and proprietary data, diagnostics messages must be protected from eavesdropping.

Additionally, the following desirable security requirements should preferably also be met:

- **Robustness.** Diagnostics communication should not easily fail due to malicious traffic.
- **Fine-Grained Access Control.** Only authorised diagnostics commands should be handled by vehicles. Some types of diagnostics should be limited with respect to the commands they are authorised to do and the information they should be able to retrieve. A fine-grained access control mechanism implemented in the vehicle shall restrict such access in accordance to a given security policy [12]. The retrieval of privacy related data can be prevented, but if such data is deem needed to be transmitted, e.g., vehicle's ID, such data should be kept confidential.
- **Prevent V2V Communication.** To prevent attacks from malicious, still authorised vehicles, communication between vehicles should be prevented.

3.4 Implementation Challenges

A security architecture for the repair shop must be attractive to the automotive industry to be implemented. The following aspects need to be considered when different security mechanisms are evaluated:

- **Easy to Deploy.** The implemented security solution should be as transparent as possible and require as little modification as possible to current protocols and standards.
- **Easy to Maintain.** As secure diagnostics should be available also to very small repair shops, it is reasonable to assume that technical staff with knowledge in security protocols and complex network infrastructures will not be available. Security mechanisms should therefore be possible to manage for non-technical persons.

– **Limited Increase in Costs.** Due to cost restrictions, it is problematic to mandate specialised hardware and software approaches that are expensive to implement.
– **Prevent Unauthorised Network Access.** Only authorised vehicles should get access to the repair shop network, i.e., those that are scheduled for maintenance.

4   Approaches to Secure Diagnostics Communication

Security mechanisms can be introduced at several layers in the communication stack as shown in Figure 2: in the security sub-layer of ISO 14229 (P4), in the application layer (P3), in the network layer (P2), or in the link layer (P1). In next section, all these possible approaches to secure ISO 14229 diagnostics messages and DoIP communication are presented. In the sections following, these approaches are evaluated against the requirements identified in Section 3.

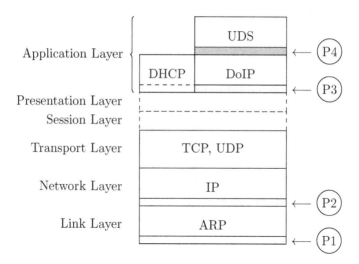

Fig. 2. Possible approaches to secure vehicle diagnostics

4.1   Possible Approaches to Secure Vehicle Diagnostics

The following possible approaches to implement security have been identified at the different layers and are presented in Table 1:

– **P4:** The ISO 14229 (UDS) security sub-layer has a well-defined interface to implement end-to-end security mechanisms for diagnostics messages. We evaluate ISO 15764 [10] and SSL/TLS [13] as two possible candidates to implement security in this sub-layer. With a security implementation at this layer, communication is secured between *diagnostics equipment* and *the in-vehicle ECU*.

- **P3:** SSL/TLS is a possible candidate to secure DoIP communication (including the encapsulated ISO 14229 diagnostics messages) by integrating the SSL/TLS protocol into the DoIP implementation. Communication is secured between *diagnostics equipment* and the *vehicle's gateway ECU*.
- **P2:** IPsec [16] is a possible candidate to secure IP communication between *diagnostics equipment* and the *vehicle's gateway ECU* at the network layer. To establish Security Associations (SAs) and exchange session keys between communicating parties of IPsec, the Internet Key Exchange (IKE)-protocol [17] can be used.
- **P1:** We evaluate Virtual LAN (VLAN) and CLL [18] as two possible candidates to secure diagnostics communication at link layer. Other approaches exist to secure Ethernet communication [19], however, we do not find them relevant in our context for different reasons:
  1. We do not consider MACsec [20] as a possible candidate because of the introduced complexity. Not only do the network infrastructure need support for MACsec, but the clients must also implement the protocol. A fall-back approach is also needed if MACsec support is lacking in one of them.
  2. Protocols for secure Address Resolution Protocol (ARP) and secure Dynamic Host Configuration Protocol (DHCP) [19] do only consider part of the problem.

  We focus on more general and less complex approaches where only one party, the clients or the network equipment, enforces the security mechanisms and not a combination of them. Moreover, communication is secured between *diagnostics equipment* and the *vehicle's gateway ECU*.

A thorough discussion of each of these possible approaches and their provided security mechanisms with respect to the requirements (as shown in Table 1) follows in the following sections.

4.2 Evaluation of Approaches: Possibilities to Fulfil Required Security Requirements

Data Integrity, Data Authenticity, and Data Freshness. Data integrity, data authenticity, and data freshness can be provided at all layers by using Message Integrity Codes (MICs), signing, and nonces.

ISO 15764 is intended to provide an implementation of data integrity, data authenticity, and data freshness in the ISO 14229 security sub-layer (P4). An adaptation of SSL/TLS may also be possible to provide these security mechanisms within the specification of the security sub-layer. Furthermore, at the application layer (P3), SSL/TLS provides the data integrity, data authenticity, and data freshness for TCP. TLS over UDP can be provided by Datagram Transport Layer Security (DTLS) [14], but multicast and broadcast messages are not supported. Thus, a secure broadcast functionality is lacking at the application layer to secure DoIP broadcast messages.

Table 1. Evaluation of diagnostics message protection and possible security mechanisms at different entry points

	P4			P3		P2	P1		
	General	ISO 15764	SSL/TLS	General	SSL/TLS	IPsec	General	VLAN	CLL
Integrity	ISO14229 diagnostics messages[1]	ISO14229 diagnostics messages	ISO14229 diagnostics messages	DoIP traffic (inc. ISO14229)[1]	**Unicast Only:** DoIP traffic: (UDP over TLS: DTLS [14])	DoIP traffic	All traffic (inc. DoIP, DHCP, ARP)[1]	No	IP (inc. DoIP), ARP, DHCP
Authenticity	-"-	-"-	-"-	-"-	-"-	-"-	-"-	-"-	-"-
Freshness	ISO14229 diag. msg.[2]	ISO14229 diag. msg.[2]	DoIP traffic (inc. ISO14229)	DoIP traffic (inc. ISO14229)[2]	-"-	-"-	All traffic[2]	-"-	-"-
Confidentiality	ISO14229 diagnostics messages[3]	-"-	-"-	**Unicast:** DoIP traffic. **Multicast:** DoIP traffic possibly by shared symmetric group key.[3]	-"-	**Unicast:** DoIP traffic. **Multicast:** DoIP traffic possibly by shared symmetric group keys.[3]	**Unicast:** All traffic by shared keys (symmetric). **Multicast:** All traffic by shared symmetric group keys.[3]	-"-	**Unicast Only:** IP (inc. DoIP)
Robustness	ARP spoofing may cause DoS by selective dropping of diverted traffic	Spoofing / manipulation of lower layer communication may cause ISO15764 to break down [15]	Spoofing of TCP packets may cause SSL communication to break down [15]	ARP spoofing may cause DoS by selective dropping of diverted traffic	Spoofing of TCP packets may cause SSL communication to break down [15]	ARP spoofing may cause DoS by selective dropping of diverted traffic	Authentication of ARP packets prevents ARP spoofing. Only AP/switch may selectively drop packets.	Possibly: one DE by ARP spoofing and one V in its own VLAN	Diversion attack by ARP spoofing not possible. Only AP/switch may selectively drop packets.
Fine-Grained Access Control	Possible	Partly	No	Possible	No	No	No	No	No
Prevent V2V Communication	No	No	No	No	No	To some extent by not allowing SAs between vehicles	Separation by encryption of L2 frames using group keys	Yes	No
Easy to Deploy	Requires modification to ISO14229, non-transparent	Follows standards	Requires modification to ISO14229, non-transparent	Requires modification to DoIP standard, non-transparent	Requires modification to DoIP standard, non-transparent	Follows standards	Non-standard solution, transparent	Follows standards, dynamic group allocation is problematic	Non-standard solution, transparent. Implementation exists.
Easy to Maintain	Depends on chosen approach	Certificates must be maintained	Certificates must be maintained	Depends on chosen approach	Certificates must be maintained	Needs PADs for managing SAs	Depends on chosen approach	Maintaining VLAN configuration is problematic	Maintaining SAs automatically created
Cost	SW implementation of security sub-layer needed	SW implementation according to standard needed	SW modification needed to security sub-layer	SW modification needed to DoIP implementation	SW modification needed to DoIP implementation	Definitions of PADs need to be established and maintained	Additional SW development needed	HW support needed, both in switches and APs	No additional HW support needed
Prevent Unauth. Network Access	No	No	No	No	No	Possible	Possible	No	No

[1] by signing   [2] by nonces   [3] by encryption

IPsec is a good candidate to implement security at the network layer (P2) that already provides data integrity, data authenticity, and data freshness. At link layer (P1), only CLL provides these security mechanisms and ensures secure IP, ARP, and DHCP communication [18]. Not surprisingly, VLAN does not provide any of the required security mechanisms since it was not designed to protect communication between devices within a virtual LAN.

Data Confidentiality. At (P4), ISO 15764 supports data confidentiality by encryption. An adaptation of SSL/TLS may also be possible within the specification of the security sub-layer.

At application layer (P3), network layer (P2), and link layer (P1), data confidentiality is provided by SSL/TLS, IPsec, and CLL, respectively. However, so far only IPsec supports data confidentiality for multicast communication [16]. If management traffic, such as the announcement of a vehicle's ID, should be kept secret from other vehicles, a secure multicast functionality is needed.

4.3   Evaluation of Approaches: Possibilities to Provide the Desirable Security Requirements

Robustness. All protocols above link layer (P1) are vulnerable to diversion of traffic by ARP spoofing attacks [7], which results in an attacker becoming a man-in-the-middle being in control of the delivery of DoIP traffic. Thus, the attacker can selectively drop packets and cause a DoS. This might not be considered a big problem, but if such a DoS attack is performed during firmware update, it may cause the update to fail and leave the Electronic Control Unit (ECU) in an inconsistent state. Since communication in a LAN is performed through direct delivery at link layer, diversion of traffic can be prevented by proper device authentication, provided the following requirements are fulfilled:

- the device's MAC address(es) is included in its certificate,
- Ethernet frames are protected against unauthorised modification, and
- Ethernet frames are signed, thus providing data authenticity,

then the receiver can verify the signature and the source MAC address against the sender's certificate. Since the MAC addresses represent the truthful sender and receiver, and the Ethernet frame is delivered through direct delivery, the frame cannot have been diverted through a malicious host by an ARP spoofing attack. Remaining devices that still can control packet delivery are switches and APs that forward packets.

SSL/TLS relies on the delivery of messages by TCP but lacks recovery mechanisms if TCP erroneously delivers messages to the SSL layer due to exploitation of features in the TCP protocol. For example, spoofing TCP data within the TCP window may cause injected packets to be delivered to the SSL layer and break the ongoing session [15].

Fine-Grained Access Control. A fine-grained access control mechanisms can only be implemented in the upper layers, (P4) and (P3), which only authorises access to diagnostics commands and data in accordance to a given security policy. So far, only ISO 15764 partly supports a fine-grained access control mechanism. With the help of an audit trail service, the standard suggests that access to the vehicle can be regulated based on previously stored information about a session and information from the ongoing session [10].

Prevention of V2V Communication. Prevention of Vehicle-to-Vehicle (V2V) communication is only possible at lower layers, i.e., (P2) and (P1). In IPsec (P2), a Peer Authorisation Database (PAD) can regulate accesses and to some extent prevent communication by denying SAs to be established between vehicles. At link layer (P1), prevention of V2V communication is possible using VLAN by allocating a separate VLAN group for each connected vehicle (together with appropriate devices). Another possible approach is separation by encryption, where each vehicle is allocated to a separate encryption group and multicast is used to send data to specific groups. CLL, however, has no mechanisms to prevent V2V communication among authenticated devices.

4.4   Implementation Aspects

Easy to Deploy. Picking a solution based on a standard protocol is preferable, however a chosen approach should also be transparent and still meet the other requirements. The ISO 14229 security sub-layer (P4) has a standard interface for incorporating security mechanisms where both ISO 15764 and SSL/TLS can be implemented. As such a security module may be replaced without any changes to the rest of ISO 14229, high transparency exists. At the application layer (P3), modifications are needed to the DoIP standard to implement security mechanisms, which limits the transparency of such an approach. At lower layers, (P2) and (P1), transparency is once again better preserved. An IPsec implementation requires no changes to DoIP to be implemented. A VLAN approach is also transparent, but it only prevents V2V communication which makes it less usable unless combined with some other approach. Furthermore, even though CLL is not a standardised approach, it is transparent to DoIP and an implementation already exists [18].

Easy to Maintain. Assuming certificates are kept up to date by external parties, knowledge in certificate management should not be needed by mechanics. For approaches implemented in upper layers, i.e., (P4) and (P3), certificate management are already integrated parts of the protocols. For IPsec, the PAD database regulates how SAs should be established between diagnostics equipment and vehicles, however, a mechanic cannot be expected to maintain a PAD in case of configuration errors or in the need for local adaptations, unless there are some additional helper application that can support, troubleshoot, and correct such problems. Similarly, CLL establishes SAs between devices, but lacks an authorisation database that restricts communication to be between diagnostics equipment and vehicles only. Furthermore, to consider VLAN a feasible approach, supporting systems are needed that can relieve mechanics from all administrative work required to manage VLAN groups.

Limited Increase in Costs. Approaches in (P4), (P3), and (P2) need to be implemented in software and new costs are mainly due to development, maintenance, and continues management of these implementations. An approach based on special hardware support, such as VLAN (P1) are not necessarily more expensive in the long run as equipment is bought once and later easily replaced by new equipment.

Prevent Unauthorised Network Access. Standard approaches exist to prevent unauthorised accesses to networks, e.g., IEEE 802.1X for wired access control and WPA2 for wireless access control. Yet, it is desirable to have an integrated solution where access control is implemented in the communication protocol, so that special hardware support is unnecessary and the loss of authentication keys in wireless APs cannot be used for impersonation of repair shops [21]. Only IPsec and link layer protocols may provide such access control and prevent unauthorised network access to the repair shop network. For example, only vehicles with valid SAs may connect using IPsec, and authentication and authorisation mechanisms may be integrated into the link layer protocols.

5   A Repair Shop Security Architecture

5.1   Meeting the Security Requirements

Based on our evaluation of possible approaches, a repair shop security architecture that best meets the security requirements can be designed. Our analysis suggest that possible security mechanisms should be selected as follows:

- *Data integrity*, *data authenticity*, and *data freshness* can be provided at any of the four entry points in the stack, however, at (P4) only the diagnostics messages are protected, while at (P3) and below, DoIP is also protected.
- *Data confidentiality* can be provided for unicast communication at any layer, but if multicast protection is desired, security mechanisms must be implemented at (P2) or below.
- ARP spoofing and TCP manipulations affect the *robustness* of the implemented security mechanisms since such activity can cause diagnostics sessions to fail and be terminated. Thus, to protect against such attacks, security mechanisms should be implemented as far down in the network stack as possible. Moreover, the robustness is also affected by the exposure of the network stack. The further down the network stack security mechanisms are implemented, the lesser amount of code is exposed with possible bugs to exploit.

104 P. Kleberger and T. Olovsson

- A *fine-grained access control mechanism* is easier to implement at higher layers in the network stack. Implementations at lower layers are possible but such implementations require understanding of how to filter diagnostics messages from the upper layer protocols.
- *Prevention of V2V communication* needs to be handled as far down the network stack as possible to prevent communication from other vehicles and discard such traffic as quickly as possible. Such an approach also limits the exposure of the network stack as much as possible.
- Even though the ISO 14229 security sub-layer (P4) is transparent, it cannot meet all desirable requirements: there is no prevention of V2V communication and it does not provide protection to all diagnostics services within the standard (as discussed in Section 2.2). At (P2) and (P1), security mechanisms may be replaced without affecting the diagnostics protocol itself, thus making them *easy to deploy*.
- The more the security mechanisms are transparently integrated in the complete diagnostics architecture, the lesser the requirements becomes on specific security knowledge for non-technical staff, thus, making it *easy to maintain*.
- From a *cost perspective*, a standardised approach (whether in hardware or software) is preferable as such an approach is easy to buy, deploy, and sign support contracts for. Specialised solutions will drive cost and should be avoided as far as possible.
- To *prevent unauthorised network access* to the repair shop network, the lower layer protocols need to restrict such access.

To conclude, most of the requirements are fulfilled when the security mechanisms are implemented as far down in the network stack as possible. However, the fine-grained access control mechanisms is one security mechanism that is simpler to implement directly into the diagnostics protocol.

5.2 Secure Vehicle Diagnostics

To decide upon the best security architecture for a repair shop network, we come to the conclusion that there are conflicting requirements that only an implementor can decide upon: *easy to deploy and maintain* vs. *robustness — IPsec* vs. *a complete link layer security architecture*. We believe that IPsec is the desirable approach since it is standardised and therefore easier to deploy and maintain, but some efforts need to be spent in developing supporting tools for easy management of the authorisation database (PAD). However, IPsec does not provide protection against diversion attacks by ARP spoofing, where an attacker becomes a man-in-the-middle and can control traffic delivery. If protection against diversion attacks is required, then we find no other approaches available than the need for a complete link layer security architecture.

Even though our analysis was directed towards a security architecture for repair shop networks, an approach based on IPsec also comes with a great benefit; it also secures remote vehicle diagnostics over the Internet. In such an architecture, we can also improve the key agreement protocol and replace IKE with a key distribution protocol specifically designed to distribute session keys and security policies (used by the fine-grained access control) only to equipment authorised to perform diagnostics, thus prevent unauthorised diagnostics of vehicles. In our previous work [12, 22], we designed such a protocol to protect vehicles from unauthorised diagnostics and the protocol has also been formally verified. Inside the repair shop network, IKE can not simply be replaced since a SA is required for communication between vehicles and diagnostics equipment before the authorisation protocol can be executed. Nevertheless, after a SA is established and the authorisation protocol has been executed, the session key used by IPsec can be replaced by the newly received and authorised session key, thus prevent unauthorised diagnostics equipment to be used.

6   Related Work

Even though quite some effort has been spent in securing the vehicular communication domain over the last years, very little has still been done in securing the protocols for vehicle diagnostics. The work that has been done in secure diagnostics has mainly focused on secure software download and firmware updates [23–26]. A first preliminary study of the DoIP protocol was performed by Lindberg [6], which focused on the security aspects of the protocol. The author concluded that even though some security mechanisms were defined in the draft specification, they were far from enough to ensure the security of the protocol. Furthermore, a test implementation for evaluation of DoIP, mainly from a safety perspective, has also been developed by Johanson et al. [27].

A few security assessments have been conducted. In [28], Nilsson et al. perform a security assessment of a wireless infrastructure used for remote diagnostics and software updates over the air. Their wireless infrastructure consists of a back-end system, a communication link, and the vehicle. Furthermore, in our previous work [21], a security assessment of the repair shop network was conducted, however, an evaluation of all possible approaches to implement the security mechanisms in the protocol stack and an analysis of these to define the most suitable security architecture was not part of that work.

In this paper, we have taken a general approach and analysed possible security mechanisms to secure *a complete vehicle diagnostics architecture* based on DoIP and ISO 14229.

7   Conclusion

In this paper, we have analysed possible approaches to secure vehicle diagnostics in repair shops for the newly standardised Diagnostics over IP (DoIP) protocol. DoIP defines a transmission protocol for diagnostics messages, but the actual diagnostics commands themselves are described in other standards. We have focused on diagnostics commands as defined by ISO 14229 Unified Diagnostic Services (UDS). Even though a security mechanism can be implemented directly into the ISO 14229 security sub-layer, we have shown that such an approach does not provide a complete protection.

Our evaluation of possible security approaches suggests that the necessary security mechanism should be implemented as far down the network stack as possible. However, one security requirement, the fine-grained access control that regulates the execution of diagnostics commands and access to information in vehicles, is best implemented at the application layer.

To conclude, we find that, although it is a compromise, the most desirable security architecture is achieved by an IPsec implementation, even though some efforts need to be spent in developing tools for easy management of the IPsec authorisation database (the Peer Authorisation Database (PAD)). Furthermore, although our analysis was directed at a local repair shop network, we can also conclude that an IPsec-based security architecture provides additional benefits: secure remote diagnostics over the Internet. However, we note that IPsec does not prevent an attacker from being in control of the delivery of (encrypted) diagnostics messages between diagnostics equipment and vehicles by spawning an ARP spoofing attack. Thus, an attacker can become a man-in-the-middle and selectively discard messages which could result in a denial of service. If such protection also is needed, we find no other approaches available than implementing a complete link layer security architecture for the repair shop network.

Acknowledgements. This research was funded by the project Security Framework for Vehicle Communication (2011-04434), co-funded by VINNOVA, the Swedish Governmental Agency for Innovation Systems

References

1. Koscher, K., Czeskis, A., Roesner, F., Patel, S., Kohno, T., Checkoway, S., et al.: Experimental Security Analysis of a Modern Automobile. In: 2010 IEEE Symposium on Security and Privacy, SP, pp. 447–462 (2010)
2. Rouf, I., Miller, R., Mustafa, H., Taylor, T., Oh, S., Xu, W., Gruteser, M., Trappe, W., Seskar, I.: Security and Privacy Vulnerabilities of In-car Wireless Networks: A Tire Pressure Monitoring System Case Study. In: Proceedings of the 19th USENIX Conference on Security. USENIX Security 2010, Berkeley, CA, USA, p. 21 (2010) (Visited on 12/18/2013)
3. Checkoway, S., McCoy, D., Kantor, B., Anderson, D., Shacham, H., Savage, S., Koscher, K., Czeskis, A., Roesner, F., Kohno, T.: Comprehensive Experimental Analyses of Automotive Attack Surfaces. In: Proceedings of the 20th USENIX Security Symposium, San Francisco, CA, USA, pp. 77–92 (August 2011)
4. ISO 14229-1:2013: Road vehicles — Unified diagnostic services (UDS) — Part 1: Specification and requirements. ISO (2013)
5. ISO 13400-1:2011: Road vehicles — Diagnostic communication over Internet Protocol (DoIP) — Part 1: General information and use case definition. ISO (2011)
6. Lindberg, J.: Security Analysis of Vehicle Diagnostics using DoIP. Master Thesis. Chalmers University of Technology. Gothenburg (2011)

7. Altunbasak, H., Krasser, S., Owen, H., Sokol, J., Grimminger, J.: Addressing the Weak Link Between Layer 2 and Layer 3 in the Internet Architecture. In: 29th Annual IEEE International Conference on Local Computer Networks, pp. 417–418 (2004)
8. ISO 27145-3:2012: Road vehicles — Implementation of World-Wide Harmonized On-Board Diagnostics (WWH-OBD) communication requirements — Part 3: Common message dictionary. ISO (2012)
9. ISO 13400-2:2012: Road vehicles — Diagnostic communication over Internet Protocol (DoIP) — Part 2: Transport protocol and network layer services. ISO (2012)
10. ISO 15764:2004: Road vehicles — Extended data link security. ISO (2004)
11. Howard, J.D., Longstaff, T.A.: A Common Language for Computer Security Incidents. In: Sandia Report: SAND98-8667 (1998)
12. Kleberger, P., Olovsson, T.: Protecting Vehicles Against Unauthorised Diagnostics Sessions Using Trusted Third Parties. In: Bitsch, F., Guiochet, J., Kaâniche, M. (eds.) SAFECOMP. LNCS, vol. 8153, pp. 70–81. Springer, Heidelberg (2013)
13. Dierks, T., Rescorla, E.: The Transport Layer Security (TLS) Protocol Version 1.2. RFC 5246 (Proposed Standard). IETF (Aug. 2008)
14. Rescorla, E., Modadugu, N.: Datagram Transport Layer Security Version 1.2. RFC 6347 (Proposed Standard). IETF (January 2012)
15. Völker, L., Schöller, M.: Secure TLS: Preventing DoS Attacks with Lower Layer Authentication. en. In: Kommunikation in Verteilten Systemen (KiVS), pp. 237–248. Informatik aktuell (2007)
16. Kent, S., Seo, K.: Security Architecture for the Internet Protocol. RFC 4301 (Proposed Standard). IETF (December 2005)
17. Kaufman, C., Hoffman, P., Nir, Y., Eronen, P.: Internet Key Exchange Protocol Version 2 (IKEv2). RFC 5996 (Proposed Standard). IETF (September 2010)
18. Jerschow, Y.I., Lochert, C., Scheuermann, B., Mauve, M.: CLL: A Cryptographic Link Layer for Local Area Networks. In: Ostrovsky, R., De Prisco, R., Visconti, I. (eds.) SCN 2008. LNCS, vol. 5229, pp. 21–38. Springer, Heidelberg (2008)
19. Kiravuo, T., Sarela, M., Manner, J.: A Survey of Ethernet LAN Security. IEEE Communications Surveys Tutorials 15.3, 1477–1491 (2013) ISSN: 1553-877X
20. IEEE 802.1AE-2006: IEEE Standard for Local and metropolitan area networks: Media Access Control (MAC) Security. IEEE (2006)
21. Kleberger, P., Olovsson, T., Jonsson, E.: An In-Depth Analysis of the Security of the Connected Repair Shop. In: Proceedings of the Seventh International Conference on Systems and Networks Communications, ICSNC 2012, Lisbon, Portugal, pp. 99–107 (November 2012)
22. Kleberger, P., Moulin, G.: Short Paper: Formal Verification of an Authorization Protocol for Remote Vehicle Diagnostics. In: IEEE Vehicular Network Conference, VNC, Boston, USA (December 2013)
23. Mahmud, S.M., Shanker, S., Hossain, I.: Secure Software Upload in an Intelligent Vehicle via Wireless Communication Links. In: Proceedings of the 2005 IEEE Intelligent Vehicles Symposium, pp. 588–593 (2005)
24. Hossain, I., Mahmud, S.M.: Secure Multicast Protocol for Remote Software Upload in Intelligent Vehicles. In: Proc. of the 5th Ann. Intel. Vehicle Systems Symp. of National Defense Industries Association (NDIA), pp. 145–155. Traverse City, Michigan (June 2005)
25. Nilsson, D.K., Larson, U.E.: Secure Firmware Updates over the Air in Intelligent Vehicles. In: IEEE International Conference on Communications Workshops, ICC Workshops 2008, pp. 380–384 (May 2008)

26. Idrees, M.S., Schweppe, H., Roudier, Y., Wolf, M., Scheuermann, D., Henniger, O.: Secure Automotive On-Board Protocols: A Case of Over-the-Air Firmware Updates. In: Strang, T., Festag, A., Vinel, A., Mehmood, R., Rico Garcia, C., Röckl, M. (eds.) Nets4Cars/Nets4Trains 2011. LNCS, vol. 6596, pp. 224–238. Springer, Heidelberg (2011)
27. Johanson, M., Dahle, P., Soderberg, A.: Remote Vehicle Diagnostics over the Internet using the DoIP Protocol. In: Proceedings of the Sixth International Conference on Systems and Networks Communications, ICSNC 2011, Barcelona, Spain, pp. 226–231 (October 2011)
28. Nilsson, D.K., Larson, U.E., Jonsson, E.: Creating a Secure Infrastructure for Wireless Diagnostics and Software Updates in Vehicles. In: Harrison, M.D., Sujan, M.-A. (eds.) SAFECOMP 2008. LNCS, vol. 5219, pp. 207–220. Springer, Heidelberg (2008)

Analysis of Persistence of Relevance in Systems with Imperfect Fault Coverage

Jianwen Xiang[1,2], Fumio Machida[2], Kumiko Tadano[2], and Yoshiharu Maeno[2]

[1] Wuhan University of Technology, Wuhan, Hubei, 430070 China
xiangjw@gmail.com
[2] NEC Corporation, Kawasaki, 211-8666 Japan
{f-machida@ab,k-tadano@bq,y-maeno@aj}.jp.nec.com

Abstract. This paper introduces the concept of persistence and analyzes its influence on reliability of systems with imperfect fault coverage (IFC). A component is persistent if it is always relevant in the system unless the system is failed, and a system is persistent if all the components are persistent. In traditional imperfect fault coverage models, simply coverage models (CMs), the coverage (including identification and isolation) is typically limited to the faulty components regardless of their relevance. The general assumption on system coherence cannot guarantee that a component will be always relevant in the system. Rather, an initially relevant component could become irrelevant later due to the failures of other components, which is unfortunately a missing issue in the traditional CMs. For systems with IFC, it is important to cover the non-persistent components whenever they become irrelevant, so as to prevent their future uncovered faults that may lead to system failure. A new coverage model incorporating the timely coverage of the irrelevant components (in addition to the faulty components) is proposed, which opens up a cost-effective approach to improve the system reliability without increasing redundancy.

Keywords: Imperfect fault coverage, relevance, irrelevance, persistence, reliability, fault tree.

1 Introduction

Fault tolerance is an essential architectural attribute for achieving high reliability in many critical applications such as flight control, space missions, and data storage systems. A fault tolerant (computer) system is typically designed to handle most of the faults that can occur in the system, including hardware-related faults, software bugs and errors, interface errors between hardware and software, and so on [1]. Fault tolerance is generally achieved by using redundancy concepts. Automatic fault detection, location, isolation, recovery, and reconfiguration mechanisms, or simply recovery mechanisms, play a crucial role in implementing fault tolerance because an uncovered component fault may lead to a system or subsystem failure and this is called an uncovered failure even when adequate redundancy exists [2]. This typically happens because the system cannot be reconfigured if the

A. Bondavalli and F. Di Giandomenico (Eds.): SAFECOMP 2014, LNCS 8666, pp. 109–124, 2014.
© Springer International Publishing Switzerland 2014

fault has not been detected or covered, and other non-faulty components may be contaminated by the non-isolated faulty component. For instance, an undetected fault may affect the subsequent calculations and operations which may lead to overall system failure, and an undetected leak, fire, or virus-infected file may corrupt the whole system and lead to catastrophic failure. The models that consider the effects of imperfect fault coverage (IFC) are known as imperfect fault coverage models, or simply coverage models (CMs) [3].

In traditional CMs, the coverage (including identification and isolation) is typically limited to the faulty components irrespective of their relevance. In other words, an irrelevant component will not be isolated from the system if it is not failed. Consequently, future uncovered faults of the irrelevant component may lead to system failure just like the uncovered faults of the relevant components.

Informally speaking, a component is irrelevant if its status (failed or not) does not affect the system state. Obviously, the irrelevance is not an issue if the component is persistent, i.e, it is *always* relevant in the system. In traditional CMs, especially the combinatorial approaches to modeling IFC (e.g., DDP [4] and SEA [5]), it is generally assumed that the system is coherent which implies that each component is relevant. This could be one reason for the omission of irrelevance in the traditional CMs. However, even with the assumption on initial relevance, the persistence of a component cannot be guaranteed. This is because an initially relevant component could become irrelevant later due to the failures of other components. For instance, let $f = x_1 \wedge (x_2 \vee x_3)$ be the fault tree of a system. f is coherent in which each variable is relevant. However, when $x_2 = 1$ (i.e., the corresponding component fails), x_3 becomes irrelevant because $f[1/x_2] = x_1 \wedge (1 \vee x_3) = x_1$, where the function f evaluated in $x = v$ ($v \in [0,1]$) is denoted by $f[v/x]$. Similarly, x_2 becomes irrelevant in $f[1/x_3]$.

A component is not persistent if it is initially irrelevant or it is initially relevant but its relevance can be changed (lost) later due to the failures of other components. A system including non-persistent components is called non-persistent, otherwise it is persistent. For a non-persistent system subjected to IFC, it is important to cover the non-persistent components whenever they are (become) irrelevant even when they are not failed. The coverage of the non-persistent components will not affect the normal functioning of the system because the coverage is carried out when the components are or become irrelevant. Rather, the coverage can prevent the future uncovered failures from the covered irrelevant components so as to enhance the system reliability. The effect is particularly significant when the system includes many non-persistent components and the uncovered failures are dominant in system unreliability. This opens up a new cost-effect way to improve system reliability without increasing redundancy.

In the work described in this paper, we first introduce and formalize the concept of persistence, and then address its significance on reliability for the systems subjected to IFC. We propose a new coverage model incorporating the coverage of non-persistent components whenever they become irrelevant for the systems subjected to IFC, called irrelevance coverage model (ICM). Given the structure function (e.g., fault tree) of the system, we present an algorithm to calculate under which conditions a component will become irrelevant, and we call the smallest conditions as the minimal irrelevance triggers (MITs) of the component. With the calculation of the MITs, the unreliability of a system in the ICM can be evaluated by a closed-form formula. The significance and effectiveness of the ICM in contrast to the traditional CM are demonstrated with a practical example with both qualitative and quantitative analysis results.

The rest of this paper is organized as follows. The background on functions, fault trees, and the traditional CM is introduced in Section 2. The concepts of persistence and irrelevance triggers are introduced in Section 3. The ICM is proposed in Section 4. A case study is presented in Section 5. The related work and concluding remarks are summarized in Sections 6 and 7, respectively.

2   Preliminaries

2.1   Functions and Fault Trees

For the purpose of this paper, fault trees are essentially considered as Boolean formulae with variables representing the covered and uncovered component failures. A literal is either a variable x or its negation $\neg x$, called positive and negative respectively. By a product we mean a conjunction of literals that does not contain both a variable and its negation. For convenience, a product is often assimilated as the *set* of its literals such that standard set operations can be applied to it.

Definition 1 (Monotonicity). *Let f be a Boolean function. f is* monotonic *if for any assignment that satisfies f, switching any variable from 0 (false) to 1 (true) cannot change the value of f from 1 to 0.*

It is clear that a Boolean formula made only of variables and connectives $\wedge$ (and) and $\vee$ (or) (without negation, $\neg$) is monotonic.

Definition 2 (Relevance). *Let $f(x_1, \ldots, x_n)$ be a Boolean function. The variable x_1 is said to be* relevant *in f and denoted by $relevant(x_1, f)$ if $f(1, x_2, \ldots, x_n) \neq f(0, x_2, \ldots, x_n)$ for some assignment over $\{x_2, \ldots, x_n\}$.*

For convenience, the irrelevance of x_1 in f is defined as the negation of the relevance, i.e., $irrelevant(x_1, f) \overset{def}{=} \neg relevant(x_1, f)$, i.e., $f(1, x_2, \ldots, x_n) = f(0, x_2, \ldots, x_n)$ for any assignment over $\{x_2, \ldots, x_n\}$.

Definition 3 (Coherence). *Let f be a Boolean function. f is* coherent *if it is monotonic and each variable is relevant.*

Definition 4 (Implicant). *Let f be a formula, and let π be a product of literals. π is an* implicant *of f if $\pi \models f$, i.e., any assignment satisfying π satisfies f. The implicant π is* prime *if there is no other implicant π' of f such that $\pi' \subset \pi$.*

If there are some assignment satisfying π that does not satisfy f, we say π is not a implicant of f, which is denoted by $\pi \not\models f$. Prime implicants (PIs) of monotonic fault trees are often called minimal cut sets (MCSs) in the reliability engineering literature. We denote by $PI[f]$ and $MCS[f]$ the set of all the PIs and the set of all the MCSs of the formula f, respectively.

In this paper, we are particularly interested in the prime implicants that consist of only positive literals (i.e., variables). This is because only positive literals represent failures in the context of fault trees, and we are interested in the failures that may make a (relevant) component become irrelevant.

Definition 5 (Positive Prime Implicant). *Let f be a Boolean formula and let π be a prime implicant of f. π is called as a* positive prime implicant *if π is a product of positive literals.*

We denote by $PPI[f]$ the Positive Prime Implicants (PPIs) of f.

2.2   Imperfect Fault Coverage Model

The appropriate coverage modeling approach depends on the type of fault tolerant techniques used and the details available on the recovery mechanisms. By considering the system behavior in response to a fault in each component at the component level, the models can be classified into single-fault (coverage) models and multi-fault (coverage) models [3]. For clarity, in this paper, we limit ourselves to the single-fault model based on the assumption that the coverage of a faulty component is independent of the status and information available at any other components. The coverage of the non-persistent components proposed in the ICM, however, can be applied to multi-fault models also.

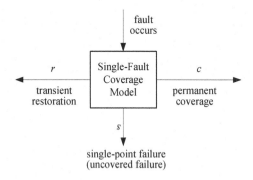

Fig. 1. General structure of single-fault coverage model

The general structure of single-fault model is shown in Figure 1. Once a component fault occurs, it leads to one of the three possible outcomes or exits, namely transient restoration, permanent coverage, and uncovered (single-point) failure. A transient restoration takes place when the offending fault is transient and the component returns to its normal working state after the restoration. A permanent coverage takes place when the fault is determined to be permanent, and the offending component is discarded and isolated from the system. A permanent (component) failure is considered as a covered failure and may lead to system failure according to the failure logic (structure function) of the system, such as the system runs out of redundancy by the covered failure. If the fault cannot be detected, located, or isolated by the recovery mechanism, the fault may lead to a system failure and this is called an uncovered (single-point) failure. This generally happens because other non-faulty components may be contaminated by the *non-isolated* faulty component, or the system cannot be reconfigured if the faulty component cannot be detected and isolated. Within the context of this paper, we refer to the exit probabilities, r, c, and s with $r + c + s = 1$. The exits are mutually exclusive and thus non-independent. Because the transient restoration does not change the overall system state, we may omit it and let $r = 0$ to simplify the analysis.

Let θ_x be a component, $\overline{x}$, $\underline{x}$, and x be the covered failure, the uncovered failure, and the failure of θ_x, respectively. Let $\mathcal{F}$ be the system failure resulting from the combinations of both covered and uncovered component failures. The single-fault model can be formalized with the following axioms [6].

$$x = \overline{x} \oplus \underline{x} \tag{1}$$

$$\overline{x} = x \wedge covered(x) \tag{2}$$

$$\overline{x} \leftrightarrow isolated(\theta_x) \tag{3}$$

$$\underline{x} = x \wedge \neg covered(x) \tag{4}$$

$$\underline{x} \rightarrow \mathcal{F} \tag{5}$$

where $\rightarrow$ and $\leftrightarrow$ stand for logic (material) implication and equivalence operators, respectively.

Suppose there are n distinct components $\theta_{x_1}, \ldots, \theta_{x_n}$, and let $\overline{\mathcal{F}}$ be the fault tree with basic events of only covered component failures (i.e., with perfect fault coverage), $\mathcal{F}$ can be defined as a disjunction of $\overline{\mathcal{F}}$ and the disjunction of all the uncovered component failures [4, 5], i.e.,

$$\mathcal{F} = \overline{\mathcal{F}} \vee \bigvee_{i=1}^{n} \underline{x_i} \tag{6}$$

For instance, let $\overline{\mathcal{F}1}$ be an example fault tree with perfect fault coverage as shown in Eq. (7).

$$\overline{\mathcal{F}1} = \overline{x_1} \vee \overline{x_2} \wedge (\overline{x_3} \vee \overline{x_4}) \tag{7}$$

The fault tree considering imperfect fault coverage, say $\mathcal{F}1$, then can be defined according to Axiom (6) below.

$$\mathcal{F}1 = \overline{x_1} \vee \overline{x_2} \wedge (\overline{x_3} \vee \overline{x_4}) \vee \underline{x_1} \vee \underline{x_2} \vee \underline{x_3} \vee \underline{x_4} \tag{8}$$

3   Persistence and Irrelevance Trigger

Suppose a system state is denoted by the fault tree representing the combinations of covered component failures that lead to system failure in that state. In the sequel, we will use $\overline{\mathcal{F}}$ to denote the original fault tree in the initial system state (in which each component is assumed to be operational, i.e., not failed), and use $\overline{\mathcal{F'}}$ to denote the updated fault tree in a specific state with the occurrences of some covered component failures. Let $\overline{\pi}$ be a set (product) of covered component failures occurred in the state denoted by $\overline{\mathcal{F'}}$, we have $\overline{\mathcal{F'}} = \overline{\mathcal{F}}[1/\overline{\pi}]$ where $\overline{\mathcal{F}}[1/\overline{\pi}]$ is the formula obtained from $\overline{\mathcal{F}}$ with $\overline{y} = 1$ for any $\overline{y} \in \overline{\pi}$. Notice that $\overline{\mathcal{F'}} = \overline{\mathcal{F}}$ when $\overline{\pi} = 0$ (or say $\overline{\pi}$ is empty in the set sense).

Definition 6 (Component Irrelevance). *A component θ_x is said to be irrelevant in a state denoted by $\overline{\mathcal{F'}}$, if the covered failure $\overline{x}$ is irrelevant in $\overline{\mathcal{F'}}$, i.e., $irrelevant(\theta_x, \overline{\mathcal{F'}}) \stackrel{def}{=} irrelevant(\overline{x}, \overline{\mathcal{F'}})$* [6].

The component irrelevance is based on the covered component failures. A component could also become irrelevant due to the uncovered failures of other components. We do not consider such an irrelevance because it is difficult or impossible to cover the irrelevant component when the "trigger" failures are undetected or uncovered.

In contrast, we say that the component θ_x is relevant in the state $\overline{\mathcal{F'}}$ if $relevant(\overline{x}, \overline{\mathcal{F'}})$, which is denoted by $relevant(\theta_x, \overline{\mathcal{F'}})$. Obviously, even if the system is originally coherent, the initial relevance of θ_x cannot guarantee that θ_x will be always relevant in the future, i.e., $relevant(\theta_x, \overline{\mathcal{F}}) \not\models relevant(\theta_x, \overline{\mathcal{F'}})$ for any $\overline{\mathcal{F'}}$. To address this issue, the concepts of persistence and non-persistence are introduced below.

Definition 7 (Component Persistence). *A component θ_x is said to be non-persistent if it is irrelevant in some state in which the system is not failed, i.e., $irrelevant(\theta_x, \overline{\mathcal{F'}})$ for some $\overline{\mathcal{F'}}$ ($\overline{\mathcal{F'}} \neq 1$), and otherwise it is called persistent.*

A non-persistent component could be either an initially irrelevant component, or a component that is initially relevant but may become irrelevant later when the system is not failed. Obviously, when the system is failed (i.e., $\overline{\mathcal{F'}} = 1$) due to the failures of some components, all the rest (operational) components are irrelevant. This is what we called trivial irrelevance. The trivial irrelevance is not considered (included) as a sub case of non-persistence, because it is useless to cover the irrelevant components when the system is failed. Moreover, the inclusion of the trivial irrelevance may introduce considerable but unnecessary calculation in reliability analysis, since the number of trivial irrelevance of a component depends on the number of MCSs that does not include the component which could be big.

For instance, as for the example fault tree $\overline{\mathcal{F}1}$ of Eq. (7), $\overline{x_2}$, $\overline{x_3}$, and $\overline{x_4}$ could become trivially irrelevant when $\overline{x_1}$ occurs because $\overline{x_1}$ is a MCS of $\overline{\mathcal{F}1}$ (that does not include $\overline{x_2}$, $\overline{x_3}$, and $\overline{x_4}$). It is not necessary to cover the components θ_{x_2}, θ_{x_3}, and θ_{x_4} when $\overline{x_1}$ occurs which leads to a system failure. Moreover, θ_{x_2} is persistent if the above trivial irrelevance is excluded.

Definition 8 (System Persistence). *A system is said to be* persistent *if each component is persistent, otherwise it is called* non-persistent.

For a non-persistent component in a non-persistent system subjected to IFC, it is important to analyze under which conditions the non-persistent component will become irrelevant, especially when it is initially relevant. Without knowing the conditions, it is impossible to cover the non-persistent component in time when it becomes irrelevant. We call such conditions the irrelevance triggers of the component.

The notion of irrelevance trigger can be generalized for the variables of general Boolean formulae (not necessary to be coherent) below.

Definition 9 (Irrelevance Trigger). *Let f be a formula and x be a variable of f, and let τ be a product (set) of other variables of f (i.e., $x \notin \tau$) with $\tau \not\models f$. Let $f[1/\tau]$ be the formula obtained from f with $y = 1$ for any $y \in \tau$. τ is called an* irrelevance trigger *of x if $irrelevant(x, f[1/\tau])$. The irrelevance trigger τ is said to be* minimal *if there is no other irrelevance trigger ρ such that $\rho \subset \tau$.*

We denote by $MIT[x, f]$ the set of all the minimal irrelevance triggers (MITs) of x in f. In the sequel, we will omit the parameter f and simply write $MIT[x]$ when the referenced formula is clear in the context, especially when f refers to the original fault tree $\overline{\mathcal{F}}$. In addition to the set form, we will also use the disjunctive normal form (DNF) to denote $MIT[x]$ by a logic product.

Two special cases are considered, namely x is originally irrelevant (in f) and x is always relevant (i.e., persistent). The MITs of these two cases can be represented by $MIT[x] = 1$ (or $\{\emptyset\}$ in the set form) and $MIT[x] = 0$ (or $\emptyset$ in the set form), respectively.

Theorem 1 (Calculation of MITs). *Let $f(x_1, \ldots, x_n)$ be a monotonic function. The MITs of x_1 can be obtained as the PPIs of $g(x_2, \ldots, x_n)$ that are not the MCSs of $f(x_1, \ldots, x_n)$, i.e.,*

$$MIT[x_1, f(x_1, \ldots, x_n)] = PPI[g(x_2, \ldots, x_n)] \setminus MCS[f(x_1, \ldots, x_n)]$$

where $g(x_2, \ldots, x_n) \stackrel{def}{=} \neg f[1/x_1] \vee f[0/x_1]$, and $\setminus$ stands for the set difference operator.

Proof (Proof Sketch). According to the Definition 9, a MIT of x_1, say τ, must be a minimal positive product and imply the logical equivalence between $f[1/x_1]$ and $f[0/x_1]$, i.e., it is a PPI of $f[1/x_1] \equiv f[0/x_1]$ (i.e., $(\neg f[1/x_1] \vee f[1/x_0]) \wedge (\neg f[0/x_1] \vee f[1/x_1])$). It is easy to verify that $\neg f[0/x_1] \vee f[1/x_1] = 1$ because f is monotonic, then τ is a PPI of $\neg f[1/x_1] \vee f[0/x_1]$. In addition, τ should not imply f according to Definition 9, and thus τ should not be a MCS of f.

For instance, as for the example fault tree $\overline{\mathcal{F}1}$ of Eq. (7), the MITs of $\overline{x_1}$ can be calculated below.

$$MIT[\overline{x_1}, \overline{\mathcal{F}1}] = PPI[\overline{x_2} \wedge (\overline{x_3} \vee \overline{x_4})] \setminus MCS[\overline{x_1} \vee \overline{x_2} \wedge (\overline{x_3} \vee \overline{x_4})]$$
$$= \{\{\overline{x_2}, \overline{x_3}\}, \{\overline{x_2}, \overline{x_4}\}\} \setminus \{\{\overline{x_1}\}, \{\overline{x_2}, \overline{x_3}\}, \{\overline{x_2}, \overline{x_4}\}\}$$
$$= \emptyset$$

i.e., $\overline{x_1}$ is persistent because all MITs are trivial (i.e., they are MCSs of $\overline{\mathcal{F}1}$).

With the calculation of MITs, the component persistence can be redefined in terms of the MITs of the component.

Proposition 1. *Let f be a Boolean function and x be a variable of f. The variable x is said to be persistent in f if it has no MIT, i.e., $MIT[x, f] = \emptyset$, otherwise it is non-persistent.*

4   Irrelevance Coverage Model (ICM)

Based on the calculation of MITs, it is possible to cover (identify and isolate) the non-persistent components whenever they become irrelevant. The coverage of the irrelevant components can be (easily) integrated into the automatic recovery and reconfiguration mechanisms of the traditional CMs, provided that the structure function (fault tree) representing the combinations of covered component failures that lead to system failure is given. In this section, we propose the irrelevance coverage model (ICM) based on the traditional single-fault coverage model by incorporating the coverage of the irrelevant components in addition to the coverage of the faulty components.

In the ICM, we assume that when a fault occurs and is determined to be permanent, not only the offending faulty component is isolated, but also the irrelevant components caused by the covered failure, if any, are isolated so that they will not contribute to the system uncovered failure anymore. Let $\mathcal{F}_{ICM}$ be the fault tree representing the combinations of covered and uncovered component failures that lead to system failure in the ICM, the axioms (3) and (5) of the traditional CM can be revised in the ICM as follows:

$$\overline{x} \vee irrelevant(\theta_x) \leftrightarrow isolated(\theta_x) \tag{3'}$$

$$\underline{x} \wedge \neg isolated(\theta_x) \rightarrow \mathcal{F}_{ICM} \tag{5'}$$

i.e., an uncovered component failure can only lead to system failure when the component is not isolated, and the isolation can be carried out whenever the component is irrelevant (or in the covered failure mode).

Let $MIT[\overline{x_i}]$ be the MITs of $\overline{x_i}$ (in the original fault tree $\overline{\mathcal{F}}$ with only covered component failures), $\mathcal{F}_{ICM}$ can be interpreted by a closed-form formula below.

$$\mathcal{F}_{ICM} = \overline{\mathcal{F}} \vee \bigvee_{i=1}^{n} (\underline{x_i} \wedge \neg MIT[\overline{x_i}]) \tag{6'}$$

in which the uncovered component failure $\underline{x_i}$ can only result in a system failure when none of the MITs of $\overline{x_i}$ occurs; otherwise the component θ_{x_i} is irrelevant and covered in the ICM.

In contrast to $\mathcal{F}$ of axiom (6), an uncovered component failure of $\mathcal{F}_{ICM}$ will no more become a single-point failure to the system if it is irrelevant. From this point of view, the system reliability can be (significantly) enhanced in the ICM, especially when the system includes many non-persistent components.

5   Case Study

The example system used in this section is the leading edge flap (LEF), a subsection of the F18 flight control system (FCS) [7]. The system was previously studied in the traditional CMs using the combinatorial DDP solution [4] and binary decision diagrams (BDDs) [8]. The LEF system is not complex but nontrivial, and the component failure rates are hypothetical but accurate in relation to each other (estimated with the help of a NASA engineer) [4], which aids in demonstrating the significance and effectiveness of our approach, the ICM.

5.1   LEF System Description

The leading edge flaps of the F18 FCS aid in takeoff & landing. The schematic diagram for both left and right LEF is presented in Figure 2 [4]. The two flight control computers (FCCs), labeled A and B (FCCA and FCCB), send signals through four channels, numbered 1 through 4 (CH1, CH2, CH3, and CH4). All four channels feed into the servo/drive unit (SERV). There are two asymmetry control units (ASYM), one for each LEF. CH2 and CH4 connect to the left and right asymmetry control units, respectively. Both the servo/drive unit and the corresponding asymmetry control unit have direct connections to each LEF. For clarity, we look specifically at the left LEF (LLEF) as studied likewise in [4, 8].

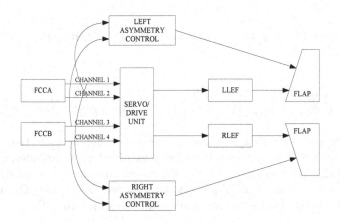

Fig. 2. Schematic Diagram of F18 FCS LEF

5.2 LLEF Fault Tree

By considering only covered component failures, the LLEF fails if either the servo/drive unit, the asymmetry control unit, or the LLEF itself fails. Other failure scenarios include all four channels failed, FCCA and CH3, FCCA and FCCB, FCCB and CH2, and CH2 and CH3 [8]. Let $\overline{\mathcal{F}}$ be the system failure of LLEF resulting from the combinations of covered component failures, $\overline{CH1}, \ldots, \overline{CH4}$ be the covered failures of the channels 1-4, respectively, $\overline{FCCA}$ and $\overline{FCCB}$ be the covered failures of the FCCs A and B, respectively, $\overline{SERV}$ be the covered failure of the servo/drive unit, $\overline{ASYM}$ be the covered failure of the left asymmetry control unit, and let $\overline{LLEF}$ be the covered (primary) failure of the LLEF itself. The fault tree and corresponding formula are shown in Figure 3 and Eq. (9), respectively.

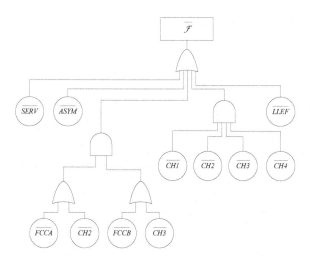

Fig. 3. Fault Tree of Covered Failures of Left LEF

$$\overline{\mathcal{F}} = \overline{SERV} \vee \overline{ASYM} \vee \overline{LLEF} \vee$$
$$(\overline{FCCA} \vee \overline{CH2}) \wedge (\overline{FCCB} \vee \overline{CH3}) \vee (\overline{CH1} \wedge \overline{CH2} \wedge \overline{CH3} \wedge \overline{CH4}) \quad (9)$$

It is easy to verify that $\overline{\mathcal{F}}$ is actually not a coherent fault tree but only a monotonic fault tree, because it includes two irrelevant variables, $\overline{CH1}$ and $\overline{CH4}$. Although the general assumption on system coherence was made in [4], the non-coherence of $\overline{\mathcal{F}}$ was somehow overlooked. Nevertheless, the DDP algorithm proposed in [4] also works for monotonic fault trees including $\overline{\mathcal{F}}$.

5.3 Assumptions and Parameters

Assumptions

1. All components have constant failure rates.
2. The system is as good as new at the start of each mission.
3. The coverage factor is the same for each component.
4. The LLEF fails iff:
   - A combination of covered component failures results in a system failure as depicted in Eq. (9), or
   - A non-isolated component experiences an uncovered fault.

Parameters

The component failure rates used in the analysis were estimated with the help of a NASA engineer. The failure rates are hypothetical but accurate in relation to each other. The one exception is the FCCs whose failure rates were thought to be underestimated at 10^{-8}/hour. A well-accepted failure rate for standard computers (processors) is 10^{-5}/hour [4]. In our analysis, we used the two rates and compared the results. The failure rates [8] are shown in Table 1.

Table 1. Exponential Failure Rates for LLEF System Component

Component	Failure Rate (/hour)
LLEF	10^{-10}
ASYM	10^{-8}
SERVO	10^{-8}
FCCs	10^{-8} or 10^{-5}
CH1-CH4	10^{-6}

Another parameter varying in our analysis is the coverage factor c, the probability of taking the permanent coverage exit given that a fault occurs. We assume that the coverage factors for all components are equal, and the values are set between 0.9 to 1. For clarity, we do not consider the transient restoration, and the exit probability r is set to 0 for all the components. Note that in Doyle et al.'s work [4, 8], the IFC was restricted to the FCCs, and the fault coverage of the other components was assumed to be perfect such that they would never experience any uncovered fault. The reason for the restriction is unclear, but we guess that to show the impact of the IFC of the FCCs on the system and on the FCCs themselves [4] could be one of the considerations.

The mission time is set to 2 hours as a typical time for a test mission. Mission times for other missions such as a combat mission could be longer [4].

5.4   Qualitative Analysis

Let $\mathcal{F}$ be the fault tree with covered and uncovered component failures in the traditional CM without coverage of non-persistent components. According to Eq. (6), $\mathcal{F}$ can be interpreted as:

$$\mathcal{F} = \overline{\mathcal{F}} \vee \bigvee_{x \in X} \underline{x} \tag{10}$$

where X is the set of component failures, i.e., $X = \{SERV, ASYM, LLEF, FCCA,$
$FCCB, CH1, CH2, CH3, CH4\}$.

Let $\mathcal{F}_{ICM}$ be the fault tree with covered and uncovered failures in our ICM
with coverage of irrelevant components. According to Eq. (6′), $\mathcal{F}_{ICM}$ can be
interpreted as:

$$\mathcal{F}_{ICM} = \overline{\mathcal{F}} \vee \bigvee_{x \in X} \underline{x} \wedge \neg MIT[\overline{x}] \qquad (11)$$

The MITs of each $\overline{x}$ can be calculated in terms of Theorem 1 because $\overline{\mathcal{F}}$ is
monotonic.

$$\begin{array}{lll}
MIT[\overline{SERV}] = 0 & MIT[\overline{ASYM}] = 0 & MIT[\overline{LLEF}] = 0 \\
MIT[\overline{FCCA}] = \overline{CH2} & MIT[\overline{FCCB}] = \overline{CH3} & MIT[\overline{CH1}] = 1 \\
MIT[\overline{CH2}] = \overline{FCCA} & MIT[\overline{CH3}] = \overline{FCCB} & MIT[\overline{CH4}] = 1
\end{array}$$

There are three persistent components, namely SERV, ASYM, and LLEF,
because their MITs are 0 (or $\emptyset$ in the set form). The other six components are
non-persistent, among them CH1 and CH4 are initially irrelevant because their
MITs are 1 (or $\{\emptyset\}$ in the set form), and the four remaining, FCCA, FCCB,
CH2, and CH3, are initially relevant but can become irrelevant afterwards due
to the occurrences of the corresponding MITs.

The MITs of a component indicate when the component should be covered
(shut down and safely isolated) in addition to the times when it fails covered in
the ICM. For instance, CH1 and CH4 should be covered in the very beginning
because they are initially irrelevant with the only MIT of 1 (true), FCCA should
be covered together with CH2 when CH2 fails covered, and FCCB, CH2, and
CH3 should be covered under the covered failures of CH3, FCCA, and FCCB,
respectively. The irrelevance coverage of the three persistent components, SERV,
ASYM, and LLEF, however, is useless because their MITs are 0 (false).

With the timely irrelevance coverage in the ICM, an uncovered component
fault can only lead to a system failure when none of its MITs occurs, otherwise
the component is safely isolated (due to the occurrence of a MIT) and will not
contribute to the system uncovered failures anymore. This is different from the
case of the traditional CM in which any uncovered component fault may lead
to system failure and become a single-point failure. The difference can be seen
more clearly by further reducing $\mathcal{F}_{ICM}$ with the MITs of each component, i.e.,
Eq. (11) can be reduced into:

$$\begin{aligned}
\mathcal{F}_{ICM} &= \overline{\mathcal{F}} \vee \bigvee_{x \in X} \underline{x} \wedge \neg MIT[\overline{x}] \\
&= \overline{\mathcal{F}} \vee \underline{SERV} \vee \underline{ASYM} \vee \underline{LLEF} \vee (\underline{FCCA} \wedge \neg \overline{CH2}) \vee (\underline{FCCB} \wedge \neg \overline{CH3}) \\
&\quad \vee (\underline{CH2} \wedge \neg \overline{FCCA}) \vee (\underline{CH3} \wedge \neg \overline{FCCB}) \qquad (12)
\end{aligned}$$

By comparing Eqs. (12) and (10), it is apparent that the $\mathcal{F}_{ICM}$ can achieve
(much) higher reliability than $\mathcal{F}$ by restricting the single-point failures of the
non-persistent components in the traditional CM. For instance, the single-point

failures, $\underline{CH1}$ and $\underline{CH4}$ of $\mathcal{F}$, are removed from $\mathcal{F}_{ICM}$ because the two components (CH1 and CH4) are initially irrelevant, and the single-point failures, $\underline{FCCA}, \underline{FCCB}, \underline{CH2}$, and $\underline{CH3}$ of $\mathcal{F}$, are no more single-point failures in $\mathcal{F}_{ICM}$ in which they can only lead to system failure with the restrictions on the non-occurrence of any of their MITs. The single-point failures, $\underline{SERV}, \underline{ASYM}$, and $\underline{LLEF}$ of $\mathcal{F}$, are, however, still the single-point failures in $\mathcal{F}_{ICM}$ because the corresponding components are persistent. This suggests that the ICM is not necessary for persistent systems in which all components are persistent.

5.5   Quantitative Analysis

The quantitative analysis results of $\mathcal{F}$ and $\mathcal{F}_{ICM}$ are shown in Table 2. The effectiveness of the ICM can be seen by the change in the coverage factor c and the change in the failure rate of the FCCs.

With $c = 1$, i.e., all the components have perfect fault coverage, there is no difference between the probabilities (unreliabilities) $Pr(\mathcal{F})$ and $Pr(\mathcal{F}_{ICM})$. This, again, verifies the observation made earlier in the qualitative analysis, i.e., when the fault coverage is perfect for every component, the ICM is useless in the sense to prevent the nonexistent uncovered faults that may lead to system failure.

Table 2. Unreliability Results of LLEF in CM and ICM

	FCCs Failure Rate			
	10^{-8}/hour		10^{-5}/hour	
c	$Pr(\mathcal{F})$	$Pr(\mathcal{F}_{ICM})$	$Pr(\mathcal{F})$	$Pr(\mathcal{F}_{ICM})$
.90	$8.44 \cdot 10^{-7}$	$4.44 \cdot 10^{-7}$	$4.84 \cdot 10^{-6}$	$4.44 \cdot 10^{-6}$
.95	$4.42 \cdot 10^{-7}$	$2.42 \cdot 10^{-7}$	$2.44 \cdot 10^{-6}$	$2.24 \cdot 10^{-6}$
.98	$2.01 \cdot 10^{-7}$	$1.21 \cdot 10^{-7}$	$1.00 \cdot 10^{-6}$	$9.20 \cdot 10^{-7}$
.99	$1.21 \cdot 10^{-7}$	$8.06 \cdot 10^{-8}$	$5.21 \cdot 10^{-7}$	$4.81 \cdot 10^{-7}$
1.0	$4.02 \cdot 10^{-8}$	$4.02 \cdot 10^{-8}$	$4.07 \cdot 10^{-8}$	$4.07 \cdot 10^{-8}$

When $c < 1$, the decrease ratio of unreliability in the ICM is significant, particularly in the case with the underestimated failure rate of 10^{-8}/hour for the FCCs. Let $UDR = (Pr(\mathcal{F}) - Pr(\mathcal{F}_{ICM}))/Pr(\mathcal{F})$ be the unreliability decrease ratio (UDR) between $Pr(\mathcal{F})$ and $Pr(\mathcal{F}_{ICM})$, the UDR with different failure rate of the FCCs and different coverage factors can be seen more clear in Figure 4. For instance, when $c = 0.9$, the unreliability can be decreased in ratio 8.28% in the ICM with the FCC failure rate of 10^{-5}/hour, and the unreliability can be decreased up to 47.39% with the underestimated FCC failure rate of 10^{-8}/hour. This interesting observation suggests that the ICM could be more effective in terms of the UDR for the systems with more reliable components. In this particular example there are only nine components, and the FCCs have a sizeable effect on the unreliability, which is one reason for the above observation. Different observations, however, may be obtained from different systems.

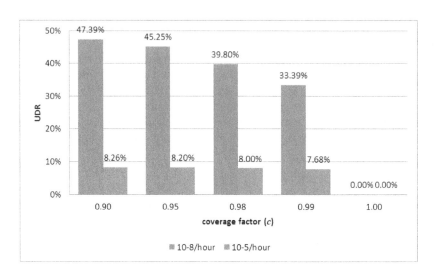

Fig. 4. Unreliability Reduction Ratio

In both cases with the failure rates of 10^{-8}/hour and 10^{-5}/hour for the FCCs, the amount (absolute value) of the decrease of unreliability in the ICM decreases with the increase of the coverage factor c. This shows that the ICM can play a more important role for the systems with "worse" fault coverage factors.

6   Related Work

The coverage concept was first introduced in the seminal paper by Bouricius et al. [9], also called as the coverage factor, as a conditional probability accounting for the efficiency of fault-tolerant mechanisms. If the identification and recovery of faults are independent of each other, the CM is called a single-fault model (e.g., [5, 10]); otherwise it is called a multi-fault model (e.g., [11, 12]). A recent survey on the status and trends of various CMs was presented in [3]. The issues of persistence and coverage of non-persistent components have not been addressed in these traditional CMs, in which the coverage was limited to the faulty components with a general assumption on system coherence [4, 5].

The relevance concept has also been used in Boolean logic driven Markov processes (BDMP) [13], in which the relevance indicator of an event is used to denote whether the Markov processes associated to the event is relevant and should not be trimmed. The relevance indicator of an event depends on the structure functions (i.e., fault trees) of other events (gates or basic events) that have edges to or triggers (a subset of edges) from the event. The relevance indicator in BDMP is analyzed without considering IFC.

A similar concept to relevance is functional dependency (FDEP) [14]. In the FDEP gate, it assumes that the system is configured such that when the trigger event (i.e., the failure of the functionally depended component) occurs, all the dependent components become inaccessible or unusable, and later faults in the dependent components do not further affect the system [14]. An approach, able to handle functional dependency in the reliability analysis of systems with IFC, has been proposed in [15]. Unlike the logical relevance which is encoded in the structure function of the system and the irrelevance triggers of each component can be evaluated automatically in the ICM as presented in this paper, the functional dependency in the FDEP gate must be specified manually.

It has been proved that the reliability of any system subjected to IFC, especially with single-fault models, decreases after certain level of redundancy [10]. Several researchers have studied the optimal redundancy problem for various systems (e.g., [16–19]). Our work is complementary to these works in terms of the common goal of reliability optimization. The ICM opens a new cost-effective way to enhance the reliability without additional redundancy, and it may even play a role in systems whose optimal redundancy limits have already been reached in the traditional CMs.

The issue of coverage of irrelevant components in the systems subjected to IFC has only been addressed in a most recent letter with a simple numerical example [6]. In this paper, we further introduce the concept of persistence at both component level and system level, refine the concept of MIT by excluding the trivial ones that also result in system failures, and propose a new and more efficient algorithm to calculate the refined MITs. Moreover, a non-trivial practical example, a subsystem of the F18 flight control system (FCS), is used to demonstrate the effectiveness of the ICM in this paper.

7 Conclusions

This paper has introduced the concept of persistence in systems subjected to IFC. The ICM has been proposed to incorporate the coverage of the non-persistent components whenever they become irrelevant, which opens up a cost-effective approach to improve the system reliability without increasing redundancy. As for the future directions, we are going to extend the ICM to non-monotonic systems and multi-fault models.

Acknowledgements. The authors are particularly grateful to Dr. Christel Seguin at ONERA and the anonymous reviewers for their detailed and constructive comments to improve the paper.

References

1. Pradhan, D.K.: Fault-tolerant computer system design, pp. 135–138. Prentice Hall (1996)
2. Arnold, T.: The concept of coverage and its effect on the reliability model of a repairable system. IEEE Trans. on Computers C-22, 325–339 (1973)
3. Amari, S.V., Myers, A.F., Rauzy, A., Trivedi, K.S.: Imperfect coverage models: Status and trends. In: Misra, K.B. (ed.) Handbook of Performability Engineering. Springer (2008)

4. Doyle, S.A., Dugan, J.B., Patterson-Hine, F.A.: A combinatorial approach to modeling imperfect coverage. IEEE Trans. on Reliability 44(1), 87–94 (1995)
5. Amari, S.V., Dugan, J.B., Misra, R.B.: A separable method for incorporating imperfect fault-coverage models into combinational models. IEEE Transactions on Reliability 48(3), 267–274 (1999)
6. Xiang, J., Machida, F., Tadano, K., Maeno, Y.: Coverage of irrelevant components in systems with imperfect fault coverage. IEICE Transactions on Fundamentals of Electronics, Communications and Computer Sciences E96-A(7), 1649–1652 (2013)
7. Doyle, S.A., Dugan, J.B., Patterson-Hine, A.: A quantitative analysis of the F18 flight control system. In: Proc. of AIAA Computing in Aerospace, pp. 668–675 (October 1993)
8. Doyle, S.A., Dugan, J.B.: Dependability assessment using binary decision diagrams (BDDs). In: IEEE Proc. of the 25th International Symposium on Fault-Tolerant Computing, FTCS 1998, pp. 249–258 (January 1998)
9. Bouricius, W.G., Carter, W.C., Schneider, P.R.: Reliability modeling techniques for self-repairing computer systems. In: 24th Ann. ACM National Conf., pp. 295–309 (1969)
10. Amari, S.V., Dugan, J.B., Misra, R.B.: Optimal reliability of systems subject to imperfect fault-coverage. IEEE Transactions on Reliability 48(3), 275–284 (1999)
11. Bavuso, S.J., Rothmann, E., Mittal, N.: Hirel: Hybrid automated reliability predictor (harp) integrated reliability tool system (version 7.0) - harp graphics oriented (go) input user's guide (1994)
12. Myers, A.F.: k-out-of-n: G system reliability with imperfect fault coverage. IEEE Trans. on Reliability 56(3), 464–473 (2007)
13. Bouissou, M., Bon, J.L.: A new formalism that combines advantages of fault-trees and markov models: Boolean logic drivenMarkov processes. Reliability Engineering & System Safety 82, 149–163 (2003)
14. Dugan, J.B., Bavuso, S., Boyd, M.: Dynamic fault tree models for fault tolerant computer systems. IEEE Transactions on Reliability 41(3), 363–377 (1992)
15. Xing, L., Morrissette, B.A., Dugan, J.B.: Efficient analysis of imperfect coverage systems with functional dependency. In: IEEE Proc. of Annual Reliability and Maintain-ability Symposium, RAMS, San Jose, CA, pp. 1–6 (January 2010)
16. Amari, S.V., McLaughlin, L., Yadlapati, B.: Optimal cost-effective design of parallel systems subject to imperfect fault-coverage. In: Proc. of Annual Reliability and Maintainability Symposium, pp. 29–34. IEEE (2003)
17. Amari, S., Pham, H., Dill, G.: Optimal design of k-out-of-n:G subsystems subjected to imperfect fault-coverage. IEEE Trans. on Reliability 53, 567–575 (2004)
18. Levitin, G.: Optimal structure of multi-state systems with uncovered failures. IEEE Trans. on Reliability 57(1), 140–148 (2007)
19. Myers, A.: Achieveable limits on the reliability of k-out-of-n:g systems subject to imperfect fault coverage. IEEE Trans. on Reliability 57(2), 349–354 (2008)

Exploiting Narrow Data-Width to Mask Soft Errors in Register Files

Jianjun Xu, Qingping Tan, Zeming Shao, and Hong Ning

School of Computer, National University of Defense Technology,
Changsha 410073, P. R. China
{jjun.xu,eric.tan.6508,szmsmile}@gmail.com,hning@nudt.edu.cn

Abstract. The dependability of computing, caused by soft errors, has become a growing design concern in the safety critical systems. Since Register Files (RFs) are very frequently accessed and errors occurred in them will propagate to other components quickly, RFs are among the major reasons for affecting systemic reliability. Current protecting techniques usually provoke significant power penalty and performance degradation. This paper proposes a lightweight software implemented method for mitigating soft errors in RFs. Based on the observation of many narrow data-width of registers' value, which indicates a large fraction of unused bits of register data, the masking operations are inserted to clear the possible errors in these bits for reducing the window of vulnerability for RFs. To improve the effectiveness, the effect of each masking range is calculated, and the covered masks analysis can remove the unnecessary masks without scarifying the errors coverage. Under the user-defined overhead constrain, the most cost-effective masking operations can be automatically selected. Experimental results from several benchmarks indicate that the reliability of programs have been averagely improved for 16.8% with only 3.3% performance overhead.

Keywords: Register file, soft error, value range analysis, masking operation, program analysis.

1 Introduction

Today, computers are widely used in many safety critical systems, such as vehicle control modules, medical systems and space applications. With the scaling of semiconductor technologies, soft errors are becoming a new challenge for them.

Soft errors, also known as single event upsets, are hardware transient faults caused by external radiation or electrical noises, for example high energy neutrons from cosmic rays and packaging impurity [1][2]. These errors may flip bits stored in storage cells or change the state of logic structures, thus affecting the correctness of program execution. With the continuing progress of VLSI towards smaller feature size, lower supply voltage, and higher frequency, microprocessors are becoming more susceptible to soft errors [3]. There have been multiple costly crash, caused by soft errors, in earth-bound computer systems [4]. Therefore, it is necessary to employ effective techniques to address soft errors.

A. Bondavalli and F. Di Giandomenico (Eds.): SAFECOMP 2014, LNCS 8666, pp. 125–138, 2014.
© Springer International Publishing Switzerland 2014

In modern processors, the original error rates of arithmetic and logic units are much smaller than those of storage structures [5]. The large storage components, such as memory and caches, are routinely protected by the ECC Codes or parity checking bits. Since Register Files (RFs) are accessed very frequently, errors occurred in them can quickly propagate to other parts. Due to the consideration of power consumption and performance loss, protecting RFs using ECC or parity bits is usually impractical. Consequently, the soft errors of RFs are among the top challenges for systemic reliability [6][7]. Moreover, current trend to employ large for better performance (e.g. IA-64) can exacerbate the reliability problem.

Recently, many methodologies have been proposed to overcome soft errors. These techniques can be mainly classified into two types: hardware-based and software-based. Comparing with the former, the latter becomes attractive because it does not incur the high economical costs and can be applied flexibly. Software-based techniques range from the basic error detection mechanisms (e.g. exception handling and assertions) to complex methodologies, including AN-codes[8], ABFT [9], data duplication [10], time redundancy [11][12] and etc. In these methods, the general strategy should be temporal or spatial redundancy, which may unfortunately have evident impact on performance and storage overhead. For example, the full duplication of data can incur double space occupation and the performance will decline significantly when redundancy computation and considerable consistency checking are introduced. The overhead is usually unacceptable in the real time systems or embedded applications.

In this paper, we present a novel lightweight approach, named MASER (MAsking Soft Errors in Register files), which can mitigate soft errors through inserting masking instructions to reset the unused binary bits of target registers. In this way, errors occurred in these bits will not impact the correctness of program execution. Exploiting the profile information, the data-width of live variables stored in registers and the masking ranges of target registers are estimated. Moreover, MASER analyzes the covered masks to remove the unnecessary masking operations. Finally, the most cost-effective masks can be selected automatically under the constrained performance overhead. To illustrate the effectiveness of MASER, we perform several experiments on a set of benchmark programs. Experimental results indicate that the average reliability of programs have been improved for 16.8% with only 3.3% runtime costs.

The content of this paper is organized as follows. Our motivation and the framework of MASER are outlined in Section 2. Section 3 introduces the detail of MASER, including masking ranges analysis, covered masks analysis and optimal masks selection. The experimental results and related works are presented in Section 4 and 5, respectively. Section 6 then summarizes the final conclusion.

2   Motivation

Since a soft error will affect a single-bit cell, we do analysis at the level of assembly code. This paper adopts the PISA instruction set [13], a 32-bit architecture, which is a MIPS-like instruction set.

Firstly, we introduce the following definition. A basic block is a sequence of instructions $\langle i_1, i_2, \ldots, i_k \mid k \geq 1 \rangle$, program executes from i_1 to i_k sequentially. For an instruction i, we define the located basic block and its successive instruction as $\beta(i)$ and $next(i)$, respectively. The set of all basic blocks in a program is denoted as $\mathcal{N}$. Using $\mathcal{N}$, a program can be associated to a control flow graph, and we define the set of connecting edges as $\mathcal{E} = \mathbb{P}(\mathcal{N} \times \mathcal{N})$, expressing all the possible execution flows. For a basic block n, $succ(n) = \{m | \langle n, m \rangle \in \mathcal{E}\}$ represents the set of immediate successors of n, and $F(n)$ denotes the executing frequency of n. For an edge $e = \langle n, m \rangle$, $P(e)$ denotes the probability about block m executing after n.

For each register r, $\omega(r)$ is denoted as its binary width (e.g. $\omega(r) = 32$ in PISA), and the data-with of actual value stored in r is defined as $\varpi(r)$, which depends on the concrete execution process of program. These execution profile and the data-width information of register value can be extracted from profiled execution, or generated from static approximations[14]. Previous work indicates that the data-width of registers' value are highly predictable [15].

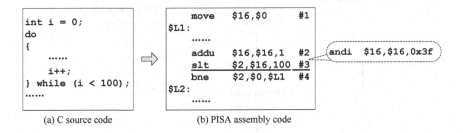

(a) C source code   (b) PISA assembly code

Fig. 1. The sample code

The idea of our approach is based on the observation that a large fraction of the data-widths of registers' actual value are narrow(i.e. less than 16 bits for a 32-bit system, or $\varpi(r) \ll \omega(r)$). Fig. 1 shows a sample code sequence of C language and the target assembly language version written in PISA. The value range of variable 'i' is $[0, 100]$), thus the corresponding stored register $16 only uses low 7 bits. If the instruction "andi $16,$16,0x3f" is inserted before #3, the semantics of snippet code will not be impacted since we know that the upper 25 bits will keep zero (called known-zero bits). However, the errors occurred in these known-zero bits will be masked out, resulting in the decrease of register $16's vulnerability ($\frac{25}{32}$ errors are cleaned). Through inserting the **andi** instructions before the source operands to clear their known-zero bits, MASER increases the reliability of program against soft errors.

It is noted that MASER can be easily extended to mask the known-one bits through **ori** instruction and sign-extensions to clean known-sign bits. Even the technique can be used to enforce the floating point registers. The exponential and decimal part can be masked distinguishingly. But, this paper only focus on the known-zero bits in general purpose registers.

Since the immediate field of `andi` instruction should be less than 16 bit-width, we focus on the value less than `0xFFFF` in the target registers (called narrow registers). The straightforward way to protect registers is to insert masking operations for each narrow register. Apparently, such an approach will be trivial but very costly. For example, masking instruction can also be inserted before #2, because the value range of source operand $16 is also $[0, 100]$. But this insertion is unnecessary because the later masking operation since #3 also clears the upper 25 bits. Based on the data flow analysis, MASER analyses the effect of error propagation to remove these non-vital masking operations. Moreover, to further reduce the performance penalty, the effect of each masking range are calculated. The most cost effective masking operations can then be selected automatically under the constrained performance overhead.

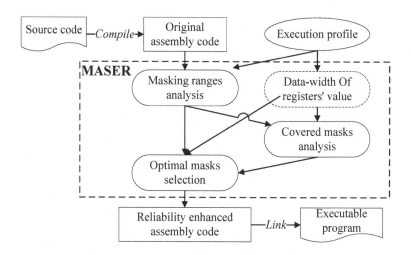

Fig. 2. The framework of MASER

Fig. 2 shows the framework of MASER, which consists of three parts: (1) Based on execution profile, analyzing masking ranges at the assembly code level using the registers' vulnerability analytical methods from work [16]. (2)Analyzing covered masks to remove the non-vital masking operations. (3) Based on previous analytical results, the most cost effective masking operations are selected through a sort algorithm. The following section will discuss these three parts in detail.

3   The MASER Approach

3.1   Masking Ranges Analysis

In this section, we want to know that how many errors can be masked when a masking operation is inserted. During the execution process of a program, a register may be read and written with new data for many times. Intuitively, the maskable errors occur in upper known-zero bits during the intervals (called maskable intervals) from latest usage (write or read) to current masking operation. Moreover, the branch and merge structures may introduce multiple latest accesses. We define the maskable domain as *masking range*, denoted formally via a quintuple, $< r, i_\perp, \varepsilon, \Gamma, \phi >$, in which:

- r: the target register.
- $i_\perp$: for instruction $i_\perp$, r is one of its source operands and the masking instruction will be inserted before $i_\perp$;
- ε: the effect will be masked by this masking operation, which is relative factor for evaluating different ranges;
- Γ: the set of latest accessing instructions;
- $\phi : \Gamma \to [0, 1]$: the masking probability function, for $i \in \Gamma$, $\phi(i)$ represents the probability of errors, which occurred in the interval starting from i, masked by this mask.

Through the use-define chain analysis, the latest accessing instructions can be determined easily. If the previous reference and $i_\perp$ located in the same basic block, the interval can be calculated with the number of intervening instructions between them within the static code. Otherwise, the maskable intervals computation will incur the inherent difficulty of path-dependence.

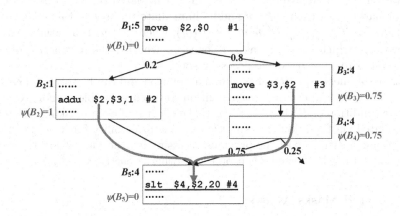

Fig. 3. The sample of masking range

Fig. 3 illustrates a sample control flow graph, where the executing frequency of basic blocks and the probability of branch edges are also marked. For example, the executing frequency of B_1 is 5, and the probability of B_2 executing after B_1 is 0.2. The target register \$2 is written in B_1 and B_2, read in B_3 and B_5 respectively. If the masking operation is inserted before instruction #4($i_\perp$), the latest accesses of \$2 include #2(write) in B_2 and #3(read) in B_3. The maskable intervals of \$2 are described by the thick arrows in Fig. 3. It should be pointed that the interval between #1 and #3 can not be masked because the errors occurred in this interval may propagate to \$3 due to #3. We only need to analyze the maskable intervals from latest usage to current mask. However, because of the inherent path dependance, tracing every possible interval is impractical.

To break away this path-dependence of maskable intervals computation, MASER adopts the idea from the static analysis method [16], which is used to analyze the vulnerability of RFs. For a masking range $< r, i_\perp, \varepsilon, \Gamma, \phi >$, the maskable intervals are decomposed into intra-block $v^\triangleleft$ for the mask inserting basic block $\beta(i_\perp)$ and inter-block $v_n^\triangleright$ for each block n. $v^\triangleleft$ is a definitely maskable interval from the entrance of $\beta(i_\perp)$ to $i_\perp$, and it can be calculated from the instruction sequence in $\beta(i_\perp)$. The latter intervals, from the possible latest accesses to the exit for each block n, are necessarily depended on the usage of r during the subsequent execution, which is defined as a **post condition function** $\psi(n)$, i.e. the probability of errors can be masked after n. The maskable intervals of r can then be simply computed by adding up the basic block attributes multiplied by its execution frequency, and the effect ε is calculated as following:

$$\varepsilon = F(\beta(i_\perp)) \times v^\triangleleft + \sum_{n \in \mathcal{N}} (F(n) \times v_n^\triangleright \times \psi(n))) \tag{1}$$

For the example of Fig. 3, the intra-block $v^\triangleleft$ is the interval from the entrance of B_5 to instruction #4, the inter-block $v_{B_3}^\triangleright$ is the interval from #3 to the exit of B_3. The most essential parameter of each basic block n, the post condition $\psi(n)$ depends on the successive blocks, and can be calculated through the system of linear equations: for each block n and its immediate successors, this relationship holds: $\psi(n) = \sum_{m \in succ(n)} P(\langle n, m \rangle) \times \psi^*(m)$, where $\psi^*(m)$ is a variable associated with m, which is defined as 1, 0, or $\psi(m)$ whether the first access of m is $i_\perp$, access(write or read), or no access, respectively.

This set of linear equations has a unique solution and can be solved efficiently. In Fig. 3, we also labels the post condition for each basic block. For example, the post condition of B_3 is 0.75. Finally, the effect ε of each masking range can be calculated via Equation (1). And the masking probability function ϕ can also be determined easily, i.e. if the previous accessing instruction i is located in the same block of mask inserted, then $\phi(i) = 1$, otherwise $\phi(i) = \psi(\beta(i))$.

3.2   Covered Masks Analysis

As introduced in Section 2, MASER tries to remove the non-vital (unnecessary) masking operations for reducing performance overhead without losing errors coverage. The non-vital masks mean that their masked errors can be covered by later masking operations. Each mask is inserted before the reading access of target register. Eliminating this mask will incur errors propagating to the destination operands, so which should be definitely masked the later ones. To ensure the safety of removing, we introduce the definition of the trusty operations and covered masks similar with the work [17].

The trusty operators are those instructions, which have a low chance to cause the original maskable errors to affect the useful bits. In other words, the maskable errors can only propagate to known-zero bits. The trusty operators thus include:

bitwise instructions (such as and, xor, or and etc), addition and subtraction, left shift and move instructions. Then the definition of covered masking range is as following:

Definition 1. *A masking range m_1 is covered by later masking range m_2 when:*

1. *m_1's next reading instruction $m_1.i_\perp$ belongs to the trusty operations, $m_1.r$ and $m_2.r$ is the source and destination operand of $m_1.i_\perp$, respectively;*
2. *$\varpi(m_1.r) \geq \varpi(m_2.r)$;*
3. *$m_2.i_\perp$ probabilistic postdominates $m_1.i_\perp$;*
4. *if $m_1.r \neq m_2.r$ and $m_1.r$ is still live after $m_1.i_\perp$, then $m_1.r$ should be masked by m_3 in addition $\varpi(m_1.r) \geq \varpi(m_3.r)$.*

Fig. 4 further explains this definition. Assume the data-width of register \$2 and \$3 to be 2 and 3 respectively. In Fig. 4-(a), m1 is obviously covered by m2 for satisfying all conditions. But in Fig. 4-(b), m1 can not be removed because of $\varpi(\$2) < \varpi(\$3)$, m2 will not cover all known-zero bits of \$2. In Fig. 4-(c), m1 also can not be eliminated, because although m1 is covered by m2 in the left branch but \$3 is read (still live) in right side. Therefore, removing m1 incurs errors propagating to \$4, which will not be masked in the later phase. Fig. 4-(d) is an interesting example, in which m1 is also partly covered by m2, \$2 is dead (written with new data) in right branch resulting in the safety of removing m1.

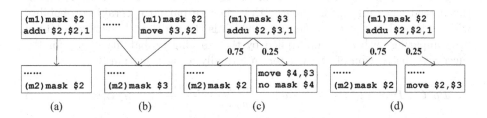

Fig. 4. Examples of covered and non-covered masking ranges

As shown in Fig. 4-(d), this kind of postdominate is different from the traditional definition (such as classic Common Sub-Expression Elimination), which often conservatively request dominating in each successive path (including the dead ones). After calculating the living probability of registers at each program point via work[16], we can use the probabilistic post-domination. It means that the living probability of target register of masking range m_1 equal to the masking probability of later m_2, then condition 3 of Definition 2 satisfy, e.g. both of two probabilities are 0.75 in Fig. 4-(d).

Based on the data-width information, we can sketch all possible masks (data-width less or equal 16 in PISA). Then the non-vital masks are removed according to Definition 2. Because of the strictness requirement of removing, we can assume that later masks may always exist (they will be safely covered by others even if they are removed) during the procedure of covered masks analysis. Finally, we get the minimum set consisted of all vital masks.

3.3   Optimal Masks Selection

During the execution process, there are obvious differences between the execute frequency of different instructions, and the data-widths of registers' value are tremendously diverse. If the overhead is predefined, it will be valuable to select the most cost-efficient masking operations to provide the optimum effectiveness.

Based on the analytical result of masking ranges, we can simply define the *masking rate* of each masking range as the masking effect divided by the execution frequency of masking operation. In this way, all masking ranges are sorted according to the masking rate and the biggest ones should have priority to be selected.

However, a masking range may be covered by others as analyzed in Section 3.2. To calculate the masking rate, the contribution of covered masks should be considered, i.e. must include its coverable masking ranges. Unlike Section 3.2, the strict condition of covered masks can be released and the partial covering is proposed. For example in Fig. 4-(b), although the data-width of \$3 is 1-bit wider than that of \$2, m2 can cover $\frac{29}{30}$ errors masked by m1. In Fig. 4-(c), according to the probability of branch, m2 can cover 75% errors originally masked by m1.

Hence, it is necessary to calculate the covered probability during selection process. The first condition of covered masks is still requested to guarantee that the propagating errors will not affect the known-one bits. Under this premise, all possible covered masks are called *partial coverable masks*. If m_2 is one of the partial coverable masks of m_1, the concrete partial coverable probability will be defined as the *coverable ratio*, which is the width of known-zero bits of m_1 comparing with m_2's, multiplied by the masking probability of m_2 for the successive instruction of m_1, written in formally using Equation (2):

$$ParCvrProb(m_1, m_2) = min(1, \frac{\omega(m_1.r) - \varpi(m_1.r)}{\omega(m_2.r) - \varpi(m_2.r)}) \times m_2.\phi(m_1.i_\perp) \qquad (2)$$

Consequently, the most cost-effective masking operations are selected according to the weight about the effects of coverable masks multiplied by the corresponding partial coverable probabilities. Algorithm 1 illustrates a greedy method of the selection procedure.

The input consists of the set of all masking ranges $\mathcal{M}$ and the predefined threshold $\mathcal{T}$, the output includes the set of selected masking ranges $\mathcal{S}$. Step $1 \sim 2$ are the initial parts and the array *prob* (remaining probability) is set to 1 for each range. Then the selection process is repeated from step 4 to 20 until the overhead $cost \geq \mathcal{T}$. For each remaining range sm, the partial covered probability of all possible coverable masks are calculated during step $6 \sim 13$. The partial coverable probabilities are set to 0 except itself (step 7). To resolve the interdependeney of coverable ranges, we use the standard worklist[18] iterating procedure (step $8 \sim 13$). Step $12 \sim 13$ describe that if the partial coverable probability is changed, then it will be inserted the worklist $\mathcal{W}$. Since the transforming functions have the attribute of monotonicity and the value range is [0, 1], the iterating procedure will terminate. Then, step 14 can compute the masking rate, and the range with maximum value will be selected finally (step 17). At the same time, the remaining probability are changed for following selection, and equaling with 0 will result in removing from $\mathcal{M}$ (step $18 \sim 20$).

Algorithm 1. Optimal masking selection

Input: The set of all masking ranges $\mathcal{M}$, the overhead threshold $\mathcal{T}$
Output: The set of selected masking ranges $\mathcal{S}$

1 $cost = 0; \mathcal{S} = \varnothing;$
2 **foreach** $m \in \mathcal{M}$ **do** $prob[m] = 1;$
3 **while** $cost < \mathcal{T}$ **do**
4      $maxMaskRate = 0;$
5   **foreach** $sm \in \mathcal{M}$ **do**
6         $\mathcal{W} = \{sm\}; cvrProb[sm] = prob[sm];$
7   **foreach** $tm \in (\mathcal{M} - \{sm\})$ **do** $cvrProb[tm] = 0;$
8   **while** $\mathcal{W} \neq \varnothing$ **do**
9            $m \leftarrow remove\ the\ first\ element\ from\ \mathcal{W};$
10   **foreach** $cm \in \mathcal{M} \wedge the\ coverable\ ranges\ set\ of\ m$ **do**
11               $cp = ParCvrProb(cm, m) \times cvrProb[m];$
12   **if** $cp > cvrProb[cm] \wedge cm \notin \mathcal{W}$ **then**
13                  $cvrProb[cm] = cp; \mathcal{W} = \mathcal{W} \cup \{cm\};$
14         $maskRate = (\sum_{tm \in \mathcal{M}}(tm.\varepsilon \times cvrProb[tm])) \div F(\beta(sm.i_\perp));$
15   **if** $maxMaskRate < maskRate$ **then**
16            $maxMaskRate = maskRate; mm = sm; maskProb \leftarrow cvrProb;$
17      $\mathcal{S} = \mathcal{S} \cup \{mm\}; cost = cost + F(mm);$
18   **foreach** $m \in \mathcal{M}$ **do**
19         $prob[m] = prob[m] - maskProb[m];$
20   **if** $prob[m] = 0$ **then** $\mathcal{M} = \mathcal{M} - \{m\};$

---

4   Experiments

In order to evaluate the capacity of MASER, we perform several experiments on a set of six numerical programs written in C. The experimental platform is SimpleScalar[13], which includes several powerful simulators. In our experiments, the concrete version of SimpleScalar is 3.0, which runs on Red Hat Linux 9.

To generate the profile information and the data-width of registers' value, we use a modified `sim-profile` simulator, which can produce detailed profiles on the data-width values and other factors. The execution frequency of each instruction is attached into the assembly code through the built-in `textprof.pl` script. And the running parameters are generated randomly for representativeness.

Firstly, we cross compiler programs into assembly codes using a GCC-based cross-compiler with 'O3' optimization level. Based on the assembly code and the transformed tool implemented by us, four versions for each program are generated: the original program (NONE), all narrow registers being masked version

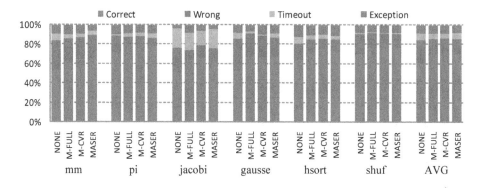

Fig. 5. The experimental results of fault injection

(M-FULL), removing covered masking ranges version (M-CVR) and the optimal selection version (MASER). Different from Algorithm 1, the threshold of the MASER versions is required to cover 90% errors of M-FULL. Comparing with the NONE versions, the proportions of inserted masking instructions are 21.6%, 14.0% and 4.2% for M-FULL, M-CVR, and MASER, respectively.

4.1 Dependability

We conduct fault injection experiments for these programs in the `sim-safe` simulator, which checks for correct alignment and access permissions for each memory reference. To be consistent with the characteristics of soft errors, we perform the injection of single bit-flip in randomly selected bits of RFs, and the concrete injection time are selected randomly according to the total execution time of target program. For each version of the studied programs, 5,000 soft errors are injected. Injected soft errors are classified into the following categories according to their effects:

– *Correct*: the injected faults do not affect the program's behavior, i.e. program completes its execution process normally with the correct result;
– *Wrong*: program exits normally, but the result is not the expected one;
– *Timeout*: program does not terminate within the given time;
– *Exception*: faults are reported by `sim-safe`, such as a segmentation fault.

The experimental results of fault injection are illustrated in Fig. 5, and the 'AVG' group describes the average value for all versions. From this figure, we find that the original versions (NONE) can also mask most of injected errors, the average value of correct category is 60.5%, which is in accordance with other researches, e.g. errors ocurred in dead variables. The average correct rates of the three enhanced versions are 70.3%, 71.5% and 70.2%, respectively. And the rates of other categories decrease in different degrees, which indicate the effectiveness of masking operations.

We attribute the correct category as the reliability of each program. The NONE versions are considered as the basis, and the improved reliability of three

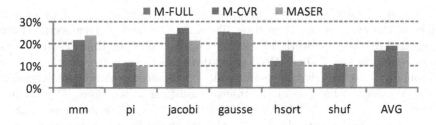

Fig. 6. The reliability improvement

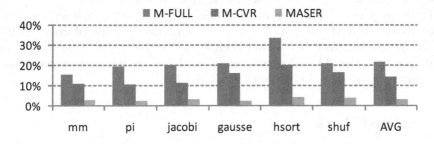

Fig. 7. Performance overhead

enhanced versions are normalized to those of the NONE versions. Fig. 6 illustrates the final results. We can find that the reliability of each enhanced program are certainly improved comparing with NONE versions. Respectively, the average rates of improvement are 16.9%, 18.9%, 16.8% for M-FULL, M-CVR and MASER versions.

Interestingly, although the M-CVR version removes some non-vital masks from M-FULL's, the reliability improvement is higher than that of M-FULL. Through preliminary analysis, we find that M-FULL inserts many extra masking instructions into programs, which expands the live intervals of registers resulting in the bigger windows of vulnerability than before.

While the MASER version adds much less masking operations than M-FULL and M-CVR, its reliability only decrease slightly and almost in common with that of M-FULL. This result indicates the effectiveness of our optimal selection strategy, i.e. data-width of different register values exist huge distinction and the correctness of program execution is closely-related with its most critical data.

4.2 Performance

We do performance evaluations using the `sim-outorder` simulator, which is the most complicated and detailed simulator in SimpleScalar. In this simulator, timing statistics are generated for a very detailed out-of-order issue superscalar processor core with a two-level cache hierarchy, which is appropriate for performance evaluations.

For every version of the six programs, we execute it for several times and recognize the average execution time. The values of performance overhead are normalized by the time overhead with the original execution time. These results are presented in Fig. 7. The 'AVG' group describes the average value.

From Fig. 7, we find that the performance of enhanced programs are decreased in varying degrees because of the inserted masking instructions. The average performance overhead of M-FULL, M-CVR and MASER versions are 21.8%, 14.3% and 3.3% respectively. Due to the relatively limit number of inserted masks and the fast speed of masking operations, the additional overhead is fewer than other traditional fault tolerance techniques against soft errors.

It is important that the overhead of MASER versions are much less than other two versions (15% of M-FULL, 23% of M-CVR), indicating the effectiveness for selecting the cost-efficient masking operations. Comparing with the results of fault injection, the MASER versions only incur 3.3% performance penalty and guarantee the same level of reliability as M-FULL.

5 Related Works

Since soft errors are a random phenomenon and the same error do not occur repetitively, the most effective and general implementation is using data duplication and time redundancy for detecting soft errors. SWIFT [12] is a representative instruction-level method, in which the original instructions are replicated to generate shadow versions with duplicated data. In the combined program, the validation checks must be inserted before including load, store, branch and syscall instructions. SWIFT averagely introduces 41% performance overhead with more than 95% errors coverage. It is noted that MASER can also cooperate with current data duplication methods, for example registers with the wide data-width values can be enhanced through duplication. Based on SWIFT, Chang et al. proposed three kinds of software-only recovery techniques [19] for soft errors. Among them, MASK is a lightweight mitigating method without adding redundancy. Similar with ours, MASK enforces statically known invariants to sketch known-zero bits, and also insert masking operations to eliminate errors in these bits. Nevertheless, MASK is only valuable for some special programs, and its capacity is mostly negligible. Based on SWIFT, work in [17] removed the non-vital checking to reduce the performance penalty through a set of compiler optimization methods.

To decrease the overhead of hardware implemented techniques, researchers tried to improve the effectiveness of protection through program analysis. Based on the partially ECC protected RFs and register lifetime analysis, work in [20] selectively protects a subset of registers through generating and decoding the ECC codes of most vulnerable registers. Lee et al. also proposed a register swapping method [16] to improve reliability based on the partially protected RFs. Memik et al. [21] proposed the duplication of actively-used registers in unused physical registers. If the primary copy can detect errors through available protection mechanism (parity or ECC), then the shadow copy can recover errors.

There are several work to address soft errors through exploiting the narrow data-width of registers' value. Work in [22] proposes the in-register duplication strategy to generate the copy of shadow versions within the upper unused bits, decreasing the requirement of additional registers for duplication. Kandala et al. extend this idea in [23], which the divides register operands into two categories: short operands and long operands. Short operands are replicated in upper unused bits, and long operands are duplicated with the unused physical registers for enhancing reliability. Work in [24] improves the immunity of register files through storing the ECC codes in the upper known-zero bits. These techniques reduce the implementing cost of area and power consumption for addressing soft errors, but they still require special hardware equipments for duplication and generating the ECC codes. But MASER is a software pure method without additional registers and other hardware resources, it can be extended to different platforms.

6   Conclusion

In this paper, we propose a low-cost software implemented method to mitigate soft errors in register files. Based on the fact of many narrow-width values of registers, we find that a large fraction of register data are known-zero bits, which originally do not affect the semantics of program. MASER inserts the masking operations to clear the unintended errors in these bits, resulting in the improvement of reliability. To increase the effectiveness, MASER analyzes the concrete masking ranges and the covered masks. Finally, the most cost-effective masking operations can be automatically selected under the overhead constrain. Experimental results indicate that the reliability of programs can be averagely improved for 16.8%, but the performance overhead is only 3.3%.

In the future, we will refine the implementation of MASER and plan to apply it in more systems, for example the 64-bit architecture.

Acknowledgments. This research was supported by National Natural Science Foundation of China (Grant No. 61202116) and Ph.D. Programs Foundation of Ministry of Education of China (Grant No. 20124307120037).

References

1. Baumann, R.C.: Radiation-induced soft errors in advanced semiconductor technologies. IEEE Trans. on Device and Materials Reliability 5(3), 305–316 (2005)
2. Ziegler, J.F., Puchner, H.: SER - History, Trends, and Challenges: A Guide for Designing with Memory ICs. Cypress Semiconductor Corp. (2004)
3. Baumann, R.C.: International technology roadmap for semiconductors 2007 executive summary (2007)
4. Michalak, S.E., Harris, K.W., et al.: Predicting the number of fatal soft errors in los alamos national laboratory's asc q computer. IEEE Trans. on Device and Materials Reliability 5(3), 329–335 (2005)

5. Shivakumar, P., Kistler, M., Keckler, S.W., Burger, D., Alvisi, L.: Modeling the effect of technology trends on the soft error rate of combinational logic. In: 32nd Int'l Conf. on Dependable Systems and Networks (DSN), pp. 389–398 (2002)
6. Blome, J.A., Gupta, S., Feng, S., Mahlke, S.A.: Cost-efficient soft error protection for embedded microprocessors. In: Int'l Conf. on Compilers, Architecture and Synthesis for Embedded Systems (CASES), pp. 421–431 (2006)
7. Wang, N.J., Quek, J., Rafacz, T.M., Patel, S.J.: Characterizing the effects of transient faults on a modern high-performance processor pipeline. In: 34th Int'l Conf. on Dependable Systems and Networks (DSN), pp. 61–70 (2004)
8. Schiffel, U., Schmitt, A., Süßkraut, M., Fetzer, C.: ANB- and aNBDmem-encoding: Detecting hardware errors in software. In: Schoitsch, E. (ed.) SAFECOMP 2010. LNCS, vol. 6351, pp. 169–182. Springer, Heidelberg (2010)
9. Huang, K.H., Abraham, J.A.: Algorithm-based fault tolerance for matrix operations. IEEE Trans. on Computers 33(6), 518–528 (1984)
10. Benso, A., Chiusano, S., Prinetto, P., Tagliaferri, L.: A c/c++ source-to-source compiler for dependable applications. In: 30th Int'l Conf. on Dependable Systems and Networks (DSN), pp. 71–78 (2000)
11. Oh, N., Shirvani, P.P., et al.: Error detection by duplicated instructions in superscalar processors. IEEE Trans. on Reliability 51(1), 63–75 (2002)
12. Reis, G.A., Chang, J., Vachharajani, N., Rangan, R., August, D.I.: Swift: Software implemented fault tolerance. In: Int'l Symp. on Code Generation and Optimization (CGO), pp. 243–254 (2005)
13. Burger, D., Austin, T., Bennett, S.: Evaluating future microprocessors: the simplescalar tool set. Technical Report 1342, UW Madison CS (1997)
14. Wu, Y., Larus, J.R.: Static branch frequency and program profile analysis. In: Proc. of the 27th Int'l Symp. on Microarchitecture (MICRO), pp. 1–11 (1994)
15. Loh, G.H.: Exploiting data-width locality to increase superscalar execution bandwidth. In: 35th Int'l Symp. on Microarchitecture (MICRO), pp. 395–405 (2002)
16. Lee, J., Shrivastava, A.: Static analysis to mitigate soft errors in register files. In: Design, Automation, and Test in Europe (DATE), pp. 1367–1372 (2009)
17. Yu, J., Garzarán, M.J., Snir, M.: Esoftcheck: Removal of non-vital checks for fault tolerance. In: Int'l Symp. on Code Generation and Optimization (CGO), pp. 35–46 (2009)
18. Kildall, G.A.: A unified approach to global program optimization. In: 1st ACM Symp. on Principles of Programming Languages (POPL), pp. 194–206 (1973)
19. Chang, J., Reis, G.A., et al.: Automatic instruction-level software-only recovery. In: 36th Int'l Conf. on Dependable Systems and Networks (DSN), pp. 83–92 (2006)
20. Montesinos, P., Liu, W., Torrellas, J.: Using register lifetime predictions to protect register files against soft errors. In: 37th Int'l Conf. on Dependable Systems and Networks (DSN), pp. 286–296 (2007)
21. Memik, G., Kandemir, M.T., Ozturk, O.: Increasing register file immunity to transient errors. In: Design, Automation and Test in Europe (DATE), pp. 586–591 (2005)
22. Hu, J.S., Wang, S., Ziavras, S.G.: In-register duplication: Exploiting narrow-width value for improving register file reliability. In: Int'l Conf. on Dependable Systems and Networks (DSN), pp. 281–290 (2006)
23. Kandala, M., Zhang, W., Yang, L.T.: An area-efficient approach to improving register file reliability against transient errors. In: 21st Int'l Conf. on Advanced Information Networking and Applications Workshops (AINAW), pp. 798–803 (2007)
24. Amrouch, H., Henkel, J.: Self-immunity technique to improve register file integrity against soft errors. In: 24th Int'l Conf. on VLSI Design (VLSID), pp. 189–194 (2011)

Towards a Clearer Understanding of Context and Its Role in Assurance Argument Confidence

Patrick John Graydon

Mälardalen Real-Time Research Centre, Mälardalen University, Västerås, Sweden
patrick.graydon@mdh.se

Abstract. The Goal Structuring Notation (GSN) is a popular graphical notation for recording safety arguments. One of GSN's key innovations is a context element that links short phrases used in the argument to detail available elsewhere. However, definitions of the context element admit multiple interpretations and conflict with guidance for building assured safety arguments. If readers do not share an understanding of the meaning of context that makes context's impact on the main safety claim clear, confidence in safety might be misplaced. In this paper, we analyse the definitions and usage of GSN context elements, identify contradictions and vagueness, propose a more precise definition, and make updated recommendations for assured safety argument structure.

Keywords: Assurance argument, safety case, safety argument, goal structuring notation, context, confidence, assured safety argument.

1 Introduction

Developers of some safety-critical systems develop a *safety case* that contains both safety evidence and an argument linking that evidence to safety claims [1,2]. The *Goal Structuring Notation* (GSN) is a popular graphical notation for recording these *safety arguments* [2,3,4]. One of GSN's key innovations is a *context* element for linking to contextual information (which is not necessarily about the system's operating context). However, definitions of context in GSN admit multiple interpretations. Moreover, a recent proposal for a clearer argument structure, namely *assured safety arguments*, demonstrates an understanding of context elements that is at odds with existing definitions [5]. If argument readers and writers do not share an understanding of the meaning of context that makes context's impact on the truth of the safety claim clear, confidence in the safety claim might be misplaced with disastrous consequences. This paper makes four contributions toward a clearer understanding of context in GSN arguments:

- A review of the definitions and uses of context elements in GSN
- Identification of contradictions and vagueness in existing notions of context
- A precise definition in terms of normative models of inductive argument
- Recommendations for applying the proposed definition, including new guidance for structuring assured safety arguments

A. Bondavalli and F. Di Giandomenico (Eds.): SAFECOMP 2014, LNCS 8666, pp. 139–154, 2014.
© Springer International Publishing Switzerland 2014

In Sect. 2, we analyse the definitions of GSN context elements given in authoritative sources and show that these admit multiple interpretations. In Sect. 3, we examine GSN context elements as used in *assured safety arguments*. In Sect. 4, we show that these definitions are inherently contradictory and explore the consequences of that contradiction. In Sect. 5, we propose and defend a definition of context in GSN given in terms of normative models of inductive argument. Finally, we discuss related work in Sect. 6 and conclude in Sect. 7.

2   Context in the Goal Structuring Notation

In some domains, developers of critical systems construct an *assurance case*. When the critical property is safety, assurance cases are known specifically as safety cases. A safety case is a 'structured argument, supported by a body of evidence, that provides a compelling, comprehensible and valid case that a system is safe for a given application in a given environment' [1, Sect. 9.1]. The argument explains how the evidence relates to safety objectives [2, Sect. 1.2.1].

GSN is one of two popular graphical notations for recording assurance arguments [3,4]. Figure 1 presents an example that the *GSN Community Standard* gives to illustrate the notation [3]. *Goal* element G1 presents the argument's main claim. Arrows with filled heads indicate that G1 is *SupportedBy* goals G2 and G3: the control system is deemed acceptably safe because all identified hazards have been eliminated or sufficiently mitigated and the software has been developed to an appropriate safety integrity level. *Strategy* S1 explains *how* goals G4–G6 support goal G2. *Solution* Sn1 provides evidence supporting the claim in G4. Context elements C1 and C2 are asserted at goal G1 using the open-ended *InContextOf* arrow. This paper considers the function of such context elements.

Consider three potential interpretations of the meaning of asserting C2 at G1: (1) the arguer asserts that the system as operated matches the referenced definition, (2) the arguer is identifying the system the argument is about, and (3) the arguer is identifying a document that the reader can refer to for details about the system. These alternatives have different impacts on the argument's soundness: (1) presents a claim that must be checked because false premises undermine conclusions; (2) is clarification that cannot be said to be true or false; and (3) has indeterminate impact because a reader could look up anything. We now turn to normative sources for help choosing the correct interpretation.

2.1   Kelly's *Arguing Safety*

One of the first specifications of GSN appeared in Kelly's DPhil Thesis [2]. Kelly introduces context elements into GSN 'in order to be able to represent the context in which a safety argument is stated and, thus, how the argument relates to, and depends upon, information from other viewpoints' [2, Sect. 3.3]. Context elements have 'two possible forms: as a reference *to* contextual information [and] as a statement *of* contextual information'. Providing context elements 'allows reference to where [the concepts used in a goal] are fully defined' [2, Sect. 3.5.2].

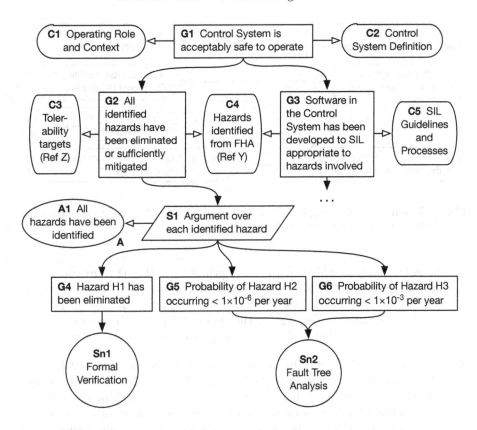

Fig. 1. Extract from 'An Example Goal Structure' (Fig. 6 from [3])

But the thesis does clearly describe how context affects the meaning and soundness of arguments. Kelly introduces Toulmin's normative model of informal, inductive argument [6] as background [2, Sect. 2.6.3], but does not describe the function of context elements in terms of any normative argument model. Instead, he gives the examples depicted in Fig. 2 [2, Sect. 3.3 (emphasis mine)]:

The claim that all applicable hazards have been complied with [sic] is set in the context of whatever is determined as an applicable standard. C1 ... refers to the set of standards identified as applicable (e.g. pointing to the document or file location / section where applicability is discussed and defined). The second example shows an argument ... (S1) ... over ... all hazards. ... S1 is only truly defined when *the basis over which it is stated is made clear*. C2 refers to where the identified hazards are discussed and defined within the supporting safety case documentation. The [third] example ... shows context being used to *communicate the basis* on which a piece of evidence (solution) is being put forward. ... C3 makes clear that the fault tree evidence referred to by Sn1 depends upon

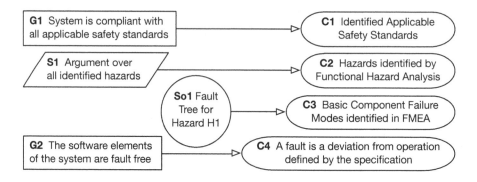

Fig. 2. Combination of 'Example Uses of GSN Context' (Fig. 26 from [2]) and 'Example Use of Context Statement' (Fig. 27 from [2])

the failure rates provided by the more primitive FMEA (Failure Modes and Effects Analysis) evidence. ... [The fourth example illustrates] an 'immediate' contextual statement used to *clarify the basis* of [a] goal .... C4 is phrased as a statement that helps *define ... the basis* of G2. Without C4, ... a reader of G2 may adopt an alternative meaning.

We will return to what might be meant by 'define the basis' in Sect. 2.3.

In GSN, context asserted at a goal is *inherited* by all goal, strategy, and solution elements supporting that goal. Considering the example of an 'argument over all identified hazards' strategy expressed in the context of a hazard log, Kelly writes that 'all the goals and solutions underneath are *also* expressed in the context of the hazard log' [2, Sect. 4.4.3.2].

2.2   The GSN Community Standard

More than a decade after GSN's introduction, a consortium of GSN users wrote the *GSN Community Standard* to 'provide a comprehensive, authoritative definition of the Goal Structuring Notation' [3]. The standard introduces context elements by noting that 'when documenting a GSN *goal* or *strategy* it can also be important to capture the context in which the claim or reasoning step should be interpreted. This is done in GSN by documenting context'. Like *Arguing Safety*, the standard explains that a context element may contain 'a reference to contextual information or a statement' [3, Fig. 7]. Part 1 (which defines GSN) offers no normative model of how context affects the meaning and validity of arguments [3]. However, Part 2 clarifies what context *isn't* [3]:

– 'In GSN, *context* elements should not be used to refer to information which is intended to support the validity of a claim. Such information ... should be represented using a GSN *solution* element' [3, Sect. 2.6.2.1].
– '*Context* elements are sometimes used where a GSN *assumption* or *justification* may be more appropriate' [3, Sect. 2.6.2.3].

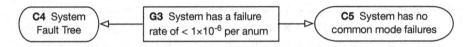

Fig. 3. Combination of 'Incorrect Use of Context (as a Solution)' (Fig. 52 from [3]) and 'Incorrect Use of Context (as an Assumption)' (Fig. 53 from [3])

Figure 3 depicts the example with which the standard illustrates these points. 'Context C4 is incorrectly associated with Goal G3 as evidence [supporting] the failure rate claim .... The correct way to represent this relationship is to associate the System Fault Tree with Goal G3 as a GSN *solution.* ... [Context C5] would be more appropriately rendered as an *assumption*' [3, Secs. 2.6.2.2–3].

Like *Arguing Safety*, the standard states that context is inherited: 'contextual information associated with a claim made in a particular goal is understood to be in scope for all sub-goals of that goal' [3, Sect. 2.3.3.4]. Discussion with Kelly suggests a fourth possible meaning of context: what is inherited is the understanding created by asserting contextual information at a claim, not the contextual information itself [7]. Returning to C2 in Fig. 1, that interpretation would be that it is the clarification of 'Control System' created by asserting C2 at G1, not the control system definition itself, that is inherited by G2, G3, etc.

Unlike *Arguing Safety*, the *GSN Community Standard* explicitly addresses conflicting context: 'nothing in the supporting argument for the goal to which the context is applied should contradict or undermine the relationship between the goal and the context' [3, Sect. 1.3.7, emphasis removed].

2.3   Interpreting GSN's Definition of Context

Arguing Safety and the GSN Community Standard are the two most authoritative definitions of GSN. Given what they say about context elements, we return to the assertion of C2 as context for G1 in example argument given in Fig. 1 and discussed in Sect. 2. Interpretation (1) of this context assertion as a claim that the system as operated matches the referenced definition cannot be correct because it contradicts the prohibition on context introducing information on which the validity of a claim depends [3, Sect. 2.6.2.1]. Interpretation (2) of the context assertion as identifying the system the argument is about seems plausible because it allows reference to where the concepts in G1 are defined [2, Sect. 2.6.3]. But interpretation (3) of context C2 *also* seems plausible. Kelly's use of the phrase 'define the basis of' [2, Sect. 3.3] and the standard's use of the phrase 'capture the context in which the claim ... should be interpreted' [3, Sect. 2] seem to suggest that the reader should keep the entire contents of the control system definition in mind when interpreting G1 and the entirety of the argument supporting it. Those contents cannot be used as a premise, but might presumably clarify the meaning of any part of the argument.

Some examples in *Arguing Safety* seem to be very clearly intended to be read using interpretation (2). For example, a context element in one example reads,

'"Sufficient" = platform meets target failure rate of 1×10^{-6} per flight hour' [2, Fig. 44]. Context C1 in Fig. 1 seems to be more consistent with interpretation (3): there is no mention of the system's operational role or operating context in goal G1. Other examples don't seem to clearly fit either of those interpretations. For example, context C3 in Fig. 2 seems to be better explained as documenting the *provenance* of an evidence item than as explaining the meaning of the text in solution So1 or offering information that would help interpret the evidence. One might regard C3 as explaining what is meant by 'fault tree', but simply knowing the failure modes would not help to interpret the strength and meaning of that evidence. It is knowing the provenance of the fault tree – which would not be documented in the referenced FMEA results – that would aid this interpretation.

3   Assured Safety Arguments

Hawkins et al. have proposed *assured safety arguments* as a means of more clearly communicating both (1) how evidence supports system safety claims and (2) why that argument establishes sufficient confidence in the main safety claim [5]. An assured safety argument contains two distinct sub-arguments:

1. 'A *safety argument* that documents the arguments and evidence used to establish direct claims of system safety'
2. 'A *confidence argument* that justifies the sufficiency of confidence in this safety argument' [5, emphasis mine]

Later discussion [7] resulted in adding a *conformance argument* to document how developers interpreted and conformed with relevant standards [8].

3.1   Structure of an Assured Safety Argument

Assured safety arguments simplify and clarify the safety rationale by relocating information that does not explain how evidence supports the safety claim. Information that increases confidence – by, for example, testifying to the quality or relevance of the evidence – is presented in a separate confidence argument. *Assurance Claim Points* (ACPs) link inferences, evidence assertions, and context assertions in the safety argument to relevant parts of the confidence argument.

Figure 4 reproduces an example used to illustrate ACPs. The square decorations ACP.A4, ACP.A1, and ACP.A3 identify the assertion of context elements DIP.A4, DIP.A1, and DIP.A3, respectively, at goal DIP.G1. ACP.S1 identifies the inference of DIP.G1 from premises DIP.G2–DIP.G6 using the argument strategy DIP.S1. ACP.A2 identifies the assertion of context DIP.A2 at that inference step. (The diamond decorations on goals GIP.G2–GIP.G6 are from GSN's pattern extension and indicate that these goals require support that is not shown here [3].)

Each ACP is a pointer to a separate portion of the confidence argument. Figure 5 reproduces an example Hawkins et al. give to illustrate assurance arguments [5, Fig. 17]. Goals CC1.3 and CC2.3 are associated with ACP.A1; together,

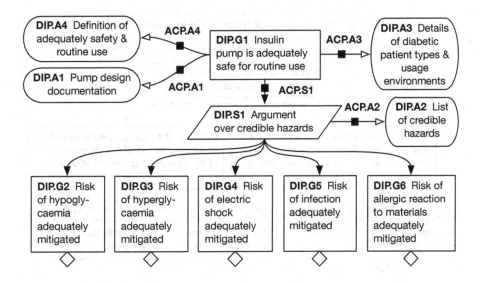

Fig. 4. 'High-level safety argument for an insulin pump' (Fig. 16 from [5])

the arguments supporting them show why we can have confidence in the assertion of 'pump design documentation' as context for the claim that the 'insulin
pump is adequately safe for routine use'. (Presumably, given other patterns in
the paper, ACP.A1 is attached to a different goal not shown in the original figure.
That goal would read 'sufficient confidence exists in the assertion of DIP.A1 as
context at goal DIP.G1' and be supported by CC1.3 and CC2.3.)

3.2 Confidence Argument Structure

Figure 6 reproduces Hawkins et al.'s illustration of a confidence argument's top-
level structure. The argument claims that confidence in the safety argument's
main safety claim is justified because each of the safety argument's components
(inferences, solutions, and context) is fit for the purpose it serves. Instantiations
of confidence patterns of the kind shown in Fig. 5 demonstrate that fitness.

There are several ways to describe confidence in assurance claims, each with its
own benefits and drawbacks [9]. Hawkins et al.'s confidence argument patterns
use a form of Baconian probability [9,10,11]. That is, they enumerate plausible
defeaters of the argument – things that might directly rebut a claim or undermine
the reasoning supporting it – and describe why those defeaters are thought to
be implausible and/or the residual likelihood of them acceptable. (Some small
degree of doubt is inevitable: even a machine checked, deductive proof might be
wrong if the proof checker is faulty or was used improperly.)

3.3 Context as Used in Assured Safety Arguments

Hawkins et al. describe the meaning of a context element linked to a goal as an

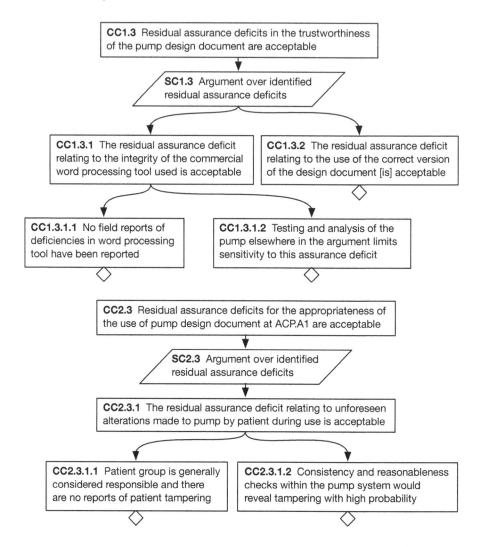

Fig. 5. 'Part of the confidence argument for ACP.A1' (Fig. 17 from [5])

assert[ion] that the context is appropriate for the elements to which it applies. For example, consider a context reference to a list of failure modes for a particular piece of equipment. The introduction of this context element when arguing about the safety of that piece of equipment implicitly asserts that the list of failure modes referred to is appropriate to the application and operating context in question.

The appropriateness of context must be considered throughout the part of the argument that inherits the context: 'the assurance of the strategy depends upon the confidence that the context ... stated is appropriate for that strategy and its

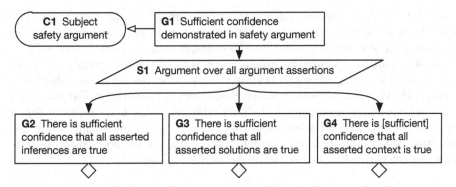

Fig. 6. 'Representing an overall confidence argument' (Fig. 15 from [5])

subgoals' [5]. But considering the appropriateness of context alone is insufficient: 'in addition to the appropriateness of the context, it is also necessary to provide an argument as to the trustworthiness of the context in question'.

Hawkins et al. do not provide a testable definitions of what it means for context to be 'appropriate' and 'trustworthy', although in the latter case they say that 'the concept of trustworthiness relates to freedom from flaw' [5]. However, they do provide examples. Referring to a generic argument over all hazards, they write that for a hazard list to be appropriate context 'there must be confidence that the hazard list is appropriate with respect to the system, application, and context'. In the case of the example shown in Fig. 4, they give the confidence argument fragment depicted in Fig. 5. They also write of the meaning of ACP.A2 that 'there is sufficient confidence that the list of credible hazards is complete and correct. Inadequate definition of a hazard or omission might invalidate the safety claim'. The context must be 'true', as goal G4 in Fig. 6 puts it.

The assertion of a context element in an assured safety argument seems to be mostly clearly defined as the making of two claims:

1. *Acceptable instantiation.* The identified thing *is* the kind of thing implied by the ordinary meaning of the term used to represent it.
2. *Fitness for role.* The identified thing has all of the properties that the entire applicable portion of argument needs it to have.

These claims then serve as implicit premises throughout the inheritance area. In Toulmin's terms [6], to assert a context element in an assured safety argument is to assert that acceptable instantiation and fitness for role are warrants that can be implicitly used in any of the affected reasoning steps.

To illustrate this definition of context, consider the example in Fig. 4. A hazard list must be *the* hazard list created for the system in question because the ordinary meaning of the words 'all credible hazards' is that they are hazards of the system in question. The hazard list must also be 'complete and correct' because inference DIP.S1 would be invalid if supporting goals DIP.G2–DIP.G6 did not accurately portray all relevant hazards. The hazard list can be assumed to have these properties throughout the argument supporting goals DIP.G2–DIP.G6.

Acceptable instantiation and fitness for role are not simply properties that must be true as prerequisites for judging whether an argument is sufficiently compelling. There are such properties, for example argument clarity and comprehensibility. But the example argument depends upon these as premises. DIP.G1 in Fig. 4 lacks a sub-goal or justification claiming that the list of hazards identified by DIP.A2 is complete and correct. Such support is used in similar reasoning steps in plain safety arguments, including in Hawkins' *High Level Software Safety Argument Pattern* [12]. The absence of such support here can only mean that the assertion of DIP.A2 is meant to demonstrate that there are no credible hazards that are not covered by one of the goals DIP.G2–DIP.G6.

4 The Problem of Conflicting Definitions of Context

Section 2.3 discussed how context is (somewhat vaguely) defined in authoritative guides to GSN. Section 3.3 showed that context elements in assured safety arguments function as claims of acceptable instantiation and fitness for role. These definitions are mutually exclusive. Clarification and identification of reference material cannot introduce new claims. Introduction of claims contradicts the prohibition on using context elements 'to refer to information which is intended to support the validity of a claim' [3, Sect. 2.6.2.1].

It is vital that all readers of an argument understand the same meaning of its context elements. If they do not, confidence in safety claims might be misplaced. For example, consider multiple reviewers collaborating to review of a large argument in parts [13]. Suppose that reviewer A examines the assertion of a hazard list document identifier as context and interprets it as explaining the term 'hazard list'. Suppose that reviewer B reviews a supporting portion of argument and interprets the context assertion as claims of acceptable instantiation and fitness for role. Because A sees no need to check either property and B assumes that they have been checked, neither will check it. The system might be put into service despite not addressing a significant hazard.

Returning to the example in Fig. 1, suppose that reviewer C interprets this 'basis' of goal G1 as simply scoping the situations to which the argument applies. Suppose that stakeholder D reads in the referenced documentation a claim about what the operating context *is*. D might assume that review had confirmed that it was acceptable to assume that the system would be used in this way while C might not see the need to check that assumption.

5 Proposed Treatment of Context and Confidence

Given the harm that misinterpretation of context might bring, GSN users should adopt a single, normative definition. This section gives and justifies our proposal.

A useful definition of GSN context elements must satisfy two requirements:

1. *Means to perform the functions that people have been using GSN context elements to perform must be preserved.* If the definition precludes using context elements to meet a need that GSN users have used them to meet, we must also propose an alternative means of meeting that need.

2. *The effect of context elements on confidence in the argument's main claim must be well defined.* Understanding this effect is a precondition for defining an effective argument review process and, ultimately, for using an argument to make certification or acceptance decisions.

5.1   Our Proposal: GSN Context Elements as Explications

We propose defining context elements as explicating terms used in the argument.

Form. Context element text must be of the form '$X: Y$' where X is a phrase and Y is its explication. Y should identify relevant documentation where appropriate.

Scope. The explication applies to (i) the element e at which the context c is asserted, (ii) any goal, strategy, or solution in the same argument module that directly or indirectly supports e through IsSupportedBy relationships, and (iii) any justification, assertion, or confidence element in the same module asserted as context to an element to which c applies as per rules (i) and (ii).

Effect. Arguments should be understood as if explicated terms were replaced by their explications.

Uniqueness. Arguers may not assert two explications for the same term that apply to the same element.

Non-circularity. Arguers may not assert explications such that any term is directly or indirectly explicated in terms of itself.

Presentation. Explicated terms appearing in GSN elements should be visually distinguished from non-explicated text. For example, explicated terms might be presented in a different font, in italics, in a different colour, underlined, or some combination of these. Hyperlinks should be used where practicable.

Loaded language. Arguers should not use context to phrase arguments in terms whose plain-language meaning might cause misunderstanding of the argument.

5.2   An Illustrative Example

To illustrate the proposal given in Sect. 5.1, consider the example given in Fig. 4. Figure 7 presents a version of that argument revised to reflect our definition of context. Context elements C1–C3 now clearly explicate terms used in goal G1. C1 clarifies which insulin pump we mean and that we mean it as delivered, not just as designed. C2 refers to documentation giving the relevant definition of 'adequately safe'. C3 clarifies what we mean by 'routine use', thus limiting the scope of the argument to that use. For clarity, we introduce goal G2 to separate (a) the inductive leap related to the relationship between safety and hazard management from (b) the argument-by-cases over the set of identified hazards.

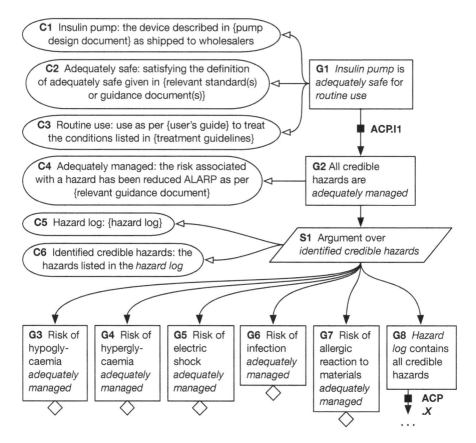

Fig. 7. Revised version of argument given in Fig. 4. The text in braces stands for details that identify the documents in question (e.g., document and version numbers).

New goal G8 is the claim of hazard log completeness that justifies strategy S1. G8 could be replaced by a justification or an away goal asserted as justification using the InContextOf relationship [12]. Those alternatives have the stylistic benefit of distinguishing the claim about hazard log completeness from the claims to have managed each hazard. However, those alternatives also have an area effect that complicates both change management and argument review.

The *scope* rule dictates that explications of 'insulin pump', 'adequately safe', and 'routine use' are applicable in all goals, strategy S1, and context elements C4–C6. The *uniqueness* rule would preclude asserting a competing explication of 'adequately managed' at goals G2–G8 or strategy S1. The *loaded language* recommendation suggested the change from 'credible hazards' in the original to 'identified credible hazards' in S1.

5.3   Assessing the Proposal: Performing All Context Functions

The examples in *Arguing Safety* [2], the GSN community standard [3], and the assured safety argument paper [5], Hawkin's software safety argument patterns [12], and our own experience suggest at least six functions that arguers *might* want context elements to perform: (1) to explain a term's meaning, (2) to link arguments to other documents, (3) to assert an implicit premise, (4) to identify background information, (5) to document the circumstances in which the argument was made, and (6) to make GSN elements less verbose.

Explaining terms. Our proposed definition clearly serves this purpose.

Linking the argument to documents. Our definition facilitates linking to explain terms more clearly. Solution elements link arguments to evidence. Linking without a clear purpose is disallowed to prevent confusion. We would replace C3 in Fig. 2 with an ACP on the solution linking to an argument that explains the fault tree's provenance and that provenance's effect on confidence.

Asserting an implicit premise. GSN offers two ways to assert a premise throughout an argument (i.e., as an implicit warrant in Toulmin's model [6]): justification elements and away goals asserted as context. In any case, this function might be overused. Local scope simplifies change and review and we might only need the goal G8 in Fig. 7 as a premise in this particular reasoning step.

Identifying background information. Background information can help to understand and validate an argument (e.g., show that it is not oversimplified [14]). But premises should be introduced using a goal, away goal, or justification element, links to details can be made as described above, and it is not clear that 'background information' serves any other useful purpose. Categorising information as either what-the-arguer-means (which can be accepted) or as evidence claims (which must be checked) facilitates argument validation.

Documenting the argument writer's circumstances. Documenting the circumstances under which an argument was made might aid interpretation. But much of this (e.g., the colour of the author's clothing) is irrelevant. Moreover, different people might interpret the remainder differently. Restricting context elements to explication forces arguers to identify which meanings are influenced by circumstance and (more importantly) what those meanings are meant to be.

Making GSN elements less verbose. A single artefact might serve multiple roles in an argument. For example, a hazard log might serve as a list of hazards, information about hazard severity, or an indication of project status [7]. Explication-only context might not reduce verbosity as well as unrestricted context because authors might have to reword element text to include the explicated term or assert context multiple times to fill multiple roles. We consider this an acceptable price for increased clarity.

Table 1. How our definition of context solves other definition's problems

Problem	Solution
The effect on argument confidence is unclear. See Sect. 4.	The assurance argument should be judged as if explicated terms had been replaced by their explications. See Sect. 5.4.
A document asserted as the basis for a goal (and possibly all of its supporting reasoning, depending on how inheritance is interpreted) could be understood by different people as explaining different things. See Sect. 2.	The context explicitly identifies the term being explicated. The *presentation* recommendation reminds readers that a term is explicated. See Sect. 5.1.
Readers might interpret different parts of a linked document as the explanation of a term. See Sect. 2.	Arguers understanding context as explication will craft explications to resist misinterpretation. Reviewers will help by pointing out vagueness. Guidance created to clarify terms used in requirements might help further, e.g. by eliminating hedge words such as 'usually' or 'generally' [15].
Readers might or might not interpret context assertion as a claim that referenced material is what its title suggests and is fit for purpose. See Sect. 3.3 and Sect. 4.	Our definition precludes this interpretation. The *loaded language* recommendation, the *presentation* recommendation, and appropriate review reduce the risk that the explicated term's plain-language meaning will colour understanding of the argument. See Sect. 5.1.

5.4   Assessing the Proposal: The Effect on Confidence

The main virtue of the definition of context in Sect. 5.1 is a well-defined impact on argument confidence: the argument should be assessed as if all explicated terms had been replaced by their explications. In Toulmin's terms, context as we define it is simply a mechanism for replacing shorthand text used in data, warrants, claims, reservations, and qualifications [6]. Table 1 shows how our proposal addresses the confidence-related problems that other definitions have.

5.5   Impact on Assured Safety Arguments

The organisation of the confidence argument (depicted at the top level in Fig. 6) must change: context as defined in Sect. 5.1 cannot be said to be 'true' or false. There is no need to argue over context elements because we argue instead over the elements and relationships whose meanings they clarify. The burden of demonstrating hazard log completeness, carried at ACP.A2 in the original formulation in Fig. 5, is carried by the evidence and inferences supporting goal G8 in Fig. 7.

But GSN also allows justification elements, assumption elements, and away goals to be the object of InContextOf relationships. Goal G4 in Fig. 6 would cover those assertions if it read 'there is sufficient confidence that all assumptions, justifications, and away goals asserted as context are true'.

One might argue the need for an assurance claim point on the inference of goal G2 from goals G3–G8 through strategy S1. The associated confidence argument fragment would cite review evidence showing that goals G3–G7 cover all of the credible hazards listed in the hazard log. It is obvious that such a review will be performed. Since the inference admits no other assurance deficit, we see no reason to burden the arguer with writing such a confidence argument fragment.

5.6 Further Recommendations: Update Review Processes

An explication cannot be either true or false, but a poor explication might admit multiple interpretations, compromising the efficacy of argument review. Existing argument review processes include steps aimed an ensuring clarity [3,13,16]. GSN argument review processes should require reviewers to consider whether terms used in the argument have multiple meanings in general use and in the relevant technical domain(s). Terms with multiple meanings should be explicated, and explications should rule out unintended meanings of the explicated terms.

6 Related Work

Arguing Safety [2] and the *GSN Community Standard* [3] define context in GSN. Examples of context in the former clearly explicate terms. What is novel about our proposed definition of context is that we limit context to this function, thus making its impact on argument confidence clear.

Matsuno and Taguchi's proposed formalisation of GSN patterns [17] defines context elements as declarations of types and variables. The definition of context proposed in Sect. 5.1 is for arguments that have not been formalised.

Because the other popular graphical argument notation, CAE, has no context element, our proposed definition of context does not apply to it [4]. For similar reasons, our proposal does not apply to plain text or tabular arguments. Any informal argument might be vague, but other causes will apply in other notations.

7 Conclusion

In this paper, we reviewed how both Kelly's thesis [2] (the original normative definition of GSN) and the *GSN community standard* [3] define context elements. Neither defines context in terms of normative models of argument and both permit multiple interpretations. But both sources are clearly at odds with how context elements are treated in assured safety arguments: the former say that context elements cannot support the validity of claims, while the latter says that they do. To resolve this contradiction and bring clarity to the meaning of GSN, we proposed a more precise definition of the semantics of GSN context elements. We illustrated this definition and its impact on the structure of assured safety arguments by reworking a published example of an assured safety argument.

Any proposed change to language semantics – whether for a natural language, a programming language, or an argument notation – will fail if people choose not to adopt it. A key factor in the adoption of this change is whether the proposal addresses all of the functions for which arguers have been using GSN context elements. We have examined examples for evidence of such functions and found none, but very few published examples exist. The only practical way forward is to make this proposal public so that arguers can judge for themselves.

Acknowledgments. This research was funded by the Swedish Foundation for Strategic Research as part of the SYNOPSIS project and by the EU/Artemis as part of the nSafeCer project (grant 295373). We thank Pierre Loisy for inspiring this work and Tim Kelly and Iain Bate for helpful discussions of this paper.

References

1. Defence Standard 00-56: Safety Management Requirements for Defence Systems, Issue 4, Part 1: Requirements (U.K.) Ministry of Defence (June 2007)
2. Kelly, T.P.: Arguing Safety — A Systematic Approach to Managing Safety Cases. DPhil thesis, University of York (September 1998)
3. Attwood, K., et al.: GSN Community Standard Version 1. Origin Consulting Limited, York (November 2011)
4. Bishop, P., Bloomfield, R.: A methodology for safety case development. In: Proc. Safety-Critical Systems Symposium (SSS) (1998)
5. Hawkins, R., Kelly, T., Knight, J., Graydon, P.: A new approach to creating clear safety arguments. In: Proc. Safety-Critical Systems Symposium (SSS), pp. 3–23 (2011)
6. Toulmin, S.E.: The Uses of Argument, Updated edn. Cambridge University Press, New York (2003)
7. Kelly, T.: Personal communication
8. Graydon, P., Habli, I., Hawkins, R., Kelly, T., Knight, J.: Arguing conformance. IEEE Software 29, 50–57 (2012)
9. Graydon, P.J.: Uncertainty and confidence in safety logic. In: Proc. Int'l System Safety Conference (ISSC) (2013)
10. McDermid, J.A.: Risk, uncertainty and software safety. In: Proc. Int'l Systems Safety Conference (ISSC) (2008)
11. Weinstock, C.B., Goodenough, J.B., Klein, A.Z.: Measuring assurance case confidence using Baconian probabilities. In: Proc. Int'l Wkshp. on Assurance Cases for Software-Intensive Systems (ASSURE) (2013)
12. Hawkins, R., Kelly, T.: A software safety argument pattern catalogue. Technical Report YCS-2013-482, University of York (2013)
13. Graydon, P., Knight, J., Green, M.: Certification and safety cases. In: Proc. Int'l Systems Safety Conference (ISSC) (2010)
14. Greenwell, W.S., Knight, J.C., Holloway, C.M., Pease, J.J.: A taxonomy of fallacies in system safety arguments. In: Proc. Int'l System Safety Conference (ISSC) (2006)
15. Wasson, K.S.: CLEAR Requirements: Improving Validity Using Cognitive Linguistic Elicitation and Representation. PhD thesis, University of Virginia (2006)
16. Kelly, T.: Reviewing assurance arguments — a step-by-step approach. In: Proc. Wkshp. on Assurance Cases for Security — The Metrics Challenge (July 2007)
17. Matsuno, Y., Taguchi, K.: Parameterised argument structure in GSN patterns. In: Proc. Int'l Conf. on Quality Software (2011)

Assurance Cases for Block-Configurable Software

Richard Hawkins[1], Alvaro Miyazawa[1], Ana Cavalcanti[1],
Tim Kelly[1], and John Rowlands[2]

[1] Department of Computer Science, University of York, York, UK
[2] BAE Systems, Warton Aerodrome, Preston, PR4 1AX, UK

Abstract. One means of supporting software evolution is to adopt an architecture where the function of the software is defined through reconfiguring the flow of execution and parameters of pre-existing components. For such software it is desirable to maximise the reuse of assurance assets, and minimise re-verification effort in the presence of change. In this paper we describe how a modular assurance case can be established based upon formal analysis of the necessary preconditions of the component. Our approach supports the reuse of arguments and evidence established for components, including the results of the formal analysis.

1 Introduction

Software maintenance and evolution is typically very costly. In the safety-critical domain, extensibility and reconfigurability have to be traded for simplicity, with impact on maintainability. We consider here what we call block-configurable software, which achieves this compromise by adopting an architecture that supports configuration via structured input data.

Block-configurable software comprises a number of components that provide particular functionality, and a manager, which uses configuration data to define how the components cooperate. The architecture resembles that of a control-law diagram with connections defined by configuration data. Block-configurable software is a convenient means of implementing control systems for which changes in dynamic behaviour can be restricted to changes in the parameters and connections of a fixed set of components.

Block-configurable software facilitates changes: to add or to change a function, it may be not be necessary to touch the code at all. It is also easier for a third-party to implement changes, since it may be enough simply to provide appropriate data. So, the integrity of the code can be maintained, whilst flexibility is still provided to the user.

This gives rise, however, to a challenge for assurance. To realise the benefits of block-configurable software, it is necessary to limit the work required for validation in the face of changes. Also from an assurance perspective, the impact should be limited to the configuration data.

The validity of the configuration data provided is a key aspect of the assurance case. We need to identify the constraints that characterise valid data, and to consider the way in which validity is established. This can be related to

A. Bondavalli and F. Di Giandomenico (Eds.): SAFECOMP 2014, LNCS 8666, pp. 155–169, 2014.
© Springer International Publishing Switzerland 2014

concerns regarding exceptional behaviour, use of resources, or any other general properties. To address both the identification and verification of constraints on the data we adopt the use of formal analysis.

Our contribution is a general pattern for assurance cases that can be made for block-configurable software using a combination of formal analysis and more traditional verification. Safety-argument patterns provide a way of documenting and reusing argument structures by abstracting the fundamental strategies from the details of a particular argument. It is possible to create specific arguments by instantiating the patterns in a manner appropriate to the application. We present a number of options for supporting various aspects of the assurance cases. We also consider the effect that changes to the software have on the assurance case, and how the impact can be minimised. We maximise reusability both at the level of the structural arguments and of the formal analysis.

Our assurance cases are not for particular properties of the system; they demonstrate that the software does not adversely affect the system in which it is embedded. We have applied our approach in an industrial case study, but use a quadratic-equation solver as an example here.

To represent assurance arguments clearly, we use a graphical notation: the Goal Structuring Notation (GSN), as it is mature, widely used, and standardised [6]. We observe, however, that our results apply to any notation that conforms to the meta-model of the OMG standard for structured assurance cases (including Adelard's CAE, for example) [12].

Section 2 defines the characteristics of block-configurable software. Our assurance-case pattern is described in Section 3. Section 4 discusses the well-behavedness arguments, and in particular termination. Section 5 discusses the effects of likely changes. Section 6 explains how the validity of configuration data can be established using a formal approach. Finally, Section 7 discusses related work and Section 8 provides conclusions.

2   Block-Configurable Software

Block-configurable software is created from generic components. It may be used to implement a solution for any problem that requires a vector of inputs to be transformed to a vector of output values. The functionality of the block-configurable software is determined at runtime through the connection of the components and the provision of parameters to them as defined using loaded configuration data specific to a particular function. A unique characteristic of this type of software, in comparison for example to data-driven software, is that data is also the means by which software is configured at design-time, through defining parameters for the code blocks and connections between them.

A key feature of block-configurable software is that it is extensible; it allows the user to employ any number of components, which can be used in any sequence to derive the required outputs. The configuration data provides all the information required to define the inputs that are needed, the outputs that are to be generated from the inputs using the components, and the parameters that are given to each component.

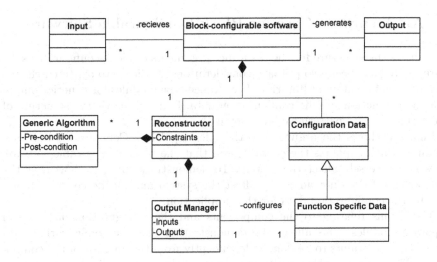

Fig. 1. Structure of block-configurable software

Figure 1 shows the structure of block-configurable software. **Inputs** and **Outputs** characterise its interface. A **Reconstructor** characterises the functions provided by the software using one or more generic components. **Configuration Data** for a function is selected at runtime. **Function Specific Data** configures the software for a particular function. **The Output Manager** is a component that defines the parameters provided to the other components and their order of execution. Each function must include an output manager, and it must be the first component executed (to define how the others are used). The design of the reconstructor and the output manager are the same in all block-configurable software. The only changes ever required to the reconstructor are small adaptations to take into account the introduction and removal of components.

A deployment of block-configurable software may include a number of different functions. Each function is reconstructed using a subset of the components available and function-specific configuration data. A deployment, therefore, consists of a set of generic components, a reconstructor that can reference all of them, and configuration data for each function. New functions can be added to the deployment by adding new configuration data, as long as only the existing components are required.

As an example, we consider a quadratic-equation solver; its Ada implementation is presented in [13]. Its inputs are the coefficients of a quadratic equation and it generates as output its solutions. The configuration data can be used to select one or both of them as output. The reconstructor uses generic components called OUTPUT_MANAGER, ADDER, MULTIPLIER, SQRT, and so on. The software may, therefore, implement different functions that uses addition, and square root, for example.

3   An Assurance Case for Block-Configurable Software

In defining the structure for the assurance arguments of block-configurable software, there have been two primary considerations: resilience to expected change scenarios and creation of libraries of assurance-case modules for generic components and function-specific configuration data. Figure 2 shows the structure of the assurance-case pattern we have defined.

Figure 3 shows the argument within the top Block-Configurable Software module, which supports the overall claim that the block-configurable software does not adversely affect the system. To demonstrate this, we show that the software itself does not adversely affect the system and all the constraints are met by the configuration data for that application.

The claims relating to the components and the configuration data are in separate modules. This allows the demonstration that the configuration data meets the constraints to be done independently from the analysis of the components. The connection between the two parts of the argument is the constraints, which are derived as part of the generic-components argument and used by the configuration-data argument. In Figure 3 this is captured by Away Context definitions (boxes with rounded top) associated with the Away Goal regarding the data constraints. The Away Goal is defined in the module Configuration Data (as named in the bottom of the Away Goal symbol). The Away Contexts are defined in the Generic-Component module (also named at the bottom).

Our approach relies on the use of the block-configurable software pattern. The assurance argument must, therefore, include evidence that the software has the

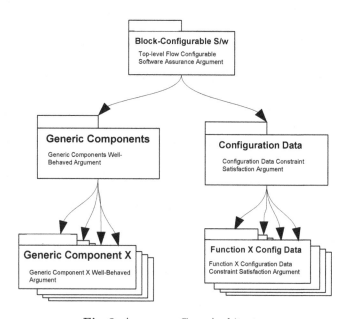

Fig. 2. Assurance-Case Architecture

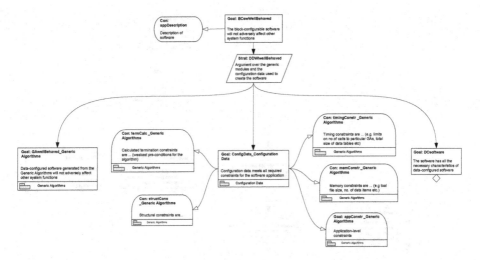

Fig. 3. Assurance Argument: BC Software Module

necessary characteristics identified by this pattern. This can be demonstrated, for example, through a simple manual check of the structure of the software modules against the pattern.

The argument regarding the generic components demonstrates that the software is "well behaved". In the argument, we assert that "if well behavedness is demonstrated, this ensures that the software does not adversely affect the system". Notions of interest for "well behavedness" are related to termination, resources, and exceptions. Here, we only consider the argument made for termination. In [13], we explore the other arguments. A confidence argument is required to show that the identification of concerns regarding well behavedness is complete and correct. The argument considers each of these concerns in turn.

The argument regarding termination must be valid for all functions of the deployment. As shown in the instantiation of our pattern for the quadratic solver example in Figure 4, the argument considers the termination guarantees of the reconstructor as well as those of each of the generic components. The claim that must be demonstrated is that the guarantee of termination is achieved for each component if the defined constraints on the configuration data are met.

An argument module (Generic Component X) is created for each of the generic components and for the reconstructor. This allows the argument for each component to be reused for different functions. The reconstructor may require small changes for different deployments. A generic component, on the other hand, may be reused, as is, for any deployment. Since it is expected that the generic components are used across different applications, this can provide a large saving in reverification effort.

We omit the pattern for the Configuration Data module; it can be found in [13]. Its argument establishes that the configuration data meets all of the constraints determined within the components argument.

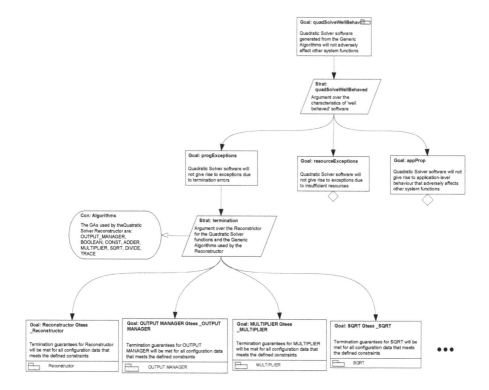

Fig. 4. Quadratic-Solver Assurance Argument: Components Module

We have a separate argument for each function, with the assumption that only one function executes at any time (otherwise combinations of functions need to be considered). This argument structure creates assurance components for function-specific configuration data, and facilitates reuse for particular functions across multiple deployments.

We envisage three strategies that can be adopted to show that the constraints are upheld by the configuration data. First, if the constraints are simple, manual review is possible. This is easy to implement and requires no specialist tools or techniques. It is, however, infeasible for more complex data and constraints, and provides low assurance.

Rather than checking the configuration data, it is possible to consider the process for its generation. A systematic process may begin with an abstract representation of the function (such as a data-flow diagram including the relevant generic components). This abstract model can be verified to check that it is structured to ensure essential properties, like the correct number of parameters are defined for each block. This can also be an effective method of establishing application-level constraints, since it provides a view of the required inputs and outputs as well as an end-to-end view of the components used. The process of transforming that abstract model into configuration data can also be used to enforce constraints on the data. This requires reliable (probably bespoke) tool support and correct encoding of the constraints within the tool.

Finally, it is possible to prove formally that the configuration data satisfies the constraints using SAT (Satisfiability) or SMT (Satisfiability Modulo Theories) solvers. There are a number of tools available that implement such techniques [7]. This has the potential to give the highest available level of assurance. Its feasibility, however, depends on the structure of both the constraints and the configuration data.

4   Termination

In this section, we consider the arguments for well behavedness as defined in the Generic Component X argument module (Figure 5). It illustrates our approach to combining structured argumentation and formal analysis.

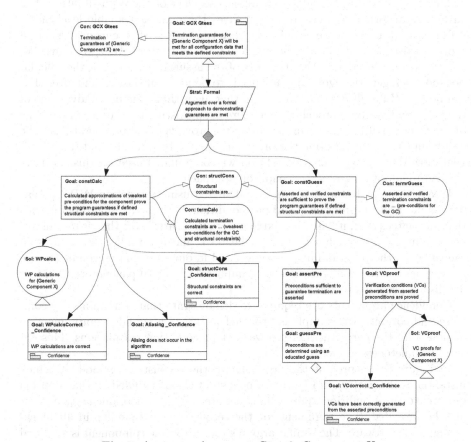

Fig. 5. Assurance Argument: Generic Component X

In arguing termination, a possible approach is to test the components. This requires test cases that provide sufficient coverage of the configuration data. Without unrealistically constraining the configuration data, however, this is extremely difficult. It is possible to use typical data, but extrapolating those test results would not provide much confidence. An alternative would be to test the components every time new configuration data is used. This, however, does not permit reuse of evidence.

In addition, testing gives no indication of the constraints that need to be satisfied, and so no guidance for the definition of configuration data. The constraints can serve as a contract between the software developers and those configuring the software to provide particular functionality.

An alternative is to use formal analysis to prove that the termination guarantees are always met. There are two possibilities: to calculate weakest preconditions that guarantee termination of the components, or assert constraints that are believed to be sufficient and then verify that they guarantee termination. The asserted preconditions can be obtained through an educated guess, based on an understanding of the code.

There are advantages and disadvantages to each of these possibilities. The advantage of formal analysis is that it gives the highest available level of assurance, as it is based on proof. The disadvantage is that currently no tool support exists for calculating the weakest preconditions of Ada programs. We note, however, that due to the structure of the assurance argument, the calculations for each generic algorithm only needs to be performed once, and after that can be reused for all functions requiring that algorithm. The main advantage of the guess-and-verify approach is that there is an existing tool set available - the SPARK toolset [21] - that can generate and prove verification conditions. The disadvantage is that guessing the precondition may be difficult, and there is no guarantee that the correct precondition will be found. Based on this, we have decided to adopt a weakest precondition approach.

Weakest preconditions [8,9] can be calculated using a function $\mathcal{WP}.\mathsf{P}.\psi$ that defines, for a given program P and postcondition ψ, the weakest precondition ϕ that guarantees that, if P is executed in a state that satisfies ϕ, then it terminates and the final state satisfies ψ. The predicates ϕ and ψ establish restrictions on the values of the programming variables, and in our case, the preconditions are restrictions on the configuration data imposed by the implementation. (More details are provided in Section 6.)

Confidence arguments are required to demonstrate that constraints are complete and correct. An example is provided in [13] of a confidence argument to demonstrate the correctness of the weakest precondition calculations. This ensures completeness as well.

In Figure 6, we present the argument in the reconstructor module, which instantiates the pattern in Figure 5. The instantiation is guided by the adoption of a weakest precondition approach. There are confidence arguments that must also be provided. The argument for the reconstructor is similar in all block-configurable software. The similar argument for a specific component is provided in [13]. The argument for the output manager is exactly the same for all block-configurable software.

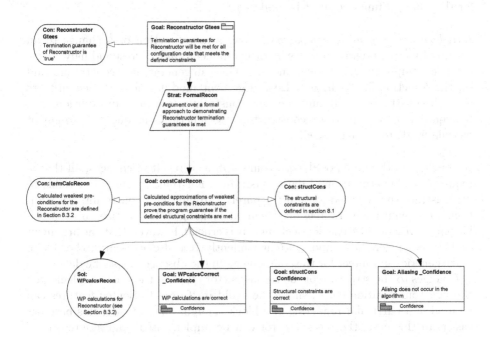

Fig. 6. Quadratic-Solver Assurance Argument: Termination Argument

As shown in Figure 3, the top-level argument requires a Configuration Data module that demonstrates that the constraints are met by all the configuration data. An argument module needs to be created for each set of configuration data. For the quadratic example, we assume that two different sets of configuration data are used by the reconstructor, which, for instance, require a different subset of the equation solutions.

5 Managing Changes to Block-Configurable Software

We consider three of the most likely change scenarios for block-configurable software, and discuss their effect on the assurance argument and evidence.

Add a new function to a deployment. In this scenario, we assume that the new reconstructor only requires the use of the existing generic components. In this case, another Function X Configuration Data module must be created for the new configuration data, and the Configuration Data module must be updated with an additional away goal reference to it.

Modify configuration data for an existing function. Here, the behaviour of a function needs to be modified, but there are no required changes to generic components. In this case, only the existing Function X Configuration Data module for the changed function must be updated.

Introduce a new generic component. Now, a new function or a change to an existing function requires a new generic component, and, correspondingly, a new Generic Component X argument module. This can generate new constraints, and so, the Function X Configured Data argument modules need to demonstrate that all constraints, including the new constraints, are met. In addition, due to required changes to the reconstructor, its Generic Component X argument module needs to be reassessed.

In conclusion, the best possible outcome is if, as a result of changes, all that is required is a reverification of data constraints. For that, it must be possible to demonstrate the required guarantees purely through data constraints. In addition, these required guarantees must remain unchanged. In practice, this is possible only in restricted scenarios of change. It is crucial, however, that the argument considers each generic component independently. It is also necessary to be able to make generic guarantees for the components in the absence of specific data.

Changes to the structure of the reconstructor (that is, those not implemented through configuration data), should be avoided. If object-oriented features can be used in a particular rendering of a block-configurable software, this becomes easier. In this case, the reconstructor can be implemented (and assured) once and for all, in terms of an abstract class that captures a generic interface for a component.

6   Validity of Configuration Data

There are different sources and kinds of constraints. Structural constraints derive from the way the block-configurable software is designed. These constraints are mostly independent of the particular application for which the software is used (except in the definition of the particular data types used in the generic components).

We have formalised the structural constraints using Z [18,1]. Our Z data model is the same for all deployments of block-configurable software, except only for the data types of the generic components. Changes are, therefore, only needed if different components are considered, and, in any case, the modelling effort required is small, since the data types are just records that can be directly represented in Z.

Our model ignores the use of pointers. For the quadratic solver, we have an Ada implementation where access types are used just to allow the use of unconstrained array types in a way that ensures absence of aliasing. In general, we need a technique to ensure that aliasing does not occur. This is addressed by a structured argument as shown in Figure 5.

To illustrate how we model the data types of generic components, we show below the model for the **ADDER** component of the quadratic solver. It is a straightforward translation of the Ada code to Z. The **DATA_PACKET_TYPE** is a record (schema) that includes the parameter and the components of the Ada record. The predicate (invariant) of the schema defines the range restriction in the declaration of the type.

$$
\begin{array}{l}
\rule{0.3cm}{0.4pt}\ RECONSTRUCTOR\_ADDER\_DATA\_PACKET\_TYPE \rule{0.6cm}{0.4pt} \\
\quad INPUT\_SIZE : POSITIVE\_WORD\_TYPE \\
\quad INPUT\_SCALING : PARAMETER\_ARRAY\_TYPE \\
\rule{7cm}{0.4pt} \\
\quad \#\ INPUT\_SCALING = INPUT\_SIZE
\end{array}
$$

Other constants, which define inputs and an identifier for the generic component, are also defined by a direct translation of the code.

More interesting is the model of the **OUTPUT_MANAGER**, which embodies the structures that allow the data configuration. This model, except in its dependency on the definitions of the *DATA_PACKET_TYPE* schemas for each of the generic components, is the same for all deployments. This is the most complex part of the model, but since the output manager is a generic component, what we have is a *DATA_PACKET_TYPE* record.

$$
\begin{array}{l}
\rule{0.3cm}{0.4pt}\ RECONSTRUCTOR\_O\_M\_DATA\_PACKET\_TYPE \rule{0.6cm}{0.4pt} \\
\quad OUTPUT\_MANAGER\_DATA : O\_M\_DATA\_TYPE \\
\rule{7cm}{0.4pt}
\end{array}
$$

The *O_M_DATA_TYPE*, however, is a record with six components that define the size of the output vector, the vector of outputs actually provided and its size, and the dependencies between the outputs and inputs. The Z model for it and all the quadratic solver components is in [13].

The configuration data is an array of *DATA_PACKET_TYPE* records.

$$
\begin{array}{c}
CONFIGURATION\_DATA\_TYPE == \\
ARRAY\,[POSITIVE\_WORD\_TYPE, \\
RECONSTRUCTOR\_DATA\_PACKET\_TYPE]
\end{array}
$$

The instantiation of this model for a particular deployment defines the type *RECONSTRUCTOR_DATA_PACKET_TYPE*, which aggregates the possible *DATA_PACKET_TYPE* records used in the components. We calculate the weakest precondition of the reconstructor, which restricts the values of a record *CONTRACT* that includes a component of type *CONFIGURATION_DATA_TYPE*, and two others to represent the input and a selection of outputs.

There may also be domain constraints on inputs that arise in the area of application. They typically restrict the range of the values of the inputs (for example, height, speed, and so on). For our example, we require that the first coefficient of the equation is different from 0, otherwise it is not a quadratic equation. It is necessary to prove that any configuration data to be used satisfies the programming and structural constraints. For that, domain constraints can be assumed to hold. This is demonstrated in the Configuration Data argument module.

To calculate weakest preconditions, we define the function $\mathcal{WP}(S).\psi$, and consider the postcondition **True**. The definition of $\mathcal{WP}(S).\psi$ is mostly standard, except that we consider that expressions can raise exceptions and prevent proper termination. We, therefore, use auxiliary functions that determine when a expression or a command terminates. Definitions are provided in [13], along with calculations for the quadratic solver.

A significant part of those calculations, namely, the treatment of the reconstructor and the output manager, is reusable, and does not need to be revisited for other software. In addition, as long as the components terminate, the calculation of the weakest precondition is compositional: if a component is added, it can be considered in isolation, and no recalculation is needed. This is despite the fact that the components can be enlisted by the reconstructor in any order.

7   Related Work

As far as we know, there has not been a lot of work on assuring software whose behaviour is configured using data. There are results on validating the data used in systems that use large quantities of data to perform their function [14,10] and on safety-related information systems [17]. They describe specification and verification techniques for data, but do not consider systems whose flow of execution is itself determined by data.

Calculation of weakest preconditions is a demanding task; an automated calculator is essential to make it practical and scalable. To our knowledge, there are almost no tools that can handle realistic languages and their types, except perhaps Java [2]. The extension of a tool like that in [4] to handle a safe language is, therefore, an interesting problem.

Weakest preconditions are the basis of the calculator in [4], which is implemented using the HOL theorem prover [11]. The simple imperative language considered includes recursive procedures; all HOL types are available. A similar calculator is described in [16], but it uses weakest liberal preconditions, which cannot be used to reason about termination.

Termination is also not treated in the more recent approach to invariant calculation in the tool in [15]. Their idea of using patterns of programs to identify invariants, on the other hand, merits further investigation. Given the constrained nature of block-configurable software, it may well be possible to identify a catalogue of program patterns and associated invariants to afford automation.

Availability of tool support is a strong point of the assert-and-verify approach, which is a clear alternative to the technique explored here. For Ada, the SPARK tools merit further investigation to assess automation. For C, the C verifier VCC [5] handles annotated concurrent programs.

Our work is concerned with a component-based verification and assurance technique. Work in this area has typically concentrated on the definition of languages for component connectors, and associated compositional techniques. For example, the approach in [20] advocates verification by model checking in a framework called X-MAN. The work in [19], on the other hand, considers object-oriented models and can be a good basis for description of our work. It is possible that we can specify the block-configurable architecture in the languages for components considered in these works to take advantage of their results for the generation of evidence. We have here, however, dealt directly with (Ada) programs, rather than a high-level modelling language. In addition, these works have not covered the construction of assurance arguments like we do here.

8   Conclusions

We have described how assurance cases can be created for block-configurable software. Our approach maximises resilience of arguments and evidence to expected changes, and enables the build up of reusable assurance-case modules for both components and configuration data. To provide evidence of termination, we have explored the use of weakest preconditions to determine the required constraints. Simple modelling and clearly prescribed adaptations are needed when the set of components changes.

The assurance case demonstrates that the software is "well behaved", by which we mean that the software does not adversely affect the rest of the system. We have identified that the notions of interest for "well behavedness" are related to termination, resources, and exceptions. In this paper we have only considered the argument made for termination. In [13], however, we also explore the arguments for resources and exceptions.

An accurate comparison between the assurance effort entailed by conventional and by block-configurable software is difficult. There is some additional effort required for a block-configurable software. Firstly, the constraints must be determined, but this is offset if a formal approach is used as testing for the particular properties needed in the assurance case is not required. Secondly, the configuration data must be verified. This is expected to be a simple task for the anticipated constraints, and the effort should, therefore, be less than is involved in testing.

For a conventional application, adding new functions requires changes to the code, and the entire program must, therefore, be reverified. For block-configurable software it is required only that the configuration data for the new functions is verified. It is when new functions are integrated into the system that savings in the assurance effort are realised.

A major drawback is the absence of tools to support weakest precondition calculations. This technique can be used to produce evidence for any functional property that can be specified by a postcondition. As we consider more elaborate properties, however, automation becomes more difficult. It is possible to use approximations like in [3]. In this case, we can ensure that invalid data is rejected, but valid data may also be rejected.

Acknowledgements. We are grateful to Jane Fenn for her support.

References

1. ISO/IEC 13568:2002. Information technology—Z formal specification notation—syntax, type system and semantics. International Standard
2. Barthe, G., Burdy, L., Charles, J., Grégoire, B., Huisman, M., Lanet, J.-L., Pavlova, M.I., Requet, A.: JACK - A Tool for Validation of Security and Behaviour of Java Applications. In: de Boer, F.S., Bonsangue, M.M., Graf, S., de Roever, W.-P. (eds.) FMCO 2006. LNCS, vol. 4709, pp. 152–174. Springer, Heidelberg (2007)
3. Cavalcanti, A.L.C., King, S., O'Halloran, C., Woodcock, J.C.P.: Test-Data Generation for Control Coverage by Proof. In: Formal Aspects of Computing (2013), doi:10.1007/s00165-013-0279-2 (online first)
4. Cavalcanti, A.L.C., Woodcock, J.C.P.: A Weakest Precondition Semantics for Circus. In: Communicating Processing Architectures 2002. IOS Press (2002)
5. Cohen, E., Dahlweid, M., Hillebrand, M., Leinenbach, D., Moskal, M., Santen, T., Schulte, W., Tobies, S.: VCC: A Practical System for Verifying Concurrent C. In: Berghofer, S., Nipkow, T., Urban, C., Wenzel, M. (eds.) TPHOLs 2009. LNCS, vol. 5674, pp. 23–42. Springer, Heidelberg (2009)
6. GSN Standardisation Committee. GSN community standard (November 2011)
7. de Moura, L., Bjørner, N.: Satisfiability modulo theories: introduction and applications. Communications of the ACM 54(9), 69–77 (2011)
8. Dijkstra, E.W.: A Discipline of Programming. Prentice-Hall (1976)
9. Dijkstra, E.W., Scholten, C.S.: Predicate Calculus and Program Semantics. Texts and Monographs in Computer Science. Springer (1989)
10. Faulkner, A.G., Bennett, P.A., Pierce, R.H., Johnston, I.H.A., Storey, N.: The Safety Management of Data-Driven Safety-Related Systems. In: Koornneef, F., van der Meulen, M.J.P. (eds.) SAFECOMP 2000. LNCS, vol. 1943, pp. 86–95. Springer, Heidelberg (2000)
11. Gordon, M.J.C., Melham, T.F. (eds.): Introduction to HOL: A Theorem Proving Environment for Higher Order Logic. Cambridge University Press (1993)
12. Object Management Group. Structured assurance case metamodel (SACM). OMG Standard Document, 2013. OMG Document Number: formal/2013-02-01
13. Hawkins, R., Miyazawa, A., Cavalcanti, A.L.C., Kelly, T., Rowlands, J.: Assurance Cases for Data-configured Software. Technical report, University of York, Department of Computer Science, York, UK (2014),
   http://www-users.cs.york.ac.uk/~rhawkins/HMCKR14.pdf
14. Knight, J.C., Strunk, E.A., Greenwell, W.S., Wasson, K.S.: Specification and Analysis of Data for Safety-Critical Systems. In: ISSC (2004)
15. Mraihi, O., Ghardallou, W., Louhichi, A., Labed Jilani, L., Bsaies, K., Mili, A.: Computing preconditions and postconditions of while loops. In: Cerone, A., Pihlajasaari, P. (eds.) ICTAC 2011. LNCS, vol. 6916, pp. 173–193. Springer, Heidelberg (2011)
16. Nipkow, T.: Winskel is (almost) Right: Towards a Mechanized Semantics. Formal Aspects of Computing 10(2), 171–186 (1998)
17. Tillotson, J.: System safety and management information systems. In: Redmill, F., Anderson, T. (eds.) Aspects of Safety Management, pp. 13–34. Springer (2001)

18. Woodcock, J.C.P., Davies, J.: Using Z—Specification, Refinement, and Proof. Prentice-Hall (1996)
19. Broy, M.: A core theory of interfaces and architecture and its impact on object orientation. In: Reussner, R., Stafford, J.A., Ren, X.-M. (eds.) Architecting Systems. LNCS, vol. 3938, pp. 26–47. Springer, Heidelberg (2006)
20. Lau, K.-K., Tran, C.M.: X-man: An mde tool for component-based system development. In: 39th Euromicro Conference on Software Engineering and Advanced Applications, pp. 158–165 (2012)
21. Barnes, J.: High Integrity Software: The SPARK Approach to Safety and Security. Addison-Wesley (2003)

Generation of Safety Case Argument-Fragments from Safety Contracts

Irfan Sljivo, Barbara Gallina, Jan Carlson, and Hans Hansson

Mälardalen Real-Time Research Centre, Mälardalen University,
Västerås, Sweden
{irfan.sljivo,barbara.gallina,jan.carlson,hans.hansson}@mdh.se

Abstract. Composable safety certification envisions reuse of safety case argument-fragments together with safety-relevant components in order to reduce the cost and time needed to achieve certification. The argument-fragments could cover safety aspects relevant for different contexts in which the component can be used. Creating argument-fragments for the out-of-context components is time-consuming and currently no satisfying approach exists to facilitate their automatic generation. In this paper we propose an approach based on (semi-)automatic generation of argument-fragments from assumption/guarantee safety contracts. We use the contracts to capture the safety claims related to the component, including supporting evidence. We provide an overview of the argument-fragment architecture and rules for automatic generation, including their application in an illustrative example. The proposed approach enables safety engineers to focus on increasing the confidence in the knowledge about the system, rather than documenting a safety case.

Keywords: Safety Case Argument-fragments, (Semi-)automatic Generation, Safety Contracts, Composable Certification, Out-of-context Components.

1 Introduction

The cost for achieving certification is estimated at 25-75% of the development costs [16]. As a part of certification, a safety case in form of a structured argument is often required to show that the system is acceptably safe to operate. To reduce cost and time-to-market, more and more safety standards are offering support for reuse within safety cases. Safety Element out of Context (SEooC) is an example of a concept for reuse proposed by the automotive ISO 26262 standard [12]. Building on such reusable elements, an approach to composable certification has been proposed [5]. The approach aims at achieving incremental certification by composing reusable argument-fragments related to safety elements, whose behaviour is specified through safety contracts. We define argument-fragments as parts of the system safety argument that argue about safety aspects relevant for the individual components.

In our previous work [15] we developed a safety contract formalism to facilitate reuse of components developed out-of-context. The safety contracts capture

A. Bondavalli and F. Di Giandomenico (Eds.): SAFECOMP 2014, LNCS 8666, pp. 170–185, 2014.
© Springer International Publishing Switzerland 2014

safety-relevant behaviours of the components in assumption/guarantee pairs. The semantics of such a pair is that if the assumption holds then the guarantee will also hold. The assumption/guarantee pairs are characterised as being either strong or weak. The strong contract assumptions are required to be satisfied in all contexts in which the component is used, hence the strong guarantees are offered in every context in which the component can be used. On the other hand, the weak contract guarantees are only offered in the contexts in which the component can be used and that satisfy the corresponding weak assumptions.

The strong and weak contracts allow us to distinguish between properties that hold for all contexts and those that are context-specific. Since every context has specific safety requirements, argument-fragments for out-of-context components may partially cover safety aspects relevant for several contexts. Creating argument-fragments for components developed out-of-context is a time-consuming activity. (Semi-)automatic generation of such argument-fragments from safety contracts would speed up the activity and allow for generation of context-specific argument-fragments. Moreover, the safety engineers would have the possibility to focus on increasing the confidence in the knowledge about the system, rather then on clerical tasks such as documenting a safety case [13].

Currently, no satisfying approach exists that facilitates generation of argument-fragments for out-of-context components. The main contribution of this paper is that we propose such an approach, capable to (semi)automatically generate argument-fragments from safety contracts and related safety requirements and evidence. As the basis for our approach we developed a meta-model that captures relationships between the safety contracts, safety requirements and evidence. To support the generation of argument-fragments from the safety contracts we provide conceptual mapping between the meta-model and argumentation notation elements. To perform the generation we provide the resulting argument-fragment architecture and a set of rules to generate the argument-fragments.

We demonstrate our approach on a Fuel Level Estimation System (FLES) and its variants that are used within Scania's trucks and busses. We focus on a single component of FLES that estimates the fuel level in the tank. This component represents a good candidate to be developed as SEooC as it is used with slight variations in many different variants. We use the safety contracts not only to capture the knowledge we have about the behaviour of the component, but also the evidence supporting the guaranteed behaviour. Moreover, by connecting in-context safety requirements with the weak safety contracts that address the requirements, we enable only those safety properties of the component relevant for the particular context to be used when developing the argument-fragment. This allows us to support more efficient creation of the argument-fragments as well as generation of context-specific arguments that contain information relevant for the context in which the component is used.

Compared to existing works, we focus on generation of argument-fragments for components developed and prepared for safety certification independently of the system in which they will be used. Approaches to generating safety case arguments [9, 3] usually extract the necessary information to build an argument from artefacts provided to satisfy some process, e.g., mandated by a safety standard. In our approach we utilise the safety contracts to capture the necessary information about a component from artefacts obtained out-of-context and show how argument-fragments can be generated for such components.

The structure of the paper is as follows: In Section 2 we present background information. In Section 3 we present the rationale behind our approach and how the generation of argument-fragments can be performed. In Section 4 we illustrate the approach for the Fuel Level Estimation System, and in Section 5 we provide a discussion of our approach. We present the related work in Section 6, and conclusions and future work in Section 7.

2   Background

In this section we introduce FLES that we use to illustrate our approach. We also provide some brief information on safety contracts based on our previous work; and Goal Structuring Notation, the argumentation notation we use for documenting safety case argument-fragments.

2.1   Illustrative Example: The Fuel Level Estimation System

In this subsection, based on [8], we provide brief but essential information related to FLES and the hazard analysis performed on it. We limit our attention to some bits of information that we use in illustrating the generation of argument-fragments.

FLES is based on a real estimation system used in Scania trucks with liquid fuel. The component-based architecture of FLES is shown in Fig. 1. The *Estimator* component estimates the volume of fuel in a vehicle's tank based on the sensor data obtained from the *Fuel Tank* and the *Engine Management System* (EMS). The received sensor values go through a series of transformations and filtering to handle any fluctuations in the sensed fuel level value. The estimated value is converted into percentage, passed to the *Presenter* and presented to the driver of the vehicle through the *Fuel Gauge* mounted on the dashboard. Due to dependencies of the transformations to the physical properties of sensors and its environment (e.g., size of the tank), these parameters are made configurable to make *Estimator* usable in different variants of the system.

The hazard analysis performed on the system reveals that if the fuel level displayed on the fuel gauge is higher than the actual fuel level in the tank then the vehicle could run out of fuel without the driver noticing, which would cause a sudden engine stop. If this happens while driving on e.g., a highway, the consequences could be catastrophic. Although there are other hazards in the system, this is the only hazard we use in illustrating our approach.

The safety analysis, as recommended by ISO 26262, starts by identifying at least one Safety Goal (SG) for each hazard, then for every safety goal, corresponding Functional Safety Requirements (FSRs) are derived and finally, Technical Safety Requirements (TSRs) are derived from the FSRs. We consider the following SGl and derived FSR:

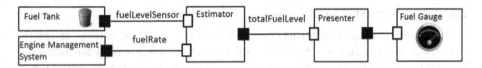

Fig. 1. Fuel Level Estimation System

- *SG1*: FLES shall not show higher fuel level on the fuel gauge than the actual fuel in the vehicle's tank;
- *FSR1*: Estimator shall not provide value of the estimated fuel level that deviates more than -5% from the actual fuel-level in the tank.

Additionally, the engine status signal provided by EMS should not be older than 0.3 seconds. An older value could result in a too high deviation from the actual fuel consumption that may cause deviation in the estimated fuel level value.

2.2   Strong and Weak Contracts

Our extension of the traditional contract-based formalism with strong and weak contracts allows for distinguishing between properties that are context-specific and properties that must hold for all contexts [14].

A traditional assumption/guarantee contract $C = \langle A, G \rangle$ is composed of assumptions A and guarantees G, where a component offers the guarantees G if its assumptions A on its environment are satisfied [6]. As an illustrative and simplified example based on the system we presented in Section 2.1, we specify a contract for Estimator with assumptions that if both the fuel level and fuel rate are provided with sufficient accuracy, Estimator guarantees that the total estimated fuel level it provides will be with certain accuracy.

Strong contracts $\langle A, G \rangle$ are composed of strong assumptions (A) and strong guarantees (G), and weak contracts $\langle B, H \rangle$ of weak assumptions (B) and weak guarantees (H) [15]. While strong assumptions must hold in order for a component to be used in any context, weak assumptions and guarantees just provide additional information for particular contexts. We say that a component, described by a set of safety contracts, is compatible with a certain context if all of its strong assumptions are satisfied by the environment. The weak contracts ensure that in all compatible contexts where the weak assumptions (B) are satisfied, the component offers the weak guarantees (H). For example, strong contracts could assume input type, range, or minimum amount of stack required and guarantee similar properties. On the other hand, weak contracts assume configurable parameters such as tank or sensor parameters in FLES and guarantee different behaviour of the component dependant on those parameters such as different accuracy of the output or specific timing behaviour.

2.3 Goal Structuring Notation

In this paper, we use Goal Structuring Notation (GSN) [2] for expressing safety case argument-fragments. GSN is a graphical argumentation notation that can be used to specify elements of any argument. Some of the basic elements of GSN are illustrated in Fig. 2 and their semantics is given in the following list:

- *Goal*: a claim or a sub-claim that should be supported by the underlying argument. It can be broken down to several sub-goals (sub-claims).
- *Strategy*: describes a method used to develop a goal into additional sub-goals.
- *Context*: represents the domain/scope of the element it is connected to.
- *Solution*: describes the evidence that the connected goal has been achieved.
- *Undeveloped element*: states that the element to which the symbol is attached requires further development.
- *InContextOf*: used to connect context with goals.
- *SupportedBy*: used to show relationship of inference between goals in the argument, or to show that certain evidence is supporting a goal.
- *Away goal*: used to specify a module in which the goal is further developed.

For the sake of clarity it must be noted that the context element can be used to simply enrich or clarify the statements of the elements it is connected to. Besides the basic symbols, we additionally use a notational extension that supports abstract argument patterns [2]. More specifically, to denote a variable we use the curly brackets within statements; to denote generalised n-ary relationships between GSN elements we use the *supportedBy* relationship with a solid circle; to denote a choice, either 1-of-n or m-of-n selection, we use a solid diamond, which can be paired, using a simple connector line, with an *Obligation* element represented by an octagon symbol, stating condition for the choice selection.

Fig. 2. Basic elements of the Goal Structuring Notation

3 Composable Arguments Generation

The aim of this section is twofold: (1) to explain the rationale underlying our approach to (semi)automatic generation of argument-fragments, and (2) to explain how the generation can be performed. The latter is done by

- providing a component meta-model, developed to capture the relationships between the safety contracts, safety requirements and evidence in an out-of-context setting, and being sufficient to provide us with the information required for argument-fragment generation,
- presenting a conceptual mapping of the meta-model elements to a subset of the basic GSN elements to provide better understanding of the transition from the meta-model to the argument-fragment,

- presenting an overview of the argument-fragment architecture, and by
- providing a set of rules for the argumentation-fragment generation.

3.1 Rationale of the Approach

In our work we focus on safety-relevant components developed and prepared for safety certification independently of the system in which they will be used. To develop such components, the engineer must assume some safety requirements that might be required when the component is used in a context. To prepare components for certification, safety engineers need to capture safety-relevant properties of the component that show how the safety requirements allocated to the component are met. To do that, we use our notion of strong and weak contracts.

It is worth to point out that the safety requirements and the safety contracts we use are closely related, but not the same. The safety contracts contain information about the actual behaviour of the component. On the other hand, the safety requirements contain information about what a particular context/system requires from the component. While the safety requirements vary between contexts, the safety contracts should be correct regardless of the context. This is important to enable reuse of out-of-context components. As an illustration, consider FLES example requirement "Estimator shall send a valid value in totalFuelLevel within 2 seconds from when the Electronic Control Unit starts". This is a requirement on Estimator in this particular context and should not be specified within the Estimator's safety contract in that form. In the safety contract we should rather specify the actual time Estimator needs to send the totalFuelLevel. This makes the contracts independent of the context in which out-of-context component can be used, which allows us to use the knowledge captured within the contracts for all contexts in which the contracts are satisfied. The strong contracts denote properties that must be argued about in argument-fragments for every context, while the weak contracts will be argued about only if associated with a safety requirement within a particular context.

In order to guarantee the actual behaviour of the component, as specified in the safety contracts, we need to provide evidence about confidence in the contract. We categorise the evidence that supports the confidence in the contracts in terms of completeness, correctness and consistency, as follows: (1) completeness refers to whether contracts have captured all the needed properties of the component and the environment, (2) correctness refers to whether the contracts are correct with respect to associated requirements and (3) consistency refers to whether the contracts are not contradicting each other.

When using an out-of-context component in a particular context, a set of actual safety requirements (e.g., FSR or TSR) is allocated to the component. One of the roles of an argument-fragment is to show that these requirements are met. As safety contracts can be used to address different types of requirements, we are developing our approach without focusing on a particular class of requirements.

The (semi)automatic generation of argument-fragments from the safety contracts enables us to reduce the effort safety engineers need to dedicate for creating a set of argument-fragments. These fragments could be created for several

contexts in which the component could be used. By speeding up both the integrator's and the developer's activities related to documenting a safety case, we
enable them to focus on activities related to their knowledge about the system,
by capturing this knowledge in the safety contracts.

3.2   Component Meta-Model

Our component meta-model in Fig. 3 is presented as an UML class diagram. This
diagram captures the relationships between the assumed requirements, safety
contracts and evidence, as described in Section 3.1. Our meta-model is based on
the SafeCer component meta-model [7], which we have adapted, focusing only
on its out-of-context part. Instead of associating argument-fragments (that may
contain information not relevant for a specific context) with a component, we
associate evidence and safety requirements directly with contracts to facilitate
generation of context-specific argument-fragments.

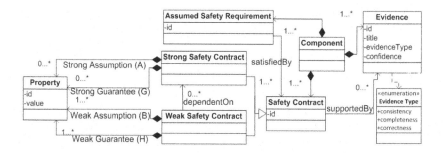

Fig. 3. Component and safety contract meta-model

The meta-model specifies a component that is composed of safety contracts,
evidence and the assumed safety requirements. Each assumed safety requirement
is satisfied by at least one safety contract, and each safety contract can have
supporting evidence. Additionally, we assume that there is at least one evidence
provided with the component supporting the consistency of the contracts. The
safety contract elements in the meta-model are covering both the strong and
weak safety contracts explained in Section 2.2. It should be noted that, based
on the SafeCer component meta-model, the components can be composite i.e.,
a set of interconnected subcomponents, and can represent a (sub)system.

3.3   Conceptual Mapping of the Component Meta-Model to GSN

As mentioned in Section 2.3, GSN is used for documenting safety cases by expressing arguments and supporting evidence to show that the safety claims are
satisfied. At the same time, as described in Section 3.2, our component meta-
model captures the component safety claims in the safety contracts, supported

by the associated evidence, with the goal to argue the satisfaction of the safety requirements. The conceptual mapping between the meta-model and GSN is depicted in Table 1.

Table 1. Conceptual mapping between the meta-model and GSN elements

The component meta-model elements	GSN-elements
Properties representing guarantee(s) Assumed safety requirement(s)	Goals
Evidence	Solutions
Properties representing assumption(s)	Contexts

In order to build an argument structure from the safety contracts, we need to map the meta-model elements to the GSN elements. Our aim is to, based on our meta-model, develop an argument-fragment that addresses the following:

1. *Compatibility of a component with a context*: to show satisfaction of strong contracts of the component by the context, as described in Section 2.2. Besides satisfaction, confidence in contracts needs to be addressed using associated evidence.
2. *Satisfaction of safety requirements*: to show that a safety requirement is satisfied we need to argue both, that weak contracts related to the safety requirement are satisfied, and that the set of the related contracts is sufficient to show that the requirement is satisfied.
3. *Confidence in contracts*: showing only that a contract is satisfied by a context is not enough. Evidence about confidence in the contract should be provided also. We provide evidence about confidence in contracts in terms of completeness, correctness and consistency as described in Section 3.1.

The satisfaction of a contract, as described in Section 2.2, means that the contract guarantees are offered. Consequently, properties representing the safety contract guarantees in the meta-model as well as the assumed safety requirements correspond to goals in GSN. Furthermore, we use evidence from the meta-model related to consistency, correctness and completeness as solutions within GSN. To clarify the context of our goals, we make context statements providing properties representing the assumptions of the safety contracts.

3.4 Overview of the Architecture of the Resulting Argument-Fragment

Given the meta-model in Section 3.2, we propose to generate the resulting argument-fragment based on the mapping provided in Section 3.3.

In the argumentation-fragment generation we will follow a pattern that for a component, say x, with a top-level goal, say $G1$, in a series of successive steps will generate the corresponding argumentation fragment. We start by decomposing the goal $G1$ into three sub-goals, as shown in Fig. 4. We first argue satisfaction of all the strong contracts of x in the goal $G2$. Then, we provide evidence for the consistency of all the contracts associated with x in the goal $G4$ and finally, we argue over satisfaction of the requirements by the related contracts in the goal $G3$. We now further develop the goal $G3$ and leave the goals $G2$ and $G4$ undeveloped, as they will be explored later.

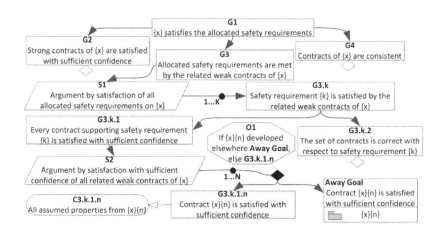

Fig. 4. Safety requirements satisfaction goal sub-structure

We further develop the goal $G3$ by applying the strategy $S1$ to argue over satisfaction of all safety requirement allocated to component x. For every safety requirement $k \in [1, K]$ where K is the number of allocated requirements, a goal $G3.k$ is created, stating satisfaction of the requirement by the related contracts. We further break down the $G3.k$ goal into two sub-goals: (1) $G3.k.1$ arguing over satisfaction of every supporting contract of the requirement k, and (2) $G3.k.2$ providing associated evidence that the related safety contracts supporting the safety requirement k are correct with respect to the requirement. We first focus on the $G3.k.1$ goal, and leave the $G3.k.2$ goal undeveloped, as it will be explored together with other parts of the argument referring to evidence.

When arguing over satisfaction with sufficient confidence of a set of contracts, we use the same strategy whether we argue over all the strong contracts ($G2$) or the weak contracts that support the safety requirements. To further develop the $G3.k.1$ goal, we apply the strategy $S2$ to argue over satisfaction with sufficient confidence over every related contract and reach the choice represented by obligation $O1$. If a goal has been developed elsewhere to support a contract n we create an away goal, otherwise we create a goal $G3.k.1.n$ for every contract n arguing over its satisfaction, where $n \in [1, N]$, with N being the number of related contracts to the requirement k. In order to further clarify the goal $G3.k.1.n$ we provide assumed properties of the contract n as a goal context.

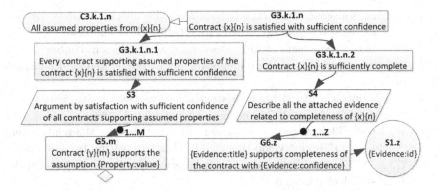

Fig. 5. Contract satisfaction with confidence goal sub-structure

As shown in Fig. 5, to argue that a safety contract n is satisfied with sufficient confidence we break down the goal $G3.k.1.n$ into two sub-goals: (1) $G3.k.1.n.1$ arguing over satisfaction of every safety contract m that supports the assumed properties of the contract n, where $m \in [1, M]$ and M is the number of contracts supporting the contract n, and (2) $G3.k.1.n.2$ providing attached evidence about the completeness of contract n. We further develop the goal $G3.k.1.n.1$ by applying the strategy $S3$ to argue over satisfaction of every supporting contract m and create a sub-goal $G5.m$ arguing that the corresponding assumed property of the contract n is satisfied by the supporting contract m. To develop the goal $G5.m$ we apply the same strategy as for the goal $G3.k.1$.

For developing the three arguments that present the attached evidence related to completeness, correctness and consistency, represented by the goals $G3.k.1.n.2$, $G3.k.2$ and $G4$, we develop the argument inspired by the "Specification Argument Pattern" [4]. Unlike in that work, we define the three types of evidence differently, as described in Section 3.1. The goal $G3.k.1.n.2$ is developed by applying a strategy $S4$ to argue over every attached evidence of the specific type. For every evidence a goal is created claiming with what level of confidence does this goal support the completeness/consistency/correctness and the evidence reference is provided as the solution to the goal.

3.5 Rules for Generation of Component Argument-Fragments

Given the argument structure in Section 3.4 and the component meta-model we can define a sequence of transformation rules that facilitate (semi)automatic generation of argument-fragments. Our goal is not only to transfer all the information provided by the safety contracts into the argument-fragment, but also to point out the goals that need further development and thus alert safety managers. For this we use undeveloped goals within the argument-fragments. We provide the rules similarly as in [9]. We create an argument-fragment for a component x by using the following rules:

R1. Create the top-level goal $G1$: "$\{x\}$ satisfies the allocated safety requirements". Develop the goal $G1$ further by creating three sub-goals:
   (a) $G2$: "Strong contracts of $\{x\}$ are satisfied with sufficient confidence".
   (b) $G3$: "Allocated safety requirements are met by the related weak contracts of $\{x\}$".
   (c) $G4$: "Contracts of $\{x\}$ are consistent".

R2. Further develop the goal $G3$ and for every allocated safety requirement k create a goal $G3.k$ "Safety requirement $\{k\}$ is satisfied by the related weak contracts of $\{x\}$" and develop this goal further by creating two sub-goals:
   (a) $G3.k.1$: "Every contract supporting safety requirement $\{k\}$ is satisfied with sufficient confidence".
   (b) $G3.k.2$: "The set of contracts is correct with respect to safety requirement $\{k\}$".

R3. Further develop the goal $G3.k.1$ by developing an argument for every safety contract n of the component x, associated with the safety requirement k. If the contract satisfaction module is developed elsewhere in the argument provide an away goal, otherwise create a sub-goal $G3.k.1.n$ "Contract $\{x\}\{n\}$ is satisfied with sufficient confidence" and provide properties representing the assumptions of the contract $\{n\}$ as the goal context $C3.k.1.n$. Further develop the sub-goal:
   (a) $G3.k.1.n.1$: "Every contract supporting assumed properties of the contract $\{x\}\{n\}$ is satisfied with sufficient confidence". For every contract m supporting the assumed property p of the contract n create a sub-goal $G5.m$: "Contract $\{y\}\{m\}$ supports the assumption $\{p\}$ ", where m is specified for a component in environment of x, say y.
   (b) $G3.k.1.n.2$: "Contract $\{x\}\{n\}$ is sufficiently complete".

R4. The goal $G5.m$ is developed further in the same way as $G3.k.1$ and the goal $G2$ is developed further in the same way as the goal $G3.k.1.n$.

R5. Goals $G3.k.1.n.2$, $G3.k.2$ and $G4$ are developed further in the same way for the list of attached evidence of the corresponding type, respectively, completeness, correctness and consistency. For every evidence z from the corresponding list of evidence type:
   (a) Create a goal $G6.z$: "$\{Evidence : title\}$ supports $\{EvidenceType\}$ of the contract with $\{Evidence : confidence\}$".
   (b) Attach a solution $S1.z$ to the goal $G6.z$ with $Evidence : id$ as reference.

R6. If no evidence of a particular type is provided, an undeveloped goal is used to indicate that the goal should be further developed.

It should be noted that, based on Rule $R4$, we can generate argument-fragments for a composite component by iterating through hierarchical structure. Applying the rules to an out-of-context component will generate an incomplete argument-fragment since not all relevant claims can be captured out-of-context. Such claims are left undeveloped, e.g., correctness of contracts with respect to a safety requirement. Hence further development of the argument-fragment is required to address all the undeveloped claims.

4   Argument-Fragment for FLES

In this section we provide safety contracts for the Estimator and EMS components of FLES, as well as show the generation of an argument-fragment for Estimator.

Table 2. Safety contracts for the Estimator component

A1: fuelLevelSensor within [0,5] AND fuelRate within [-1,3212]
G1: totalFuelLevel within $[-1, 100]$
E$_{A1,G1}$: Sw architecture design specification, Sw architecture verification report
B1: (fuelLevelSensor within correct range AND fuelLevelSensor does not deviate more than 10% from the actual fuel level value AND fuelLevelSensorParameter=10) OR (fuelRate within [0,3212] AND fuelRate does not deviate more than 1% from the actual engine consumption value AND Tank size within [230-1000])
H1: totalFuelLevel does not deviate more than -1% from the actual fuel level value
E$_{B1,H1}$: Simulation of the Estimator component under assumed conditions

4.1   The Safety Contracts

The strong and weak contracts for Estimator addressing the requirement $FSR1$ of FLES are shown in Table 2. The strong contract assumes the allowed ranges of inputs and guarantees the possible outputs of the component. The evidence supporting the completeness of strong contract $\langle A1, G1 \rangle$ includes the software architecture design specification and the corresponding verification report.

As described in Section 2.1, the quality of the totalFuelLevel output of the Estimator component is dependent on relevant parameters and the quality of inputs. The weak contract $\langle B1, H1 \rangle$ of Estimator guarantees that the deviation of the totalFuelLevel from the actual fuel level is less than or equal to -1% if assumptions on either fuelLevelSensor and parameters related to it, or fuelRate and parameters related to it, are satisfied. The corresponding evidence is obtained by simulation of Estimator under the assumed conditions, and the simulation report is attached as evidence supporting the contract completeness.

The EMS component safety contracts related to the Estimator component are provided in Table 3. The EMS strong contract is similar to the one for the Estimator component, ensuring the input and output port ranges. The weak contract $\langle B2, H2 \rangle$ guarantees that the deviation of the estimated fuel consumption does not exceed 0.4% of the actual fuel consumption under the assumed engine parameters and freshness of the information obtained from the engine. A simulation of the EMS component's behaviour under the stated conditions is attached as an evidence to support contract completeness.

4.2   The Resulting Argument-Fragment for the Estimator
         Component

In Fig. 6 we provide a part of the argument-fragment for $FSR1$ of FLES, allocated to the Estimator component and associated with the Estimator contract

Table 3. Safety contracts for the EMS component

A2: engineStatus within [a,b] **G2**: fuelRate within [-1,3212] **E**$_{A2,G2}$: Sw architecture design specification, Sw architecture verification report
B2: Engine parameters=20 AND engineStatus delay under 0.3 seconds **H2**: fuelRate does not deviate more than 0.4% from the actual fuel consumption **E**$_{B2,H2}$: Simulation of the fuel consumption estimation under assumed conditions

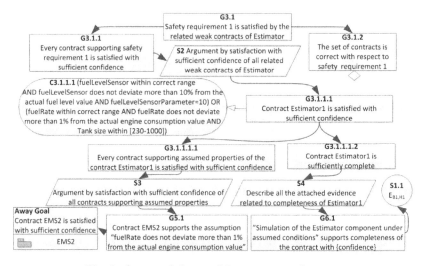

Fig. 6. A part of the resulting argument-fragment

$\langle B1, H1 \rangle$ denoted as $Estimator1$ within the argument. By using the rules from Section 3.5, we generate an argument-fragment from the provided safety contracts to argue over satisfaction of $FSR1$ by showing that the requirement is satisfied by the related $Estimator1$ contract. The argument for satisfaction of $Estimator1$ contract is developed to show the associated evidence supporting its completeness, and point to the away goals supporting its assumed properties. Due to space limitations we show only an away goal supporting $Estimator1$ assumed property related to the fuelRate deviation and supported by the EMS $\langle B2, H2 \rangle$ contract, denoted as $EMS2$ within the argument. The generated argument-fragment contains some properties that could be captured in an out-of-context setting and should be further developed to cover all relevant properties not captured within the contracts.

5   Discussion

As seen in the example in Section 4 we are able to generate a partial argument-fragment based on the component meta-model in Section 3.2. We support the confidence in contract completeness by associating the supporting evidence with the contracts. At the same time, by making the contracts related to the actual behaviour of the component and not to particular safety requirements, we are able to use the contracts to address different context-specific safety requirements.

The presented approach allows us to use the safety claims captured for an out-of-context component to develop context-specific argument-fragments. The resulting argument-fragment for a particular context should not include information relevant for all contexts, but only the information relevant for the particular context. By automating the generation of argument-fragments from safety contracts we speed up the creation of such argument-fragments for different contexts. The argument presented in Section 4 does not present all the aspects an argument should cover, such as failure modes or process-based arguments, but it provides an illustration of how the contracts can be used to generate argument-fragments. Contracts can be used to capture different safety aspects of components, e.g., failure behaviour. The resulting argument quality depends on the quality and variety (e.g., in terms of aspects) of the provided contracts.

The amount of work that still needs to be performed for a specific system depends on the abstraction level at which we allocate the safety requirements to components that have their safety contracts specified. If we connect the requirements with the contracts at higher levels of abstraction, based on the compositional nature of our approach a more complete argument-fragment could be generated. According to ISO 26262, SEooC cannot be an item, i.e., a system implementing a complete functionality, but it can be a subsystem or a subcomponent of an item. Hence we focused on lower level components and how to reduce efforts needed to generate their argument-fragments.

The problem of automation and reuse of safety analyses and safety reasoning within the safety cases is a sensitive issue, especially since safety is a system property and needs to be reasoned about for the particular system. As mentioned in [13], the goal of automation is not to replace human reasoning, but to focus it on areas where they are best used. Similarly, in this work we are not aiming at eliminating human reasoning from the process of safety reasoning and argumentation, but to support it by providing automation of more clerical tasks.

6   Related Work

Generating safety case arguments to increase efficiency of safety certification has been a topic of many recent works. While some consider different notions of assumption/guarantee contracts for that purpose [17, 10] others directly build upon safety requirements [9, 3].

Assume/guarantee contracts are used in [17] to capture the vertical dependencies between a software application and a hardware platform that enables automatic generation of application specific arguments. The work presents a model-based language for specifying demanded and guaranteed requirements between the applications and platforms. The language allows for capturing restricted set of properties, whereas the contract formalism we base our work on is more expressive and offers support for easier out-of-context to in-context reuse of components. Also, [17] does not provide means for generating arguments from the captured contracts.

An approach where "informal" contracts are used for safety-case generation is proposed in [10]. The approach uses Dependency-Guarantee Relationships (DGRs) that correspond to our contracts. It derives an argument for a module by using all the DGRs of the module to build an argument relying on dependencies from other modules. In contrast to this approach, we take in consideration different types of evidence that need to be provided with the safety contracts and components, including compatibility of a component with a particular context.

A method for automated generation of safety case arguments based on an automatic extraction of information from existing work-products is presented in [3]. The generated argumentation consists of summaries of different work-products created within a project. Similarly, a methodology for safety case assembly from artefacts required to satisfy some process objectives is presented in [9]. The work provides a set of transformation rules from captured safety requirements to safety case arguments. While these methods are useful for generating a safety case argument from a set of safety requirements that are related to existing work-products, they do not as we do consider reuse of out-of-context components developed and prepared for certification.

7   Conclusion and Future Work

In this paper we have presented an approach for generating safety case argument-fragments from safety contracts for out-of-context components developed and prepared for safety certification independently of the system in which they will be used. The approach allows us to speed up the creation of context-specific argument-fragments. More specifically, we have presented an overview of the argument-fragment architecture and provided a set of rules for generating the argument-fragments from the safety contracts, including illustrating the application of the rules with an example. We can conclude that safety contracts provide a good basis for generating argument-fragments and in that way allow safety engineers to focus more on capturing the knowledge about the system rather than spending time on documenting a safety case.

In our future work, we plan to refine our component meta-model, e.g., to provide support for different classes of requirements. Consequently, this refinement entails co-evolution of the generation rules. We also plan to implement the provided rules within an existing tool that supports a contract formalism, e.g., the CHESS-toolset [1]. To show the scalability of our approach we aim at using it for more complex case studies, e.g., for a larger number of safety requirements. Further more, we plan to explore how our approach could be used to reduce some of the common argument fallacies [11] related to the structure of arguments. Moreover, it is worthwhile investigating usage of our approach for safety case maintenance and change management.

Acknowledgements. Thanks to Iain Bate for useful discussions and comments. This work is supported by the Swedish Foundation for Strategic Research (SSF) via project SYNOPSIS as well as EU and Vinnova via the Artemis JTI project SafeCer.

References

[1] CHESS-toolset: http://www.chess-project.org/page/download
[2] GSN Community Standard Version 1. Technical report, Origin Consulting (York) Limited (November 2011)
[3] Armengaud, E.: Automated safety case compilation for product-based argumentation. In: Embedded Real Time Software and Systems (ERTS) (February 2014)
[4] Bate, I., Conmy, P.: Assuring Safety for Component Based Software Engineering. In: 15th IEEE International Symposium on High Assurance Systems Engineering (HASE) (January 2014)
[5] Bate, I., Hansson, H., Punnekkat, S.: Better, faster, cheaper, and safer too - is this really possible? In: 17th IEEE Int'l Conf. on Emerging Technologies for Factory Automation (ETFA). IEEE (September 2012)
[6] Benveniste, A., Caillaud, B., Ferrari, A., Mangeruca, L., Passerone, R., Sofronis, C.: Multiple viewpoint contract-based specification and design. In: de Boer, F.S., Bonsangue, M.M., Graf, S., de Roever, W.-P. (eds.) FMCO 2007. LNCS, vol. 5382, pp. 200–225. Springer, Heidelberg (2008)
[7] Carlson, J., et al.: Generic component meta-mode, Version 1.0 SafeCer, Deliverable D132 (November 2013)
[8] Dardar, R.: Building a Safety Case in Compliance with ISO 26262 for Fuel Level Estimation and Display System. Master's thesis, Mälardalen University, School of Innovation, Design and Engineering, Västerås, Sweden (2014)
[9] Denney, E., Pai, G.: A lightweight methodology for safety case assembly. In: Ortmeier, F., Daniel, P. (eds.) SAFECOMP 2012. LNCS, vol. 7612, pp. 1–12. Springer, Heidelberg (2012)
[10] Fenn, J.L., Hawkins, R.D., Williams, P., Kelly, T.P., Banner, M.G., Oakshott, Y.: The who, where, how, why and when of modular and incremental certification. In: 2nd International Conference on System Safety (ICSS). IET (2007)
[11] Greenwell, W.S., Knight, J.C., Holloway, C.M., Pease, J.J.: A taxonomy of fallacies in system safety arguments. In: 24th International System Safety Conference, ISSC (2006)
[12] ISO 26262-10. Road vehicles — Functional safety — Part 10: Guideline on ISO 26262. International Organization for Standardization (2011)
[13] Rushby, J.: Logic and epistemology in safety cases. In: Bitsch, F., Guiochet, J., Kaâniche, M. (eds.) SAFECOMP 2013. LNCS, vol. 8153, pp. 1–7. Springer, Heidelberg (2013)
[14] Sljivo, I., Carlson, J., Gallina, B., Hansson, H.: Fostering Reuse within Safety-critical Component-based Systems through Fine-grained Contracts. In: International Workshop on Critical Software Component Reusability and Certification across Domains (CSC) (June 2013)
[15] Sljivo, I., Gallina, B., Carlson, J., Hansson, H.: Strong and weak contract formalism for third-party component reuse. In: IEEE 3rd International Workshop on Software Certification (WoSoCer) (November 2013)
[16] Storey, N.R.: Safety Critical Computer Systems. Addison-Wesley Longman Publishing Co., Inc., Boston (1996)
[17] Zimmer, B., Bürklen, S., Knoop, M., Höfflinger, J., Trapp, M.: Vertical safety interfaces–improving the efficiency of modular certification. In: Flammini, F., Bologna, S., Vittorini, V. (eds.) SAFECOMP 2011. LNCS, vol. 6894, pp. 29–42. Springer, Heidelberg (2011)

Estimating Worst Case Failure Dependency with Partial Knowledge of the Difficulty Function

Peter Bishop[1,2] and Lorenzo Strigini[1]

[1] Centre for Software Reliability, City University, London, UK
{pgb,strigini}@csr.city.ac.uk
[2] Adelard LLP, London, Exmouth House, London, UK
pgb@adelard.com

Abstract. For systems using software diversity, well-established theories show that the expected probability of failure on demand (*pfd*) for two diverse program versions failing together will generally differ from what it would be if they failed independently. This is explained in terms of a "difficulty function" that varies between demands on the system. This theory gives insight, but no specific prediction unless we have some means to quantify the difficulty function. This paper presents a theory leading to a worst case measure of "average failure dependency" between diverse software, given only partial knowledge of the difficulty function. It also discusses the possibility of estimating the model parameters, with one approach based on an empirical analysis of previous systems implemented as logic networks, to support pre-development estimates of expected gain from diversity. The approach is illustrated using a realistic safety system example.

Keywords: Safety, software reliability, fault tolerance, failure dependency, software diversity, difficulty function.

1 Introduction

Software diversity has been advocated as a means of improving the reliability of safety related software and in particular safety systems that react to a demand, where a 1 out of 2 or a 2 out of 3 voting scheme can be used to ensure that some safety action is performed. This approach is used in industry (e.g. for railway interlocking), but development and maintenance is costlier than for a non-diverse system and it is not easy to predict in advance the likely safety improvement that can be achieved.

Theory as well as experimental studies indicate that failures of diverse implementations ("versions") are not necessarily independent [3, 7, 15]. The challenge is to determine *how much* improvement should be expected with diversity. Early theoretical work by Eckhardt and Lee [4] showed that variations in the degree of "difficulty" for different inputs (or "demands") will result in the expected *pfd* for a pair of diverse programs being greater than the product of the expected *pfd*s of the two programs and thus limit the effectiveness of diversity. Littlewood and Miller [8] later showed that, if diversity in development results in different "difficulty functions" for the two diverse

A. Bondavalli and F. Di Giandomenico (Eds.): SAFECOMP 2014, LNCS 8666, pp. 186–201, 2014.
© Springer International Publishing Switzerland 2014

programs, the expected *pfd* for common failures of a diverse pair can also be *less* than the product of the expected *pfd*s of the single versions.

To quantify via these theories the improvement in expected *pfd* for a diverse safety system, one would need to specify both the difficulty for every demand, and the demand profile. Difficulty functions will normally be impossible to estimate for real projects (although *a posteriori* difficulty estimates have been obtained [1, 15] for some "toy" applications where many different versions were developed [12]). In addition, if the safety system is used in different operational contexts, the demand profile might also be different and this can change the expected *pfd*s.

In this paper we examine an approach for a more modest, but still useful, goal of estimating the worst case improvement in average *pfd*, by deriving a worst case demand profile that only requires knowledge about two points on the difficulty function rather that characterizing the whole function.

The paper will first summarize the theory underlying the difficulty function, then identify the worst demand profile that maximizes the expected *pfd* for a pair of diverse programs, relative to the expected *pfd* of a single version for a given difficulty function. We then consider what estimates for the expected *pfd* can be derived given different types of knowledge about the difficulty function. We also discuss means, and difficulties, for estimating the model parameters and tentatively suggest an approach for systems implemented as logic networks.

2   The Difficulty Function

In these models, the process that delivers a program, with its unknown faults (if any), is modelled as the random sampling of a program from a "population of all possible programs". The (unknown) probability of "drawing" each specific possible program depends on the specification, the development process, the development team, etc. Given these factors, the "difficulty function" $\theta(x)$ is defined as the probability that such a "randomly drawn" program will fail on a given demand x.

The mean *pfd*s of a single program (pfd_1) and of common failure for a pair of diverse programs (pfd_2) depend on the difficulty function $\theta(x)$ and the demand profile $p(x)$. For a difficulty function $\theta(x)$, the expected *pfd* of a single program version is:

$$pfd_1 = \sum \theta(x)\, p(x) \qquad (1)$$

We consider the case in which the two versions for a 1-out-of-2 system are developed from the same process for the same specification: the two developments have the same "difficulty function" (Eckhardt and Lee model [4]). Thus pfd_1 is the same for both programs; among all the scenarios where this holds, this scenario, of identical difficulty functions, yields the highest (i.e., the worst) value of pfd_2.

Assuming conditional independence between failures of the versions for each demand [4] (i.e., the two developments are independent [11]), the expected *pfd* for a randomly drawn pair of programs is then:

$$pfd_2 = \sum \theta(x)\, \theta(x)\, p(x) \qquad (2)$$

pfd_2 increases with the variance of the difficulty function $\theta(x)$. Intuitively, if the difficulty function is very "spiky", there is a high probability that the diverse programs will fail on the same, "difficult" demands: the average benefit from diverse programs will be lower than otherwise. Conversely if the difficulty function is "flat" (the same value for all demands), there is nothing that forces the diverse programs to fail on similar inputs, so the gain in average reliability is higher. In this case, pfd_2 does equal the product between the expected pfd values for the two versions. For brevity, when this equality holds we will say there is "independence on average"[1].

Clearly the mean pfd depends upon the demand profile $p(x)$ as well as the demand difficulty $\theta(x)$. In the next section we use this dependence on the demand profile to derive the worst case value of pfd_2 for a given value of pfd_1.

3   Estimating the Worst Case Expected pfd

We compare the expected pfd for this system with that of a single-version (i.e., non-diverse) system used in the same function (hence with the same demand profile).

To determine the worst-case impact of the profile on the expected pfd, we choose the family of the most extreme profiles possible: the ones in which the only demand values with non-zero probabilities are $x=hi$ and $x=lo$ that have the highest and lowest values of the difficulty function, $\theta(hi)$ and $\theta(lo)$. For this profile, we can write:

$$pfd_1 = z\,\theta(hi) + (1-z)\,\theta(lo) \tag{3}$$

$$pfd_2 = z\,\theta(hi)^2 + (1-z)\,\theta(lo)^2 \tag{4}$$

where $z = p(lo)$ and $(1-z) = p(hi)$. So pfd_1 and pfd_2 can vary between their minimum and maximum values depending on z, i.e.:

$$\min(pfd_2) = \theta(lo)^2, \quad z = 0 \tag{5}$$

$$\max(pfd_2) = \theta(hi)^2, \quad z = 1 \tag{6}$$

No other profile can achieve this range, as non-zero probabilities for demands with intermediate θ values would reduce the maximum and increase the minimum value achievable. There is also another sense in which these profiles are "extreme". Given a certain difficulty function, a given value of pfd_1 can in general be the result of many different profiles, only one of which is "extreme"[2]. This "extreme" profile is the one where pfd_2 is largest, i.e., the advantage of diversity is smallest. Under this profile, the

---

[1] We underscore that "independence on average" is a property of expected values, not of individual program pairs. If independence of failures held for every pair of diverse programs, "independence on average" would also hold. However, "independence on average" could hold even if independence does not hold within each pair; and we can have $pfd_2 > pfd_1{}^2$ even in a population of pairs in which pairs with negative or zero correlation between failures of their component versions are more common than pairs with positive correlation [10].

[2] To be precise, we should consider the cases in which more than one demand values have values of θ equal to $\theta(hi)$ (or equal to $\theta(lo)$). The reasoning presented here remains valid: we can treat all the demands with an identical value of θ as one demand.

expected *pfd* of a diverse pair, pfd_2, is a linear combination of $\theta(lo)^2$ and $\theta(hi)^2$ and hence a linear combination of $(\min pfd_1)^2$ and $(\max pfd_1)^2$. This can be compared with the "best case" profile that only selects demands x with exactly the same difficulty, i.e. where $\theta(x)=pfd_1$, so from (2) that $pfd_2=pfd_1^2$ which represents "independence on average". The expected *pfd*s for the best and worst profiles are shown in Fig. 1 below for the case where $\theta(hi)=0.04$, and $\theta(lo)$ takes different values from zero to 0.02.

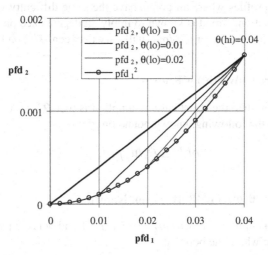

Fig. 1. Variation in pfd_2, given the extreme profile and $\theta(hi)=0.04$

To understand this graph, we consider that for a given value of $\theta(lo)$, the lowest possible value of pfd_1 is $\theta(lo)$, given by setting $z=0$ in equation (3), and the corresponding value of pfd_2 equals $\theta(lo)^2$ (equation 4). This is why the straight lines for $\theta(lo)=0.01$ and $\theta(lo)=0.02$ do not continue to the left of these points.   The maximum values of pfd_1 and pfd_2 are given by setting $z=1$, and correspond to the rightmost point in the graph, $pfd_1=\theta(hi)$, $pfd_2=\theta(hi)^2$. All the intermediate "extreme" profiles for the same values of $\theta(lo)$ and $\theta(hi)$ give the $\{pfd_1, pfd_2\}$ pairs represented by the points of the straight line   joining these maximum and minimum points on the pfd_1^2 curve.

We now study the effects of various levels of knowledge about $\theta(hi)$ and $\theta(lo)$.

3.1   Case where $\theta(hi)$ and $\theta(lo)$ are Known

When $\theta(hi)$ and $\theta(lo)$ are known, the endpoints of the linear combination are known and changing z changes the ratio of pfd_2 to pfd_1, since from equation (3):

$$z = \frac{\theta(hi) - pfd_1}{\theta(hi) - \theta(lo)} \quad \text{and} \quad 1 - z = \frac{pfd_1 - \theta(lo)}{\theta(hi) - \theta(lo)}$$

From equation (4) we can calculate pfd_2 as a linear function of pfd_1, i.e.:

$$pfd_2 = \theta(lo)^2 + \frac{(\theta(hi)^2 - \theta(lo)^2)(pfd_1 - \theta(lo))}{\theta(hi) - \theta(lo)} \quad (7)$$

We note that if $pfd_1 = \theta(lo)$ or $pfd_1 = \theta(hi)$, then $pfd_2 = pfd_1^2$. This is not surprising: these cases select profiles where all points have the same difficulty value: effectively a flat difficulty function, which is known to imply "independence on average". It also follows that the reduction factor pfd_2/pfd_1 will vary between $\theta(lo)$ and $\theta(hi)$.

3.2   Case Where Only θ(hi) is Known

If $\theta(lo)$ is unknown, then the worst case assumption is that $\theta(lo) = 0$, and hence equation (7) reduces to the following, known bound on pfd_2:

$$pfd_2 \le \theta(hi)\, pfd_1 \quad (8)$$

3.3   Case Where θ(hi) and θ(lo) are not Known

The worst case assumption is now $\theta(lo) = 0$, $\theta(hi) = 1$ and hence equation (8) reduces to the extreme case where the bound is:

$$pfd_2 \le pfd_1 \quad (9)$$

In this case, the mean *pfd* of a diverse pair could be no better than that for a single version. The worst case – the equality in (9) holds – would mean that the programs developed have fail on some specific demands and no others (with probability 1). Comparison with the previous cases highlights how knowledge about the difficulty function allows us to reduce the mean value of pfd_2 as a proportion of pfd_1.

3.4   Case Where the Ratio between θ(hi) and θ(lo) is Known

In this case we only know the maximum "roughness" of the difficulty function, k, the ratio of $\theta(hi)$ to $\theta(lo)$, but not the absolute difficulty values. Hence:

$$k = \frac{\theta(hi)}{\theta(lo)} \quad (10)$$

In this model, there is no constraint on the x axis endpoints $\theta(hi)$ and $\theta(lo)$ apart from the ratio k (and the fact that $0 \le \theta(lo) \le pfd_1 \le \theta(hi) \le 1$). The worst case value of pfd_2 lies on the chord between the two endpoints: as illustrated in Fig. 2 below.

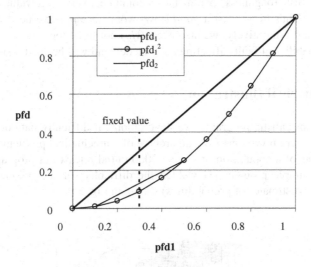

Fig. 2. Worst case given a known difficulty ratio k

To get the worst case for a given pfd_1, we effectively slide the linear combination chord for pfd_2 along the pfd_1^2 curve, while keeping the ratio between the endpoints of the chord (on the pfd_1 axis) equal to k. Then we choose the chord that gives maximum (worst) possible value of pfd_2 for a given value of pfd_1. Since pfd_1 is held constant, maximizing the ratio pfd_2/pfd_1 also maximizes pfd_2/pfd_1^2 (the worst case increase relative to independence on average). The analysis in Appendix A shows that pfd_2 is bounded by:

$$pfd_2 \leq \frac{(k+1)^2}{4k} pfd_1^2 \tag{11}$$

So the worst case reduction factor for pfd_2 relative to pfd_1 is $pfd_1 \cdot (k+1)^2/4k$, rather than the factor of pfd_1 that would result from "independence on average".

This worst case bound equation is only applicable up to the point where $\theta(hi)=1$ (as we cannot slide the pfd_2 chord any further to the right). From the analysis in Appendix A, it can be shown that this limit is reached when:

$$pfd_1 \geq \frac{2}{k+1} \tag{12}$$

If pfd_1 exceeds this constraint, a variant of equation (7) has to be used instead where $\theta(hi)=1$ and $\theta(lo)=1/k$, i.e.:

$$pfd_2 = k^{-2} + \frac{(1-k^{-2})(pfd_1 - k^{-1})}{1-k^{-1}}, \qquad pfd_1 \geq \frac{2}{k+1} \tag{13}$$

The difficulty "roughness" parameter, k, could be a very large value or even infinity if $\theta(lo)=0$. Thus to forecast a *good* (low) worst-case pfd_2 we need $\theta(hi)$ to be not too high; counter-intuitively, we also need $\theta(lo)$ not to be too *low*: we need evidence that the probability of faults affecting any one demand will be "bad enough".

4   Numerical Illustration

For some non-realistic programs, we have empirical difficulty data derived from an analysis of program versions from an archive of mathematical problems and solutions [12]. Analysis of a population of around 3000 initial releases of program versions for a relatively simple problem [1] yielded the difficulty surface (taking the observed frequencies as estimates of probabilities) shown in Fig. 3 below.

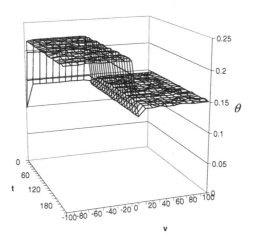

Fig. 3. Empirical difficulty function from around 3000 program versions [1]. These programs receive two inputs, t and v, hence the difficulty function is plotted as a surface.

Analysis showed that $\theta(hi)=0.2282$ and $\theta(lo)=0.1012$. That is, in this case $k = 0.2282/0.1012 = 2.25$.

Inserting these values into equations 7, 8 and 9, the relationship between these bounding equations is illustrated in Fig. 4.

The bound based on knowledge of both $\theta(hi)$ and $\theta(lo)$ (equation 7) represents the least pessimistic worst case bound on pfd_2. It can be seen that the curve based on an estimate of k (equation 9) touches the least conservative bound line at the maximum dependency point when $pfd_1 = 0.140$ (see Appendix A for details).   Unlike equation 7, equation 9 allows the maximum dependency point that defines pfd_2 to be shifted if a new estimate of pfd_1 is made. This is equivalent to defining new values for $\theta(hi)$ and $\theta(lo)$ which retain the same ratio k.

The pfd_2 bound based on $\theta(hi)$ alone (equation 8) tends to be the most pessimistic, although it does intersect with the least conservative bound when $pfd_1 = \theta(hi)$

(0.2282) when equations 7 and 8 agree with the "independence on average" result when $pfd_2 = pfd_1{}^2 = \theta(hi)^2$.

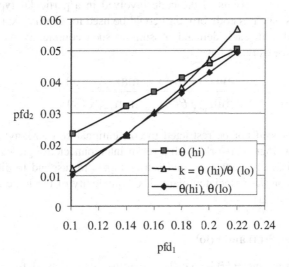

Fig. 4. Comparison of worst case bound equations. The labels for the three plots indicate which parameters are assumed known, with the values derived *a posteriori* for the study in **Fig. 3**.

5   Parameter Estimation

In the analysis above we have identified alternative ways of deriving a worst case value for pfd_2 given pfd_1 by using different kinds of information about the difficulty function. To apply these models for prediction, as opposed to generic insight, we require realistic model parameters. At the current state of knowledge, there are no means for deriving credible difficulty values to support prediction (estimation of expected pfd) for a specific safety application. In the following subsections we examine some potential directions for deriving model parameters, and difficulties to be overcome for them to become applicable in the future.

5.1   Estimating k

Estimation of k could be based on relative complexity, if one assumed the demand difficulty for demand x proportional to some measure of demand logic complexity[3],

$$\theta(x) \propto c(x) \tag{14}$$

---

[3]   We accept that this could only be a first-cut assumption. One of the possible objections is that higher complexity may lead to more effort to avoid or remove faults, so that the difficulty function might not be a linear function (or maybe not even a monotonic function) of a measure of complexity [5].

where $c(x)$ is a measure of the logic complexity required to process a given demand x. For example, the complexity measure could based on the number of lines of code or number of decision points in the code involved in a particular type of demand. Program analysis (such as code pruning) could be used to identify the relevant subset of code involved with each demand. Assuming such complexity measures can be derived, k would be estimated as:

$$k = \frac{\max_{x \in X} \theta(x)}{\min_{x \in X} \theta(x)} \approx \frac{\max_{x \in X} c(x)}{\min_{x \in X} c(x)} \tag{15}$$

This approach need not be restricted to conventional code. Many safety systems are represented as logic networks with a set of interconnected logic gates. Each type of demand requires different logic and sensor inputs to respond to different safety-related incidents on the associated plant. The complexity of the logic network could be used to estimate $c(x)$.

5.2   Estimating θ(hi) and θ(lo)

One means of estimating $\theta(hi)$ is to make use of the fact that, by definition:

$$\theta(hi) \leq p_{faulty} \tag{16}$$

where p_{faulty} is the probability that a program selected from the population of all possible program versions is faulty. The value of p_{faulty} could be estimated via a range of methods including an analysis of the development process [2] and the level of test coverage achieved [9], however they are not mature methods and confidence in their predictions will be especially low when few faults are expected to be present.

Alternatively, estimates of $\theta(x)$ could be made directly based on some expected fault density f [13] and an estimate of the amount of code or logic $n(x)$ needed to respond to a particular demand. There can be many demands x that exercise the same logic, but if we make a (strong) assumption that all demands are equally likely to fail if the logic is faulty (on average over the whole population), then:

$$\theta(x) = n(x)f \tag{17}$$

So the maximum and minimum values of $n(x)$ over all types of demand x can be used to obtain $\theta(hi)$ and $\theta(lo)$.

5.3   Empirical Data Analysis

Data sets that can be used for empirical parameter estimation are quite limited, but there is survey of programmable logic controller (PLC) logic faults undertaken for the UK Health and Safety Executive [14]. Such PLCs are not programmed using conventional code but as an interconnected set of logic elements (like AND, OR, NOT) or relay "coils" (that simulate the behavior of hardware relays). Field reliability data was collected from a range of industrial applications from the nuclear, chemical, oil and gas and electrical industrial sectors (but predominantly nuclear). A full set of data was collected for 125 PLCs which included the number of:

- inputs
- outputs
- coils
- failures
- years of use

No PLC "platform" failures were recorded in over 600 PLC-years of operation, suggesting that PLC platforms are fairly reliable. We should also note that "coils" were used as the measure of the number of logic elements, but we cannot be sure the actual logic network contained coils or whether an "equivalent coils" estimate was calculated for alternative types of logic. In addition, the term "failures" in this data set might actually be a misnomer for "number of faults", as the failure counts are typically zero or one. We assumed "failures" indicate the number of different faults. This is conservative from the viewpoint of estimating maximum difficulty as it can only over-estimate the number of network logic faults. Furthermore, if over-estimation of faults were consistent, it would not affect the k ratio derived in Section 3.4.

On further analysis, we found that some of the PLCs contained identical logic network metrics and identical fault counts. This was interpreted to mean that the same logic network was installed on multiple PLCs, which could bias the result by counting the same logic network several times over. These duplicates were eliminated from the analysis, leaving size and fault data for 96 different PLC programs. The results are presented in Fig. 5 below.

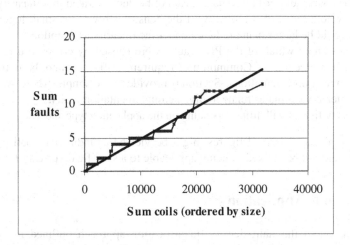

Fig. 5. Logic faults vs. network coils (cumulative)

As the fault data are relatively sparse, the graph presents a cumulative count of faults versus the number of "coils". The summation is performed in program size order, as this will reveal a non-linear relationship between PLC program size and faults by an increasing or decreasing gradient. As can be seen in Fig. 5, the relationship does appear to be roughly linear (to 95% in a chi-squared test). Perhaps surprisingly, the slope seems to be slightly less for the larger PLC programs (at the right hand side of the graph).

A very similar graph was obtained when we used the sum of inputs and outputs (*io*) as the network size measure. Again, the correlation is better than 95% in a chi-squared test.

Given the evidence of a linear relationship between network size and logic faults, it may be legitimate to use an average fault density to estimate the number of faults in a logic network. The logic density estimates derived from the linear regression analysis of faults against the coil and *io* measures are shown in Table 1 below.

Table 1. Logic fault density estimates

Logic fault density measure		Value
f_{io}	(faults/io)	$3.0 \ 10^{-4}$
f_{coil}	(faults/coil)	$5.0 \ 10^{-4}$

Some caveats need to be placed on these fault density estimates, notably:

- The fault density is based on the number of fault *discovered* which could be an underestimate if some of the faults have yet to be found. The data in [14] shows the mean operating time is 5.9 years. It is not certain that all defects would have been detected over that period of time.
- Given the sparseness of failure data it cannot be demonstrated that linearity applies over the whole range of complexity. If the density is lower for small logic subsystems, k would be larger than predicted under the linearity assumption.
- We do not know which of the PLC faults were caused by errors in user requirements or implementation. Common user requirement flaws cannot be mitigated by diverse logic implementations. Section 6 provides an example where we assume the fault density estimates relate to diverse implementation faults.
- Fault density figures will differ depending on the application type and safety criticality.

So the empirically derived figures might be viewed as indicative "ball-park" figures, but should not be viewed as being applicable to a specific diverse system.

6   Example Application

The application of the fault density quantification approach outlined in Section 5 is illustrated on an actual industrial safety system with two independent safety trains that control functionally diverse plant shutdown mechanisms[4]. The A and B train subsystems and logic element counts (taken from the logic specification sheets) are shown in Table 2 below.

---

[4] The details have been anonymised at the request of the system operators.

Table 2. A and B Train subsystem network complexity measures

A Train subsystem	I/O	Gates
A1	24	16
A2	22	9
A3	49	28
A4	31	23
Total	126	76
B Train subsystem	**I/O**	**Gates**
B1	17	9
B2	28	16
B3	15	7
Total	60	32

We will use the data to illustrate the mean *pfd* estimation approach, using arbitrary (and quite extreme) assumptions about the variation of logic use with demands. Let us assume some logic subsystems are unnecessary for some demands. For example a standby electrical supply subsystem might be essential if connection to the grid power supply is lost but not otherwise.

So the extreme level of variation in number of subsystems with demand might be:

- One (the smallest) logic subsystem in A and B
- All logic subsystems in A and B

Using the *io* complexity measure we set an upper bound on the difficulty for a logic sub-network x containing $n_{io}(x)$ *io* elements as:

$$\theta(x) = f_{io}\, n_{io}(x)$$

Based on the $n_{io}(x)$ numbers assumed for the assumed maximum and minimum logic networks needed for a demand we derive the bounding values for θ and k shown in Table 3 below. Note that, in this particular example, the specified logic differs between trains A and B, so we are assuming that there are no common specification flaws and the difficulty values estimate the likelihood of implementation flaws only.

Table 3. A and B Train difficulty and difficulty variation estimates

Subsystem	A Train		B Train		Worst case
Demand x requires:	#io	$\theta(x)$	#io	$\theta(x)$	$\theta(x)$
Smallest single subsystem	22	$6.6\ 10^{-3}$	15	$4.5\ 10^{-3}$	$6.6\ 10^{-3}$
All subsystems	126	$3.78\ 10^{-2}$	60	$1.8\ 10^{-2}$	$3.78\ 10^{-2}$
k	5.7		4		5.7

For the A and B trains, different logic is involved, so the values are not identical, but we conservatively assume the worst case value applies to both trains. In the following calculation, we assume that the expected value pfd_1 is 10^{-2} for each train. This is combined with the bound formulae for pfd_2 from Section 3 and the worst case values in Table 3 above to yield the bounds on the expected value of pfd_2 shown in Table 4 below.

Table 4. Worst case A and B Train pfd estimates

Bound equation	pfd_2 bound
a) $pfd_2 \leq p_{faulty} pfd_1$	$3.8 \ 10^{-4}$
b) $pfd_2 \leq \theta(hi) \ pfd_1$	$3.8 \ 10^{-4}$
c) $pfd_2 \leq (\theta(hi)+\theta(lo)) \ pfd_1 - \theta(hi)\theta(lo)$	$2.5 \ 10^{-4}$
d) $pfd_2 \leq ((k+1)^2/4k) \ pfd_1^2$	$2.6 \ 10^{-4}$

It can be seen that in this example the results are very similar. The results for a) and b) are identical because the $\theta(hi)$ estimate is based on all the logic in the train and hence is identical to p_{faulty} for the train. The results for c) and d) are also similar since the pfd_1 value chosen is close to the maximum dependency point.

7   Discussion

It should be noted that the analysis in this paper relates to *expected values*. The analysis seeks to estimate the improvement we might expect between the *averages* pfd_1 and pfd_2 by using diversity, under worst case assumptions about the operational profile. It *does not* predict the improvement ratio that will actually be achieved by a *specific pair* of program versions under a specific operational profile—clearly the actual reduction achieved could be better or worse than a model based on averages [10].

It is also important to note that this analysis describes the effects of those parts of development that are indeed diverse. For example, if there is a common specification, the possibility of a specification flaw would invalidate the conditional independence assumption required in the Eckhardt and Lee model [4]. Accounting for such common factors requires more complex models [11] and we have not checked how the approach would extend to those models.

The paper also explores possible directions for quantifying the model parameters. The analysis of PLC failure data in Section 5 illustrates how one might attempt to estimate ranges of difficulty. However the method discussed should be viewed as "work in progress", as it has not been validated or substantiated. In particular:

- It assumes that difficulty can be estimated from predicted fault density. This is not supported by deduction and could only be validated experimentally.
- There is an assumption of linearity between logic complexity and logic faults. This is not contradicted by the available empirical data but it would require far more empirical data to validate the assumption over the whole range of complexity.
- There are no fault density and complexity data for systems of higher criticality, so we have no support for an assumption of linearity for such systems, and we cannot derive "typical" fault density figures for such systems.

Clearly further empirical studies are needed to check the underlying assumptions and to derive realistic faults density values before the models can be applied to high criticality systems. For validating this approach to estimating the difficulty function, the main obstacle is that direct empirical assessment of difficulty functions means counting faults affecting each demand in a large population of programs developed independently for the same specification. The rarity of such populations, outside laboratory experiments on toy problems, is the usual problem in empirical software engineering. Given instead sets of realistic, but practically unique programs, a feasible form of weaker validation would be to select sets of programs that are assessed to have the same parameters for the estimation method used, and then, within such a set of programs, measure fault frequencies over sets of demands estimated to have the same difficulty.

More generally, the current models assume a common difficulty function and further work is needed to generalize this approach to the case where the difficulty functions differ for the two versions (the Littlewood and Miller model [8]).

We also note that these bounding methods also apply to the models by Hughes [6] that explain correlation between random failures in redundant hardware in terms of variation of failure rates with environmental stress. Variation of failure rates with environmental factors will typically be easier to assess than variation of difficulty between demands.

8   Conclusions

We have developed models for estimating the worst case reduction in mean *pfd* achievable by diverse program pairs that require only a partial knowledge of the difficulty function. These models can give qualitative insight, e.g. about the effects of development decisions thought to increase or to reduce maximum or minimum difficulty. We have also discussed ways for estimating the parameters required for these models, and their difficulties; in particular, an approach for estimating difficulty values and difficulty variation for applications defined in terms of a logic diagram.

We note that the methods discussed for deriving the difficulty parameters are very preliminary. Much more empirical support, especially for the high criticality systems where diversity is likely to be employed, would be needed before they could be applied for quantitative prediction (e.g. for pre-development decisions about diversity). Further work is also needed to generalize the theory to cases where the difficulty functions differ for the diverse program versions.

References

1. Bentley, J.G.W., Bishop, P.G., van der Meulen, M.J.P.: An Empirical Exploration of the Difficulty Function. In: Heisel, M., Liggesmeyer, P., Wittmann, S. (eds.) SAFECOMP 2004. LNCS, vol. 3219, pp. 60–71. Springer, Heidelberg (2004)
2. Bloomfield, R.E., Guerra, A.S.L.: Process Modelling to Support Dependability Arguments. In: IEEE Dependable Systems and Networks, DSN 2002, pp. 113–122 (2002)
3. Eckhardt, D.E., Caglayan, A.K., et al.: An experimental evaluation of software redundancy as a strategy for improving reliability. IEEE Trans. Software Eng. 17(7), 692–702 (1991)

4. Eckhardt, D.E., Lee, L.D.: A theoretical basis for the analysis of multiversion software subject to coincident errors. IEEE Transactions on Software Engineering 11(12), 1511–1517 (1985)
5. Hatton, L.: Reexamining the fault density-component size connection. IEEE Software 14(2), 89–97 (1997)
6. Hughes, R.P.: A New Approach to Common Cause Failure. Reliability Engineering 17(3), 211–236 (1987)
7. Knight, J.C., Leveson, N.G.: Experimental evaluation of the assumption of independence in multiversion software. IEEE Trans. Software Engineering 12(1), 96–109 (1986)
8. Littlewood, B., Miller, D.R.: Conceptual Modelling of Coincident Failures in Multiversion Software. IEEE Transactions on Software Engineering 15(2), 1596–1614 (1989)
9. Malaiya, Y.K., Denton, J.: Estimating the number of residual defects in software. In: Third IEEE International High-Assurance Systems Engineering Symposium, pp. 98–105. IEEE (1998)
10. Popov, P., et al.: Software diversity as a measure for reducing development risk. In: IEEE Tenth European Dependable Computing Conference, EDCC 2014, pp. 106–117 (2014)
11. Salako, K., Strigini, L.: When does 'Diversity' in Development Reduce Common Failures? IEEE Transactions on Dependable and Secure Computing 11(2), 193–206 (2014)
12. Skiena, S., Revilla, M.: Programming Challenges. Springer (2003) ISBN: 0387001638
13. Sherriff, M., Williams, L.: Defect Density Estimation Through Verification and Validation. In: The 6th Annual High Confidence Software and Systems Conference, Lithicum Heights, MD, pp. 111–117 (2006)
14. Wright, R.I., Pilkington, A.F.: An Investigation into PLC Reliability. HSE Software Reliability Study, GNSR/CI/21. Risk Management Consultants (RMC), Report R94-1(N), Issue B (1995)
15. van der Meulen, M.J.P., Revilla, M.A.: The Effectiveness of Software Diversity in a Large Population of Programs. IEEE Transactions on Software Engineering 34(6), 753–764 (2008)

Appendix A   Worst Case *Pfd* Model Details

This analysis compares the mean *pfd* of a pair, pfd_2, with the "independence on average" value $pfd_1{}^2$ by defining a dependency factor D as $pfd_2 / pfd_1{}^2$

An extreme profile is assumed where only $p(hi)$ and $p(lo)$ can be non-zero. From the expressions of pfd_1 in (3) and pfd_2 in (4), the ratio of pfd_2 to $pfd_1{}^2$ is:

$$D = \frac{(\theta(hi))^2 z + (\theta(lo))^2 (1-z)}{(\theta(hi)z + \theta(lo)(1-z))^2} \tag{18}$$

By definition $\theta(hi) = k\theta(lo)$, so the dependency equation can be re-written as:

$$D = \frac{(k^2 - 1)z + 1}{((k-1)z + 1)^2} \tag{19}$$

Differentiating with respect to z we obtain:

$$\frac{dD}{dz} = \frac{-(k-1)^2(z(k+1)-1)}{(z(k-1)+1)^3} \tag{20}$$

Hence the differential is zero when either $k=1$ or $z=1/(k+1)$. When $k=1$, the difficulty function is flat, $\theta(hi)=\theta(lo)=pfd_1=D$: the best case ("independence on average").

The $z=1/(k+1)$ case is the situation where the dependency factor D is highest. Substituting $z=1/(k+1)$ into (19), the maximum dependency value D can be shown to be:

$$D = \frac{(k+1)^2}{4k} \tag{21}$$

This can be used the set the worst case value of pfd_2 relative to pfd_1^2, i.e.:

$$pfd_2 = \frac{(k+1)^2}{4k}pfd_1^2 \tag{22}$$

Substituting $z=1/(k+1)$ into (3), this occurs when:

$$pfd_1 = \frac{2k}{k+1}\theta(lo) \tag{23}$$

Or expressed in entirely terms of $\theta(hi)$ and $\theta(lo)$, it can be shown that the maximum dependency occurs when:

$$pfd_1 = \frac{2\theta(hi)\theta(lo)}{\theta(hi)+\theta(lo)} \tag{24}$$

So that:

$$pfd_2 = \theta(hi)\theta(lo) \tag{25}$$

Hence at the maximum dependency point, the ratio of the mean pfds is:

$$\frac{pfd_2}{pfd_1} = \frac{\theta(hi)+\theta(lo)}{2} \tag{26}$$

Proving the Absence of Stack Overflows

Daniel Kästner and Christian Ferdinand

AbsInt GmbH, Science Park 1, 66123 Saarbrücken, Germany
{kaestner,ferdinand}@absint.com

Abstract In safety-critical embedded systems the stack typically is the only dynamically allocated memory area. However, the maximal stack usage must be statically known: at configuration time developers have to reserve enough stack space for each task. Stack overflow errors are often hard to find but can cause the system to crash or behave erroneously. All current safety standards, e.g., ISO-26262, require upper estimations of the storage space; due to its dynamic behavior the stack is an especially critical storage area.

Typically neither testing and measuring nor static source code analysis can provide safe bounds on the worst-case stack usage. A safe upper bound can be computed by whole-program static analysis at the executable code level. When an Abstract Interpretation based static analyzer is used, it can be formally proven that the maximal stack usage will never be underestimated. The challenge for binary-code level analyzers is to minimize the necessary amount of user interactions, e.g., for function pointer calls. To minimize user interaction, the analysis has to be precise, and the annotation mechanism has to be flexible and easy-to-use. The analyzer configuration has to be done once for each software project; afterwards the analysis can be run automatically, supporting continuous verification.

In this article we describe the principles of Abstract Interpretation based stack analysis. We present an annotation language addressing all properties of typical automotive and avionics software and report on practical experience.

1 Introduction

In embedded systems, the run-time stack (often just called "the stack") typically is the only dynamically allocated memory area. It is used during program execution to keep track of the currently active procedures and facilitate the evaluation of expressions. Each active procedure is represented by an activation record, also called stack frame or procedure frame, which holds all the state information needed for execution. Usually the stack grows towards lower addresses. The procedure frame typically consists of the return address, space for saved registers, local variables, temporaries and outgoing function arguments. In consequence the frame size depends on the number of local variables, and the number of temporary variables and parameters at each specific call site. The stack size at a given program point then depends on the program path executed and the sizes of the frames of all currently active functions. The frame layout is defined by the calling conventions, which are either defined with the instruction set architecture, or by the individual compiler.

In a multi-tasking system, in general each task and each interrupt service routine (ISR) can be assigned their own stack. The maximal stack usage then results from

A. Bondavalli and F. Di Giandomenico (Eds.): SAFECOMP 2014, LNCS 8666, pp. 202–213, 2014.
© Springer International Publishing Switzerland 2014

adding the stack maxima of all relevant tasks and ISRs at a critical instant, i.e., the worst-case interruption scenario. Operating systems for safety-critical systems typically use static-priority scheduling strategies. The overall worst-case stack usage then can be determined from the priorities of tasks and the interrupt hierarchy. In the case of OSEK [20] the necessary information can be derived from the OS configuration (cf. Sec. 6).

Precisely determining the maximum stack usage before deploying the system is important for economical reasons and for system safety. Overestimating the maximum stack usage means wasting memory resources. Underestimation leads to stack overflows: memory cells from the stacks of different tasks or other memory areas are overwritten. This can cause crashes due to memory protection violations and can trigger arbitrary erroneous program behavior, if return addresses or other parts of the execution state are modified. In consequence stack overflows are typically hard to diagnose and hard to reproduce, but they are a potential cause of catastrophic failure. The accidents caused by the unintended acceleration of the 2005 Toyota Camry illustrate the potential consequences of stack overflows: the expert witness' report commissioned by the Oklahoma court in 2013 identifies a stack overflow as probable failure cause [7].

In safety-critical systems stack overflows should be avoided in order to prevent damage to health or property of people. Updating an embedded system typically is very costly once the system is deployed. Also liability questions have to be considered as all current safety standards, e.g., DO-178B/C or ISO-26262, require upper bounds of the used storage space used to be given, which includes the stack usage.

A safe upper bound of the maximal stack usage can be computed by whole-program *static analysis at the executable code level*. When an *abstract interpretation* based static analyzer is used, it can be formally proven that the maximal stack usage of each task will never be underestimated. From the per-task stack maxima the system-level stack maximum can be determined from the priorities of the tasks and the interrupt hierarchy. The challenge for binary-code level analyzers is to minimize the necessary amount of user interactions, e.g., for function pointer calls. To minimize user interaction, the analysis has to be precise, and the annotation mechanism has to be flexible and easy-to-use. The analyzer configuration has to be done once for each software project; afterwards the analysis can be run automatically, supporting continuous verification.

2 Methodology Overview

Measurement-based techniques to investigate the maximum stack usage are typically based on stack pollution checks: the stack area is pre-filled with a fixed bit pattern and then a set of test cases is executed. Afterwards in the used parts of the stack the initial pattern has been overwritten: they have been polluted. The amount of polluted stack space represents the maximal observed stack usage. The limitation of this approach is that memory overwrites caused by stack overflows which are outside the stack area are not detected. In the simplest case, the size of the polluted area is determined manually by using a debugger. The stack pollution checks can also be automatically performed at run-time [13,8,23]. The drawback is that when a stack overflow occurs the system might crash before the stack overflow is detected and handled.

The basic problem of all measurement-based techniques is that the worst-case input typically is unknown. So even repeated measurements with various inputs cannot guarantee that the maximum stack usage is ever observed. This is already true for the sequential code of a single task, as in general all potential program paths have to be investigated. In a multi-tasking context the problem is exacerbated: the worst-case stack usage occurs for a specific interruption scenario where a number of preempted or blocked tasks and possibly nested interrupt service routines are active at the same time. Moreover, the preemptions have to occur at program points where the task/ISR stack usage is maximal. On realistic systems no full test coverage covering all potential scenarios can be achieved [25].

To circumvent the coverage problem some approaches advocate to continuously monitor the used stack during 'normal' operation of the system for a given period in time, aiming at a reliability metrics based on the time spent for measurements. However, in contrast to hardware metrics, the results are inconclusive since there is no indication how often a specific execution path has been exercised during the observation period, or whether it has been exercised at all. In consequence for software-based systems no statistical failure rates are available which are comparable to those used for hardware components with typical requirements between maximally 10^{-5} and 10^{-9} failures per hour of operation [22].

In interrupt-driven systems execution is mainly controlled by event handlers and non-blocking tasks which are atomic with respect to other tasks [15]. Typically there is only one stack. For this execution paradigm advanced testing methods have been developed which aim at automatically creating critical interruption scenarios [24,9]. There is also a number of static approaches to compute the worst-case stack usage at the system level [4,5,25]. However these approaches target small devices like networked sensors whereas our focus is on safety-critical control-centric aerospace and automotive applications which require more complex system architectures. In the same context also static analyses to compute the maximum stack usage at the task level are discussed [5,25,18]. Their focus is on system-level aspects like automatically determining enabling/disabling of interrupts to limit the number of potential interruption scenarios. The value analysis used to determine stack usage of sequential code typically is not very elaborate so that, e.g., indirect function calls and memory accesses cannot be handled.

Static analysis at the source code level typically is unsafe as the effects of the code generation tool chain including compiler, assembler and linker cannot be taken into account. *Compilers* can exploit knowledge about the code generation process in order to provide information about stack usage. However they typically do not take into account the effects of inline assembly code or link-time optimizations. Moreover nowadays embedded control software, especially in the automotive domain, is often composed of libraries and object code integrated from different suppliers. Stack effects of such software parts cannot be safely estimated by the compiler. Another aspect relevant for functional safety certification is the independence between stack usage verification and the code generation tool chain.

Other approaches aim at monitoring the stack size and increasing it, if required. In [3,21] the compiler is modified to check the available stack size at function entry. If the stack grows too high, a stack overflow handler is invoked, and additional stack space can be provided. [21] additionally proposes to modify the compiler to emit the current stack maximum at function entries as an alternative to stack pollution checks. However, since no precise information about the stack size of the function is computed the size check cannot prevent stack overflows in all cases. Moreover dynamic stack size checking and resizing can cause significant runtime overhead.

Our approach is to compute sound and precise information about the maximal stack usage at the task level which minimizes the need for user interaction to provide indirect function call targets and recursion bounds. All required user information can be specified concisely in the formal language AIS [1]. In the safety-critical domain from this information the system-level maximum can be calculated from the per-task maxima and the OS configuration information. This approach supports non-preemptive and preemptive static-priority scheduling schemes with multiple levels of interrupt handling.

3   Static Analysis

Static program analyzers compute information about the software under analysis without actually executing it. The analyzers can work at the source code level, or at the object or executable code level. Semantics-based static analyzers use a program semantics that is a model of the program executions in all possible or a set of possible execution environments. Applied at the binary machine code level they do not compute an approximation of a programming language semantics, but an approximation of the semantics of the machine code of the microprocessor. Based on the program semantics, information about data and control flow is obtained. The most important characteristics of static analyzers is whether they are *sound* or *unsound*. A static analyzer is called *sound* if the computed results hold for any possible program execution.

A program analyzer is unsound when it can omit to signal an error that can appear at runtime in some execution environment. Unsound analyzers are *bug hunters* or *bug finders* aiming at finding some of the bugs in a well-defined class. Their main defect is unreliability, being subject to false negatives thus claiming that they can no longer find any bug while many may be left in the considered class.

The theory of *abstract interpretation* [6] is a mathematically rigorous formalism providing a semantics-based methodology for static program analysis. The semantics of a programming language is a formal description of the behavior of programs. The most precise semantics is the so-called concrete semantics, describing closely the actual execution of the program. Yet in general, the concrete semantics is not computable. Even under the assumption that the program terminates, it is too detailed to allow for efficient computations. The solution is to introduce an abstract semantics that approximates the concrete semantics of the program and is efficiently computable. This abstract semantics can be chosen as the basis for a static analysis. Compared to an analysis of the concrete semantics, the analysis result may be less precise but the computation may be significantly faster. By skillful definition of the abstract semantics, a suitable trade-off between precision and efficiency can be obtained. This makes it possible even for complex analyses to scale up to industry-size software projects (cf. Sec. 7).

Abstract interpretation supports formal correctness proofs: it can be proved that an analysis will terminate and that it is sound, i.e., that it computes an over-approximation of the concrete semantics. Moreover it can be shown that imprecisions always occur on the safe side. Examples of such proofs can be found in [10,27,19]. For stack usage analysis soundness means that the computed stack height must never be below the stack usage in any concrete execution: If no potential stack overflow is signaled the absence of stack overflows has been formally proven, i.e., there are *no false negatives*. Furthermore, as a static technique abstract interpretation can be easily automatized and can reduce the verification and validation effort.

4 Stack Usage Analysis by Abstract Interpretation

As discussed above, for safe stack size analysis it is important to work on fully linked *binary code*, i.e., here the static analysis is not based on the source code but on the executable code. It approximates the semantics of the machine code of the microprocessor by using an abstract model of the processor architecture. The abstract model does not need to cover the entire state of the microprocessor, only the parts affecting the stack are needed. The hardware state relevant for worst-case stack analysis includes the processor registers and the memory cells. For a naive analysis only the stack pointer register is needed, but for precise results it is important to perform an elaborate value analysis on the contents of processor register and memory cells (cf. Sec. 4.2). In the following we will give an overview of the structure and analysis phases of the tool StackAnalyzer [14,11].

4.1 Decoding

The input for the decoding phase is the fully linked binary executable that contains the task to be analyzed. The instruction decoder identifies the machine instructions and reconstructs the control-flow graph [26]. To ensure safety of later analysis results, the reconstructed CFG itself must be safe, i.e., all possible paths that can occur during execution of the program must be represented. Finding the target addresses of absolute and PC-relative calls and branches is straightforward, but determining target addresses computed from register contents can become difficult. Examples of such computed addresses are, e.g., indirect calls via function pointers or the implementation of high-level programming language constructs like switch tables. Uncertainties may lead to over-approximations of the actual control flow of the analyzed task which reduces analysis precision. To deal with this, StackAnalyzer uses specialized decoders that are adapted to certain code generators and/or compilers. They usually recognize branches to a previously stored return address, and know the typical compiler-generated patterns of branches via switch tables. Yet non-trivial applications may still contain some computed calls and branches (in hand-written assembly code) that cannot be resolved by the decoder; these unresolved computed calls and branches are documented by appropriate messages and require user annotations. Such annotations may list the possible targets of computed calls and branches, or tell the decoder about the address and format of an array of function pointers or a switch table used in the computed call or branch. The annotations are written in the formal language AIS and can be supplied in a dedicated input file (cf. Sec. 5).

4.2 Value Analysis

Value analysis aims at statically determining the contents of the registers and memory cells at each program point and for each execution context. The results of the value analysis are used to predict the addresses of data accesses, computed calls and branches, and to find infeasible paths caused by conditions that always evaluate to true, or always evaluate to false in a specific context. By concentrating on the value of the stack pointer during value analysis, the analysis can figure out how the stack increases and decreases along the various control-flow paths. This information can be used to derive the maximum stack usage of the entire task.

Contexts Disambiguating contexts is important to achieve high analysis precision. Consider a value analysis that computes an interval of possible values for every register r. The interval for r is a correct approximation of a concrete program state if it contains the value of r in this program state. Suppose now a routine R is called twice, once with parameter 0 and once with parameter 3. Then the best abstract information that can be obtained for the parameter register is the interval $[0,3]$, which indicates that the value of the register might be 0, or 1, or 2, or 3. The precision of the analysis can be improved considerably if the analysis does not compute a single abstract value for each program point in R, but two different ones, one for each call of R. In the example considered above, these are the intervals $[0,0]$ for the call with parameter 0 and $[3,3]$ for the call with parameter 3. The values 1 and 2 are thus excluded successfully. To be more general again, StackAnalyzer computes an abstract information for every pair of a program point p and a possible calling context of p. All program points in a given routine R have the same set of calling contexts. Each calling context indicates a particular way of calling R. The context is represented as a *call string* which is essentially composed from the addresses of all call instructions to currently active functions together with the corresponding function names. The context information is further refined by distinguishing between different iterations of a loop. By default, the length of the call string is not bounded, but for efficiency reasons, StackAnalyzer offers a way to restrict the number of contexts by limiting the length of the call strings. If a call string exceeds this limit, the first elements are omitted. The consequence is then that contexts are only disambiguated until a given calling depth. The information from the additional contexts will be unified, leading to a potential loss of precision of the analysis.

Loop Bound Analysis As a part of the value analysis a so-called loop bound analysis is performed. It uses the results of value analysis to determine lower and upper bounds for the number of iterations of loops. Knowing such bounds can improve the precision of value analysis, e.g., if the loop iterates through an array. For stack analysis the loop bound analysis can be restricted to loops that increase or decrease the stack in every iteration. If the iteration bound of a loop cannot be determined automatically, users can provide it in the AIS file or as source code annotations (see Sec. 5).

Iteration Between Decoding and Value Analysis The target of an indirect call or branch depends on the value of some register. Sometimes, an explicit value is written to the register some time before the call so that the call target can in principle be determined automatically. Unfortunately, the setting of the register often does not occur immediately before the call, but some time earlier, e.g., before a loop containing the call, so that matching of a simple code pattern is not sufficient to find the target address. The executable reader, which should follow function calls to decode the reachable instruction sequences, is not aware of the register values. These values are determined by value analysis, which however cannot construct control-flow graphs. The solution of the problem is to iterate between decoding and value analysis. If value analysis has found some register values needed by the decoder to resolve some indirect calls or branches, then the decoder is run again so that it can use these register values. Since this changes the control-flow graph, the value analyzer is run again to take care of the changes. If it finds more register values or the information about the values already found changes, a third iteration is performed, etc.

5   Refining the Analysis

Additional input to StackAnalyzer can be supplied in a formal language called AIS [1] in a dedicated input file. Alternatively, for executables built with debug information, AIS annotations can also be provided as source code comments.

AIS annotations often refer to program points. In the simplest cases, program points are described by an address or a routine name. More complicated descriptions are also possible, e.g., to denote the third computed call in a particular routine, or the loop beginning in a specific source code line. In the following we will only summarize annotations for call and branch targets, and loop bounds. Other AIS annotations allow path and dependency information to be specified, recursion bounds, reachability information, effects of external functionality, etc. For a complete reference see [1].

If user specifications are needed, StackAnalyzer issues a notification which describes the type of annotation needed (e.g., loop bound annotation) and the instruction (block) for which it is needed. If the executable has been build with debug information, also the corresponding source code construct is shown. An annotation wizard assists users to create the annotations in the correct syntax.

5.1   Indirect Calls and Branches

A call or branch is computed or indirect if its target depends on the value of some register. Computed calls often result from the usage of function pointers, while computed branches often correspond to switch tables. Computed targets which cannot be resolved automatically have to be resolved by annotations. Either the possible targets of the call or branch can be listed, or the list of targets can be extracted automatically from a given array or table.
Example:

```
instruction 0xc0f8 calls "disable";
instruction 0x9024 calls 0xa4, "go", "munch";
```

Program points are not restricted to simple addresses. A program point description particularly suited for calls and branches specifications is "R" + n COMPUTED which refers to the nth computed call or branch in routine R.
Example:

```
instruction "MC" + 1 computed branches to
    "MC" + 0x5C bytes, "MC" + 0x6C bytes;
```

Further syntactical variants support expressing branch targets relative to the address of the computed branch instruction, and branches via function pointer tables.

Example: Assume the first computed call or branch in `main` is a call via array A with 10 elements. Each array element is a target address of 4 bytes. The number and size of the array elements can be read from the symbol table. This is covered by the following AIS annotation:

```
instruction "main" + 1 computed calls via "A";
```

Sometimes, the situation is more complex because there are some steps of indirection: there is a master table containing not the function pointers themselves, but pointers to some other tables containing the function pointers, or pointers to yet other tables etc. The AIS declaration language can describe all these cases.

5.2 Loop Bounds

Stack analysis does not need loop bounds unless the loop body has a non-zero stack effect. Such loops, e.g., are generated by some compilers for pushing function parameters onto the stack before a function call. The parameters are removed from the stack by a single instruction after the call.

If a loop bound is missing StackAnalyzer issues a corresponding warning. Loop bound specification can be written in the following form:

```
LOOP ProgramPoint Bounds Type;
```

A `ProgramPoint` is either an address or a loop expression. The address must be the start address of the loop; this is the same address as in the messages about missing loop bounds. A loop expression looks like `"R" + n LOOPS` which means the nth loop in routine R, counted from 1.

The `Bounds` information can be supplied in several forms, e.g., by providing the minimum and maximum execution count for the loop body in the executable, or by specifying the maximum execution count only. The `Type` expression specifies the location of the loop test, i.e., whether it is at the beginning or at the end of the loop.
Example: The following annotation specifies that the first loop in `prime` has the loop test at the end and is executed at most 10 times.

```
loop "prime" + 1 loop end max 10;
```

Furthermore AIS permits to specify parametric loop bounds, i.e., the loop bound can be expressed as a formula depending on function parameters or auxiliary variables.

6   The System Level

We focus on complex safety-critical systems as used for Control&Command programs in the aerospace and automotive domains. Common system architectures are synchronous systems, or dynamically scheduled systems based on static-priority scheduling. In synchronous systems tasks are invoked from a cyclic executive and the schedule is completely static. They typically use one stack and, hence, for the purpose of stack height analysis they can be considered as a single piece of sequential code. The stack height analysis of StackAnalyzer directly yields the global maximum.

One example of a dynamically scheduled system architecture is the architecture defined by the OSEK standard [20] which is commonly used in automotive industry. Applications are composed of tasks and interrupt service routines. OSEK requires tasks to be scheduled by static-priority scheduling according to the priority ceiling protocol [20]. Tasks can be configured to be non-preemptable, or fully preemptive. Each task is associated with a run-time context which includes the stack. Tasks which can never preempt each other may be executed in the same run-time context, i.e., depending on the OS there may be one stack per task, or one stack per priority level. At the task level the run-time context is occupied at the beginning of execution time and is released again once the task is finished. The interrupt processing level consists of one or more interrupt priority levels. Interrupts take precedence over tasks; interrupt service routines have a statically assigned interrupt priority level. There are two ISR categories, depending on whether they use an operating system service, or not.

The maximal stack usage of the entire system is influenced by the maximal stack size of each task and ISR, by the preemptability of tasks, the task priority, category and priority of the ISRs, and the extend of the run-time context (per task or per priority level). In consequence the maximal stack usage can be calculated from the per-task maxima by a simple formula depending on information about implementation and configuration of the OS which is statically available. In general, the maximum stack usage S^{max} of the entire system can be calculated as:

$$
\begin{aligned}
S_{max} = {} & s^{init} \\
& + \sum_{0 \leq p < p_{max}} (max_i\{Stack(T_i) \mid p(T_i) = p\} + s^{TCF}) \\
& + max_i\{Stack(T_i) \mid p(T_i) = p_{max}\} \\
& + \sum_{0 \leq p' \leq p'_{max}} (max_i\{Stack(I_i) \mid p(I_i) = p\} + s^{ICF})
\end{aligned}
$$

where s^{init} is the size of the initialization frame, $Stack(T_i)$ is the maximal stack usage of task T_i, $Stack(I_i)$ is the maximal stack usage of ISR I_i, $p(T_i)$ denotes the priority of task T_i, p_{max} denotes the maximal task priority, p'_{max} is the maximal interrupt priority, s^{TCF} denotes the size of the task context switch frame, and s^{ICF} denotes the size of the ISR context switch frame.

In StackAnalyzer such formula can be specified using the so-called ResultCombinator view. For the analysis of the tasks and ISRs separate analysis objects are created. The results of these analysis can be referenced in the formula editor of the ResultCombinator to compute the global stack maximum.

7   Practical Experience

StackAnalyzer depends on the instruction set architecture and is available for a wide range of targets, including ARM, Infineon C16x, Infineon TriCore/Aurix, TI C28x, TI C33, Fujitsu FR81S, M68k, PowerPC, and V850. It has been successfully used for certification according to various contemporary safety standards. Qualification Support Kits and Qualification Software Life Cycle Data Reports enable the tool qualification to be performed automatically [17].

Experience shows that even for large applications precise stack bounds can be calculated within short computation time. The computation time is mainly influenced by the program structure and the task size; no significant variations between different instruction set architectures could be observed. In Tab. 1 stack analysis results are shown for some tasks from different industry sectors and for different target architectures. The tasks have been arbitrarily chosen among the largest available tasks of industrial production software. Colum *Arch* denotes the target architecture, column *Industry* the application area (E: electronics, AU: automotive, AE: aerospace). In column *Task Size* the code size of the task under analysis is shown in kilobytes; column $Stack^{max}$ shows the computed maximal stack size in bytes. The number of required AIS annotation is shown in column *Annotations*, the analysis time is given in column *Analysis Time*. Some processors like the Infineon C16x, TriCore, and Aurix have separate user and sys-

Table 1. Stack analysis results

Arch	Industry	Task Size [KB]	$Stack^{max}$ [B]	Annotations	Analysis Time
ARM	E	24.67	2184	5	8s
ARM	AU	124.86	396	0	1m 12s
M68020	AE	48.34	34752	1	1m 50s
M68020	E	0.96	128	2	1s
PowerPC	AE	681.63	67728	28	2m 52s
PowerPC	AU	82.94	1312	187	12m 25s
C16x	AU	93.55	168u/56s	1	2m 31s
C16x	AE	25.84	394u/32s	77	7s

tem stacks; StackAnalyzer computes separate maxima for both the user and the system stack. In the table above 'u' denotes the user stack while 's' denotes the system stack.

The graphical user interface of StackAnalyzer provides different views of the result, including visualizations of the call graph and control flow graph, and enables the information contained in the executable to be browsed in a user-friendly way. Creating AIS annotations is facilitated by a dedicated annotation wizard. These mechanisms help users to efficiently set up the analysis and evaluate the analysis results. After the configuration of the analysis and the assessment of the results the analysis can be executed in batch mode as a part of continuous verification processes or regression tests.

A dedicated XML-based exchange format (XTC format [2]) enables StackAanalyzer to be seamlessly integrated in other development tools. Tool couplings are available with model-based code generators including Esterel SCADE [12] and dSPACE TargetLink [16]. They make it possible to detect stack problems early in the development process. Another benefit of the tool couplings is that all required AIS annotations can be automatically generated from the model level without any user interaction being required.

8 Summary

Stack overflows are serious errors which can cause embedded software to crash or to behave erratically. They are typically hard to identify and fixing them can be very cost-intensive, especially when the system has already been deployed. All current safety standards, including DO-178B/C or ISO-26262, require upper bounds of the storage space used to be given, which explicitly includes the stack usage.

Whole-program static analysis at the executable code level can provide upper bounds on the maximal stack height of tasks. When an abstract interpretation based static analyzer is used, it can be formally proven that the bound is safe, i.e., that the maximal stack usage will not be underestimated. To be practically usable the analyzer must be able to handle indirect function calls, stack-relevant loops, and recursions. The tool

StackAnalyzer addresses this goal by performing a sophisticated value analysis which enables the control flow to be precisely reconstructed and provides precise information about the potential values of registers and memory cells. However, in general, it is not possible to statically resolve all indirect calls, and to compute bounds for every loop and recursion. For any unresolved issues user annotations can be provided in the formal annotation language AIS in a flexible and concise way. From the maximal stack usage of each task and ISR and static information about the OS configuration, the global stack maximum can be computed.

Practical experience shows that industry-size projects from different industry sectors for various target processors can be analyzed in short time with precise results. Static analyses can be easily automatized, supporting continuous verification. This way, stack overflows can be detected early, preventing late-stage integration problems. The analysis results also provide valuable feedback in optimizing the stack usage of an application so that the most cost-efficient hardware can be chosen. With dedicated Qualification Support Kits the tool qualification for StackAnalyzer can be done automatically with respect to any contemporary safety standard. In summary, using a sound static stack usage analysis enables safety to be improved and development time to be reduced.

Acknowledgement. The work presented in this paper has been supported by the ITEA2 project TIMMO-2-USE and the EU ARTEMIS Joint Undertaking under grant agreement no. 269335 with the German BMBF (MBAT project).

References

1. AbsInt. AIS Quick Reference Guide (2013)
2. AbsInt. XTC Language Specification Version 2.1 (2013),
   http://www.absint.com/xtc/
3. Biswas, S., Simpson, M., Barua, R.: Memory overflow protection for embedded systems using run-time checks, reuse and compression. In: Proceedings of the 2004 International Conference on Compilers, Architecture, and Synthesis for Embedded Systems, CASES 2004, pp. 280–291. ACM, New York (2004)
4. Brylow, D., Damgaard, N., Palsberg, J.: Static checking of interrupt-driven software. In: Proceedings of the 23rd International Conference on Software Engineering, ICSE 2001, pp. 47–56. IEEE Computer Society Press, Washington, DC (2001)
5. Chatterjee, K., Ma, D., Majumdar, R., Zhao, T., Henzinger, T.A., Palsberg, J.: Stack size analysis for interrupt-driven programs. In: Cousot, R. (ed.) SAS 2003. LNCS, vol. 2694, pp. 109–126. Springer, Heidelberg (2003)
6. Cousot, P., Cousot, R.: Abstract interpretation: a unified lattice model for static analysis of programs by construction or approximation of fixpoints. In: POPL 1977: Proceedings of the 4th ACM SIGACT-SIGPLAN Symposium on Principles of Programming Languages, pp. 238–252. ACM Press, New York (1977)
7. Dunn, M.: Toyota's killer firmware: Bad design and its consequences. EDN Network (October 2013), http://www.edn.com/design/automotive/4423428/Toyota-s-killer-firmware--Bad-design-and-its-consequences
8. Engelschall, R.S.: Portable multithreading: The signal stack trick for user-space thread creation. In: Proceedings of the Annual Conference on USENIX Annual Technical Conference, ATEC 2000, p. 20. USENIX Association, Berkeley (2000)
9. Eslamimehr, M., Palsberg, J.: Testing versus static analysis of maximum stack size. In: Proceedings of the 2013 IEEE 37th Annual Computer Software and Applications Conference, COMPSAC 2013, pp. 619–626. IEEE Computer Society Press, Washington, DC (2013)

10. Ferdinand, C.: Cache Behavior Prediction for Real-Time Systems. PhD thesis, Saarland University (1997)
11. Ferdinand, C., Heckmann, R., Franzen, B.: Static Memory and Timing Analysis of Embedded Systems Code. In: Groot, P. (ed.) Proceedings of the 3rd European Symposium on Verification and Validation of Software Systems (VVSS 2007), Eindhoven, The Netherlands, March 23. TUE Computer Science Reports, vol. 07-04 (2007)
12. Ferdinand, C., Heckmann, R., Le Sergent, T., Lopes, D., Martin, B., Fornari, X., Martin, F.: Combining a high-level design tool for safety-critical systems with a tool for WCET analysis on executables. In: 4th European Congress ERTS Embedded Real Time Software, Toulouse, France (January 2008)
13. Guillemin, P.: Stack overflow detection using the ST9 timer/watchdog. Doc id 2476 rev 2, STMicroelectronics (2011)
14. Heckmann, R., Ferdinand, C.: Stack Usage Analysis and Software Visualization for Embedded Processors. In: Grote, C. (ed.) Vorträge und Begleittexte zur Embedded Intelligence 2002. Grundlagen, Architekturen, Werkzeuge und Lösungen, Nürnberg, Poing, Februar 19-21. Design & Elektronik (2002)
15. Hill, J., Szewczyk, R., Woo, A., Hollar, S., Culler, D., Pister, K.: System architecture directions for networked sensors. SIGARCH Comput. Archit. News 28(5), 93–104 (2000)
16. Kästner, D., Kiffmeier, U., Fleischer, D., Nenova, S., Schlickling, M., Ferdinand, C.: Integrating Model-Based Code Generators with Static Program Analyzers. Embedded World Congress (2013)
17. Kästner, D., Pister, M., Gebhard, G., Schlickling, M., Ferdinand, C.: Confidence in Timing. In: Safecomp 2013 Workshop: Next Generation of System Assurance Approaches for Safety-Critical Systems, SASSUR (September 2013)
18. Kim, H., Cha, H.: Multithreading optimization techniques for sensor network operating systems. In: Langendoen, K.G., Voigt, T. (eds.) EWSN 2007. LNCS, vol. 4373, pp. 293–308. Springer, Heidelberg (2007)
19. Miné, A.: Weakly Relational Numerical Abstract Domains. PhD thesis, École Polytechnique, Palaiseau, France (December 2004),
    http://www.di.ens.fr/~mine/these/these-color.pdf
20. OSEK/VDX. OSEK/VDX Operating System. Version 2.2.3 (2005)
21. Park, S.H., Lee, D.K., Kang, S.J.: Compiler-assisted maximum stack usage measurement technique for efficient multi-threading in memory-limited embedded systems. In: Lee, R. (ed.) Computers,Networks, Systems, and Industrial Engineering 2011. SCI, vol. 365, pp. 113–129. Springer, Heidelberg (2011)
22. Radio Technical Commission for Aeronautics. RTCA DO-178B. Software Considerations in Airborne Systems and Equipment Certification (1992)
23. Real Time Engineers Ltd. FreeRTOS^{TM} web page: Stack Usage and Stack Overflow Checking (2010), http://www.freertos.org/Stacks-and-stack-overflow-checking.html
24. Regehr, J.: Random testing of interrupt-driven software. In: Proceedings of the 5th ACM International Conference on Embedded Software, EMSOFT 2005, pp. 290–298. ACM, New York (2005)
25. Regehr, J., Reid, A., Webb, K.: Eliminating stack overflow by abstract interpretation. ACM Trans. Embed. Comput. Syst. 4(4), 751–778 (2005)
26. Theiling, H.: Extracting Safe and Precise Control Flow from Binaries. In: Proceedings of the 7th Conference on Real-Time Computing and Applications Symposium (RTCSA 2000), Cheju Island, South Korea, December 12-14, pp. 23–30. IEEE Computer Society Press (2000)
27. Thesing, S.: Safe and Precise WCET Determinations by Abstract Interpretation of Pipeline Models. PhD thesis, Saarland University (2004)

Trust-Based Intrusion Tolerant Routing in Wireless Sensor Networks

Francesco Buccafurri[2], Luigi Coppolino[1], Salvatore D'Antonio[1],
Alessia Garofalo[1], Gianluca Lax[2], Antonino Nocera[2], and Luigi Romano[1]

[1] University of Naples Parthenope,
Department of Engineering, Naples, Italy
{alessia.garofalo,luigi.coppolino,luigi.romano,
salvatore.dantonio}@uniparthenope.it
[2] DIIES, University Mediterranea of Reggio Calabria,
Via Graziella, Località Feo di Vito, 89122 Reggio Calabria, Italy
{bucca,lax,a.nocera}@unirc.it

Abstract. Wireless Sensor Networks (WSNs) are being increasingly
adopted in several fields because of their advantages with respect to
classic sensor networks. However, nodes in a WSN cooperate and this
exposes them to several security threats. Trust-based systems constitute an established solution to ensure security of distributed systems. In
this work, a trust-based approach is discussed to make WSNs tolerant
against attacks targeting their routing layer. We show how such attacks
are tolerated with low overhead in comparison to unprotected systems.
Preliminary experimental results are presented confirming the validity of
the proposed approach.

Keywords: Trust-based systems, trust, reputation, intrusion prevention, Wireless Sensor Network, Ad hoc On-Demand Distance Vector.

1 Introduction

Wireless Sensor Networks (WSNs) are composed of battery-powered tiny sensors with wireless connection capabilities. Sensor nodes in WSNs are capable of
connecting to each other, exchanging information, routing packets according to
the specific WSN technology chosen. Nodes in WSN can interact with computer
networks through a Base Station (BS).

WSN adoption in Critical Infrastructures (CIs) [4][1] has advantages as eas-
iness of deployment in hostile environments and no need for underlying infrastructures. However, their adoption is limited due to their security weaknesses;
for instance, the most widely adopted WSN routing protocols such as Ad hoc
On-Demand Distance Vector (AODV) [13], Collection Tree Protocol (CTP) [5],
Destination Sequenced Distance-Vector Routing (DSDV) [14] are designed without considering security mechanisms.

Cyber defense of wireless transmissions in general is challenging because the
communication channel itself is easy to monitor without being detected. Additional

A. Bondavalli and F. Di Giandomenico (Eds.): SAFECOMP 2014, LNCS 8666, pp. 214–229, 2014.
© Springer International Publishing Switzerland 2014

issues are experienced in WSNs, since nodes are equipped with low computational resources and limited energy supply, so computation-intensive defense mechanisms (e.g. encryption with large key size, public key cryptography) that are typically used in computer networks can hardly be adopted on an 'as is' basis in WSNs. A consequence is that WSNs are also exposed to cyber threats [8].

This work proposes a trust-based layer enhanced architecture designed to tolerate intrusion attempts. In this context, by tolerance we mean the capability of the WSN to keep providing the service it is intended to even when a malicious entity compromises successfully a legitimate WSN node and then routing attacks occur in the network. The proposed solution allows us to improve resilience to cyber-attacks by incurring in little overhead in terms of additional messages exchanged between WSN nodes. We focus on the *sinkhole attack* [8] since it can have major consequences when successful, and also (importantly) because it is often used as a preliminary attack to more severe intrusions. A preliminary experimental campaign was performed, where the trust-based architecture was tested against sinkhole attacks to AODV routing protocol, which is a widely adopted WSN routing protocol (e.g., in ZigBee and Bluetooth). Preliminary experimental results show the effectiveness of the proposed architecture.

The remainder of this paper is organized as follows. Section 2 provides background definitions needed for understanding of this work and details existing solutions for ensuring cyber security in WSNs. Section 3 details the attack model considered. Section 4 discusses the trust-based architecture designed to tolerate cyber attacks to WSNs routing protocols. Section 5 details the trust-based model chosen. Section 6 provides a security analysis of the proposed architecture including the robustness of the trust and reputation layer. Section 7 gives some interesting implementation details and describes the testbed chosen for the execution of the experimental campaign whose results are shown in Section 8. Finally, in Section 9, we draw our conclusions.

2   Related Work

In WSNs different routing protocols exist. The most popular ones are Ad-hoc On Demand Distance Vector (AODV)[13] and MultiHop. AODV is a reactive routing algorithm. It is the routing scheme adopted by ZigBee and Bluetooth. When a WSN node using AODV protocol receives a packet addressed to an unknown destination, it starts to send "'route discovery"' packets (Route Request message - RREQ). A "'route discovery"' message is propagated throughout the network until a node finds an entry in its routing table matching the address, and responds to the request with a Route Reply message (RREP). Each message brings the receiving device to set a path in its routing table, if the sender of that message is an in-sight node. When the message reaches its destination, a backward path has been set along the intermediate nodes. In AODV, when two valid routes are available to the same destination the "'freshness"' of the route and the number of hops to the destination (called *hop count*) are considered to choose which one has to be used.

Different solutions have been introduced in literature to detect and tolerate routing attacks against the WSN[4][11][9], some of which specifically focus on sinkhole attack as [7][3]. In this paper we present a new solution which aims at tolerating routing level attacks through a trust and reputation based protocol. In [20], the authors propose a Trust-Aware Routing Framework (TARF) for protecting routing activities in WSNs. This is achieved by evaluating a tradeoff between trust perceived and energy consumed for a specific route. When attacks are not occurring in the system, the trust-aware framework proposed is shown to have acceptable performances with reference to an unprotected system. An experimental testbed shows that the behavior of the TARF-enabled system under attack is comparable to the behavior of an unprotected system when attacks are not occurring. The framework presented in this work makes use of several information related to data delivery, loop detection, energy consumption. WSN routing protocols may be natively able to provide a part of such information; in some cases instead, most of the data required by TARF need to be estimated by the framework itself, thus requiring an additional effort in terms of packets overhead or computational resources. However, considerations about the effective deployment of this architecture on different WSNs are not provided by the authors. The survey provided in [19] discusses works related to trust models for secure routing and they are detailed in the following. The purpose of Reliable Adaptive serviCe-driven Efficient Routing (μRACER) [15] is to provide a suite for sensor-actuator networks that provides different features at once, as context-aware task scheduling and direction-aware routing. The suite is not designed to ensure cyber security; however, in [19], μRACER is stated to resist to attacks since trusted nodes are chosen by taking into account the ratio of messages forwarded. Since both the system design and experimental results do not take into account cyber attacks, the effectiveness of this approach in presence of malicious nodes cannot be estimated. In [10], a strategy called Efficient Monitoring Procedure In Reputation System (EMPIRE) is proposed. EMPIRE aims to detect blackhole attacks, i.e. attacks where packets forwarded to a malicious node are dropped. The solution proposed is only resilient to blackhole; our architecture instead is capable of detecting both sinkhole and blackhole attacks. In our work, trust measurements are used to estimate fast and successful delivery of messages; those estimations are affected under different attacks, as sinkhole and blackhole. In [17], a k-parent Flooding Tree Model is proposed. The model provides resilience to Denial-of-Broadcast Message attacks, i.e. attacks where a malicious user attempts to deny broadcast message to all nodes in the network. The model is designed only for broadcast messages and it proposes a k-parent tree model: each node is given k parents, and each parent is given a reputation. The reputation is not estimated through interactions with neighbors, but only through direct trust; also, the direct trust can only assume values 0 or 1. So, the estimation of trust perceived is highly relevant when reputation is updated. If such estimation is incorrect for any reason, there is no other mechanism available to adjust such an error. This is prevented in our model because trust and reputation are both taken into account when computing the *dependability* of nodes [2].

In [18], a trust-based model for trusted routing called Trust Routing for Location-Aware Sensor Networks (TRANS) is proposed. Such model assumes that knowledge of geographic locations is available in the WSN routing protocol considered. The trust model takes into account geographic information and considers trusted geographic locations. The model proposed in our work instead is independent of geographic locations. In [6] a framework is proposed called Reputation-based Framework for Sensor Networks (RFSN) whose purpose is to mitigate wrong sensor readings. Such errors are supposed to have any cause, as low energy available on the mote or malicious nodes attacking the network. About the trust model, a pessimistic approach is chosen, where the network does not trust unknown nodes. This allows malicious nodes not to take advantage of the trust initially granted. However, this approach incurs in an high overhead of packets especially in the system setup, since all nodes need to exchange information until e.g. high value of trust is estimated for legitimate nodes. Our work instead proposes an optimistic approach; this is because: i) cyber attacks to WSNs are much less frequent than normal, non-malicious activities; ii) initially, attackers are often not present in the WSN (when the initial trust is set); iii) when attackers are initially present in the WSN, they initially behave correctly so to gain trust of the remaining nodes in the network.

To the best of our knowledge, trust-based models currently proposed on WSNs use passive approaches, i.e. they only make use of information provided by the routing protocol in use. This implies that the features of the routing protocol in use pose limitations to the trust-based architecture. Our work instead proposes a proactive, event-driven approach, so that relevant information can be collected by the trust-based architecture independently of the specific features of the considered routing protocol. Also, the choice of an event-driven approach allows a significant reduction of the introduced overhead, with respect to the one obtained by periodically exchanging collected measurements.

3   Attack Model

The trust-based architecture presented in this work aims at tolerating *sinkhole attack*, where the attacker lures legitimate nodes to route their packets through a malicious node. When this attack is successful, the malicious node is able to launch more severe attacks such as altering or dropping packets sent from legitimate nodes. In order to successfully perform a sinkhole attack, a malicious node pretends that it represents a high quality route with reference to the routing protocol in use. As already mentioned, cyber defense mechanisms are not provided in the most common WSN routing protocols (e.g. AODV). Thus, legitimate nodes typically just receive routes advertised and no security check is performed on them. After that, the advertised quality is compared with the quality of an already known route (if any). So, if an old route is replaced with a forged route (received by a malicious node), the attack is successful.

A way to perform sinkhole attack is the following:

1. The network is initially composed of legitimate nodes only, as shown in Figure 1.a.

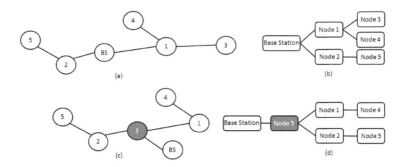

Fig. 1. Evolution of a sinkhole attack: (a) A WSN where nodes are not compromised (BS = Base Station), (b) The hierarchy of routing data towards the Base Station, (c) The WSN state when the attack is successfully performed by node 3, (d) The hierarchy of routing data as obtained by the sinkhole attacker through forged packets

2. Each node establishes its own routing tables according to the routing protocol in use. The tree in Figure 1.b represents the routes established by nodes to reach the BS when no attack is yet affecting the network. In the figure, each node has chosen the closest node to the BS to route packets directed to the BS itself. So, e.g. node 3 is a leaf of the routing tree since it has the lowest quality link to the BS.
3. After that, a legitimate node is compromised e.g. through reprogramming and sinkhole attack begins.
4. The compromised node requests a route to a given destination.
5. The compromised node sends a forged response to the previously sent request; the purpose of this message is to advertise a (false) high quality route to the same destination as claimed at previous step. This misleads neighboring nodes, which can choose to replace their older route with the new advertised one.

Figures 1.c and 1.d show an example of topology and routes established after a successful sinkhole attack. In the example, node 3 is a legitimate node that is compromised by an attacker and so it forges information about the quality of its link from the BS. After the attack succeeds, any packet can be compromised by node 3 since all packets are forwarded through that node. In this way, more severe attacks can be launched on the target system.

4   Trust and Reputation Layer

IP-based WSNs make use of a modified version of the OSI model, as an example Figure 2.a shows AODV used as routing protocol, e.g. as in ZigBee Libelium Waspmote[1]. Our architecture is designed as an additional layer on top of which AODV is available (Figure 2.b). The purpose of this new layer is to provide

---

[1] http://www.libelium.com/products/waspmote/

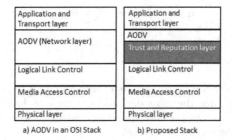

a) AODV in an OSI Stack   b) Proposed Stack

Fig. 2. (a) OSI stack protocol for IP-based WSNs; (b) the intrusion-tolerant trust and reputation layer

functionalities required to ensure intrusion tolerant routing. Specifically, the Trust and Reputation (T&R) layer in Figure 2.b makes use of the dependability L, which represents a global estimation of all knowledge related to a node under test, and acts as follows on any node in the WSN:

1. Data sent to the routing protocol from its underlying level (and vice versa) are monitored.
2. When the T&R layer detects routing operations that could result in a topology change, a *test* procedure is started to estimate the dependability of nodes involved in the current operation. The test procedure is not triggered in two cases: i) when the same test was already recently performed; ii) when the dependability of the node triggering the test procedure is lower than a fixed threshold. In both these conditions, current path is instead preserved. The following steps refer to the case when the test procedure is allowed.
   (a) Test results are used to estimate the trust of involved nodes.
   (b) The evaluated trust is shared with neighboring nodes, which store the information and compute the reputation of tested nodes.
   (c) The T&R layer of the node that launched the test estimates the global dependability of tested node/s. Subsequent routing interactions will be performed with the most dependable node. When the tested node is considered trustworthy, the event producing the topology change is forwarded 'as is' to the routing layer. Otherwise, such a change is masked to the routing layer.

The test procedure should choose the most dependable node by taking into account the link quality Q, which represents the effective quality of the route the tested node belongs to. However, estimations of Q cannot be assumed as trustworthy; so, the dependability L introduced is used as an unforgeable estimator and it is defined as $L = f(T, R)$. In this expression, T and R represent trust and reputation; trust is measured through a test procedure, dependent on the kind of attack that must be tolerated, instead reputation is obtained by combining the trust measures received by neighboring nodes during previous tests of the node currently tested.

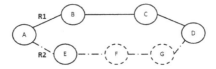

Fig. 3. An example of WSN topology where a route update is requested and the trust-based architecture estimates the most dependable source to be chosen. (Solid line = route established and saved in the corresponding routing tables; dashed line = candidate route to replace the established route)

For the sinkhole attack, the purpose of the *test* procedure is to check the quality of the route containing the node under test against the quality of the route currently used by the node performing the test. Figure 3 provides an example of the test procedure. In the figure, node A is initially aware of one route to node D, and such route is composed of two intermediate nodes (B and C). After that, node E advertises itself to node A as a single hop route to node D. Assuming that the routing protocol considers the route with the minimum hops to the destination as the best route; in that case, route R2 would be the best candidate to reach node D. The T&R layer intercepts the potential change of route and triggers a test: two packets are sent from node A to node D, each of them through one of the candidate routes. When the packets are received back, the round trip time of both packets is estimated. If the packet through node E has the lower round trip time, the advertised route is indeed the best one and so trust about node E is raised; on the contrary, E is punished (i.e., its trust is reduced). Security aspects related to the testing procedure are discussed in Section 6.

In a typical WSN deployment, nodes send data to the BS; in that case, the purpose of the test procedure is to test candidate routes to the BS. BS authentication has then to be ensured to guarantee the authenticity of the test. We explicitly emphasize that our purpose is only to ensure integrity of the test procedure; however, packet integrity can be ensured with existing methods which are orthogonal to our work. In the following section, more details are provided about the T&R model designed to provide intrusion tolerance to sinkhole attack for AODV routing protocol.

5   The Trust and Reputation Model

In this section, we discuss how node dependability is computed. We make use of the concepts of trust and reputation: Trust measures the degree to which one node trusts another on the basis of past interactions, reputation is based on a collection of opinions that other nodes hold about a given node. Both scores range in the interval $[0, 1]$.

We assume given a WSN with a set $N = n_1, ..., n_w$ of nodes. We show how trust and reputation of nodes are computed and updated after each node interaction, which consists in the execution of the test procedure described in Section 4.

Consider an interaction between the nodes n_i and n_j and let $F_{i,j}$ be the score, assigned by n_i to n_j, that quantifies the result of this interaction from the point of view of trust [16]. $F_{i,j}$ ranges in the interval $[0,1]$: 0 (resp., 1) is the score assigned to a bad (resp., good) interaction. After this interaction, the trust that n_i deserves to n_j is: $T_{i,j} = F_{i,j}$.

At this point, n_i forwards this score, say feedback about n_j, to each of its neighbors, which, in turn, update their reputation about n_j. In particular, a node n_z that receives the d-th feedback $F_{k,j}^d$ (for any $1 \leq j, k \leq w, k \neq j, d \geq 1$) about n_j, updates the reputation deserved to n_j as follows:

$$
R_{z,j}^d =
\begin{cases}
(1 - \alpha) \cdot R_{z,j}^{d-1} + \alpha \cdot F_{k,j}^d & \text{if } n_j^d \neq n_j^{d-1} \wedge F_{k,j}^d < R_{z,j}^{d-1} \\
\\
R_{z,j}^{d-1} & \text{otherwise}
\end{cases}
\tag{1}
$$

where n_j^x is the node providing the x-th feedback about n_j, and $R_{z,j}^0$ is the default value of reputation. We assume $R_{z,j}^0 = 1$ because, in normal conditions (i.e., when no attack occurs), all nodes are trustworthy. This choice is aimed at favoring the dynamic of the routing protocol, which, otherwise, would be very reluctant to route changes for a long working time (until reputation values grow sufficiently).

In Equation 1, the new value of the reputation of a node is computed weighting, by means of the parameter $\alpha \in [0,1]$, two contributions: (1) the reputation value computed on the basis of the previous feedback, and (2) the current feedback. α allows us to modulate the weight of the two components.

Once trust and reputation of a node are computed, the (global) dependability that the node n_z deserves to n_j is computed as:

$$
L_{z,j} = (1 - \beta) \cdot T_{z,j} + \beta \cdot R_{z,j}
\tag{2}
$$

where $T_{z,j}$ and $R_{z,j}$ are the current values of trust and reputation, resp., computed by the node n_z towards n_j. In words, dependability is computed weighting in a complementary way, by means of β, trust and reputation. β lies in the interval $[0,1]$ and modulates the importance given to trust w.r.t. reputation.

The parameters α and β need to be set on the basis of simulation, once security policies are established (this issue is addressed in Section 7). Here, we provide some general considerations. As for the parameter α, we argue that its value should depend on the dependability of the node (say n_f) providing the feedback. For instance, when n_z receives a feedback from a node n_f whose dependability $L_{z,f}$ is zero, the value of reputation should not be affected by this feedback. Thus, α should be 0. Conversely, if $L_{z,f} = 1$ (i.e., maximum dependability), we have to take into account the feedback for updating dependability (so, $\alpha > 0$), and depending on how much the system has to keep memory of the past, the value of α will be close to 1. The higher the value of α, the lower the inertia of the update mechanism of reputation. We may set $\alpha = \gamma \cdot L_{z,f}$ with $\gamma \in (0,1]$, and use as starting value $\gamma = 0.5$, in such a way that, at most, feedbacks are weighted in the same way as reputation. The parameter β balances trust and reputation: its value should be low ($\beta \leq 0.5$) so to prevent attackers from forging reputation of non-malicious nodes.

A final observation is that, according to our model, only feedbacks able to reduce reputation produce effects. Hence, to save traffic, feedbacks with score 1 are not forwarded. The negative role of feedbacks (w.r.t. the reputation values) results in pushing node reputation towards low values. To contrast this effect, we introduce an *aging* mechanism producing a *bonus*: the reputation of each node is increased (up to 1) by δ each τ time, where δ and τ are parameters suitably fixed. For example, setting $\delta = 0.1$ and $\tau = 360$ seconds, a node that has reputation score 0 (for example, because of a network problem occurred) and that does not interact with other nodes recovers a reputation score equal to 1 after 1 hour.

We explicitly note that the optimal tuning of parameters $\alpha, \beta, \gamma, \delta, \tau$ is outside the scope of this work and will be the object of a future work. Thus the experimental campaign of Section 7 will be using for such parameters the reference values reported in this section.

6   Security Analysis

In this section, we analyze the security of our approach against the attack model presented in Section 3. We proceed by analyzing a number of significant security aspects.

Security of the Test. Suppose node z receives a malicious advertisement from node j (assumed compromised) aimed at forcing z to update its routing path to the BS in favor of j. Let i be the node currently included in the routing table of z. Recall that our approach is based on the triggered execution of a test consisting in the measurement, by z, of the round trip time of two messages from z to the BS through two different routes, of which only one includes the tested node j (the other includes the node i). The aim of the test is estimating the quality of the two routes, to evaluate the trustworthiness of the advertisement of j in promoting itself as a better route towards the BS.

The test procedure can be compromised by an attacker that replies to a test message pretending to be the BS. This requires that the testing procedure uses authentication of the destination node. It is worth noting that such an authentication would not avoid routing level attacks such as the sinkhole attack. Also with destination authentication, the testing procedure is vulnerable to a *replay* attack, that is the reply message to the testing procedure can be recorded by the attacker and reused later. To avoid the *replay* attack the testing procedure must guarantee the freshness of messages (e.g. by using a challenge/response protocol). Observe that the overhead introduced by the authentication is limited to the testing procedure while the remaining messages do not require any authentication or encryption.

Obviously, the compromised node j could selectively delay the round-trip message routed through i, but only in case j belongs to both the routes of the test. If we consider the case in which there is a single node compromised that performs the attack, and assuming that no successful step of j towards sinkhole has been already done, this is impossible, as both j and i are neighbors of z, and thus i cannot see j as an *ancient node* towards the BS because this would mean that i has been already deceived by j (contradiction). Thus, j cannot belong to both routes of the test and then cannot delay the message routed through i. In general, assuming that a partial sinkhole is done by the node j, it is easy to see that the breaking of the test cannot add new victim nodes.

Lack of Memory of Trust. Assume that both trust and reputation of z towards j are 1. Our protocol requires that z, before deciding whether j may replace i in its routing table, runs a test (see Section 4) involving nodes i and j. The feedback $F_{z,j}$ is obtained from the result of the above test so that, in case of failure, the update rule $T_{z,j} = F_{z,j}$ decreases the trust value of j, drastically reducing the chance of j to be selected by z, as the dependability function is strongly dependent on the trust. This positive effect is obtained because trust is computed only on the basis of the last interaction, meaning that this measure has no memory of the past. The reason of this choice is that even one bad interaction with a node could be the symptom of a malicious behavior of this node.

Self-Promoting Attacks. This attack occurs when an attacker manipulates its own reputation by falsely increasing it. As in our model positive feedbacks are uninfluential, there is no way for a node to force self-promoting.

Whitewashing Attacks. In this family of attacks, attackers try to repair maliciously their reputation. Once they restore their reputation, the attackers can continue the malicious behavior. As in our system positive feedbacks are uninfluential, the only way to whitewash reputation is to use the aging mechanism of the *bonus*, which increases periodically (but slowly) the reputation of nodes. This succeeds only if, for a long time, the node stops any action that can generate new negative feedbacks. This means that the reputation system keeps memory of a malicious behavior only for a (large) time window. After that, this memory is erased, but it is decreased again (i.e., the reputation is drastically reduced) as soon as another malicious action is done. The long time period required to whitewash the reputation and the high dinamics of the network make the attacks that can be performed periodically (i.e., each time the reputation is whitewashed) uneffective. This prevents the attacker to have benefits from the whitewashing attack because no escalation is allowed.

Slandering Attacks. In this case, attackers manipulate the reputation of other nodes by reporting false data to lower the reputation of the victim nodes. In this case, the attacker, say j, generates false negative feedbacks about a victim node, say i, to increase its relative value of dependability and emerge w.r.t. the other nodes. Suppose that the false feedback is provided by j to z and regards node i. The reputation value is changed by the d-th feedback $F_{j,i}^d$ only if $n_i^d \neq n_i^{d-1}$, where n_i^d is the node that provided the d-th feedback about i. Thus, if the previous and current feedbacks come from the same node, the latter is ignored. So, the effect of a slandering attack is seriously limited (in practise, cancelled) by the combination of this strategy with the aging mechanism of the *bonus* recalled above. Indeed, after a false feedback about the victim node i is given, the attacker should wait the arrival of another feedback concerning i coming from a different node, which is not controllable by the attacker. In the meantime, the aging mechanism will vanish the attempt by restoring the reputation of the victim node. Observe that, in our attack model, we assume that suitable strategies are already applied in the network in order to prevent sybil attacks. Therefore, the above countermeasure cannot be vanished by the generation of multiple identities corresponding to the compromised physical node. It remains to consider change-identity and re-entry techniques. Actually, in these cases the attacker may successfully perform slandering attacks by generating unfair ratings about a victim node. This vulnerability can be eliminated by relying on authentication and integrity services of the network. In particular, it suffices to require that feedbacks are processed only if authenticated by the BS. Even though this issue is out of the scope of the paper, we may highlight that the message authentication mechanism here required is very little expensive. Indeed, it is needed only for the messages generated by the BS for the test procedure. Moreover, even cheap hash-based methods can be used requiring only that every node shares with the BS a secret key. Thus, the BS may send the result of the test equipped with a number of message authentication codes, one for each neighbor of the tester node. To do this, the tester node includes the list of its neighbors in the starting message of the test procedure. Once the tester node receives the authenticated result of the test from the BS, it forwards this to its neighbors according to our model.

Sleep Deprivation Attacks. In this case, the target of the intruder is to maximize the power consumption of a victim, so that its lifetime is minimized. In particular, a power-consuming action is required every time a node is called to perform the test. Therefore, the compromised node could force continuously a victim node z to perform the test, thus implementing a sleep deprivation attack against it. This attack is prevented in two ways. The first is that the test is executed by a node z on the basis of the advertisement of a node j only if the reputation of j is greater than a suitable threshold. But, after the first test failures, the reputation of j will go under the threshold. The second way is that, as described in Section 4, each node keeps the timestamp of the last performed test on a node. The test can be repeated only if the new request arrives at a time not too close to that of the last request.

7   Implementation Details and Testbed Setup

The proposed T&R layer was implemented in the network simulator NS-3 [12], whose source code is open and available and where a WSN on AODV routing protocol can be simulated.

With respect to Figure 2, the new layer was placed at routing level. So, information useful to the trust mechanism has to be added to standard routing information provided by AODV. In particular, AODV [13] allows us to do this through *extensions* to standard packets. Extensions format is defined by the RFC. They are aimed at creating custom data types with custom length and transmitting their values to nodes in the network. At the time of writing this

Table 1. AODV extensions implemented (for IPv4)

Extension	Fields	Type	Extension Length
Test request	Test ID, Tested IP Address	1	80 bit
Test response	Test ID, Tested IP Address	2	80 bit
Trust propagation	Measured Node,Trust value	3	64 bit

paper, NS-3 does not implement extensions[2], so we implemented this feature by modifying the simulator and used it to exchange trust information; Table 1 shows the AODV extensions implemented. It is worth noting that encryption is not included in our implementation because the key size to be used is highly application-dependent and resources-dependent on limited devices as WSN nodes. The testbed in Table 2 simulates a WSN on top of NS3 where nodes perform environmental monitoring and they periodically send sensed data to the BS. The architecture proposed was tested by simulating a dense WSN, where different couples of nodes could reach each other directly. A dense (but not fully meshed) configuration was chosen in order to simulate a deployment where e.g. a node A needs to reach the BS but: i) A cannot communicate directly with the BS and so a route with intermediate nodes has to be established; ii) A has different neighbors, so it may obtain different routes to the same destination. This forces A to choose a trusted node to send sensed data.

Table 2. Testbed configuration for simulation of the trust-based architecture

Network Simulator	NS-3 [12]
Implemented Attack	Sinkhole [8]
Number of devices	$w = 10$
Routing Protocol	Ad hoc On-Demand Distance Vector [13]
Feedback levels allowed	$F_{min} = 0$, $F_{max} = 1$
Initial trust, reputation,	$T_{i,j}\vert_{t=0} =1$, $R^0_{i,j}\vert_{t=0} = r_s =1$,
dependability	$L_{i,j}\vert_{t=0} =1 \ \forall \ 1 \leq i,j \leq w, i \neq j$
Avg. no. of neighbors per node	4.2
T&R Model Parameters	$\beta = 0.5$, $\gamma = 0.5$, $\alpha = \gamma * L_{i,j}$

8   Experimental Results

This section provides the results of a preliminary experimental campaign conducted with respect to settings detailed in Table 2. In our experiments we compared the behavior of the network in safe conditions and under the attack, both in the case of an unmodified AODV stack and when the T&R layer is deployed. It is worth noting that to make measurements comparable we implemented a "passive" sinkhole attack. In a passive attack, the attacker does not inject additional packets, rather it executes the attack by modifying legitimate traffic.

---

[2] http://www.nsnam.org/docs/release/3.19/models/html/aodv.html

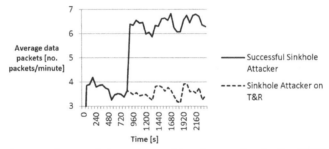

Fig. 4. Average data packets exchanged by the attacker in the WSN testbed

The effectiveness of the proposed approach against sinkhole attacks is demonstrated by the experimental results illustrated in Figure 4, where the number of packets traversing the attacker node before and after the attack is shown. It should be noted that in the unmodified AODV stack (solid line) after the launch of the attack (starting after about 800 seconds) the number of packets traversing the attacker node suddenly increases. This is a direct effect of the success of the attack, since a number of neighbor nodes are now using the attacker node to forward their traffic. In the same conditions, when the AODV stack is enhanced with the T&R layer (dashed line), the traffic traversing the attacker node does not present any significant change, indicating that the attack has been tolerated by the WSN.

Figure 5 shows the behavior of some nodes during the sinkhole attack when the T&R layer is deployed. First of all, it is worth noting that the attacker node is located at the edge of the network. As such, it handles a small number of routing packets (since it does not have any child node). We can also note that when the sinkhole attack is launched (after about 800 seconds), there is a peak in the number of routing packets exchanged. This overhead can be easily tied to the start of the test procedure. After the test procedure is completed, the routing packets profile of nodes returns to its normal behavior.

Finally, we evaluated the overhead introduced by the adoption of the T&R layer. It is worth noting that since cryptographic procedures are only used once during every test (while common traffic does not need cryptography) the overhead

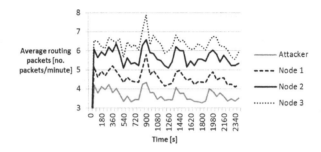

Fig. 5. Average routing packets exchanged per node in the WSN testbed

due to the T&R layer is mainly represented by the additional packets exchanged. To get an estimate of such an overhead, we modified the T&R layer so that the test procedure is performed every time a potential change of topology is detected by the T&R layer. This allowed us to consider the measured overhead as an upper bound of the one due to the introduction of the T&R layer. We simulated the network in three different conditions (Figure 6): i) without attacks and without deployment of the T&R layer (dash-dot line); ii) T&R layer is deployed, but no attack is performed on the WSN (dashed line); iii) T&R layer is deployed and sinkhole attack is performed (solid line). During the time window ($t \in [0, 780]\, s$), the T&R layer was not activated. In this initial time window, nodes start sending data to the BS and they populate their own routing tables; also, each node establishes its best route to the BS with respect to all information known to the node itself. During this initial time window, all of the three conditions considered are characterized by the same amount of routing packets exchanged. At time 780s the T&R layer is activated and an overhead of packets is experienced with respect to normal operating conditions. Specifically, an approximately constant overhead of 1% was measured. When the sinkhole attack is launched, the compromised node tries to force the update of routing tables and so an average additional overhead of 0.3% is detected. Such additional overhead is related to the additional tests performed in the network and can be considered acceptable.

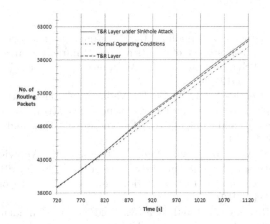

Fig. 6. The routing packets exchanged over time by nodes in the WSN testbed

9   Conclusions

In this work, a trust-based approach was proposed to ensure intrusion tolerant routing in WSNs. For this purpose, an additional layer was introduced in the WSN protocol stack; such layer performs intrusion tolerance activities and masks information to routing layer when more dependable information are estimated to be already available. The layered approach proposed allows us to provide tolerance capabilities to existing protocols. This cannot be ensured when instead the routing protocol is improved or when a new protocol is proposed; in those cases, the protocols proposed are not compliant to RFCs or instead a corresponding standard is not defined. The Trust and Reputation layer proposed also presents a proactive approach, where a potentially not trusted node is explicitly tested so to obtain a direct measurement of corresponding trustworthiness. A specific trust and reputation model was designed for tolerating sinkhole attack on AODV routing protocol, and it was implemented on NS3. Preliminary experimental results show the low packets overhead when the proposed layer was added to the WSN protocol stack. In the future we plan to include further tests and to validate the behavior of the layer proposed under different conditions, e.g. a different deployment of nodes and a different traffic pattern. Moreover a thorough experimental campaign will be performed to show the best tuning of the threshold values characterizing the proposed trust and reputation model.

Acknowledgements. This work has been partially supported by the TENACE PRIN Project (n. 20103P34XC) funded by the Italian Ministry of Education, University and Research. This project has received funding from the European Union's Seventh Framework Programme for research, technological development and demonstration under grant agreement no 313034 (SAWSOC Project).

References

1. Afzaal, M., Di Sarno, C., Coppolino, L., D'Antonio, S., Romano, L.: A resilient architecture for forensic storage of events in critical infrastructures. In: 2012 IEEE 14th International Symposium on High-Assurance Systems Engineering (HASE), pp. 48–55 (October 2012)
2. Bondavalli, A., Ceccarelli, A., Falai, L., Vadursi, M.: Foundations of measurement theory applied to the evaluation of dependability attributes. In: 37th Annual IEEE/IFIP International Conference on Dependable Systems and Networks, DSN 2007, pp. 522–533 (2007)
3. Coppolino, L., D'Antonio, S., Garofalo, A., Romano, L.: Applying data mining techniques to intrusion detection in wireless sensor networks. In: 2013 Eighth International Conference on P2P, Parallel, Grid, Cloud and Internet Computing (3PG-CIC), pp. 247–254 (2013)
4. Coppolino, L., Romano, L., Bondavalli, A., Daidone, A.: A hidden markov model based intrusion detection system for wireless sensor networks. Int. J. Crit. Comput.-Based Syst. 3(3), 210–228 (2012)
5. Fonseca, R., Gnawali, O., Jamieson, K., Kim, S., Levis, P., Woo, A.: The collection tree protocol (ctp) (2006)
6. Ganeriwal, S., Balzano, L.K., Srivastava, M.B.: Reputation-based framework for high integrity sensor networks. ACM Trans. Sen. Netw. 4(3), 15:1–15:37 (2008)
7. Garofalo, A., Di Sarno, C., Formicola, V.: Enhancing intrusion detection in wireless sensor networks through decision trees. In: Vieira, M., Cunha, J.C. (eds.) EWDC 2013. LNCS, vol. 7869, pp. 1–15. Springer, Heidelberg (2013)
8. Karlof, C., Wagner, D.: Secure routing in wireless sensor networks: attacks and countermeasures. In: Proceedings of the First 2003 IEEE International Workshop on Sensor Network Protocols and Applications, pp. 113–127 (2003)

9. Li, Z., Gong, G.: A survey on security in wireless sensor networks. Department of Electrical and Computer Engineering. University of Waterloo, Canada, pp. 2008–2020 (2011)
10. Maarouf, I., Baroudi, U., Naseer, A.: Efficient monitoring approach for reputation system-based trust-aware routing in wireless sensor networks. IET Communications 3(5), 846–858 (2009)
11. Min, W., Kim, K.: Intrusion tolerance mechanisms using redundant nodes for wireless sensor networks. In: 2014 International Conference on Information Networking (ICOIN), pp. 131–135 (2014)
12. National Science Foundation, Planète group: ns-3 (2012)
13. Perkins, C., Belding-Royer, E., Das, S.: et al.: Rfc 3561-ad hoc on-demand distance vector (aodv) routing. Internet RFCs, pp. 1–38 (2003)
14. Perkins, C.E., Bhagwat, P.: Highly dynamic destination-sequenced distance-vector routing (dsdv) for mobile computers. In: Proceedings of the Conference on Communications Architectures, Protocols and Applications, SIGCOMM 1994, pp. 234–244. ACM, New York (1994)
15. Rezgui, A., Eltoweissy, M.: μRACER: A reliable adaptive service-driven efficient routing protocol suite for sensor-actuator networks. IEEE Transactions on Parallel and Distributed Systems 20(5), 607–622 (2009)
16. Schillo, M., Funk, P., Stadtwald, I., Rovatsos, M.: Using trust for detecting deceitful agents in artificial societies (2000)
17. Srinivasan, A., Wu, J.: Secure and reliable broadcasting in wireless sensor networks using multi-parent trees. Security and Communication Networks 2(3), 239–253 (2009)
18. Tanachaiwiwat, S., Dave, P., Bhindwale, R., Helmy, A.: Location-centric isolation of misbehavior and trust routing in energy-constrained sensor networks. In: 2004 IEEE International Conference on Performance, Computing, and Communications, pp. 463–469 (2004)
19. Yu, Y., Li, K., Zhou, W., Li, P.: Trust mechanisms in wireless sensor networks: Attack analysis and countermeasures. Journal of Network and Computer Applications 35(3), 867–880 (2012); special Issue on Trusted Computing and Communications
20. Zhan, G., Shi, W., Deng, J.: Design and implementation of tarf: A trust-aware routing framework for wsns. IEEE Transactions on Dependable and Secure Computing 9(2), 184–197 (2012)

A Petri Net Pattern-Oriented Approach for the Design of Physical Protection Systems

Francesco Flammini[1], Ugo Gentile[2], Stefano Marrone[3],
Roberto Nardone[2], and Valeria Vittorini[2]

[1] AnsaldoSTS, Naples, Italy
francesco.flammini@ansaldo-sts.com
[2] Università di Napoli "Federico II", DIETI, Italy
{ugo.gentile,roberto.nardone,valeria.vittorini}@unina.it
[3] Seconda Università di Napoli, Dip. di Matematica e Fisica, Italy
stefano.marrone@unina2.it

Abstract. The design of complex Physical Protection Systems (PPSs) still raises some challenges despite the high number of technologies for smart surveillance. One reason is the lack of effective methodologies able to support the PPS designer in evaluating the effectiveness of the system on varying design choices. Indeed, an estimation of the system vulnerability should be performed in the early phases of the PPS design. This paper introduces a model-based methodology for the quantitative estimation of the vulnerability of a PPS. The proposed methodology clearly defines a compositional approach which takes advantage from the usage of predefined patterns for the creation of vulnerability models. In particular, the paper proposes some Petri Net patterns able to capture the behavioural aspects of several assets and actors involved in attacking/defending scenarios.

Keywords: Pattern Oriented Modelling, Model-Based Vulnerability Assessment, Generalized Stochastic Petri Nets, Physical Protection Systems Design.

1 Introduction

Nowadays, there is an increasing interest in system protection against intentional threats of physical nature [8,19]. On those regards, model-based vulnerability assessment is a crucial phase in the risk analysis of critical infrastructures. In fact, typical risk models include the computation of three logically sequential factors: probability or frequency of threats (P); probability that threats are successful in their intent (i.e., vulnerability, V); consequences of successful threats (i.e., expected damage, D). Therefore, in order to evaluate infrastructure risks (R), it is essential to be able to compute the vulnerability of the system with respect to the threats [11]. One of the most widespread and intuitive model for the evaluation of the risk is [21]: $R = P * V * D$. This model is based on a quantitative notion of vulnerability, different from other definitions also commonly used,

A. Bondavalli and F. Di Giandomenico (Eds.): SAFECOMP 2014, LNCS 8666, pp. 230–245, 2014.
© Springer International Publishing Switzerland 2014

both in information system security and physical security [3,14]. We will return on this point in the related work.

While threat occurrence rates and expected damages are rather easy to evaluate basing respectively on historical threat data and cause-effect analysis, vulnerability is often very difficult to account for since it requires the evaluation of the effectiveness/efficiency of possibly novel technological countermeasures. Unfortunately, it is not rare that new security technologies and related management procedures are justified only by intuition, and reveal in practice to be much less effective than expected or advertised. In order to quantitatively assess the effectiveness of protection systems, stochastic models are needed that are able to represent the dynamic/temporal aspects of threat and countermeasure evolution in the specific installation context.

Other essential requirements for such models to be usable in real industrial settings is the ease of use, maintainability and scalability to large problems. The Stochastic Petri Net (SPN) model we have proposed in [13] in order to cope with vulnerability assessment had the advantage of being simple and easy to customise in terms of parameters; however, it was much less suited to be customised in terms of structure due to the underlying formalism constraints that prevent the modeller from easily performing some structural modifications that could be required in real-word analyses, like addition of attack/defence phases, concurrent threats, fail-prone/redundant countermeasures, etc.

To cope with those issues, in this paper we propose a modular and compositional approach for quantitative vulnerability assessment based on SPNs using the ORIS tool [6]. The justification for adopting the SPN formalism has already been given in [13] and relates to the very high expressive power that allows modellers to easily overcome the limitations of other formalisms (e.g. Bayesian Networks) in modelling dynamic aspects of the system. Despite of the expressive power, modelling with SPN is also easier with respect to other suitable formalisms (e.g. Continuous Time Markov Chains) since it allows to easily represent the possibly concurrent phases of activity diagrams when used as scenario views. On the other hand, Petri Nets (PNs) have demonstrated their capability to cope with extensible and compositional modelling. Compositionality and model reuse are two crucial aspects in order to deal with heterogeneous problems as the ones considered in this paper: this is the main motivation of the pattern based approach here proposed. ORIS is one of the most recent tools for SPN modelling, featuring several advantages ranging from the user-friendly GUI to a wide range of possible analyses. Furthermore, the combination of the formalism and the tool enables the possibility of instantiating and composing reference patterns by means of an automatic process based on model-driven techniques and to optimise design parameters by techniques like evolutionary algorithms.

Hence, with respect to our previous work [13] in which a single model is described, this paper introduces a methodology for model-based vulnerability analysis and provides guidelines for vulnerability modelling, also in the direction of enabling the automated generation of the models within a more general model-driven process supporting the design of Physical Protection Systems (PPSs).

The ideas on which the methodology is founded are not new if separately considered (e.g., the usage of patterns, models composition, component based model development). Nevertheless, they are integrated and applied to the quantitative evaluation of physical vulnerability leading to an original way of addressing this problem.

The approach is demonstrated by evaluating the vulnerability of a metro station against a typical attack event. This case study has been already described in other papers (see e.g. [12]) and constitutes a non-trivial scenario involving several smart-sensors integrated in a Physical Security Management System [18].

The rest of this paper is organised as follows. Section 2 and Section 3 respectively contain related work and a brief introduction to the the class of SPNs used in the paper (namely Generalized Stochastic Petri Nets). Section 4 sets the approach in the general context of physical protection system design and fine tuning. Section 5 describes the reference high-level model and the compositional approach addressed in this paper. Section 6 provides details on constituent submodels and some GSPN patterns for recurrent behaviours. Section 7 applies the methodology on a realistic example coming from mass transit security. Finally, Section 8 draws conclusions and provides some hints about future developments.

2 Related Work

Vulnerability assessment mainly relies on compliance-based approaches (presence of proper components) and performance-based approaches (effectiveness evaluation of PPS against the consequences of a successful attack). Two well-known definitions of vulnerability, which well pertain to information system security, say that vulnerability is a flaw or weakness (in any aspect of the system) that can be exploited by a threat [3,28]. These definitions are widely used in risk assessment methodologies designed to be *qualitative* and based on the work of skilled security analysts. In fact, vulnerability is commonly qualitatively evaluated, also relying on the availability of historical data related to past threat events. In this paper we rather adopt a quantitative notion of vulnerability, in order to define a model-driven process supporting PPS design and evaluation. Several concepts are borrowed from model-based dependability and security evaluation [24] and applied to vulnerability analysis. We consider a definition similar to the one provided by the The Open Group [16] where vulnerability is the probability that an attacker exceeds the defensive capabilities of the targeted asset. In other word, the (conditional) probability that an attack is successful. The process is based on a modeling approach that specifies the three main aspects involved in effective physical protection system design, according to what stated in the Mary Linn Garcia's work [14,15], i.e., attacks, assets and protection technologies and devices. Hence, our approach considers vulnerability with the respect to the threats, as also in [20] where a complete attack tree-based language is proposed. Specifically, with reference to a specific threat, our work is based on the following quantitative definition of risk (R) [21]: $R = P * V * D$, where: P is the expected frequency of occurrence of the threat, which can be measured in [events/year];

"V" is the vulnerability of the asset with respect to the threat, that is to say the likelihood that an attack is successful, given that it is attempted; D is an estimate of the expected damage occurring after a successful attack, which can be quantified and expressed in any currencies, e.g. Euros. The vulnerability "V" is a non-dimensional parameter, since it represents the conditional probability *P(success|threat)*. Therefore, a quantitative way to express the risk associated to a specific threat is to measure it in lost Euros per year: [€/year]. Though subject to criticism in some applications [10], the risk model defined above has been widely accepted by risk analysts, including the ones belonging to US national laboratories [1]. In this paper we propose a model-based approach to the evaluation of the vulnerability term, with the ultimate goal of supporting the design and the evaluation of PPSs. Our approach also exploits the usage of Petri Net (PN) patterns. Several works in the literature present PN patterns. In particular, in [23] the definition of some design patterns is given (e.g., event sequence, token multiplier and token removal); other works focus on specific contexts, such as Van der Aalst's workflow patterns [29]. We re-use some design solutions from [23] to define a PN security-oriented set of patterns.

3 An Overview of Generalized Stochastic Petri Nets

Generalized Stochastic Petri Nets (GSPNs) are a well known modeling paradigm introduced in 1984. GSPNs extend Petri Nets with a temporal specification allowing the description of both the temporal and logical evolution of a system within the same model. A GSPN consists of *places*, *transitions* and *arcs*. Graphically a GSPN model is a directed bipartite graph in which places are drawn as circles and transitions are drawn as bars or boxes. The arcs are the oriented edges of the graph. *Tokens* are markers within places and are used to specify the state of a PN. They are drawn as black dots. The dynamic behavior of the PN is defined by the *firing rule*. If a transition may fire (i.e., if all its input places contain at least as many tokens as the multiplicities of the corresponding arcs from the places to the transition) the transition is said to be enabled. Its firing removes a number of tokens from all its input places and generates a number of tokens in each output place according to the multiplicity of the arcs connecting the places and the transition. An *inhibitor arc* is a circle-headed arc from a place to a transition which prevents the transition to be enabled if the place contains a number of tokens equal or greater than the multiplicity of the arc. Timing is associated with transitions. They belong to two classes: *timed transitions* (representing timing consuming activities) whose delays are exponentially distributed random variables (here drawn as empty boxes), and *immediate transitions* with a null delay which fire as soon as they become enabled (here drawn as thin bars). An immediate transition always has precedence over a timed transition if they are concurrently enabled. The reader may refer to [9] for an introduction to GSPN modeling.

4   Designing Physical Protection Systems

In this Section we introduce the overall PPS model-driven design process which is the frame where the proposed pattern-based modelling approach is situated.

The process presented in this paper moves from Garcia's work, trying to take advantage of the integration of the available information about the infrastructure, the threats and the features of the protection devices.

The design process is represented in Fig. 1. The ultimate goal is to automate the generation of a suitable vulnerability model and the optimisation of the PPS design, starting from a tentative configuration, according to given objectives. The process starts with the development of high level specification models of the three main components to be considered in evaluating the system vulnerability: the infrastructure to protect, the configuration of its protection system and the attack scenarios to cope with. The activity *System definition* represents the analysis phase which must be performed to enable the *High Level Modelling* activity. The high level models are UML models or they may be expressed by means of a Domain Specific Modeling Language (DSML, in [22] a UML profile is proposed), then proper model transformations [26] are defined and applied to automate the generation of a formal vulnerability model (*Formal Modelling*) and the set of parameters to be used in the optimisation phase (*Tuning Problem Definition* and *Problem Tuning*). Hence, the defined process is formalism-independent as different formal modelling languages may be used to express the vulnerability model, depending from the indices the user wants to evaluate and the objectives he wants to reach (*Indices choice*). For example, a PPS designer could be interested in minimising both the probability that a threat is not detected and the cost of the protection system. The vulnerability model takes into account the three components specified above; the set of parameters gathered from the high level models contains the attributes which have to be considered by the optimisation algorithms and used to instantiate the vulnerability model (e.g., MTTF of devices, rates, delays, etc.). This set of parameters is the input for the *Tuning Problem Definition* phase as well as the vulnerability model. The last is used in the *Problem Tuning* phase as it was an heuristic function: an optimisation algorithm explores the design space by varying the parameter values and it is guided by the results obtained by solving the vulnerability model. The optimisation algorithm may be a Multi-Objective Evolutionary Algorithm (MOEA) such as Particle Swarm Optimization (PSO), Multi-Objective Genetic Algorithms (MOGAs) or Firefly Algorithm (FA) [30].

The automated generation of the vulnerability model is a tricky step as we believe that it may be successfully implemented only if proper modelling guidelines and patterns are defined and implemented within the transformational approach, in order to guarantee both the feasibility of the translation and the correctness of the resulting model. Hence, in the next Section a general structure for the vulnerability model is proposed, and a specific realisation by means of Petri Net patterns is described. Of course, the sub-nets convey the fact that they must be used within an automated process, as a trade-off must be made between the modelling style and the effectiveness of the model transformation.

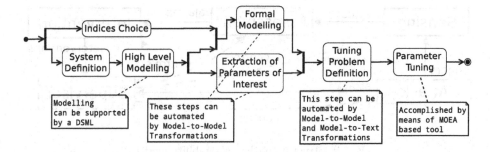

Fig. 1. A model-driven process supporting the PPS design

5   A Generic Vulnerability Model

This Section introduces the structure of the vulnerability model that should be used in the transformation step to generate a specific formal model. The model is influenced by the work of Mary Linn Garcia [14,15] and it is defined as a composition of five modules, each of them consisting of one or more sub-models expressed through the target formal language. It is shown in Fig. 2 where four modules (the white boxes) contain the sub-models whose composition describes the dynamics of the overall system in case of attack, the fifth module (the grey box) plays the role of a supervisor. The data flow among the modules is represented by oriented arcs (solid lines). The dashed arrows model a control flow enabling the possibility of monitoring and resetting the state of the entire model.

The *Attack* module is in charge of modelling the evolution of the attack inside the physical infrastructure to protect. As the occurrence of an attack may be detected by sensing devices (security cameras, chemical sniffers, etc.), the *Sensing* module is responsible of modelling the devices (that may be activated by *triggers*) and generating events. The *Assessment* module may model the presence of a security management system capable of assessing (and in case of correlating) the events produced by the sensing devices and generating *alarms*. The *Intervention* module models the actions performed in order to block the attack (e.g., the intervention of guards or other countermeasures). This model receives as input the assessed *alarms* from the *Assessment* module. The *Supervisor* module also acts as an observer and evaluates the vulnerability of the system by taking into account the information coming from both the *Attack* and *Intervention* modules (i.e., the percentage of successful attack events).

At the state, we have chosen the GSPN formalism to instantiate the modules defined above, because the proposed vulnerability model requires to describe both static and dynamic features of the system as well as timing information.

5.1   Sub-models Composition

An agent-based paradigm is adopted in order to realize a loosely coupled communication between the components of the model. This approach is not new in

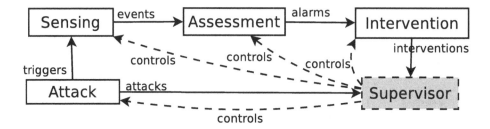

Fig. 2. Structure of the vulnerability model

security modeling: several scientific works use agent-based paradigm for both methodologies and practical tools [25]. The application of this communication and interaction mechanism to the generic model previously described fits the distributed and asynchronous nature of infrastructures, attacking scenarios and PPSs: attacking and defending activities run concurrently. The sub-models expose proper interfaces and they are composed by connecting the output to the input interfaces.

We use the Communicative Networks principles described in [27] in order to realize the communication between modules. According to this approach, output interfaces are transitions while input interfaces are places.

Fig. 3 depicts the composition to realize the $ModelA - to - ModelB$ communication by using a *composition network*. The composition is performed by superposing the transition *outInterface* of the Model A with the transition T of the composition network, and the place P of the composition network with the place *inInterface* of the Model B. The communication is guaranteed by the added arc. Superposition techniques are described in the literature, e.g. in [4].

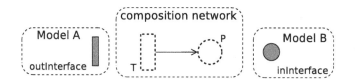

Fig. 3. Composition of GSPNs

6   Petri Net Patterns for the Vulnerability Model

In this Section, the definition of GSPN patterns capturing the behaviours of some actors of Physical Protection Systems is provided. In the graphical representations of patterns, the dashed elements and their names in italics represent the model elements to superpose with interface elements according to the Subsection 5.1.

6.1   Attack Model

Fig. 4 defines the interface of the Attack model; it is constituted by the *init* input place (that means the phase may start), the *start* output transition (the action has started) and the *end* output transition (the action has ended). Fig. 5 proposes a simple GSPN pattern for a single-phase attack.

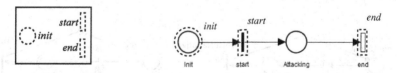

Fig. 4. Interface of the Attack model   **Fig. 5.** The single phased attack

As it is clearer by the case of multiple phased attack, the *end* transition of a single phase submodel can be connected to the *init* place of another one. Moreover, the output interfaces serve as starting conditions for the *Sensing* model.

6.2   Sensing Model

The *Sensing* model represents an abstraction of the layer of sensors that monitor a sensitive target. Fig. 6 shows the interfaces exposed by the *Sensing* model: *event* and *reset* that are input interfaces *detected* that is the output interface.

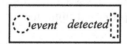

Fig. 6. Interface of the Sensing model

One of the simplest GSPN pattern *Sensing* model can be constituted by is depicted in Fig. 7. In this model, the *InputEvent* is the destination place of a token when a detectable attacking event is conducted. According to the *Attack* model, *InputEvent* is coupled with the *start* output transition. Regarding the output interface, the *NoFalseNegative* represents the normal functioning of the sensor; nevertheless, this GSPN pattern also considers the possibility of undetected events (false negatives) that are modelled by the *FalseNegative* transition.

This simple GSPN pattern can be extended by introducing, as example, traditional up-down SPN cycles modelling the failure-repair evolution of real components. This second solution is depicted in Fig. 8. This pattern uses an inhibitor arc, so that the transition "Detecting" is not enabled if the sensing device is not working. The addition of inhibitor arcs makes PN systems Turing equivalent, in case the reachability set is *not* finite they enhance the expressive power of PNs but they prevent some analysis techniques [7]. In case the PN system is bounded they just allow for a compact representation and might be avoided. Here we deal with bounded systems, the inhibitor arc may be automatically removed and replaced by a proper sub-net according to the pattern-based approach within an automated process, if needed.

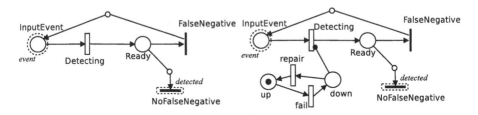

Fig. 7. Simple Sensing   **Fig. 8.** The Faulty Sensor

6.3   Assessment Model

The assessment model is in charge of elaborating the events raised by the Sensing layer in order to assess them into real alarms. Fig. 9 depicts the interface of this model: there are n input places in_1, ..., in_n, one for each *Sensing* model in input to this model. The other element is the *out* transition that communicates with *Intervention* model giving (assessed) alarms.

Three GSPN patterns are proposed fulfilling the scope of this model:

- *dummy assessment*: the assessment phase is constituted by the simple propagation of the events detected by the Sensing model (see Fig. 10);
- *logical assessment*: the assessment is provided by combining input events by means of logical operators (Fig. 11 represents the AND assessment but OR and KooN are easily implementable);
- *human assessment*: the assessment is provided by guard who controls periodically the sensor: in case of event, he spends some time raising the alarm (see Fig. 12).

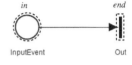

Fig. 9. Interface of the Assessment model   **Fig. 10.** Dummy assessment

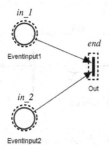

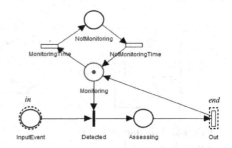

Fig. 11. AND based assessment

Fig. 12. Human based assessment

6.4 Intervention Model

The Intervention model is in charge of modelling the defending process (i.e. the movement of the guards towards the place of the threat, or the procedure of activation of the countermeasures). The interface of this model is represented in Fig. 13. The model has two interfaces: an input *start* place and an output *end* transition. As for the Attack model, we can structure a defending process in phases. Thus, Fig. 14 depicts the GSPN pattern for a single simple phase. Composition of phases (and of GSPNs) is possible as for the Attack model is Subsection 6.1.

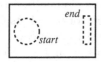

Fig. 13. Interface of the Intervention model

Fig. 14. Single phase intervention

6.5 Supervisor Model

The *Supervisor* model exposes three interface elements as depicted in Fig. 15. The interface elements are the input places *defender* and *attacker*, that receive tokens respectively from the *Intervention* and the *Attack* submodels, and the *reset* output transition, in charge of restoring the initial state of the entire network.

A possible implementation of this module is detailed in Fig. 16: the PN sub-net is a slight modification of the *A-before-B* pattern from [23] (an event sequencing pattern). According to [23], this pattern addresses the case that *"on synchronizing two concurrent subnets it may be interesting to know the order in which the enabling tokens arrive at the synchronization point"*. Here, the events *A* and *B* are the conclusion of the attacking and defending sequences of actions; it is necessary to know which sequence ends first in order to evaluate the success/failure

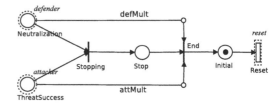

Fig. 15. Interface of the Supervisor model

Fig. 16. Supervisor model

of the protection system. This evaluation is made as follows. Starting from the definition of vulnerability in [13], $V = 1 - P_E$ where P_E is the probability that the physical protection system is effective against the threat and by interpreting probability in a frequentist way:

$$P_E = \overline{tk(Neutralization)}/[\overline{tk(Neutralization)} + \overline{tk(ThreatSuccess)}]$$

Where $\overline{tk(p)}$ is the mean number of tokens over time in p. Hence, it holds:

$$V = \overline{tk(ThreatSuccess)}/[\overline{tk(Neutralization)} + \overline{tk(ThreatSuccess)}]$$

The initial marking of the sub-net (one token in Initial place) represents the state where no attack has started yet: when the Reset timed transition fires, the Supervisor module passes the token to the Attack module (see Fig. 2). Reset (labeled *reset*) is the output interface of the Supervisor model: its timing nature is due to the necessity to have an initial tangible state. Moreover, the model is characterized by two arcs: from Neutralization to End and from ThreatSuccess to End. If we consider N_A the number of the different ways the modelled attack can success, $attMult = N_A - 1$ is the multiplicity of the arc from ThreatSuccess to End; in a similar way, if N_D is the number of the ways an attack may fail, $defMult = N_D - 1$ is the multiplicity of the arc from Neutralization to End. This mechanism is necessary to consume all the tokens representing attacking and defending "threads". The arcs also restore the initial marking of the network enabling a steady state analysis of the network.

7   Applications to Mass-Transit Transportation

The effectiveness of the modelling approach described in the previous Sections is demonstrated using a case-study in the mass transit domain, whose assets are vulnerable to several threats, including terrorist attacks. Therefore, surveillance systems for mass transit feature a growing number of heterogeneous sensing devices. In such a context, the quantitative evaluation of the PPS effectiveness is very important to design robust surveillance systems and to reduce the overall risk associated to the considered threats.

Let us consider a threat scenario similar to the chemical attack with Sarin agent occurred in the Tokyo subway on March 20, 1995, which caused 12 fatalities and 5500 injured [2]. The available technologies to early detect and assess the threat include intelligent cameras, audio sensors and specific standoff CWA (Chemical Warfare Agents) detectors. The main CWA detection technologies include Ion Mobility Spectroscopy (IMS), Surface Acoustic Wave (SAW), Infrared Radiation (IR), etc. They are employed in ad-hoc standoff detectors, characterised by different performances. One of the most accurate devices, the automatic passive IR sensor, can recognize a vapor cloud from several kilometres. Obviously, it is possible to combine heterogeneous detectors (e.g. IMS/SAW and IR) and to correlate their alarms according to different criteria (e.g. logic, temporal, and spatial), in order to increase the CWA detection reliability. The same considerations apply to the alarms detected by the other sensing devices. The threat scenario consists of a simultaneous drop of CWA in subway platforms. Let us assume the following set of events: (1) attackers enter in the atrium bringing chemical agents; (2) attackers enter on the platform and free chemical agents: (3) first contaminated persons fall down on the floor; (4) people around the contaminated area run away and/or scream; (5) the chemical agent spreads in the platform level and possibly reaches higher levels.

In order to show the effectiveness of the approach, we compare some possible defensive scenarios counteracting such an attack:

- *S1*: a smart-camera, a microphone and a IMS/SAW sensor are present only on the platform, an alarm is raised if all the three sensors detect events;
- *S2*: a smart-camera, a microphone and a IMS/SAW sensor are present only on the platform, an alarm is raised only if at least two of the three sensors detect events;
- *S3*: only IMS/SAW and IR sensors are in the atrium, an alarm is raised if all the three sensors detect events;
- *S4*: only IMS/SAW and IR sensors are on the platform, an alarm is raised if all the three sensors detect events.

To build all the scenario models, we considered a two-phase pattern for the *Attack* model. Each sensor is modelled by a simple sensing pattern. AND-based models are proposed to implement the *Assessment* model (scenarios S1, S3, S4) while a 2-out-of-3 GSPN pattern is used with reference to scenario S2. As *Intervention* model, we choose a single phased pattern. For the sake of the space, only the first scenario is shown: Fig. 17 represents high level model as an instantiation of the formalism independent schema in Fig. 2; Fig. 18 shows the GSPN resulting from the substitution of the specified patterns.

The models have been populated with the realistic values listed in Table 1. The analyses have been conducted using the ORIS tool [6] and the results, computed by means of the formula in Subsection 6.5 are reported in Table 2. For this specific case study, the results may (quantitatively) show us that:

- early detection dramatically improve the effectiveness of the PPS: comparing the S3 and S4 scenarios, vulnerability varies from 0.8974 to 0.4074 by moving the sensors from the platform to the atrium;

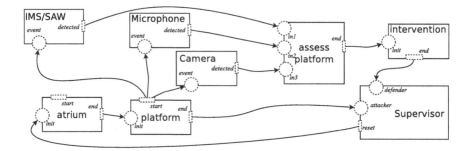

Fig. 17. The S1 scenario formalism independent model

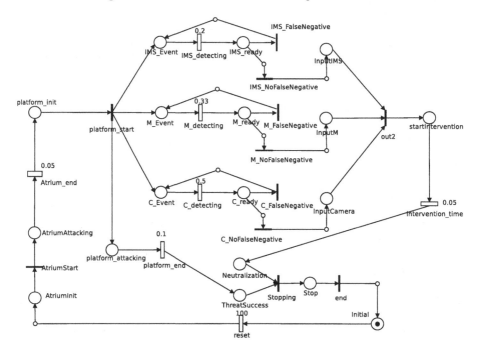

Fig. 18. The S1 scenario GSPN model

– assessment method does not play a crucial role for the three sensors cases: the difference between S1 and S2 scenarios is of 1 point percent.

Table 2 also indicates the feasibility of the approach in terms of computational complexity by illustrating the dimension of the state spaces for the scenarios.

After evaluating the vulnerability, it is rather straightforward to obtain risk estimation. For instance, if the frequency of the specific threat is estimated to be 0.1 events per year (P) and the expected damage is estimated to be 10M (D), then we get the following risk estimations:

Table 1. Description of model parameters

Description	Value
Attack	
Atrium crossing time	20 *s*
Attack accomplishment time on platform	10 *s*
IMS/SAW	
Detection time	5 *s*
False Negative Probability	0.05
IR	
Detection time	2 *s*
False Negative Probability	0.03
Smart camera	
Detection time	3 *s*
False Negative Probability	0.1
Microphone	
Detection time	2 *s*
False Negative Probability	0.1
Intervention	
Intervention time	20 *s*

Table 2. Analyses results

Scenario	*Vulnerablity*	*Vanishing markings*	*Tangible markings*
S1	0.0579	19	17
S2	0.0454	82	42
S3	0.4074	15	9
S4	0.8974	11	9

Scenario S2: R = 0.1 * 0.0454 * 10.000.000 = 45.400 €/ year
Scenario S3: R = 0.1 * 0.4074 * 10.000.000= 407.400 €/ year

Of course, while for rare events like terrorist strikes those values provide relative yet useful indications, for less rare events like thefts and vandalism, those values correspond more realistically to the expected/average annual loss in monetary terms.

8   Conclusions and Future Developments

In this paper we have presented an extensible model-driven approach to formal modeling for the quantitative evaluation of physical vulnerability. The approach first introduces some GSPN security oriented patterns that can be instanciated and composed to build security models: this allows a good balance between flexibility and usability.

This work started on the track laid down by the METRIP project[1] where the problem of vulnerability evaluation in the context of physical security has been approched by means of an UML model annotated with the CIP_VAM UML Profile [22] and automatic generation of a Bayesian Network model. Moving to GSPNs was necessary in order to capture dynamical aspects.

Further research effort will be addressed in the following directions. First, this work is a starting point to build libraries of PN patterns able to consider more complex situations. The usage of these patterns will also be supported by transformational approaches for their automatic generation from high level models as successfully done in the reliability field [5]. Moreover, optimization algorithms may exploit the solution of vulnerability models as heuristics [17] in order to tune the parameters of protection mechanisms (response times, failure rates, number of replicas, etc.).

References

1. A risk assessment methodology for physical security. white paper. Technical report, SANDIA National Laboratories (2008)
2. Global terrorism database [199503200014]. Technical report, National Consortium for the Study of Terrorism and Responses to Terrorism, START (2012)
3. Information technology security techniques information security management systems overview and vocabulary. Technical report, ISO/IEC (2014)
4. Bernardi, S., Donatelli, S., Horvath, A.: Compositionality in the GreatSPN tool and its application to the modelling of industrial applications. In: DAIMI PB: Workshop Proceedings Practical Use of High-level Petri Nets, University of Aarhus, Department of Computer Science, pp. 127–146 (2000)
5. Bernardi, S., Flammini, F., Marrone, S., Merseguer, J., Papa, C., Vittorini, V.: Model-driven availability evaluation of railway control systems. In: Flammini, F., Bologna, S., Vittorini, V. (eds.) SAFECOMP 2011. LNCS, vol. 6894, pp. 15–28. Springer, Heidelberg (2011)
6. Bucci, G., Carnevali, L., Ridi, L., Vicario, E.: Oris: a tool for modeling, verification and evaluation of real-time systems. International Journal on Software Tools for Technology Transfer 12(5), 391–403 (2010)
7. Busi, N.: Analysis issues in petri nets with inhibitor arcs. Theor. Comput. Sci. 275(1-2), 127–177 (2002)
8. Carney, J.: Why integrate physical and logical security? Technical report, Cisco (2011)
9. Chiola, G., Ajmone-Marsan, M., Balbo, G., Conte, G.: Generalized stochastic petri nets. a definition at the net level and its implications. IEEE Transactions on Software Engineering 19(2), 89–107 (1993)
10. Cox Jr, L.A.: Some limitations of risk = threat × vulnerability × consequence for risk analysis of terrorist attacks. Risk Analysis 28(6) (2008)
11. Flammini, F., Gaglione, A., Mazzocca, N., Pragliola, C.: Optimisation of security system design by quantitative risk assessment and genetic algorithms. Int. J. of Risk Assessment and Management 15, 205–221 (2011)

---

[1] http://metrip.unicampus.it

12. Flammini, F., Marrone, S., Mazzocca, N., Pappalardo, A., Pragliola, C., Vittorini, V.: Trustworthiness evaluation of multi-sensor situation recognition in transit surveillance scenarios. In: Cuzzocrea, A., Kittl, C., Simos, D.E., Weippl, E., Xu, L. (eds.) CD-ARES Workshops 2013. LNCS, vol. 8128, pp. 442–456. Springer, Heidelberg (2013)
13. Flammini, F., Marrone, S., Mazzocca, N., Vittorini, V.: Petri net modelling of physical vulnerability. In: Bologna, S., Hämmerli, B., Gritzalis, D., Wolthusen, S. (eds.) CRITIS 2011. LNCS, vol. 6983, pp. 128–139. Springer, Heidelberg (2013)
14. Garcia, M.L.: Vulnerability Assessment of Physical Protection Systems. Butterworth-Heinemann (December 2005)
15. Garcia, M.L.: Design and Evaluation of Physical Protection Systems. Butterworth-Heinemann (October 2007)
16. The Open Group. Risk taxonomy. Technical report, The Open Group (2009)
17. Güdemann, M., Ortmeier, F.: Model-based multi-objective safety optimization. In: Flammini, F., Bologna, S., Vittorini, V. (eds.) SAFECOMP 2011. LNCS, vol. 6894, pp. 423–436. Springer, Heidelberg (2011)
18. Hunt, S.: Physical security information management (PSIM): The basics. Technical report, Cisco (2011)
19. Johnson, R.G.: Physical Security Assessment. Critical Infrastructure Security - WIT Press (2011)
20. Kordy, B., Mauw, S., Radomirović, S., Schweitzer, P.: Foundations of attack–defense trees. In: Degano, P., Etalle, S., Guttman, J. (eds.) FAST 2010. LNCS, vol. 6561, pp. 80–95. Springer, Heidelberg (2011)
21. Lewis, T.G., Darken, R.P., Mackin, T., Dudenhoeffer, D.: Model-Based Risk Analysis for Critical Infrastructures. Critical Infrastructure Security - WIT Press (2011)
22. Marrone, S., Nardone, R., Tedesco, A., D'Amore, P., Vittorini, V., Setola, R., Cillis, F.D., Mazzocca, N.: Vulnerability modeling and analysis for critical infrastructure protection applications. International Journal of Critical Infrastructure Protection 6(34), 217–227 (2013)
23. Naedele, M., Janneck, J.W.: Design patterns in petri net system modeling. In: Proceedings of the Fourth IEEE International Conference on Engineering of Complex Computer Systems, ICECCS 1998, pp. 47–54 (1998)
24. Nicol, D.M., Sanders, W.H., Trivedi, K.S.: Model-based evaluation: from dependability to security. IEEE Transactions on Dependable and Secure Computing 1(1), 48–65 (2004)
25. Pederson, P., Dudenhoeffer, D., Hartley, S., Permann, M.: Critical infrastructure and interdependency modeling: A survey of US and international research. Technical report, Idaho National Laboratory (2006)
26. Sendall, S., Kozaczynski, W.: Model transformation: the heart and soul of model-driven software development. IEEE Software 20(5), 42–45 (2003)
27. Sibertin-Blanc, C.: Cooperative nets. In: Valette, R. (ed.) ICATPN 1994. LNCS, vol. 815, pp. 471–490. Springer, Heidelberg (1994)
28. Stoneburner, G., Goguen, A.Y., Feringa, A.: Sp 800-30. risk management guide for information technology systems. Technical report, Gaithersburg, MD, United States (2002)
29. Van der Aalst, W.M.P., Ter Hofstede, A.H.M., Kiepuszewski, B., Barros, A.P.: Workflow patterns. Distributed and Parallel Databases 14(1), 5–51 (2003)
30. Zhou, A., Qu, B.-Y., Li, H., Zhao, S.-Z., Suganthan, P.N., Zhangd, Q.: Multi-objective evolutionary algorithms: A survey of the state of the art. Swarm and Evolutionary Computation 1(1), 32–49 (2011)

On Two Models of Noninterference: Rushby and Greve, Wilding, and Vanfleet

Adrian Garcia Ramirez[1], Julien Schmaltz[1], Freek Verbeek[2],
Bruno Langenstein[3], and Holger Blasum[4]

[1] Department of Computer Science
Eindhoven University of Technology
Postbus 513, MB 5600, Eindhoven, The Netherlands
[2] School of Computer Science
The Open University of The Netherlands
Postbus 2960 6401 DL Heerlen, The Netherlands
[3] German Research Center for Artificial Intelligence (DFKI GmbH)
Saarbrücken, Germany
[4] SYSGO AG
Klein-Winternheim, Germany

Abstract. We formally compare two industrially relevant and popular
models of noninterference, namely, the model defined by Rushby and the
one defined by Greve, Wilding, and Vanfleet (GWV). We create a mapping between the objects and relations of the two models. We prove a
number of theorems showing under which assumptions a system identified as "secure" in one model is also identified as "secure" in the other
model. Using two examples, we illustrate and discuss some of these assumptions. Our main conclusion is that the GWV model is more discriminating than the Rushby model. All systems satisfying GWV's Separation
also satisfy Rushby's noninterference. The other direction only holds if
we additionally assume that GWV systems are such that every partition
is assigned at most one memory segment. All of our proofs have been
checked using the Isabelle/HOL proof assistant.

Keywords: Noninterference, information flow security, formal models.

1 Introduction

Critical devices found in cars, aircrafts and medical devices are becoming more
and more interconnected. In this context, a design and validation environment
offering secure decomposition of embedded systems becomes key to safety and
security [11,3]. A key issue is to control failure propagation when multiple functions share a processor. In an ideal environment, every function should have its
own processor with controlled communication channels with the other processors running other functionalities. The left part in Figure 1 shows an example
of a gateway application running on three different processors. A function with
a high level of criticality (H) sends information to a function with a low level of
criticality(L) via a downgrader (D). Every function has its own processor and

A. Bondavalli and F. Di Giandomenico (Eds.): SAFECOMP 2014, LNCS 8666, pp. 246–261, 2014.
© Springer International Publishing Switzerland 2014

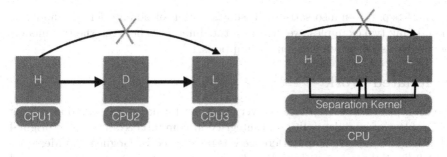

Fig. 1. Gateway example with dedicated vs. shared resources

communications happen via explicit dedicated channels. Instead of having separate processors for separate functions, modern systems integrate several functions on a single shared processor, e.g., Integrated Modular Avionics. Separation kernels are at the heart of these modern safety and security critical systems [18]. Their main purpose is to provide an operating system foundation simulating the ideal multiple processor environment on a single shared one. The right part in Figure 1 shows the same gateway example implemented on one processor. Both security and safety require the assurance that one function only affects the others using specified communication channels. In the integrated case, the separation kernel provides this assurance. *Noninterference* is a model used to extract verification requirements for the separation kernel. Such a model allows the expression that application H can *interfere* with D and that D can interfere with L. In the transitive case, H can also interfere with L. Intransitive noninterference is required to express the requirement that H cannot directly interfere with L. The definition and study of transitive and intransitive noninterference has been an active research field for the last three decades. Several definitions have been proposed together with verification methodologies. These definitions are all slightly different. Today, these differences mostly remain unexplored. Still, knowing these details is key in selecting a particular definition and methodology.

Rushby and GWV are two popular models of noninterference. Both have been applied in practice. To the best of our knowledge, there exist only informal comparisons between these models. In contrast, we take a precise and formal approach. We give formal proofs expressed in the logic of a proof assistant, namely, Isabelle/HOL [15]. These proofs show in detail where these models differ and where they coincide. Our main contribution is to show that all systems satisfying GWV's definition of Separation are secure under the Rushby model of noninterference. The other direction requires the additional assumption that GWV systems are such that partitions are assigned at most one memory segment. The source of this difference mainly originates from the granularity of the two models. GWV expresses security at the level of memory segments, while Rushby considers security at the level of partitions. Different assignments between partitions and segments may yield the same security policy. Our proofs consider both transitive and intransitive policies. For each type of policy, we prove theorems showing under which conditions a system satisfying GWV's notion of Separation also satisfies Rushby's notion of noninterference, and vice versa. Using two examples, we illustrate the differences between the two models and the necessity of some of our assumptions.

2   Related Work

The concept of noninterference is a very abstract formalization aimed at solving the problem of confidentiality and integrity in computer systems. The original definition of transitive noninterference was introduced by Goguen and Meseguer in 1982 [5]. Subsequently, John Rushby [19] proposed the first widely accepted definition of noninterference for intransitive policies based on the idea of an `ipurge` function, originally introduced by Haigh and Young [9]. Since its introduction noninterference definitions have been widely discussed, and some modifications have been proposed. Van der Meyden argued that the classic notion of intransitive noninterference (`ipurge`) allows some cases where a low security domain can infer information from higher security domains without the intermediation of the trusted downgraders [13]. He proposed new definitions of security to overcome this limitation and manually proved relations between his new definitions and purge-based ones [14,4]. Von Oheimb [16] proposed a generalization of the original Rushby's model to ensure noninterference in non-deterministic state machines.

Schellhorn et al. have applied Rushby's definition to smart cards that run multiple applications that may not interfere which each other [21]. Their approach applies to, e.g., IBMs SmartXA, a smart card with both a supervisor- and a user-mode, but to other multiapplicative systems such as cell phones or PDAs as well. Krohn and Tromer adopt a process algebraic version of Rushby's definition formulated by Ryan and Schneider [12,20]. They prove noninterference for Flume, a 30,000-line extension to a standard Linux kernel that provides decentralized information flow control.

The model proposed by Greve, Wilding and Vanfleet (GWV [7]) ensures a security property called Separation. Greve proposed a later revision of the GWV model called GWVr1 [1]. GWVr1 defines the notion of agents with the purpose of adding accountability properties into the original model. Another generalization called GWVr2 [6] was defined to cover security policies for dynamic and distributed systems. A description and comparison between the GWV variants was published by Greve [8]. Alves-Foss and Taylor clarified some of the concepts proposed in the GWV model [2]. After informally comparing the GWV model concepts and the notions of noninterference, they suggested that the GWV model is at least as strong as the noninterference definition. We show in this paper that the GWV model is stronger.

The GWV model has been applied to several industrial systems. Whalen et al. use model checking to verify the Turnstile high-assurance cross-domain guard platform of Rockwell Collins [1]. Richards applies GWVr2 to verify INTEGRITY-178B, an operating system developed by Green Hills Software [17]. Wilding et al. use the GWV framework in the ACL2 theorem prover to verify partition management for the AAMP7G microprocessor [22].

3   Two Models of Noninterference

We give a brief presentation of the Rushby and the GWV models. All proofs are omitted in this section. They are available in the original publications [19,7] and in our Isabelle proof scripts[1].

3.1   Rushby Transitive Noninterference

We consider Rushby's model of noninterference with access control [19]. We first define the system model and Rushby's notion of "secure". After that, we introduce the elements needed for access control and define noninterference for intransitive policies and the definition of "isecure".

Systems are modelled using Moore machines. A Moore machine is a 6-tuple $(\mathcal{S}, s_0, \mathcal{A}, \mathcal{O}, \text{step}, \text{output})$, where $\mathcal{S}$ is a finite state of states, $\mathcal{A}$ is a finite set of actions which are the inputs of the machine, $\mathcal{O}$ is a finite set of outputs, $\text{step} : \mathcal{S} \times \mathcal{A} \to \mathcal{S}$ is a finite transition relation, and $\text{output} : \mathcal{S} \to \mathcal{O}$ computes the current outputs from the current states.

Please note that from this point on, the first letters of the alphabet $(a, b, ...)$ are used to denote actions, the letters $s, t, ..$ to represent states and the letters of the Greek alphabet $\alpha, \beta, ...$ to indicate sequences of actions.

Function run computes the state reached after executing a sequence of actions. Let $[]$ be the empty sequence of action, $\alpha[0]$ the first action, and $\alpha[1...]$ be α without the first action.

$$\text{run}(\alpha, s) = \text{if } (\alpha = []) \; s \text{ else } \text{run}(\alpha[1...], \text{step}(s, \alpha[0]))$$

A security policy is defined as a relation between *domains*. The security policy defines which domains are allowed to *interfere* with other domains. Intuitively two domains u and v have an "interference" relation if u is allowed to flow information to v. Let $\mathcal{D}$ be the set of domains. Interference is defined as the relation $\leadsto : \mathcal{D} \times \mathcal{D}$. Noninterference is simply defined by its negation, noted $\not\leadsto$.

Rushby's definition of security is based on function $purge(\alpha, u)$. This function returns a subsequence of α, resulting of deleting all the actions of the domains that are not allowed to interact with v. In other words, it removes all actions of domains u that have a "noninterference" relation with v $(u \not\leadsto v)$.

$$\text{purge}(\alpha, u) = \text{if } (\text{dom}(\alpha[0]) \not\leadsto u) \; \text{purge}(\alpha[1...], u) \text{ else } \alpha[0]; \text{purge}(\alpha[1...], u)$$

A system being "secure" is then defined as the equality between a run and its purged version. The intuition is that from the point of view of a given domain, running the entire system or running this system without the actions of the domains not interfering with this domain should not be distinguishable. This notion of secure is defined by the following equation:

$$\forall a, \alpha.\text{output}(\text{run}(\alpha, s_0), a) = \text{output}(\text{run}(\text{purge}(\alpha, \text{dom}(a)), s_0), a) \quad (1)$$

---

[1] http://www.win.tue.nl/~jschmalt/publications/safecomp14/safecomp14.html

A system is *view-partitioned* if for any domain u there exists an equivalence relation – noted $\overset{u}{\sim}$ – on the set of state $\mathcal{S}$. Related to this view partition equivalence relation, three unwinding conditions are introduced:

- **Output Consistency:** $s \overset{\text{dom}(a)}{\sim} t \rightarrow \text{output}(s, a) = \text{output}(t, a)$
- **Step Consistency:** $s \overset{u}{\sim} t \rightarrow \text{step}(s, a) \overset{u}{\sim} \text{step}(t, a)$
- **Locally Respects:** $\text{dom}(a) \not\rightsquigarrow u \rightarrow s \overset{u}{\sim} \text{step}(s, a)$

The main theorem in Rushby's theory is the "Unwinding Theorem". The latter shows that security follows from the three unwinding conditions.

Theorem 1. Unwinding Theorem. *Let $\rightsquigarrow$ be a security policy and M a view partitioned system that is*

1. *output consistent,*
2. *step consistent,*
3. *locally respects $\rightsquigarrow$,*

then M is secure for $\rightsquigarrow$.

The Unwinding Theorem can be used to represent systems with access control mechanisms. In this context, the state is assumed to be composed of individual storage locations, called "objects". Each object has a name and a value. Access control functions determine for each domain which locations can be read or written. This read and write accesses are defined using functions observe and alter, with the interpretation that $\text{observe}(u)$ returns the locations that domain u can read, and $\text{alter}(u)$ returns the locations that domain u can write.

Definition 1. Structured State. *A machine has a structured state if there exist:*

- *a set $\mathcal{N}$ of names*
- *a set $\mathcal{V}$ of values*
- *a function* contents $: \mathcal{S} \times \mathcal{N} \rightarrow \mathcal{V}$

with the interpretation that contents(s, n) *is the value of the object named n in state s.*

An access control policy is enforced when the behavior of the system matches the intended interpretation of the observe and alter functions. This requires the following conditions – called the "Reference Monitor assumptions" – to be satisfied.

Definition 2. Reference Monitor Assumptions

- *Reference Monitor 1 (RMA1):*

$$s \overset{u}{\sim} t \equiv \forall n \in \text{observe}(u).\text{contents}(s, n) = \text{contents}(t, n)$$

− *Reference Monitor 2 (RMA2):*

$$s \overset{u}{\sim} t \wedge$$
$$(\texttt{contents}(\texttt{step}(s, a), n) \neq \texttt{contents}(s, a) \vee$$
$$\texttt{contents}(\texttt{step}(t, a), n) \neq \texttt{contents}(t, a))$$
$$\rightarrow \texttt{contents}(\texttt{step}(s, a), n) = \texttt{contents}(\texttt{step}(t, a), n)$$

− *Reference Monitor 3 (RMA3):*

$$\texttt{contents}(\texttt{step}(s, a), n) \neq \texttt{contents}(s, n) \rightarrow n \in \texttt{alter}(\texttt{dom}(a)))$$

From these reference monitor assumptions, Rushby shows that the three unwinding conditions can be derived. These conditions are therefore sufficient to ensure security. For transitive security policies, the main theorem in the Rushby model is the following:

Theorem 2. *A system with structured state that satisfies the Reference Monitor Assumptions and the following two conditions*

1. $u \rightsquigarrow v \rightarrow observe(u) \subseteq observe(v)$
2. $n \in alter(u) \wedge n \in observe(v) \rightarrow u \rightsquigarrow v$

is secure for the policy $\rightsquigarrow$.

3.2 Rushby Intransitive Noninterference

In the case of intransitive policies, function *purge* is re-defined to purge actions with no *indirect* interference with a given domain. From this new definition of purge, called `ipurge`, the definition of security is obtained by replacing occurrences of *purge* with `ipurge`. Let us call this definition *isecure*.

After several technical lemmas, Rushby proves an Unwinding Theorem for intransitive policies. The only difference to the transitive case (Theorem 1) is the assumption of *weak step consistency* instead of step consistency. Formally, weak step consistency is defined as follows:

$$s \overset{u}{\sim} t \wedge s \overset{\text{dom}(a)}{\sim} t \rightarrow \texttt{step}(s, a) \overset{u}{\sim} \texttt{step}(t, a)$$

It basically adds the requirement of view partition equivalence for the current active domain. This is needed to ensure that information only flows between domains with an indirect interference relation.

From this Unwinding Theorem, Rushby proves that the Reference Monitor Assumptions are also sufficient to ensure *isecure*.

Theorem 3. *A system with structured state that satisfies the Reference Monitor Assumptions and the following condition*

1. $n \in alter(u) \wedge n \in observe(v) \rightarrow u \rightsquigarrow v$

is isecure for the policy $\rightsquigarrow$.

3.3   Greve, Wilding, Vanfleet

In the Rushby model, the current action is an input to the system. In the GWV model, the current action is part of the system state. We define a GWV state as a tuple made of a Rushby state and an action. Let $\mathcal{S}_g$ denote the set of GWV states. Given $s_g \in \mathcal{S}_g$, we let $s_g.s$ denote the Rushby state part of s_g and $s_g.a$ the action part of s_g.

The GWV model uses the term *partitions* to denote what Rushby calls *domains*. Both terms denote the same concept. We keep notation $\mathcal{D}$ to denote the set of partitions. Function `current` returns the current active partition from a GWV state: $\texttt{current} : \mathcal{S}_g \rightarrow \mathcal{D}$. A number of memory segments is associated to each partition. Function `segs` takes as input a partition and returns the memory segments associated to it: $\texttt{segs} : \mathcal{D} \rightarrow \mathcal{P}(\mathcal{M})$. The values stored in memory segments are given by function `select`. Let $\mathcal{V}$ be the set of possible values of memory segments. Function `select` takes as input a state and a memory segment. It returns the value of this segment in the state: $\texttt{select} : \mathcal{S}_g \times \mathcal{M} \rightarrow \mathcal{V}$. Finally, function *next* models one system execution step, that is, the execution of one action and the computation of the next state: $next : \mathcal{S}_g \rightarrow \mathcal{S}_g$.

The security policy is defined by function `dia`. This function takes a memory segment – say n – as input and returns all memory segments allowed to *directly affect* memory segment n. Function `dia` is formally defined as follows:

$$\texttt{dia} : \mathcal{M} \rightarrow \mathcal{P}(\mathcal{M})$$

In the GWV model, *separation* denotes the notion of "secure".

Definition 3. Separation. *Let $s, t \in \mathcal{S}_g$ and $n \in \mathcal{M}$,*

$\texttt{current}(s) = \texttt{current}(t) \wedge$
$\texttt{select}(s, n) = \texttt{select}(t, n) \wedge$
$\forall m \in \texttt{dia}(n) \cap \texttt{segs}(\texttt{current}(s_g)).\texttt{select}(s, m) = \texttt{select}(t, m)$
$\rightarrow$
$\texttt{select}(\texttt{next}(s), n) = \texttt{select}(\texttt{next}(t), n)$

This definition states that for any segment n, its value is only affected by the memory segments that (1) are allowed to directly interfere with it and (2) are part of the current active partition. In our comparison, we need a variant, which also assumes equality of the action in states s and t. We shall denote by "Separation with Action Equality" the definition above where $s.a = t.a$ is added to the assumptions.

4   Formal Comparison

4.1   Proof Overview

Figure 2 gives an overview of the comparison between the two models. Lemma 2 shows that Separation implies weak step consistency. From this lemma, Theorem 6 shows that for any GWV system satisfying Separation there exists a

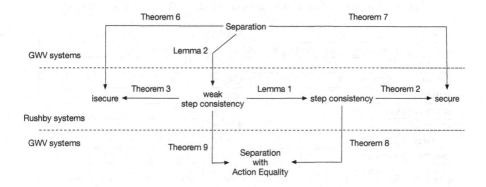

Fig. 2. Relation between the GWV and the Rushby models

corresponding Rushby system that is *isecure*. Lemma 1 shows which additional assumptions are required to recover step consistency from weak step consistency. Using these additional assumptions, Theorem 7 shows that Separation also implies a Rushby system that is *secure*. Theorems 8 and 9 show under which assumptions Separation with Action Equality can be derived from a secure or isecure Rushby system. The main assumption requires that any segment is assigned to a partition and that all partitions have at most one segment. In Section 5, we discuss these assumptions in more details.

4.2   Mapping between the Two Worlds

We give a mapping between the objects and relations defined in the two models. We first show how we map states and the transition functions. After that, we show mappings for the security policy and the view partition equivalence relation. Table 1 gives an overview of this mapping.

In the Rushby model, systems are modelled using Moore machines. From such a machine, the corresponding GWV system model is defined as the following 5-tuple $(\mathcal{S}_g, s_{g_0}, \mathcal{O}, \texttt{next}, \texttt{output}_g)$, where:

- $\mathcal{S}_g : \mathcal{S} \times \mathcal{A}$: a GWV state is a tuple composed of a Rushby state and a Rushby action.
- $\texttt{next} : \mathcal{S}_g \rightarrow \mathcal{S}_g$: computes the next state. We assume that $\texttt{next}(s_g).s = \texttt{step}(s_g.s, s_g.a)$ for all state s_g.
- $\texttt{output}_g : \mathcal{S}_g \rightarrow \mathcal{O}$: computes the observable output from the current state. We assume that $\texttt{output}_g(s_g) = \texttt{output}(s_g.s, s_g.a)$ for all state s_g.

We assume that the set of memory segments of the GWV model equals the set of objects of the Rushby model, that is, we have $\mathcal{M} = \mathcal{N}$. We then identify function $\texttt{select}$ with function $\texttt{contents}$, that is, $\texttt{select}(s_g, n) = \texttt{contents}(s_g.s, n)$ for all states s_g and memory segment n.

Table 1. Mapping between the elements of the GWV and Rushby models

GWV	Rushby
$S_g : S \times A$, with $s_g.s \in S$ and $s_g.a \in A$	states in S, actions in A
Partition,$\mathcal{D}$	Domain, $\mathcal{D}$
Memory segment, $\mathcal{M}$	Object, $\mathcal{N}$
output$_g$	output
current(s_g)	dom$(s_g.a)$
segs(p)	alter(p)
select(s_g, n)	contents$(s_g.a, n)$
next$(s_g).s$	step$(s_g.s, s_g.a)$
$\{s \mid \exists s' \in \text{segs}(u).s \in \text{dia}(s')\}$	observe(u)
$s \overset{u}{\sim}_g t$	$s \overset{u}{\sim} t$
$u \rightsquigarrow_g v$	$u \rightsquigarrow v$

We assume that a GWV partition can write to all its segments, that is, we have $\text{alter}_g(u) = \text{segs}(u)$ for all partition u. A partition can read all segments in direct interference with its own segments, that is, we define $\text{observe}_g(u) = \{s \mid \exists s' \in \text{segs}(u).s \in \text{dia}(s')\}$. Assuming reflexivity of dia, we can easily prove that $\text{segs}(u) \subseteq \text{observe}_g(u)$.

The definition of dia induces a security policy at the level of partitions. Such a policy is defined such that two domains have an interference relation if there exists a pair of segments that are in direct interaction. We can phrase this definition using alter_g and observe_g as follows:

$$u \rightsquigarrow_g v \overset{\triangle}{=} \text{alter}_g(u) \cap \text{observe}_g(v) \neq \emptyset \qquad (2)$$

This definition implies the condition corresponding to Condition 2 in Theorems 2 and 3. The following equation directly follows from this definition:

$$\forall u, v.n \in \text{alter}_g(u) \wedge n \in \text{observe}_g(v) \rightarrow u \rightsquigarrow_g v \qquad (3)$$

Finally, the GWV model does not define a view partition equivalence relation. This is a central concept in the Rushby model and we need to define such a concept for the GWV model. We say that two states are view partition equivalent for domain u in the GVW model if and only if the value of the segments of u and the current active partition are equal in these two states. We define relation $s \overset{u}{\sim}_g t$ as follows:

$$(\forall m \in \text{segs}(p).\text{select}(s, m) = \text{select}(t, m)) \wedge \text{current}(s) = \text{current}(t) \qquad (4)$$

4.3   Reformulation of Rushby's Theorems

In its original formulation, Rushby defines three reference monitor assumptions. The second monitor assumption is mainly used to derive (weak) step consistency. In our formulation, we replace this assumption with weak step consistency. We now prove a lemma showing how to recover step consistency from weak step consistency. We show that any system that is weak step consistent and that satisfies the third reference monitor assumption and the two conditions in Theorem 2, is also step consistent.

Lemma 1. *Let M be a system that is weak step consistent and satisfies the following conditions:*

1. $u \rightsquigarrow v \rightarrow observe(u) \subseteq observe(v)$
2. $n \in alter(u) \land n \in observe(v) \rightarrow u \rightsquigarrow v$
3. *RMA3:* $\texttt{contents}(\texttt{step}(s,a),n) \neq \texttt{contents}(s,n) \rightarrow n \in \texttt{alter}(\text{dom}(a)))$

then, M is step consistent.

Using this lemma, we can reformulate the main theorem of the Rushby model for transitive and intransitive security policies.

Theorem 4. *A system with structured state that satisfies weak step consistency, the first and third Reference Monitor Assumptions and the following conditions*

1. $u \rightsquigarrow v \rightarrow observe(u) \subseteq observe(v)$
2. $n \in alter(u) \land n \in observe(v) \rightarrow u \rightsquigarrow v$

is secure for the policy $\rightsquigarrow$.

Theorem 5. *A system with structured state that satisfies weak step consistency, the first and third Reference Monitor Assumptions and the following condition*

$$n \in alter(u) \land n \in observe(v) \rightarrow u \rightsquigarrow v$$

is isecure for the policy $\rightsquigarrow$.

4.4   From GWV to Rushby

Our main lemma is to show that the GWV view partition equivalence is weakly step consistent. This lemma is key in proving implication to the transitive and intransitive models of Rushby. To prove this lemma, we introduce the notion of "current respects", which states that if two states are equivalent, the next current active partition is the same in these two states.

$$\textbf{CurrentRespects} \equiv s \overset{u}{\sim}_g t \rightarrow \texttt{current}(\texttt{next}(s)) = \texttt{current}(\texttt{next}(t))$$

We now state and prove our main lemma. A system satisfying the definition of Separation (Definition 3) also satisfies weak step consistency.

Lemma 2. *Given a system M satisfying the definition of separation by GWV and Current Respects, then $\overset{u}{\sim}_g$ is weakly step consistent, that is,*

$$s \overset{u}{\sim}_g t \land s \overset{\texttt{current}(s)}{\sim}_g t \rightarrow \texttt{next}(s) \overset{u}{\sim}_g \texttt{next}(t)$$

Proof. Assume $s \overset{u}{\sim}_g t \wedge s \overset{\texttt{current}(s)}{\sim}_g t$. We then need to derive two facts to obtain our conclusion: (1) equality of the segments in the next states and (2) equality of the next current active partition. The second fact directly follows from the assumption $s \overset{u}{\sim}_g t$ and Current Respects. We are left with proving the first fact.

Let n be a memory segment such that $n \in \texttt{segs}(u)$. From the assumptions $s \overset{u}{\sim}_g t$ and $s \overset{\texttt{current}(s)}{\sim}_g t$, we derive the three conditions of the definition of GWV secure. By definition, $s \overset{u}{\sim}_g t$ gives us the equality of the value of n in states s and t and the equality of the current partition in s and t. By definition, $s \overset{\texttt{current}(s)}{\sim}_g t$ gives us equality in states s and t of all the segments of the current active partition. Hence, the segments at the intersection of $\texttt{dia}(n)$ with the segments of the current active partition are also equal. We just derived the following:

1. $\texttt{select}(s, n) = \texttt{select}(t, s)$
2. $\texttt{current}(s) = \texttt{current}(t)$
3. $\forall n' \in \texttt{dia}(n) \cap \texttt{segs}(\texttt{current}(s)).\texttt{select}(s, n') = \texttt{select}(t, n')$

Then, Definition 3 gives us $\texttt{select}(\texttt{next}(s), n) = \texttt{select}(\texttt{next}(t), n)$. □

Using this Lemma, we prove that any GWV system that is secure for an intransitive policy $\rightsquigarrow$ is also Rushby secure for this security policy. In this proof, we assume that GWV systems satisfy reference monitor assumptions similar to the first and third assumptions in the Rushby model. Formally, we define the following properties:

Definition 4. GWV Reference Monitor Assumptions

- *GWV Reference Monitor 1 (GWVRMA1):*

$$s \overset{u}{\sim}_g t \equiv \forall n \in \texttt{observe}_g(u).\texttt{select}(s, n) = \texttt{select}(t, n)$$

- *GWV Reference Monitor 3 (GWVRMA3):*

$$\texttt{select}(\texttt{next}(s), n) \neq \texttt{select}(s, n) \rightarrow n \in \texttt{alter}_g(\texttt{current}(s))$$

The first assumption is needed to provide a definition of $\overset{u}{\sim}_g$. The second assumption states that only the current active partition is allowed to write a memory segment. This is a basic underlying assumption of the GWV model, which is often left implicit. In our formal comparison, we need it to be explicit. Using our mapping, it is easy to check that these two assumptions map to RMA1 and RMA3 (Definition 2) of the Rushby model.

Theorem 6. *Let M_g be a GWV system satisfying the GWV Reference Monitor Assumptions and Current Respects. Let M be the Rushby system corresponding to M_g. Then M is isecure for $\rightsquigarrow_g$.*

Proof. From the assumptions, the mapping from the GWV model to the Rushby model, and Equation 3, we obtain all assumptions of Theorem 5. □

We now show any GWV secure system is also Rushby secure for transitive policies. The proof uses our reformulations of the main theorems of the Rushby model.

Theorem 7. *Let M_g be a GWV system that satisfies Current Respects, weak step consistency, the GWV Reference Monitor Assumptions, and the following condition:*

$$\forall u, v.u \leadsto_g v \rightarrow \mathsf{observe}_g(u) \subset \mathsf{observe}_g(v)$$

Let M be the Rushby system corresponding to M_g. Then, M is secure for $\leadsto_g$.

Proof. From the assumptions, the mapping from the GWV model to the Rushby model, and Equation 3, we obtain all assumptions of Theorem 4.   □

4.5 Rushby Step Consistency Implies GWV Secure

We now prove that for any Rushby system satisfying step consistency there exists a GWV system satisfying Separation with Action Equality. The main assumption states that in the GWV system partitions are assigned at most one segment and that all segments are assigned to a partition.

Theorem 8. *Let M be a view partitioned system that is step consistent. Let M_g be the mapping of M to the GWV model such that in M_g all partitions have exactly one segment and all segments have a partition, i.e., the following condition holds:*

$$\forall n \in \mathcal{M}.\exists p \in \mathcal{D}.n \in \mathsf{segs}(p) \wedge \forall n' \in \mathcal{M}.n' \in \mathsf{segs}(p) \rightarrow n' = n$$

Then, M_g satisfies Separation with Action Equality.

Proof. The main idea of the proof is to show that the hypotheses of Separation with Action Equality implies $\overset{p}{\sim}_g$ for some partition p. From this fact, we use the assumption that the system is step consistent to derive segments equality after execution of an action. We then map this back to the GWV world.

Let $s_g, t_g \in \mathcal{S}_g$ and $n \in \mathcal{M}$. The hypothesis of our conclusion for n gives:

$$\mathsf{current}(s_g) = \mathsf{current}(t_g)$$
$$\wedge \mathsf{select}(s_g, n) = \mathsf{select}(t_g, n)$$
$$\wedge s_g.a = t_g.a$$
$$\wedge \forall m \in \mathsf{dia}(n) \cap \mathsf{segs}(\mathsf{current}(s_g)).\mathsf{select}(s_g, m) = \mathsf{select}(t_g, m)$$

From the second condition and the assumption that all partitions have exactly one segment, it follows that all segments of p have the same value in states s_g and t_g, i.e., we obtain: $\forall m \in \mathsf{segs}(p).\mathsf{select}(s_g, m) = \mathsf{select}(t_g, m)$.

From the third condition, we derive equality of the current active partition, i.e., $\mathsf{current}(s_g) = \mathsf{current}(t_g)$.

We now have obtained that s_g and t_g are GWV view partition equivalent for partition p, i.e., $s_g \overset{p}{\sim}_g t_g$. Using the mapping, we translate this condition to

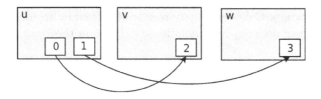

Fig. 3. Rushby secure but GWV insecure system

the Rushby model and obtain $s_g.s \overset{p}{\sim} t_g.s$. From step consistency, we obtain view partition equivalence for the successor states: $\mathtt{step}(s_g.s, s_g.a) \overset{p}{\sim} \mathtt{step}(t_g.s, s_g.a)$.

By definition of $\overset{p}{\sim}$ for structured states, it follows that the observable contents of partition p is equal in the two successor states, i.e.:

$$\forall m \in \mathtt{observe}(p).\mathtt{contents}(\mathtt{step}(s_g.s, s_g.a), m) = \mathtt{contents}(\mathtt{step}(t_g.s, s_g.a), m)$$

The mapping translates this statement to the GWV model:

$$\forall m \in \mathtt{observe}_g(p).\mathtt{select}(\mathtt{next}(s_g), m) = \mathtt{select}(\mathtt{next}(t_g.s), m)$$

Let p be the partition to which n is assigned. We then derive the right hand side of our conclusion, i.e., $\mathtt{select}(\mathtt{next}(s_g), n) = \mathtt{select}(\mathtt{next}(t_g), n)$. $\square$

4.6   Rushby Weak Step Consistency Implies GWV Secure

For the intransitive case, the relation between Rushby and GWV is similar. The only difference in the statement is that Rushby systems are weak step consistent. The main difference with the previous proof is that one needs to also derive GWV view partition equivalence for the current active partition.

Theorem 9. *Let M be a view partitioned system that is weakly step consistent. Let M_g be the mapping of M to the GWV model such that in M_g all partitions have exactly one segment and all segments have a partition, i.e., the following condition holds:*

$$\forall n \in \mathcal{M}.\exists p \in \mathcal{D}.n \in \mathtt{segs}(p) \land \forall n' \in \mathcal{M}.n' \in \mathtt{segs}(p) \to n' = n \qquad (5)$$

Then, M_g satisfies Separation with Action Equality.

5   Counter-Examples and Discussion

5.1   On the Direction Rushby to GWV

We justify the assumption that partitions must have no more than one segment. Consider the example in Figure 3. There are three partitions, namely, u, v, and w. Partition u has two segments, named 0 and 1. Partition v has segment 2, and partition w has segment 3. Consider the following assignments in the GWV model. We have $\mathtt{segs}(u) = \{0,1\}$, $\mathtt{segs}(v) = \{2\}$, and $\mathtt{segs}(w) = \{3\}$. We consider two different assignments for $\mathtt{dia}$. First, we define $\mathtt{dia}_1(0) = \mathtt{dia}_1(1) = \emptyset$, $\mathtt{dia}_1(2) = \{0\}$, and $\mathtt{dia}_1(3) = \{1\}$. We then define $\mathtt{dia}_2$ to be equal to $\mathtt{dia}_1$, except for segment 3, where we define $\mathtt{dia}_2(3) = \{0\}$. Using our definition of $\leadsto_g$, these two definitions of $\mathtt{dia}$ imply the following security policy: $u \leadsto_g v$, $u \leadsto_g w$. Let us call this policy $\leadsto_g^e$.

In the Rushby model, the two different assignments of $\mathtt{dia}$ would produce two different definitions of $\mathtt{observe}(w)$: $\mathtt{observe}_1(w) = \{0,3\}$ and $\mathtt{observe}_2(w) = \{1,3\}$. Assume these two systems are secure in the Rushby model. This means that they are secure for policy $\leadsto_g^e$. Assume that in the GWV model a system satisfying $\mathtt{dia}_1$ satisfies Separation, but a system with $\mathtt{dia}_2$ does not. Then, we have two secure systems in the Rushby model, but only one of them maps to a GWV secure system. Therefore, to map Rushby secure systems to GWV secure systems, it is required that GWV partitions have at most one memory segment.

The intuition behind this assumption is that defining interactions between segments is more fine-grained than defining interactions between partitions. In that sense, the GWV model is more expressive than the Rushby one. This might be of interest for hardware which allows to directly specify access control between memory segments. However, most commercial off-the-shelf Memory Management Units (MMUs) only allow to assign memory segments to address spaces. They do not support direct control mechanisms between memory segments.

All segments must be assigned to a partition. The reason is that a segment not under control of a partition may contain secret data, but there is no way to control the flow of this data. This secret segment may influence any other one without violating the security policy.

5.2   Transitive GWV Security Policy

For transitive policies, the proof going from a GWV secure system to a Rushby secure one needs an assumption, which is not needed in the case of intransitive policies. This condition states that if two domains u and v have an interference relation, the set of observable objects of u must be a subset of the observable objects of v. This is condition 1 in Theorem 4. We give a counter-example of a GWV system from which the derived Rushby system violates this condition.

Consider the system pictured in Figure 4. Partition V is assigned one segment. It can write this segment using information from segments 2 and 3. Partition U is assigned segments 2 ,3, 4, and 5. Let consider the following definition of $\mathtt{dia}$: $\mathtt{dia}(4) = \{5\}$, $\mathtt{dia}2 = \{3\}$, and $\mathtt{dia}1 = 2$. For any other segment, its $\mathtt{dia}$ is the empty set. The issue is that our mapping defines $\mathtt{observe}_g(v) = \{1,2,3\}$ and $\mathtt{observe}_g(u) = \{2,3,4,5\}$. Also, our mapping gives $v \leadsto_g u$. Hence, $\neg(\mathtt{observe}_g(u) \subseteq \mathtt{observe}_g(u))$. Here again, the different granularity of the two models prevents the translation of some GWV systems to Rushby ones. In this example, the Rushby model cannot express the fact that within a partition some segments may not flow information to other ones. Note that supporting this notion of intra-partition flow restrictions is in practice difficult to ensure.

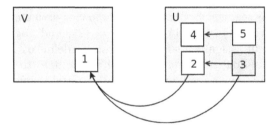

Fig. 4. Transitive Rushby secure but GWV insecure system

A reason for this is that all memory segments of a partition are loaded in the same kernel working area. Special hardware is then needed to restrict information flows between two particular segments of the same partition.

6   Conclusion and Future Work

We formally compared the GWV and the Rushby models by proving theorems showing under which conditions a system satisfying the notion of Separation defined by GWV also satisfies the notion of noninterference defined by Rushby, and vice versa. We proved that from any system satisfying Separation, one can construct a system satisfying Rushby's noninterference. The other direction only holds for GWV systems such that partitions have at most one segment. This assumption lifts the granularity of the GWV model to the granularity of the Rushby model. We provided a counter-example showing that without this assumption, Rushby systems which are secure may not satisfy Separation. If a separation kernel allows partitions to have several non-contiguous memory segments, the GWV model must be used. Otherwise, the two models are equivalent.

There are many different definitions of noninterference. The formal relations between these definitions is mostly unexplored. In particular, we still need to study of the relation of the Rushby and GWV models to the one of Van der Meyden. In the future, our plan is to extend our formal comparison to other definitions of noninterference.

Acknowledgment. We acknowledge funding from the European Union's Seventh Framework Programme (FP7/2007-2013) under grant agreement n° 318353 (EURO-MILS project: http://www.euromils.eu).

References

1. Hardin, D.S. (ed.): Design and Verification of Microprocessor Systems for High-Assurance Applications (2010)
2. Alves-Foss, J., Taylor, C.: An analysis of the GWV security policy. In: Fifth International Workshop on ACL2 Prover and its Applications (2004)

3. Brygier, J., Fuchsen, R., Blasum, H.: PikeOS: Safe and secure virtualization in a separation microkernel. Technical report, SYSGO (2009)
4. Eggert, S., van der Meyden, R., Schnoor, H., Wilke, T.: Complexity and unwinding for intransitive noninterference. CoRR abs/1308.1204 (2013)
5. Goguen, J.A., Meseguer, J.: Security policies and security models. In: IEEE Symposium on Security and Privacy, pp. 11–20 (1982)
6. Greve, D., Wilding, M., Richards, R., Vanfleet, W.M.: Formalizing security policies for dynamic and distributed systems (September 2004) (unpublished), http://hokiepokie.org/docs/sstc05.pdf
7. Greve, D., Wilding, M., Vanfleet, W.M.: A separation kernel formal security policy. In: Fourth International Workshop on the ACL2 Theorem Prover and its Applications, ACL2 2003 (July 2003)
8. Greve, D.: Information security modeling and analysis. In: Hardin, D.S. (ed.) Design and Verification of Microprocessor Systems for High-Assurance Applications, pp. 249–299. Springer, US (2010), http://dx.doi.org/10.1007/978-1-4419-1539-9_9
9. Haigh, J.T., Young, W.D.: Extending the noninterference version of mls for sat. IEEE Trans. Software Eng. 13(2), 141–150 (1987)
10. Hardin, D.S. (ed.): Design and Verification of Microprocessor Systems for High-Assurance Applications. Springer (2010)
11. Kaiser, R., Wagner, S.: Evolution of the PikeOS microkernel. In: First International Workshop on Microkernels for Embedded Systems, p. 50 (2007)
12. Krohn, M., Tromer, E.: Noninterference for a practical DIFC-based operating system. In: IEEE Symp. Security & Privacy, pp. 61–76 (2009)
13. van der Meyden, R.: What, indeed, is intransitive noninterference? In: Biskup, J., López, J. (eds.) ESORICS 2007. LNCS, vol. 4734, pp. 235–250. Springer, Heidelberg (2007)
14. van der Meyden, R., Zhang, C.: A comparison of semantic models for noninterference. Theor. Comput. Sci. 411(47), 4123–4147 (2010)
15. Nipkow, T., Paulson, L.C., Wenzel, M.: Isabelle/HOL. LNCS, vol. 2283. Springer, Heidelberg (2002)
16. von Oheimb, D.: Information flow control revisited: Noninfluence = Noninterference + Nonleakage. In: Samarati, P., Ryan, P.Y.A., Gollmann, D., Molva, R. (eds.) ESORICS 2004. LNCS, vol. 3193, pp. 225–243. Springer, Heidelberg (2004)
17. Richards, R.J.: Modeling and security analysis of a commercial real-time operating system kernel. In: Hardin (ed.) [10], pp. 301–322
18. Rushby, J.: Design and verification of secure systems. ACM SIGOPS Operating Systems Review 15, 12–21 (1981)
19. Rushby, J.: Noninterference, transitivity and channel-control security policies. Tech. rep., Computer Science Laboratory, SRI International (1992)
20. Ryan, P.Y.A., Schneider, S.A.: Process algebra and non-interference. Journal of Computer Security, 214–227 (1999)
21. Schellhorn, G., Reif, W., Schairer, A., Karger, P., Austel, V., Toll, D.: Verification of a formal security model for multiapplicative smart cards. In: Cuppens, F., Deswarte, Y., Gollmann, D., Waidner, M. (eds.) ESORICS 2000. LNCS, vol. 1895, pp. 17–36. Springer, Heidelberg (2000)
22. Wilding, M., Greve, D., Richards, R., Hardin, D.: Formal verification of partition management for the AAMP7G microprocessor. In: Hardin (ed.) [10], pp. 175–191

Specifying Safety Monitors for Autonomous Systems Using Model-Checking

Mathilde Machin[1,2], Fanny Dufossé[1,2], Jean-Paul Blanquart[3],
Jérémie Guiochet[1,2], David Powell[1,2], and Hélène Waeselynck[1,2]

[1] CNRS, LAAS, 7 avenue du colonel Roche, F-31400 Toulouse, France
[2] Univ de Toulouse, LAAS, F-31400 Toulouse, France
`firstname.lastname@laas.fr`
[3] Airbus Defence and Space, 31 rue des cosmonautes, 31402 Toulouse, France
`jean-paul.blanquart@astrium.eads.net`

Abstract. Autonomous systems operating in the vicinity of humans are critical in that they potentially harm humans. As the complexity of autonomous system software makes the zero-fault objective hardly attainable, we adopt a fault-tolerance approach. We consider a separate safety channel, called a monitor, that is able to partially observe the system and to trigger safety-ensuring actuations. A systematic process for specifying a safety monitor is presented. Hazards are formally modeled, based on a risk analysis of the monitored system. A model-checker is used to synthesize monitor behavior rules that ensure the safety of the monitored system. Potentially excessive limitation of system functionality due to presence of the safety monitor is addressed through the notion of permissiveness. Tools have been developed to assist the process.

Keywords: Safety Monitoring, Safety Rules, Autonomous Robotics.

1 Introduction

Autonomous systems such as robots and unmanned vehicles are widely studied and technically feasible. An important bottleneck for their effective deployment in human environments is the safety concerns of both users and certification authorities. Various ad-hoc safety measures have been designed, often focused on particular risks, such as collision. However, if autonomous systems are to be certified, the method needs to be generalized. We propose here a general method to build high-level safety specifications based on hazard analysis.

The autonomous systems of interest to us offer a wide range of features and operate in a diverse unstructured environment. They can thus be complex, which makes them difficult to verify. Moreover, diversity of the environment implies that testing cannot significantly cover the situations that the system will face. Here, we choose a classical fault tolerance approach by considering online safety measures implemented in a device called a *safety monitor*, that is simple and independent from the main control channel, and thus easier to verify. The monitor is solely responsible for safe system behavior. To this end, the monitor is

A. Bondavalli and F. Di Giandomenico (Eds.): SAFECOMP 2014, LNCS 8666, pp. 262–277, 2014.
© Springer International Publishing Switzerland 2014

equipped with means for context observation (i.e., sensors) and is able to trigger safety interventions. The monitor behavior is specified declaratively by a set of *safety rules*, each defining one intervention to apply in certain observation conditions. However, safety interventions may also prevent the system from fulfilling its functions. For instance, a vehicle whose emergency brakes are permanently engaged is useless. We require the monitor to be *permissive* with respect to the possibility for the system to perform useful tasks.

Continuing the work of Mekki-Mokhtar *et al.* [1], we propose a process based on hazard analysis to specify safety monitors and extend it by means of formal methods. Once a hazard is identified, it is necessary to specify what the monitor has to do to avoid it, i.e., the safety rules. We aim to explore solutions very early in the autonomous system design process. Thus, many observations and interventions can be considered in a first design iteration, whereas only the most appropriate ones are actually developed and implemented. We propose to use model-checking to explore and check the specifications.

The main contributions of this paper are:
 - A method to explore possible safety specifications by using model-checking.
 - A method for modeling permissiveness in temporal logic.
 - A set of tools to support the methodology[1].

First, we present the overall concepts and process in Section 2. Section 3 details the exploration of possible safety rules in a discrete model, which is applied in Section 4 to a mobile manufacturing robot. Related work is discussed in Section 5 and Section 6 presents conclusions and future work.

2   Baseline and Concepts

We introduce here the underlying concepts of our work, based on definitions adapted from [1], and then present the overall process.

2.1   Concepts

Taking inspiration from the IEC 61508 standard [2], we define a *safety monitor* as a device responsible for safety, in opposition to the main control channel which is responsible for all other functional and non-functional requirements of the system. The monitor is equipped with means for context observation (i.e., sensors) and able to trigger safety interventions. The safety monitor is independent from the main control channel, as regards its means of observation, computation and intervention. It is required to protect against all faults that adversely affect safety, including interaction faults. The whole safety channel is assumed fault-free (for example, we consider that the sensors available to the monitor are perfect, without uncertainty.) In practice, this must be achieved through classical redundancy and verification techniques. We focus in our work on the upstream task of obtaining a correct high-level specification with respect to safety and permissiveness.

---

[1] Available at `http://webhost.laas.fr/TSF/archives/safety_rule_synthesis`

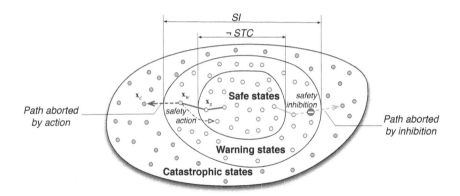

Fig. 1. Partition of system states in catastrophic, warning and safe states

A **safety invariant (SI)** is a necessary and sufficient condition to avoid a hazardous situation. If a safety invariant is violated, we assume that damage is immediate and irreversible, with no possible recovery. We refer to any state violating the safety invariant as a *catastrophic state*.

> *Example: "the robot speed shall not exceed 3 m/s" (where 3 m/s is the speed beyond which harm is considered to be inevitable).*

A **safety intervention** is an activity carried out explicitly to prevent the system from violating a safety invariant by constraining the system behavior. An intervention is only applicable in states satisfying its associated *precondition*. We distinguish two types of interventions: inhibitions and actions.

A **safety inhibition** prevents a change in system state. When triggered, an inhibition is assumed to be immediately effective.

> *Example : "lock the wheels" (with "robot stationary" as precondition).*

A **safety action** triggers a change in system state (and implicitly prevents other state changes).

> *Example : "apply emergency brake".*

A **safety trigger condition (STC)** is a condition that, when asserted, triggers a safety intervention. The intervention is applied when the STC is true. The STC is chosen such that it becomes true before the safety invariant is violated.

> *Example: "the robot speed is greater than 2 m/s (i.e., less than the safety invariant threshold of 3m/s)".*

A **safety rule** defines a way of behaving in response to a hazardous situation. A safety rule can be operationalized as an if-then rule:

Safety rule $\triangleq$ *if* [safety trigger condition] *then* [safety intervention].

> *Example: "if the robot speed is greater than 2 m/s then apply emergency brake."*

As illustrated in Figure 1, the safety invariant defines the partition between catastrophic states and non-catastrophic states of the monitored system. Interventions have to be applied before the catastrophe, i.e., in non-catastrophic

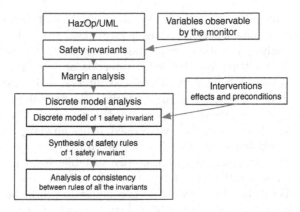

Fig. 2. Overview of the process

states. Now, interventions add constraints to the system behavior. So the set of non-catastrophic states is partitioned into warning states, where interventions are applied, and safe states, in which the system operates without constraint. The warning states are defined such that every path from a safe state (e.g., x_s on Figure 1) to a catastrophic state, e.g., x_c, passes through a warning state, e.g., x_w. The warning state enables triggering of an intervention to abort the path to the catastrophic state.

We assess the monitor and its safety rule set according to the following three properties:

Safety is the ability to ensure that the safety invariants are never violated, i.e., that catastrophic states are unreachable.

Permissiveness is the ability to allow the system to perform its tasks.

Validity specifies that no intervention is applied while its precondition is false.

Safety and permissiveness are antagonistic. We take this antagonism into account by designing the monitor to be *maximally permissive with respect to safety*, i.e., to restrict functionality only to the extent necessary to ensure safety.

2.2   Process Overview

Figure 2 presents the overall process. We base our process on a HAZOP-UML hazard analysis, which outputs safety invariants expressed in natural language. We consider as a running example a mobile robot with a manipulator arm and the informal safety invariant *The arm must not be extended beyond the base when the speed is greater than V_0.*

The safety invariant is then expressed formally with predicates on variables that are observable by the monitor. We focus for now only on predicates involving a variable compared to a fixed threshold. This type of safety threshold is amenable to formal verification and is used in many real systems. Considering the two monitor observations: the absolute speed v, and a Boolean observation of the arm position a (*true* when the arm is above the base, *false*, when the arm is extended), the example safety invariant is formalized as $v < V_0 \lor a = true$.

The margin analysis partitions non-catastrophic states into safe states and warning states by splitting variable value intervals or sets. This is done one variable after another. For example, the speed interval $[0, V_0[$ from the safety invariant is partitionable according to a margin m in two intervals $[0, V_0 - m[$ and $[V_0 - m, V_0[$. In the case of arm position, the observation is Boolean. The singleton value set $\{true\}$ cannot be partitioned, hence no margin exists. Formal conditions for the existence of a margin are studied in [1].

From the margin analysis, we can discretize variables involved in the safety invariant in order to synthesize safety rules. We call this the discrete model analysis, which is detailed in Section 3. It is composed of three main steps: creation of a discrete model, rule synthesis, and rule consistency checking. In order to keep models simple enough to be validated, each safety invariant is modeled separately. The state variables of the model are the observable variables discretized by intervals according to the thresholds of the safety invariant and the existing margins. The discrete model (e.g., Figure 3) is the Cartesian product of the variable partitions. A catastrophic state is one that violates the safety invariant (there is one catastrophic state on Figure 3, labeled C). The warning states (W) are those that lead the system to the catastrophe in one step. Interventions are modeled using the same discretized variables. In the example the monitor is able to brake (action) and to prevent the arm from extending (inhibition).

The monitor is responsible for neutralizing every transition leading to a catastrophic state. For instance, Figure 4 illustrates a satisfying safety rule set, which applies braking in $s3$ and arm inhibition in $s1$ and $s2$. Additionally to the transitions leading directly to the catastrophic state, several other transitions are deleted. The safety rule set respects the safety properties, as the system cannot enter the catastrophic state. All non-catastrophic states are reachable. Nevertheless, there is some loss of permissiveness as the system cannot stay in $s3$. We consider this to be acceptable. In Sections 3.4 and 3.5, we propose two methods to find systematically such safety rule sets.

As safety invariants are processed separately, the final step is to check the consistency between the safety rule sets from different safety invariants. This is addressed in Section 3.6.

3   Discrete Model Analysis

Given a safety invariant, several safety rules are usually needed to avoid violation of the safety invariant. We call a *safety strategy* a set of rules applied with respect to a single safety invariant. In this section, we aim to synthesize a safe, permissive and valid strategy based on the discrete model.

We propose two approaches to synthesize strategies (Figure 5). The *automatic method* finds strategies fast, given permissiveness requirements, by exploring automatically the various combinations of safety rules. The *interactive method* enables the user to adapt permissiveness requirements, and to build or modify a strategy rule by rule.

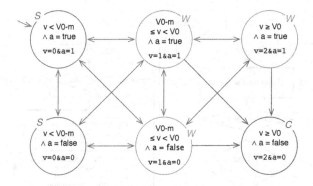

Fig. 3. The example discrete model from the partitions $\{true, false\}$ for arm position, and $\{[0, V_0 - m[, [V_0 - m, V_0[, [V_0, V_{max}[\}$ for speed

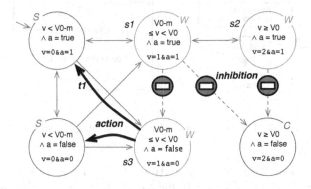

Fig. 4. The example model with a safety rule set

The interactive method is used whenever there is no solution to the given model and requirements. It informs the user on how to adapt the submitted problem. The automatic method can then be used on the new problem to find all possible strategies

3.1 Tools

We use the modeling language SMV and the model-checker NuSMV2 [3]. SMV enables the declaration of integer variables and constraints on their behavior. NuSMV builds transparently the Cartesian product of the ranges of all variables. When no constraint is declared, all the combinations of variable values (i.e., states) are possible and all transitions between each pair of states are implicitly declared. Constraints are then added to delete undesired states and transitions. As for variables, time is discrete. It is modeled by the operator next(). NuSMV is well-adapted to our variable-oriented modeling approach. Moreover, the implicit transition declaration is convenient for modeling the whole physically possible behavior.

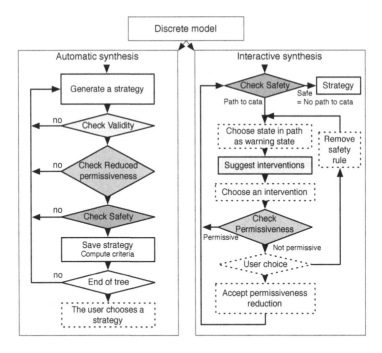

Fig. 5. The two methods for safety strategy synthesis

In the following, SMV code and output of NuSMV are given in typewriter font. We have developed a template file to facilitate the modeling and to allow the process to be automated.

3.2   System and Intervention Modeling

The domain of each variable of the safety invariant is partitioned according to the thresholds of the safety invariant and the margin (if it exists), and the resulting elements are numbered. For instance $\{[0, V_0 - m[, [V_0 - m, V_0[, [V_0, V_{max}[\}$ is encoded as $\{0,1,2\}$ (see Figure 3). Continuity of variables, i.e., contiguity of partition elements, is modeled as the constraint: `next(x) = x | x+1 | x-1`, i.e., a variable `x` can stay in the same interval or move to an adjacent interval, but it cannot jump from one interval to another that has no common boundary.

We then model possible dependencies between variables. Nevertheless, some dependencies cannot be modeled in a discrete way or with a given partition. If a dependency is not modeled, the discrete model has less constraints than it should, or from another point of view, it has too many transitions. If this "super-graph" is safe, so is the "true" model. On the contrary, the permissiveness results of the super-graph are not trustworthy. The resulting strategies are always safe; but their level of permissiveness depends on the dependency modeling effort.

Interventions are always effective (when their preconditions are true), provided some environmental and dimensioning assumptions. A safety braking action requires to consider for example a maximum slope rate, a maximum torque from the motors. Safety interventions are then modeled as constraints that may be applied or not. Consider a discretized speed v. The braking action and the acceleration inhibition can be modeled by:

```
braking ->  ( (v!=0 -> next(v)=v-1) & (v=0 -> next(v)=0) )
acc_inhibition -> next(v)!=v+1
```

As these examples show, an intervention usually adds a constraint on only one variable, and leaves the others free. For example, at the same time step: speed can be decreased by braking, and the arm can fold (as in transition $t1$ in Figure 4).

We make no restrictive assumption about the behavior of the main control channel. The system model represents what is physically possible in the system without a monitor. Therefore, safety interventions only remove transitions, i.e., possible behaviors, and cannot add transitions, i.e., add physically impossible behaviors.

Unlike classical model-checking, an integer value does not model a single interval width of an observable variable. Consequently, the time step has no determined value. The **next** operator models an elastic future, which can be very close or far away.

3.3   Safety, Permissiveness and Validity Modeling

Monitor properties are expressed in CTL (*Computation Tree Logic*), which is entirely supported by NuSMV without any syntax change. Time along paths is modeled by three operators: X for a property to hold in the next state, G to hold on the entire path, F to hold eventually. The branching aspect is modeled by A, all the branches, and E, there exists a branch. A CTL operator is composed of one branching operator and one time operator. It is applied on states, or more generally on statements on the system state.

To model safety, we use the atomic property *cata* to denote the catastrophic states. *cata* is the negation of the safety invariant, e.g., **cata := speed=2 & arm_pos=0**. Safety is modeled as the unreachability of the catastrophic states, i.e., in CTL, $AG \neg cata$. The expression of *cata* is the only user task in the initial property modeling. Permissiveness and validity properties are generated automatically. During the synthesis, the user is supposed to remove some permissiveness properties according to the accepted permissiveness loss choices.

Permissiveness is translated by three liveness properties applied to each non-catastrophic state s_{nc}:

- SIMPLE REACHABILITY $EF\, s_{nc}$
  The state is reachable from the initial state.
- UNIVERSAL REACHABILITY $AG\, EF\, s_{nc}$
  The state is reachable from any reachable state.
- CONTINUOUS (and universal) REACHABILITY $AG\, EF\, \left(s_{nc} \wedge EG\, s_{nc}\right)$
  The state is reachable and the automaton can stay (indefinitely) in this state. If an action is applied to the state, the system cannot stay in the state. It is only a transient state, so the system cannot carry out tasks in this state.

Continuous reachability is stronger than universal reachability, which is stronger than simple reachability. The three properties checked separately on each warning state enable permissiveness to be assessed in a more detailed way than with a single binary value. It is usually impossible to obtain safety without some loss of permissiveness, and particularly with respect to continuous reachability.

It is possible but highly unlikely for variables to change their values simultaneously and independently. Such changes are called *diagonal transitions* by reference to the two variable case (cf. Figure 3). As permissiveness should not depend on such unlikely transitions, we choose to ignore diagonal transitions when checking permissiveness. *diag* denotes that the immediately fired transition was a "diagonal" transition. $mem(diag)$ is the memorization of *diag*, i.e., *diag* and $mem(diag)$ are initially false and as soon as *diag* is true, $mem(diag)$ becomes true and stays true even if the value of *diag* changes. To ignore diagonal transitions during permissiveness checking, the properties are modified using $mem(diag)$ as follows:

- SIMPLE REACHABILITY $EF(s_{nc} \land \neg mem(diag))$
  The state is reachable by a path that always satisfies $\neg diag$, i.e., a path that has no simultaneous value changes of independent variables.

- UNIVERSAL REACHABILITY $AG\Big(\neg mem(diag) \to EF\Big(s_{nc} \land \neg mem(diag)\Big)\Big)$

  The implication selects the part of the model without diagonal transitions and checks the reachability property only in this part. From the previous simple reachability property, we already know that this part is non-void.

- CONTINUOUS (and universal) REACHABILITY

$$AG\Big(\neg mem(diag) \to EF\Big(s_{nc} \land \neg mem(diag) \land EG(s_{nc})\Big)\Big)$$

The automaton without any safety rule is usually permissive because it is only a structure without specified behavior. Variables can change freely their values. Similarly, it is unsafe, as catastrophic states are reachable.

Validity specifies that interventions are not applied in states that violate their preconditions. We express this as:

$$AG \bigwedge_{i \in Interventions} i \to precondition_i$$

where *Interventions* is the set of the candidate interventions and $precondition_i$ is the precondition associated to intervention i.

Once the safety invariant and the interventions have been defined, and the properties have been generated, we can synthesize a strategy using either the interactive method (Section 3.4) or the automatic method (Section 3.5).

3.4   Interactive Method

The interactive method (right side of Figure 5) uses the command-line interface of NuSMV and alias commands. The model-checker finds a path to a catastrophic state as a counter-example to the safety property. The user chooses a warning state in this path to apply an intervention. The warning state is by default the state immediately preceding the catastrophic state. Then the model-checker determines whether each intervention is *locally* relevant. To this end, the warning state is declared as the initial state and additional properties, called *suggestion* properties, are checked. Suggestion properties are of the form $i \rightarrow (precondition_i \wedge AX \neg cata)$ where i is the intervention. The intervention is suggested if its precondition is satisfied (i.e., the rule is valid) and if it renders the catastrophic state unreachable in one step. If the state immediately preceding the catastrophic state is not suitable (e.g., no intervention can be applied), the user chooses an earlier state. When the nth state before the catastrophic state is selected, the property has to be modified to apply the AX operator n times to check that the catastrophic state is unreachable in n steps.

The user chooses an intervention among those suggested. The model-checker checks the permissiveness of the system with the new safety rule.

This is done iteratively until there are no more paths to catastrophic states, i.e., the system is safe. The selected safety rules constitute a satisfying strategy.

If the permissiveness test returns false, the user has three choices: accept the loss of permissiveness; try another intervention; or try another warning state. Selecting an earlier warning state in the path implies that downstream states will be unreachable, which negatively impacts permissiveness. It may however be relevant if a combination of safety rules makes many states unreachable.

The interactive method enables the user to customize in what states and to what extent permissiveness is required. But exploration can be slow, which is the reason why we have also developed an automatic method.

3.5   Automatic Method

The automatic method (left side of Figure 5) runs on the same model. It outputs all safe and valid strategies that satisfy the permissiveness requirements (if any such strategies exist). If full permissiveness is required, no result is obtained. On the contrary, the lower the requirements, the more results there are. We thus consider by default only simple and universal reachability, and compute criteria that help the user to choose. When there is no solution, the interactive method enables the user to find the blocking point and locally reduce the permissiveness requirement. The automatic method is then run with customized requirements.

The automatic method is based on the enumeration of the strategies through a branch-and-cut algorithm and the verification of properties by NuSMV [4]. The method is implemented using NuSMV scripts and a C program.

3.6   Consistency between Strategies

Different strategies may apply interventions simultaneously, which may be incompatible, e.g., braking and acceleration. To check strategy consistency, the previous models (with their strategies) are merged into a single model. When observable variables are common to several models but with different domain partitions, a new domain partition is defined by taking the union of the thresholds from the different models.

There are two types of inconsistency. For example, braking and acceleration impose incompatible constraints on speed, so the model-checker cannot compute a next state. This type of inconsistency is detected by a basic command. Other inconsistencies are not visible in the model because they cannot be modeled with the chosen partition or there is no impact on an observable variable. In these cases, we propose to list concurrent interventions to enable an expert to determine inconsistencies.

4   Case Study

Our case study is part of the SAPHARI (*Safe and Autonomous Physical Human-Aware Robot Interaction*) project [5]. The robot is composed of a mobile base and an articulated arm. It is an industrial co-worker in a manufacturing setting. It takes and places part boxes on shelves, work stations, or on the robot base in order to convey them. It operates in the human workspace. We study here two safety invariants from this robot.

4.1   Human/Arm Collision during Base Motion

Collision avoidance of the base trajectory relies only on base-to-obstacle distance sensor. Consequently, if the arm is unfolded and extends beyond the base during base motion, a collision between the arm and a human is possible. A very slow base movement is tolerated. This case is the same as the example of Section 2.2. The safety invariant is: *The arm must not be extended beyond the base when the base is moving (with speed higher than V_0).*

Discrete Model. The available observations are: 1) a Boolean observation of the arm position a; 2) linear absolute base speed v (to simplify we ignore rotation speed). a and v are independent. The safety invariant is formalized as $a = true \lor v < V_0$. The considered interventions are: 1) braking (of base wheels); 2) inhibit the arm motion to prevent it from extending beyond the base, this is possible only when the arm is above the base. A margin exists for the speed. The following excerpt of the SMV module encodes the discrete model of Figure 3. No other template modification is required.

```
MODULE Collision_SI
VAR -- Variable declarations
--Continuity(low bound, high bound, initial value, mode)
base_speed : Continuity(0,2,0,mode);
    -- 0:<V0-m,  1:V0-m<v<V0,  2:>V0
arm_pos : Continuity(0,1,1,mode);
    -- 1:above the base, 0:extended beyond

DEFINE cata:= (base_speed.v=2 & arm_pos.v=0);

VAR -- Intervention declarations
```

```
--Interv(precondition, flag to apply interv, effect, mode)
brake_base : Interv( base_speed.v!=0, flag_brake_base, next
    (base_speed.v)=base_speed.v - 1, mode);
inhib_arm : Interv( arm_pos.v=1, flag_inihb_arm, next(
    arm_pos.v)=1, mode);
```

The effect of brake_base is to decrease the speed. However, when speed.v=0, decreasing it violates the variable range, so speed!=0 is set as precondition.

Interactive Method. We apply the algorithm of the right side of Figure 5. Checking for safety returns a path to the catastrophic state. The state immediately preceding the catastrophic state, chosen as a warning state, is defined by base_speed.v = 1 & arm_pos.v = 0. With this state as initial, suggestion properties are checked. The only suggested intervention is brake_base. We thus define its trigger flag_brake_base in a safety rule:

```
DEFINE flag_brake_base := base_speed.v=1 & arm_pos.v=0;
```

Permissiveness properties are true except for the continuous reachability of the warning state. This is expected since braking is an action intervention.

Another path to the catastrophic state results in defining base_speed.v = 1 & arm_pos.v = 1 as a warning state. Both possible interventions are suggested. The inhibition inhib_arm is chosen since it does not decrease permissiveness:

```
DEFINE flag_inhib_arm := base_speed.v=1 & arm_pos.v=1;}
```

We check that permissiveness is indeed unchanged.

A third path to catastrophe defines the warning state base_speed.v = 2 & arm_pos.v = 1 where both interventions are again suggested. We choose inhib_arm again and therefore add the warning state to flag_inhib_arm.

```
DEFINE flag_inhib_arm := (base_speed.v=1 & arm_pos.v=1) | (
    base_speed.v=2 & arm_pos.v=1);}
```

Checking for safety now returns true. The strategy so defined is valid, safe, and acceptably permissive. It is the same strategy as in Figure 4.

Automatic Method. From the same model Collision_SI the automatic method returns three strategies. Among the three generated strategies, two have two non-continuously reachable states and the last has only one such state. To minimize loss of permissiveness we choose the strategy with only one non-continuously reachable state.

```
STRATEGY #2
--Criteria
non continuously reachable states 1
states with intervention 3
states with combined interv 0
total nb of interv 3
interv_brake_base used in 1 states
```

```
interv_inhib_arm  used  in  2  states
--Strategy  definition
DEFINE  flag_brake_base  :=  flag_cinterv_1  |  flag_cinterv_3;
DEFINE  flag_inhib_arm  :=  flag_cinterv_2  |  flag_cinterv_3;
DEFINE  flag_st_1  :=  base_speed.v  =  1  &  arm_pos.v  =  0;
DEFINE  flag_st_4  :=  base_speed.v  =  1  &  arm_pos.v  =  1;
DEFINE  flag_st_5  :=  base_speed.v  =  2  &  arm_pos.v  =  1;
DEFINE  flag_cinterv_1  :=  flag_st_1 ;
DEFINE  flag_cinterv_2  :=  flag_st_4  |  flag_st_5 ;
DEFINE  flag_cinterv_3  :=  FALSE ;
```

The other computed criteria are: number of states where an intervention is applied, use of combined interventions, i.e., application of several interventions on the same state, the type of intervention. For example, our strategy makes use of the two defined interventions **brake_base** and **inhib_arm** and uses no combination of interventions. This strategy is the same as in Figure 4.

Our modeling and synthesis methods find the same strategy that was previously found intuitively on the graphical representation. Interventions are clearly modeled, contrary to the graphical method. Moreover, as our modeling is textual we can solve the same problem type with three or more variables.

4.2   Boxes Sliding from the Base

The robot arm has an impactive gripper as an end-effector that takes and places boxes on its base, which can be used to convey part boxes. In this case, the robot must respect a speed limit V_1 that is less than the general speed limit.

Discrete Model. The available observations are: 1) *box*, a Boolean (*true* in presence of box), and 2) base speed v (the same as in Section 4.1). The safety invariant is $box = false \lor v \leq V_1$. A safety margin value can be placed on speed. The resulting integer ranges are $[\![0,1]\!]$ for *box* and $[\![0,2]\!]$ for speed (with **cata:=box=1 & speed=2**). The only possible intervention is braking, since the presence of boxes is not controllable.

Synthesis. Running the automatic method returns no strategy. During interactive exploration, braking is suggested and applied, leading to a complete loss of permissiveness in the state **box=0 & speed=2**. In other words, the robot cannot go faster than V_1 even if there is no box on the base. This is clearly not acceptable. The user can choose either another suggested intervention (not possible in this example) or an earlier state in the path (which brings here no benefit). The current model and requirements admit no satisfying strategy. The intuitive cause is that the presence of a box is uncontrollable.

Now, according to the robot service hypotheses only the robot arm is allowed to place a box on the base. We add to the model the observable variable **gripper** with values {**closed_empty**, **open**, **closed_with_box**} and the associated interventions: **inhibit_opening** and **inhibit_closing**. The variable is continuous in the sense that from the value **closed_empty** to **closed_with_box**, the gripper always transits by **open**. We model that a box cannot arrive on the base without being in the gripper, and symmetrically a box can only be removed by the (open) gripper.[2]

```
TRANS box.v=0 & next(box.v)=1 -> gripper.v=closed_with_box
TRANS box.v=1 & next(box.v)=0 -> gripper.v=open
```

Due to perception latency, gripper and box sensors may not be synchronized. Therefore, the likely next **gripper** values (**open** in the first constraint) are not specified.

The automatic method returns 32 strategies (which is a lot, so the selectivity of the method should be improved). For every strategy, 5 states are not continuously reachable and braking is applied in every warning state. One strategy uses only braking. The other strategies add some inhibitions to this minimal strategy. For instance, we consider the strategy that adds `inhibit_opening` in warning states with no box on the base (`inhibit_closing` is not used).

In this example, the safety invariant is first ensured, with a high impact on permissiveness. The gripper hypothesis makes the safety invariant feasible without any impact on permissiveness at the expense of lower safety coverage. Even if modeled safety is fully checked, the strategy does not cover all cases, e.g., when workers disobey service regulations and place boxes on the robot base.

4.3 Consistency between Strategies

The two models with their strategies make every intervention pair reachable. By modeling that $V_0 < V_1 - m$, the braking triggered by the first strategy is no longer concurrent with interventions of the second invariant. In our example, `inhib_arm` is compatible with `brake` and `inhibit_opening`.

5 Related Work

Several safety monitoring approaches have been proposed in the literature. For instance [6] argues for a small and simple component in charge of guaranteeing system safety, in particular with respect to hazardous sequences of function invocations. We actually extend this conceptual approach proposing a systematic methodology for the identification of the properties to ensure, while focusing only on invariants.

Runtime verification (RV) typically generates code instrumentation from temporal logic properties to verify execution traces at runtime [7]. Runtime verification can be seen as a downstream process of our workflow: it could implement the monitor from the specification that we generate. Some runtime verification work explores the issue of independence between the monitor and the monitored system. For example, Pike *et al.* [8] consider time-triggered monitoring of a set of global variables, which avoids code instrumentation, achieves time-isolation, and consequently does not require re-certification of the system due to the presence of the monitor. A concept close to permissiveness is defined as functionality: *"the monitor cannot change the monitored system's behavior, unless the latter*

---

[2] For clarity, the gripper variable is given textual values rather than integer values.

has violated its specification." Another relation between RV and our work is the use of formal verification for monitoring purposes. We check offline the tree of all possible executions (of the model) by using the branching logic CTL whereas RV checks concrete executed traces with respect to linear temporal properties. The reaction to trigger when detecting an error is called the steering problem in the runtime verification community. It is a potential feature of monitors, but it remains much less developed than the detection part. Error detection typically returns information to the monitored program or raises an exception. Other possible reactions are considered as ad-hoc to particular systems because they are not formally captured.

A parallel can be established between game theory and the way the system is modeled, as possible physical behaviors. The monitor player is able to fire or inhibit some transitions whereas the opponent, which can be regarded as the environment or the main controller, is able to fire any transitions. Safety rules are then the monitor strategy to achieve the winning condition (safety, permissiveness and validity) whatever the opponent plays. In particular, we take inspiration from *supervisor synthesis* [9], which is close to game theory.

Supervisor synthesis is based on language theory. It outputs directly the maximally permissive monitor, i.e., the monitor resulting in the system automaton that recognizes the largest language. Therefore, permissiveness is taken into account but the user cannot customize it, by preferring one state instead of another. In [10], Fotoohi *et al.* use supervisor synthesis to check the safety requirements of a semi-autonomous wheel-chair.

Woodman *et al.* [11] present a very similar workflow to monitor autonomous systems. They use HAZOP to identify hazards and determine (intuitively) the corresponding safety rules, which are if-then-else rules. From sensor observations, the monitor (safety layer) sends actuation inhibitions to both the controller and the software actuator interface. The strong point of the method is to take into account sensor uncertainty. Permissiveness is implicit.

6   Conclusion

We have described a method for obtaining a high-level safety monitor specification, taking into account the specific features of autonomous systems. We base it on hazard analysis, which is non-formal. Thanks to formal methods, we ensure that the derivation from formal safety invariants to safety rules is correct, provided the modeling of safety invariants is valid. Safety invariants are modeled separately in order to maintain model validability and to ensure scalability.

Our method justifies the modeling effort in that it does not only check the specification but also guides the user in building it. Compared with related work, both actions and inhibitions are allowed, resulting in a more generic method. Another strong point is the explicit modeling of permissiveness. The user has no permissiveness requirement to provide and can choose precisely the permissiveness trade-off (provided variable dependency is modeled). By using the template, the modeling approach is scalable to many variables and interventions.

As future work, the algorithm selectivity is to be improved and the method extended to process safety invariants other than those based on thresholds. The method has yet to be applied on real and complete systems. Implementation of the monitor would show how to adapt our hypotheses to the real system, or vice versa. The implemented safety interventions have to comply with the temporal hypothesis of the method taking into account the system dynamics and the environment: 1) inhibitions have to be effective "instantaneously"; 2) margin values have to cater for possible action latency. Note that the permissiveness analysis always prefers inhibitions to actions whereas actions may be preferred from an implementation viewpoint. Future work concerns customization of the fault independence assumption by implementing safety rules at different levels in the system architecture, resulting in several safety monitors instead of one.

Acknowlegment. This work is partially supported by the SAPHARI Project, funded under the 7th Framework Programme of the European Community.

References

1. Mekki-Mokhtar, A., Blanquart, J.P., Guiochet, J., Powell, D., Roy, M.: Safety trigger conditions for critical autonomous systems. In: 18th Pacific Rim Int'l Symp. on Dependable Computing (PRDC), pp. 61–69. IEEE (2012)
2. ISO/IEC 61508-7: Functional safety of electrical / electronic / programmable electronic safety-related systems - part 7: Overview of techniques and measures (2010)
3. Cimatti, A., Clarke, E., Giunchiglia, E., Giunchiglia, F., Pistore, M., Roveri, M., Sebastiani, R., Tacchella, A.: Nusmv 2: An opensource tool for symbolic model checking. In: Brinksma, E., Larsen, K.G. (eds.) CAV 2002. LNCS, vol. 2404, pp. 359–364. Springer, Heidelberg (2002)
4. Dufossé, F., Machin, M., Guiochet, J., Powell, D., Roy, M., Waeselynck, H.: Safety strategy synthesis: Game theory versus model-checking. LAAS-CNRS, Tech. Rep. 14059 (2014)
5. Saphari project, http://www.saphari.eu
6. Rushby, J.: Kernels for safety. Safe and Secure Computing Systems, 210–220 (1989)
7. Leucker, M., Schallhart, C.: A brief account of runtime verification. Journal of Logic and Algebraic Programming 78(5), 293–303 (2009)
8. Pike, L., Niller, S., Wegmann, N.: Runtime verification for ultra-critical systems. In: 2nd Int'l Conf. on Runtime Verification, San Francisco, California, USA (2011)
9. Wonham, W.M.: Supervisory control of discrete event systems (2005)
10. Fotoohi, L., Gräser, A.: A supervisory control approach for safe behavior of service robot case study: Friend. In: Proceedings of the 2010 ACM Symposium on Applied Computing, pp. 1305–1306. ACM (2010)
11. Woodman, R., Winfield, A.F., Harper, C., Fraser, M.: Building safer robots: Safety driven control. Int'l J. Robotics Research 31(13), 1603–1626 (2012)

Automatically Generated Safety Mechanisms from Semi-Formal Software Safety Requirements

Raphael Fonte Boa Trindade, Lukas Bulwahn, and Christoph Ainhauser

BMW Car IT GmbH
Petuelring 116, 80809 München
{raphael.trindade,lukas.bulwahn,christoph.ainhauser}@bmw-carit.de

Abstract. Today's automobiles incorporate a great number of functions that are realized by software. An increasing number of safety-critical functions also follow this trend. For the development of such functions, the ISO 26262 demands a number of additional steps to be performed compared to common software engineering activities. We address some of these demands with means to semi-formally express software safety requirements, tools to automatically implement these requirements, and artifacts and traceability information that can be used for safety case documentation. Through a hierarchical classification of safety mechanisms, a semi-formal specification language for requirements, a generation engine and a case study on a production-model automotive system, we demonstrate: first, how expert knowledge of the functional safety domain can be captured, second, how the tedious and error prone task of manually implementing safety mechanisms can be automated, and third, how this serves as a basis for formal safety argumentation.

1 Introduction

Today's automobiles incorporate an increasing number of functions that are realized by software. Developers design, implement and integrate the software-based functions using, amongst others, model-driven development.

Following this trend, an increasing number of safety-critical functions are implemented in software as well. To ensure the functional safety of these software implementations, the safety engineering workflow defined by the safety standard for road vehicles, ISO 26262 [8], requires that safety engineers perform a number of steps during the development of a specific safety-critical function. Safety engineers analyze possible hazards that a system can cause, define high-level safety goals to prevent hazards and analyze malfunctions that can lead to the violation of safety goals. They then develop the functional and technical safety concepts for a specific system, where the safety goals are refined to functional and technical safety requirements. The technical safety requirements are written in informal prose, consisting of software and hardware safety requirements, and specify how the system implementation realizes the high-level safety goals.

Software developers realize the software safety requirements using mechanisms for error detection and error handling. They ensure their correct implementation by well-established design and implementation principles and by diligent

A. Bondavalli and F. Di Giandomenico (Eds.): SAFECOMP 2014, LNCS 8666, pp. 278–293, 2014.
© Springer International Publishing Switzerland 2014

verification activities. In today's safety engineering, the realization of software safety requirements is done by software developers. Although developers work carefully, development remains susceptible to human error. Moreover, the link towards technical safety requirements is mostly established through verbal communication and usually some informal documentation. This makes it difficult to argue on traceability of implementation and specification artifacts.

We address these issues with means to semi-formally express software safety requirements and with tools to automatically implement these requirements. Moreover, the tools provide semi-formal artifacts and traceability information that can be used for safety case documentation.

Our first contribution is a hierarchical classification of safety mechanisms (Section 3.1) based on the properties inherent to different kinds of mechanisms. Our second contribution is a semi-formal specification language (Section 3.2) for software safety requirements. Our third contribution is a generation engine (Section 3.3) for transforming semi-formal software safety requirements into software and system architecture enhancements, such as model elements and source code. Furthermore, we evaluate our approach on a case study (Section 4) of a production-model automotive system. Finally, we discuss related work (Section 5) and show how our approach can be applied to automate the realization of more complex safety requirements (Section 6).

In sum, our contributions automate a laborious step of the safety engineering workflow. Thereby, we reduce the manual effort of safety verification steps, and make iterative safety-critical software development more efficient.

2   The AUTOSAR Standard and Tooling

To integrate our contributions smoothly into the existing automotive tooling, we base our work on the widely-used and commonly-accepted AUTOSAR standard [4]. AUTOSAR is an open system architecture providing a meta-model implementation, which allows car manufacturers and their software suppliers to collaborate and standardize several elements of automotive platforms, such as scheduling, communication paradigms and system services.

The AUTOSAR architecture abstracts from the low-level details of electronic control units (ECUs) using a component model and a virtual function bus (VFB), which provides abstract communication concepts between components. The component model allows developers to specify software modules, compositions of modules, ports, and port interfaces.

The VFB enables the interconnection of these modules via ports independent of the actual hardware topology and system deployment, which is not known at the VFB level. Furthermore, ports can provide different communication paradigms, such as sender-receiver or client-server.

The system model defines a concrete layout of ECUs and the buses connecting them. Additionally, software components are deployed to specific ECUs in the system model and the component interconnections are mapped to concrete communication channels, such as a CAN or FlexRay bus.

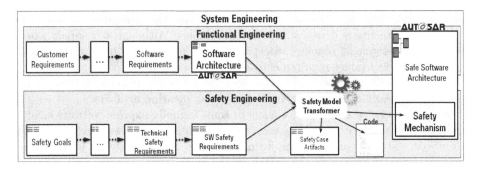

Fig. 1. Workflow for the automatic generation of software safety mechanisms

To develop AUTOSAR-compliant systems, the model authoring tool Artop [2] provides basic functionality to create AUTOSAR system models, software architecture models, and ECU configurations. Furthermore, the ARText framework [3] supports the definition of textual languages for AUTOSAR. For example, ARText's software component language allows developers to describe software architectures at the VFB level. We use ARText's capabilities to define a textual language for software safety requirements.

3   Safety Model Transformation

In this section, we describe our approach for automatic realization of software safety requirements based on semi-formal specifications and model transformations. We briefly show how it fits into typical safety-critical software development workflow and we describe the three steps for its realization.

Figure 1 depicts how our solution fits into a typical automotive system engineering workflow. Note that this figure shows the artefact evolution, and not the related process steps. On the one hand, functional engineering is responsible for a software/system architecture that satisfies customer requirements. On the other hand, safety engineering is responsible for defining the safety goals and the requirements to fulfill these goals, among which are software safety requirements. The software safety requirements (expressing *what* shall be done) lead to the enhancement of the pre-existing software architecture through safety mechanisms implementing these requirements (expressing *how* it shall be done).

3.1   Classification of Safety Mechanisms

As a first step towards the automated realization of software safety requirements, we identified and classified existing safety mechanisms in a hierarchy. Our classification in Figure 2 is based on Wu and Kelly's classification [19], the ISO 26262 recommendations, literature and expert knowledge from the functional safety domain. This classification serves as the foundation for the requirements language and model transformations discussed in Sections 3.2 and Section 3.3.

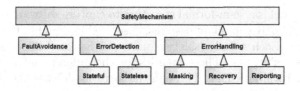

Fig. 2. Hierarchical classification of safety mechanisms

It groups mechanisms by provided functionality and by properties related to the functionality. For example, the program control-flow mechanism has the functionality of *detecting errors* by observing the *logical order of program execution*. Our classification has three main categories: fault avoidance, error detection and error handling. We focus on error detection and error handling.

Error detection is further divided into *stateless* and *stateful* detection. The stateless safety mechanism subcategory contains, for instance, checksum mechanisms, such as CRC and parity checks, software or hardware based self-test algorithms, and read-back mechanisms such as message read-back or challenge response. The stateful subcategory contains, for example, elements for logical monitoring, such as message counters or control-flow monitoring, as well as for temporal monitoring, such as aliveness supervision, and data maximum age.

Moreover, the error handling category is also subdivided into masking, recovery and reporting. Corresponding elements of these subcategories are, for example, filtering, voting, defaulting, and correction codes for masking; device reset, memory partition reset, and degradation for recovery.

Our complete classification contains more than thirty mechanisms. Based on this classification, we have also assessed which mechanisms are realizable in software in the context of an AUTOSAR-compliant system. The classification and assessment is described in detail in the deliverable D3.6.b [9] developed within the SAFE project [10].

As previously mentioned, software safety mechanisms implement software safety requirements. Our classification of mechanisms and their formalization has taken into account their attributes, semantics, and also the technology platform in which they are realized (i.e. AUTOSAR). This resulted in patterns that can be applied by safety engineers in order to satisfy technical safety requirements. These patterns are closely related to safety mechanisms. This is consistent with traditional engineering methods, since engineers tend to specify implementation requirements very close to the solution domain. We use these patterns to define our specification language and meta-model relations from the identified patterns to AUTOSAR elements.

3.2 Semi-Formal Specification of Software Safety Requirements

The approach proposed in this paper enables engineers to define requirements intuitively and consists of three main elements: a meta-model, a textual modeling language and a generation engine.

The meta-model is a semi-formal structure to capture software safety requirements for AUTOSAR-compliant systems, described in detail in the SAFE deliverable D3.6.b [9]. Each software safety requirement has a specified semantics, also defined in this deliverable. The semantics for the different safety requirements is defined in natural language. Through the meta-model and the semantics, we achieve the formalization of our software safety requirements.

With this semantics, we capture the generally-accepted intuitions about the safety mechanisms in a semi-formal manner. As we focus on the application of this language for writing software safety requirement and realizing them automatically in software, this semi-formal semantics suffices to establish a common understanding for language designers, tool developers and users. Investigation of the meta-theory, the formal verification of properties and the proof of correctness of tool implementations are not the focus of this work.

The meta-model defines the structure and attributes of our requirements in a machine-friendly format. The textual modeling language is a human-friendly interface to the meta-model. It provides access to all meta-model attributes, and its simple textual form makes it easier for safety engineers to use. The generation engine applies model transformations to generate source code, AUTOSAR models and traceability artifacts.

Meta-Model. Our current meta-model is limited to a selection of nine types of software safety requirements, which we derived from the mechanisms captured in our classification, briefly described in Section 3.1. This selection of software safety requirements was driven by our evaluation scenario and it covers all relevant mechanisms for our case study described in Section 4. Each requirement from our selection corresponds to one mechanism in our classification, but not all mechanisms in our classification have been included in the meta-model. For the formalization of this selection, we captured the necessary attributes in a meta-model and specified their semantics in natural language.

Our approach assumes that technical safety requirements are specified semi-formally. This means that these requirements can be individually referenced within a model. Our meta-model in turn allows traces from software safety requirements to technical safety requirements and software safety requirements to architectural elements to be established, as recommended by the ISO 26262 norm, part 8, clause 8.4.5.

The formalization of software safety requirements using our meta-model and their semantics is the first step towards our approach of automatically realizing such requirements. The graphical UML class diagrams of meta-model are bulky and their proper presentation would exceed the limits of this paper. Hence, we limit ourselves to the description of the textual language, which nevertheless contains all attributes of the meta-model. A proper and detailed description of the meta-model can be found in the SAFE deliverable D3.6.b [9].

Textual Modeling Language. In this section, the basic building blocks of our textual modeling language are described. These building blocks allow engineers

```
ssr limitRangeOfBrakeTemperature satisfies brakeTemperatureRequirement
using {
    check range of root::ptSensorAbstraction::ppSensorTPC → brakeTemp
within {
    (min := -20.0 , max := 120.0 , tolerance := 0.2)
    }
    handle {
    VALUE_ABOVE_RANGE ⇒ default (120)
    VALUE_BELOW_RANGE ⇒ default (-20)
    }
}
```

Fig. 3. Range check software safety requirement

to specify formalized software safety requirements that fulfill technical safety requirements. Figure 3 shows an exemplary software safety requirement for a range checker. The range checker is an error-detection requirement, protecting the value range of a given variable or interface.

The basic building block of the language is a software safety requirement statement. This statement is the formalization of a requirement that realizes the related technical safety requirements. The syntax is:

ssr ⟨name⟩ **satisfies** ⟨reference to technical safety requirement⟩ **using**
{⟨expectation⟩ **handle** ⟨reaction⟩}

The reference to the corresponding technical safety requirement that is realized by the software safety requirement enables traceability and can be used in the safety case argumentation.

The ⟨expectation⟩ describes the expected behavior, e.g., timing, input-output relations, and internal state of elements, for a given element. A deviation from the expectation triggers the corresponding ⟨reaction⟩ statement. In the range checker example, it is expected that the value range of the data element *brakeTemp* lies between -20 and $+120$. The value is provided by the port *ppSensorTPC* of the software component *ptSensorAbstraction* in the software composition *root*; our language references the AUTOSAR model through the pattern ⟨software composition⟩ :: ⟨software component⟩ :: ⟨port⟩ → ⟨data element⟩.

In the case of violation of the expected behavior, the ⟨reaction⟩ handles the resulting errors. Within the ⟨reaction⟩ block, a set of ⟨malfunction⟩ ⇒ ⟨action⟩ pairs can be specified. The malfunctions determine which corresponding ⟨action⟩ shall be executed. Malfunctions are derived from the specific effects of errors detected by the software safety requirement. For example, the malfunctions detected by a range checker are lower and upper limits violations, denoted by VALUE_BELOW_RANGE and VALUE_ABOVE_RANGE, resp. Similarly, a control-flow requirement has temporal and logical state-transition violations as malfunctions.

For each malfunction specified, the following action statements are available in our language: (i) produce a default value, (ii) produce a value according to a given formula, (iii) send a signal to the AUTOSAR diagnostics event manager, (iv) invoke an operation on an AUTOSAR server port prototype or (v) reset the ECU. These actions have shown to be sufficient for our purposes. Nevertheless, the list of actions can be extended if necessary. For some of the ⟨action⟩ statements, further parameters are needed. For example, in Figure 3, the engineers must provide default values for each default value action.

Moreover, engineers are allowed to specify further nested error handling requirements within *actions*. Hence, a software safety requirement can nest error detection and error handling requirements. This allows engineers to define chains of detection and handling requirements for realizing a given technical safety requirement within the structure of a single software safety requirement.

In general, software safety requirements are directly related to specific model elements, e.g., ports or components. Therefore, these cannot be reused by other requirements. However, some software safety requirements can be reused, e.g., a filtering requirement. A filtering requirement defines that value errors are masked from the receiving component during a given time interval. If two software safety requirements need the same filtering behavior, they can reuse the same filtering requirement. The reuse is achieved by defining an action referring to the same filtering requirement within the reaction block of the two software safety requirements. The syntax for filtering software safety requirements is:

filter ⟨name⟩ { **previous** := ⟨identifier list⟩, **current** := ⟨identifier⟩, **tolerance** := ⟨integer⟩, **value** := ⟨expression⟩ } **handle** { ⟨reaction⟩ }

The filter ⟨name⟩ is used to refer to a given filter within the reaction block of other requirements, e.g., as shown in Figure 5. The ⟨identifier list⟩ defines how many previous values shall be stored for the filter, the *current* identifier refers to the current value received by the filter, *tolerance* defines how many times the filter is allowed to be consecutively triggered before the reaction block is executed and the *value* expression defines how the masked value is computed by the filter. The reaction block of the filter has the same syntax and semantics as described previously.

With the support of our textual modeling language engineers can define software safety models. The definition of software safety models is the second step towards the automated realization of software safety requirements.

3.3   Model Transformations

The third step towards the automated realization of software safety requirements are the model transformations. There are two model transformations provided by our safety model transformer, a model-to-model (M2M) transformation and a model-to-text (M2T) transformation. The M2M transformation produces AUTOSAR model artifacts and SAFE model artifacts. The M2T transformation generates C source code. Both transformations take the semi-formally defined software safety requirements and the AUTOSAR software architecture as input.

The safety model transformation uses the M2M transformation to enhance the pre-existing AUTOSAR software architecture by adding the new architectural elements: software components, wrapper software components, software component interconnections, executable entities, and system and basic software (BSW) configurations. In addition, it uses the M2T transformation to generate the source code implementing the required executable entities.

The integration of the generated elements requires the software design to be adapted in different ways. In the following, the result of adding some of the elements listed previously is described using the exemplary range checker software safety requirement.

Following the workflow depicted in Figure 1, the safety engineer defines software safety requirements according to the formalism proposed in Section 3.2. At this point, the software architecture is known but not yet enhanced with safety mechanisms. The software safety requirement in Figure 3 states that a range check shall be implemented for a specific data element of a sender-receiver port.

The realization of the range check for the given port is independent from the behavior of the component providing data and also from the one requiring data. Therefore, the M2M transformation generates a modular AUTOSAR solution composed of a software component, the executable entities of this software component and a connector adaptation.

The generated solution is modular since the safety requirement is realized as a single component, instead of being generated as part of a pre-existing component. It is important to note that such a solution might not be suitable for all cases and might impose requirements on the hardware platform, for example, a safe communication between the component implementing the safety requirement and the pre-existing component. The presented solution exemplarily describes one possible realization of a safety requirement and highlights all elements created in the generation process.

The software component created by the M2M transformation represents the range checker mechanism and contains a required port for the incoming data and a provided port for forwarding the checked value.

Two executable entities for the range checker software component are generated: one for initializing the software component and another one for performing the range check.

The software component interconnections require the software architecture to be adapted and pre-existing elements related to the software safety requirement are affected. In this example, the existing connector for the sender-receiver port pair is re-routed through the range checker software component instance.

The system configuration is enhanced to map the range checker software component instance to the ECU instance where the receiver software component is executed. This information is obtained from the models provided as input to the transformation.

The M2T transformation then generates the source code for the two executable entities of the range checker. The code is responsible for initializing the safety mechanism and for checking the value range as well as triggering the specified reactions in case of an error.

The source code is generated from C-code templates. The templates were implemented manually by a software engineer and capture the typical implementation patterns for software safety requirements. They take into account properties of the software safety requirements, e.g., buffers, ranges and specified reactions and are defined having in mind properties such as ISO 26262 requirements on coding standards (i.e., MISRA C [15]).

Moreover, there are other possible adaptations to the initial software architecture than the ones described in the range checker example. Simple mechanisms only require adding a new executable entity to a pre-existing software component. However, for more intrusive safety mechanisms, e.g., control-flow monitoring, the monitored executable entities or software components are adapted to provide interfaces for the reporting of checkpoints. Furthermore, if no modification to the application software level is allowed, specific configuration or enhancement of basic software modules are required. Such more complex enhancements of the architecture require more contextual information (e.g., the AUTOSAR system configuration).

While our approach automates the realization of software safety requirements, it does not automate the task of validation and verification. For validating the implementation of software safety requirements, regular software engineering efforts, as recommended by the ISO 26262, are still required.

4   Evaluation

In order to demonstrate our approach, we have applied it to a real-world example. We have partially re-engineered the existing realization of a torque-vectoring rear axle system by replacing pre-existing software safety mechanisms with automatically generated mechanisms.

We have conducted a preliminary comparison of the regular development efforts and the efforts required by our approach. The full results of this comparison are described in SAFE project deliverable [11] to be released at the end of 2014. It indicates that significant effort reductions during the development and integration phases are possible in some cases. In the comparison, the benefits of fulfilling the traceability and formalism requirements of the ISO 26262 could not be quantified; only a more extensive evaluation in future projects allows a quantitative comparison.

The torque-vectoring system has the task of applying different torques to the rear axle to reduce the risk of under-steering and to increase agility while cornering. For this purpose, the technical system architecture is realized with the three main modules: *torque handling, torque position calculation* and *position control*. In order to perform its functionality, the three modules together read several data sources, either sensor, e.g., the disk temperature, or external units, e.g., the nominal torque value, realize a set of computations and finally operate the actuators to distribute the calculated torque to both wheels of the rear axle.

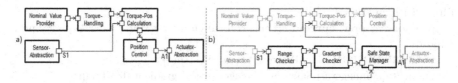

Fig. 4. Torque Vectoring System Software Architecture: a) without safety mechanisms b) enriched with safety mechanisms

The technical safety concept contains more than 100 requirements that shall be realized in software. In the following, we apply our proposed approach for one concrete technical safety requirement:

TSR1: *"In case of errors during sensor data acquisition of the disk temperature, the torque-vectoring system shall be disabled within 100 milliseconds (ms)"*

This requirement has several implications on the technical solution. First, some kind of error detection during data acquisition shall be performed. Second, a corresponding error handling strategy (disable the system) has been defined. Our approach supports safety engineers during the refinement and fulfillment of technical safety requirements providing patterns that safety engineers select while taking their domain expertise and the system's properties into account.

In the software architecture shown in Figure 4 (a), the input data named $S1$, provided by the "Sensor Abstraction" component, is carrying the disk temperature referenced by TSR1. We assume the safety engineer defines two software safety requirements according to the formalism we have proposed in Section 3.2, in order to assure that the technical safety requirement TSR1 is fulfilled. Firstly, a range checker shall detect possible violations of lower and upper value boundaries of $S1$. Secondly, a gradient checker shall detect improper value changes from $S1$ within a given time window, i.e., more than 2 degrees within 10 ms.

Both software safety requirements lead to the degradation of the torque-vectoring system if sensor data is invalid for more than 50 ms. The approach chosen by the safety engineer is to fulfill the 50 deadline by scheduling the range check and gradient check tasks with a period of 10 ms. After detecting the error within 50 ms, the system disables the torque-vectoring during the subsequent 50 ms, and hence, satisfies the time interval required by TSR1.

Figure 5 depicts the software safety requirements for the range and gradient checkers as well as the filtering requirement. The filter reacts if five consecutive errors in the 10-ms-period task occurs, and therefore, reacts within 50 ms as required.

Using both software safety requirements, the AUTOSAR software design and system deployment information, the generative approach adapts the software architecture as shown in Figure 4 (b).

According to the software safety requirements, the software component *Range Checker* obtains the disk temperature from the providing software component

```
filter diskTempFilter {
    previous := prev, current := cur, tolerance := 5, value := cur + prev / prev
} handle {
    FILTER_ERROR ⇒ call root::ptTorqueSystem→
    ptSafeStateManager::spSafeStateManager→error_gradient_diskTemp
}

ssr limitGradientOfDiskTemperature satisfies TSR1 using {
    limit gradient of root::ptSensorAbstraction::ppSensorTPC→diskTemp {
        min := −2.0, max := 2.0,tolerance := 0.001, period := 10 ms
    } handle {
        GRADIENT_TOO_HIGH ⇒ diskTempFilter()
        GRADIENT_TOO_LOW ⇒ diskTempFilter()
    }
}
ssr limitRangeOfDiskTemperature satisfies TSR1 using {
    check range of root::ptSensorAbstraction::ppSensorTPC → diskTemp within {
        (min := -20.0 , max := 120.0 , tolerance := 0.2)
    } handle {
        VALUE_ABOVE_RANGE ⇒ diskTempFilter()
        VALUE_BELOW_RANGE ⇒ diskTempFilter()
    }
}
```

Fig. 5. Gradient and range check and corresponding filtering for the disk temperature

Sensor-Abstraction, performs the necessary value range validations and forwards the value to the *Gradient Checker* component. The *Gradient Checker* component gathers the disk temperature provided by the *Range Checker*, performs the plausibility check and provides a filtered value to the receiving software component *Torque-Pos Calculation*.

The decision made by the safety engineer refining the technical safety requirement implies that, in case of invalid data, both requirements filter erroneous values for the specified time interval (five erroneous values for the range checker and 50 ms divided into five 10 ms cycles for the gradient checker). If the invalid data persists for more than five range checks or 50 ms for the gradient check, the checkers invokes the software component *Safe State Manager*, which is responsible for the degradation of the actuator.

Figure 6 provides a small excerpt of the code corresponding to the implementation of the gradient checker safety mechanism. The generated code has been integrated into the production software of the rear axle torque-vectoring system and its functionality has been tested against the real mechanical system and on the real target ECU. In the evaluation scenario, the generator focuses on the relevant adaptations of the software architecture, the system configuration and the C-code implementation. The generated artifacts provide traceability information and support the safety case argumentation.

```
//runnable for AUTOSAR
void swcGradientChecker_check_rp_ptRestECU_ppSensorTPC_diskTemp () {

    SInt16 current_value;
    int check_gradient_result;

    //read current value
    Rte_Read_rp_ptRestECU_ppSensorTPC_diskTemp(&current_value);
    if (b_swcGradientChecker_check_rp_ptRestECU_ppSensorTPC_diskTemp_init == TRUE) {
        b_swcGradientChecker_check_rp_ptRestECU_ppSensorTPC_diskTemp_init = FALSE;
        state.last_value = current_value;
        Rte_Write_pp_ptRestECU_ppSensorTPC_diskTemp(current_value);
    } else {
        check_gradient_result = swcGradientChecker_check_rp_ptRestECU_ppSensorTPC_diskTemp_check_gradient(current_value);
        if (check_gradient_result == FALSE){
            //set error
            b_swcGradientChecker_check_rp_ptRestECU_ppSensorTPC_diskTemp_gcError = TRUE;
            if (state.error & swcGradientChecker_check_rp_ptRestECU_ppSensorTPC_diskTemp_ERROR_GRADIENT_TOO_HIGH){
                SInt16 _filterReturnValue = swcGradientChecker_check_rp_ptRestECU_ppSensorTPC_diskTemp_diskTempFilter
                    (current_value);
                Rte_Write_pp_ptRestECU_ppSensorTPC_diskTemp(_filterReturnValue);
                state.last_value += swcGradientChecker_check_rp_ptRestECU_ppSensorTPC_diskTemp_MAX_VALUE;
                SetStateMessage(DBG_ID_swcGradientChecker_check_rp_ptRestECU_ppSensorTPC_diskTemp,
                    swcGradientChecker_check_rp_ptRestECU_ppSensorTPC_diskTemp_ERROR_GRADIENT_TOO_HIGH,current_value);
            }

            if (state.error & swcGradientChecker_check_rp_ptRestECU_ppSensorTPC_diskTemp_ERROR_GRADIENT_TOO_LOW){
                Rte_Call_cp_ptTVHAG2_ptSafeStateManager_spSafeStateManager_error_gradient_swcRestECU_ppSensorTPC_diskTemp();
                state.last_value += swcGradientChecker_check_rp_ptRestECU_ppSensorTPC_diskTemp_MIN_VALUE;
                SetStateMessage(DBG_ID_swcGradientChecker_check_rp_ptRestECU_ppSensorTPC_diskTemp,
                    swcGradientChecker_check_rp_ptRestECU_ppSensorTPC_diskTemp_ERROR_GRADIENT_TOO_LOW,current_value);
            }
        } else {
            if (b_swcGradientChecker_check_rp_ptRestECU_ppSensorTPC_diskTemp_gcError) {
                //reset all handling mechanisms used
                swcGradientChecker_check_rp_ptRestECU_ppSensorTPC_diskTemp_diskTempFilter_reset();
                b_swcGradientChecker_check_rp_ptRestECU_ppSensorTPC_diskTemp_gcError = FALSE;
            }
            Rte_Write_pp_ptRestECU_ppSensorTPC_diskTemp(current_value);
            state.last_value = current_value;

            SetStateMessage(DBG_ID_swcGradientChecker_check_rp_ptRestECU_ppSensorTPC_diskTemp,
                swcGradientChecker_check_rp_ptRestECU_ppTPC_diskTemp_ERROR_NOERROR,current_value);
        }
    }
}
```

Fig. 6. Excerpt of generated code realizing the gradient checker requirement

The final result of artefacts and architectural adaptations largely depends on the implementation of the generator and is also influenced by the system configuration. The results are mainly driven by design decisions of the safety engineer, software developer, or system integrator. For example, for certain patterns, they might prefer the generation of new runnables instead of the generation of new software components.

5   Related Work

Much literature and research addresses the safety engineering process from safety goals to software safety requirements, but the realization of software safety requirements has only been addressed sparsely.

The structure of our safety mechanisms classification for the specific classes of technical safety requirements is influenced by Wu and Kelly's hierarchy [19]. Guidelines on safety-critical and fault-tolerant systems [7,12,16] were important sources during the development of our safety-mechanism hierarchy.

Our M2M/M2T approach exploiting a formalized structure for software safety requirement specification was mainly driven by software safety mechanisms in existing implementations of current safety-critical systems. Contrary to our pattern-based solution, Erkkinen and Conrad [6] assume a general-purpose modeling language including a code generation engine, and restrict the use of blocks of the language and configuration settings of the code generator, to fulfill safety-relevant properties. Mader et al. [13] propose a generation environment that, given a static system model, generates Simulink [17] models for specified safety mechanisms. In this approach, the generator does not produce the dynamic behavior of the safety mechanism, but requires the engineer to manually refine the model in a subsequent step providing the implementation of the behavior.

Arora and Kulkarni [1] describe a theory of how the combination of detectors and correctors lead to fault-tolerant systems. Roughly, our approach makes their theoretic considerations practically applicable, as using our approach, engineers combine and nest detection and handling requirements in similar way and our tools provide argumentation on certain fault-tolerance aspects.

The Mbeddr tool platform [18] supports different aspects of embedded software development. For example, it allows its users to customize the C programming language for certain industrial domains, and to integrate further information, such as requirements, into the programming language. While Mbeddr focuses on programming language extensions in general, our approach focuses specifically on formalizing safety requirements and safety mechanisms. It is worthwhile to use Mbeddr's functionality for integrating our specific approach into the C programming language. This makes our approach also applicable in a non-AUTOSAR context. As a result, any developer using Mbeddr can easily realize safety mechanisms using our textual description language.

Masci et. al. [14] describe an approach to formally specify the user interface of PCA infusion pumps that also supports verification and demonstration of proof obligations. While our approach assumes that the safety engineer realizes the refinement of technical safety requirements through the use of our formalized software safety requirements, Masci et. al. relies on the formalization of natural language requirements using higher-order logic together with an executable model of the system based on finite state machines. Formal languages, such as higher-order logic, provide a flexible and extendable language to formalize the requirements. However, this requires in-depth experts for the use of the formal language. In contrast, in our work, we aim for a simple domain-specific language tailored for safety engineers untrained in formal specification.

6   Outlook: Freedom from Interference

One challenging aspect of safety-critical software in the automotive domain is the coexistence of software components with different criticality on the same system. This is often called mixed-criticality. The ISO 26262, part 6, clauses 7.4.10 and 7.4.11 requires such cases to be analyzed and to provide sufficient evidence of *freedom from interference*, namely, the absence of cascading faults between components. In this section, we consider this aspect from the software perspective and describe an approach to address mixed criticality.

ISO 26262, part 6, Annex D provides guidance regarding faults whose occurrence could lead to the violation of freedom-from-interference requirements. In this case, the main aspects to consider are timing, execution, memory and communication.

We investigated approaches to automatically guarantee the fulfillment of freedom from interference requirements based on this paper's work and on the ISO 26262 recommendations. Our approach involves the analysis of AUTOSAR software architectures where safety requirements are allocated to software components and are enhanced with ASIL annotations. After the analysis, a set of software safety requirements for the architecture is defined and proposed to the safety engineer. This set of requirements can be automatically realized by our approach, as described in Section 3.

The ASIL annotations are used to check for mixed-criticality situations between components. In such case, the highest ASIL of the components being checked is taken as basis and all other software components are analyzed regarding this highest ASIL.

First, the analysis takes into account communication. The required ports of each software component are analyzed and, whenever data is being provided by a component with lower ASIL, requirements for safety mechanisms to deal with communication faults are suggested. Examples of such requirements are default value, checksums and filters. Furthermore, temporal properties of communication, i.e., time outs, are considered as well. If components with the same ASIL are deployed to different ECUs, the analysis adds safety requirements related to the configuration of the AUTOSAR Communication Stack, which ensures safe inter-ECU communication between components through the end-to-end protection (E2E) library.

Second, the analysis continues with software execution aspects. For this aspect, the analysis checks if components with different ASIL share ECU partitions or ECUs. For different ASIL components sharing only the same ECU, but exist in different partitions, mechanisms, such as aliveness monitoring, are suggested. If components with different ASIL share the same ECU partition, more care shall be taken regarding execution, since a fault in a software component can change the flow of another one. In this case, requirements, such as control-flow monitoring, are suggested for error detection. Alternatively, such errors can also be avoided by defining requirements on the operating system scheduler; however, our analysis currently does not take this solution into account.

Last, the analysis considers the use of dynamic storage (main memory) in the software architecture. If components with different ASIL share the same partition, the analysis suggests, among other solutions, storing the component data inversely in the memory. This is relevant if the components interfere with components having a lower ASIL. In case the ECU supports partitions, allocating components with the same ASIL to a common partition is suggested. This avoids cascading faults between software components through memory.

The suggestions from the analysis refer directly to the software mechanisms identified in our classification (Section 3.1). Since the analysis currently does not take into account any extra information about the system, the number of suggested requirements become quite large and can become a burden to the safety engineer instead of supporting safety activities. A possibility for improvement is to take into account the error model of the system. Such an error model would describe the static malfunction propagation through system components, as described in Cuenot et. al.'s work[5]. This allows the analysis to suggest extra requirements exploiting information about the system architecture and the errors that actually occur in the system.

7   Conclusion

The realization of safety-critical software functions consists of more than just implementing a few lines of code for the error detection and error handling mechanisms, it rather requires that developers and engineers provide evidence of the correctness of those lines and fulfillment of safety requirements.

Our approach captures expert knowledge of the functional safety domain and automates the tedious and error prone task of manually implementing safety mechanisms, while providing a basis for formal safety argumentation. Hence, developers and engineers can focus on the adequacy of the software safety mechanism rather than the technical matter of its implementation. Furthermore, extending our approach to other platforms can be achieved by simply extending the meta-model and providing corresponding generators.

In future work, we want to further investigate how complex software safety requirements, such as freedom from interference, are formalized using our approach, and we want to identify suitable safety patterns for them. These complex safety patterns are challenging, since they are composed by different mechanisms and ensure safety through their collaborative behavior. Moreover, we want to conduct a controlled experiment to quantify the benefits our approach and understand the concrete benefits in terms of effort saving when applying it to the development of the complete software for a given safety-critical function.

Regarding formal verification, we want to better understand the required formalization of the AUTOSAR meta-model and programming language for providing a formal proof of correctness of software safety requirements' implementations. Moreover, we want to investigate the integration of more expressive formalisms and use of interactive theorem provers, as described by Masci et al. [14].

Furthermore, to enhance our analysis for freedom from interference, we want to investigate the benefits of integrating error model information into the decisions when suggesting safety requirements.

Acknowledgements. We thank Andreas Baak, Michael Knapp, Tilmann Ochs, Thomas Schutzmeier and Kazi Zahid for their valuable contributions. We express our gratitude to the anonymous reviewers for their constructive comments. We gratefully acknowledge the full support from Harald Heinecke, Michael Rudorfer, Tillmann Schumm, Reinhard Stolle and Michael Würtenberger. This work has been conducted within the SAFE project in the ITEA2 framework, EUREKA cluster program $\Sigma!3674$, and has been funded by the German Ministry for Education and Research (BMBF) through ID 01|S11019, and by the French Ministry of the Economy and Finance (DGCIS).

References

1. Arora, A., Kulkarni, S.S.: Detectors and correctors: A theory of fault-tolerance components. In: Int. Conf. on Distributed Computing Systems, pp. 436–443 (1998)
2. Artop User Group: Artop – AUTOSAR tool platform, http://www.artop.org
3. Artop User Group: Artext – an AUTOSAR textual language framework (2013), http://www.artop.org/artext
4. AUTOSAR Development Partnership: Main requirements (v 2.1.0, rel 4.0, rev 1)
5. Cuenot, P., Ainhauser, C., Adler, N., Otten, S., Meurville, F.: Applying model based techniques for early safety evaluation of an automotive architecture in compliance with the ISO 26262 standard. In: Embedded Real-Time Software and Systems, ERTS (2014)
6. Erkkinen, T., Conrad, M.: Safety-critical software development using automatic production code generation (technical paper). In: SAE World Congress 2007 (2007)
7. ISO: ISO/FDIS 26262, Part 6 - product development at the software level (2011)
8. ISO: ISO/FDIS 26262 road vehicles – functional safety (2011)
9. ITEA2 Project SAFE: Deliverable D3.6.b: Safety code generator specification (2013), https://itea3.org/project/workpackage/document/download/1556/10039-SAFE-WP-3-SAFED36b.pdf
10. ITEA2 Project SAFE: Safe - Safe Automotive software architecture (2013), http://www.safe-project.eu/
11. ITEA2 Project SAFE: Deliverable D5.6.c: Evaluation of safety code generation, http://www.safe-project.eu/SAFE-Download.html (to be published, 2014)
12. Kirrmann, H., Grosspietsch, K.: Fault-tolerant control systems (survey paper). Automatisierungstechnik 50(8), 362–374 (2002)
13. Mader, R., Griessnig, G., Armengaud, E., Leitner, A., Kreiner, C., Bourrouilh, Q., Steger, C., Weiss, R.: A bridge from system to software development for safety-critical automotive embedded systems. In: 38th EUROMICRO Conference on Software Engineering and Advanced Applications, SEAA 2012, pp. 75–79 (2012)
14. Masci, P., Ayoub, A., Curzon, P., Lee, I., Sokolsky, O., Thimbleby, H.: Model-based development of the generic PCA infusion pump user interface prototype in PVS. In: Bitsch, F., Guiochet, J., Kaâniche, M. (eds.) SAFECOMP. LNCS, vol. 8153, pp. 228–240. Springer, Heidelberg (2013)
15. MIRA Ltd.: MISRA-C:2004 Guidelines for the use of the C language in critical systems (2004), http://www.misra.org.uk
16. NASA: NASA software safety guidebook. NASA (2004)
17. The MathWorks Inc.: Simulink (2013)
18. Voelter, M., Ratiu, D., Schätz, B., Kolb, B.: mbeddr: An extensible C-based programming language and IDE for embedded systems. In: Proc. of the 3rd Ann. Conference on Systems, Programming, and Applications: Software for Humanity, SPLASH 2012, pp. 121–140. ACM (2012)
19. Wu, W., Kelly, T.: Safety tactics for software architecture design. In: Proc. of the 28th Annual Int. Computer Software and Applications Conference, COMPSAC 2004, pp. 368–375. IEEE (2004)

Querying Safety Cases

Ewen Denney[1], Dwight Naylor[2], and Ganesh Pai[1]

[1] SGT / NASA Ames Research Center
Moffett Field, CA 94035, USA
{ewen.denney,ganesh.pai}@nasa.gov
[2] Rensselaer Polytechnic Institute
Troy, NY 12180, USA
naylod@rpi.edu

Abstract. Querying a safety case to show how the various stakeholders' concerns about system safety are addressed has been put forth as one of the benefits of argument-based assurance (in a recent study by the Health Foundation, UK, which reviewed the use of safety cases in safety-critical industries). However, neither the literature nor current practice offer much guidance on querying mechanisms appropriate for, or available within, a safety case paradigm. This paper presents a preliminary approach that uses a formal basis for querying safety cases, specifically Goal Structuring Notation (GSN) argument structures. Our approach semantically enriches GSN arguments with domain-specific metadata that the query language leverages, along with its inherent structure, to produce *views*. We have implemented the approach in our toolset AdvoCATE, and illustrate it by application to a fragment of the safety argument for an Unmanned Aircraft System (UAS) being developed at NASA Ames. We also discuss the potential practical utility of our query mechanism within the context of the existing framework for UAS safety assurance.

Keywords: Safety cases, Queries, Views, Formal methods, Automation.

1 Introduction

A safety case essentially provides an audit trail, which can assist in convincing the various stakeholders of a system, including regulators, that the system is acceptably safe [1]. One of the motivations to use structured arguments in developing a safety case is to provide a means to explicitly justify safety considerations from concept, through requirements, to the evidence of risk mitigation/control. Additionally, argument structures are intended to make a safety case easier to comprehend and, thereby, more efficient to review critically [2]. To improve clarity in presenting the underlying reasoning, the Goal Structuring Notation (GSN) [3] provides a graphical syntax with which to specify the appropriate argument structures.

Previously [4], we identified the need to present role-specific information to subject-matter experts to improve the comprehensibility of a safety argument. Furthermore, as a system evolves through its lifecycle, so should its safety case, i.e., system changes, assumptions that are validated/invalidated, and observations of safety performance, for example, should translate into updates of the safety case so that the system and its safety

A. Bondavalli and F. Di Giandomenico (Eds.): SAFECOMP 2014, LNCS 8666, pp. 294–309, 2014.
© Springer International Publishing Switzerland 2014

case are mutually consistent. We believe that one of the first steps to address these needs is through an approach for safety case *queries*. Although the potential to query a safety case has been put forth previously as one of the benefits of using safety cases, and as a way for stakeholders to understand how safety concerns have been addressed [5], to the best of our knowledge there is scant guidance on a principled way for querying safety cases.[1]

The application domain motivating our work is Unmanned Aircraft Systems (UASs). We are interested in creating a framework for argument-based assurance of airworthiness and flight safety of UAS, which augments the existing processes and reuses the artifacts produced to the extent possible, so as to ease its adoption in practice. A broad goal is to be able to address the requirements from the relevant regulations/standards. An additional goal is to be able to support safety case development. In general, safety engineers and system developers need to understand and communicate what they (or others) have already done, that which remains to be done, and how different parts of the argument may relate to each other and to the system.

These issues are also critical for safety/assurance case assessors. To determine safety case fitness for purpose, it is necessary to involve all the relevant stakeholders so that they may understand the (safety) claims made, and challenge the reasoning and evidence presented. However, safety cases typically contain heterogeneous reasoning [6] and a wide variety of evidence, e.g., the mandated work products which show compliance to the relevant regulations and standards, the results of analyses (safety, system, and software), various inspections, audits, reviews, simulations, verification activities including various kinds of subsystem/system tests, and, if applicable, also the evidence of safe performance from prior operations. In other words, safety cases can easily amass a large amount of information. For example, the preliminary safety case for ADS-B airport surface surveillance applications [7] is about 200 pages long. Thus, partly due to the size and diversity of information contained in a safety case it may not be straightforward (or possible) for all stakeholders to locate and/or understand all the arguments presented along with their different elements.

In this paper, our main contribution is a preliminary approach (Section 2), and a formal basis for querying GSN safety case argument structures (Section 3). We define queries as properties of GSN nodes, constructed from unary and binary relations, and take the result of executing a query to be an *argument structure view*, rather than simply the list of nodes which satisfy the query. We also describe the *Argument Query Language*, AQL[2], and give formal semantics for both queries and views based on an earlier semantics for argument structures. We have implemented the approach in our toolset AdvoCATE [8], and illustrate its application on a fragment of a safety case argument structure for the Swift UAS, under development at NASA Ames (Sections 4 and 5).

In this first implementation, we have limited ourselves to querying the argument structure, rather than the entire assembly of artifacts comprising a safety case. Next, we describe our approach for querying and how it can help to address the problem of accessing (and understanding) the rich variety of information contained in a safety case.

---

[1] However, we acknowledge that existing safety case tools may provide a search functionality to locate the information of interest.

[2] In Islamic philosophy, *'aql* is the use of logical inquiry as a basis for law.

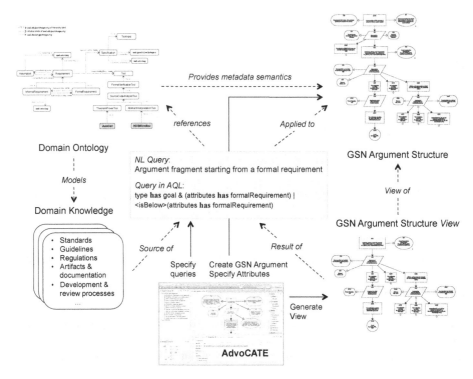

Fig. 1. Methodology for querying safety cases using AdvoCATE: Enrich GSN argument structures with metadata drawn from domain ontologies and use Argument Query Language (AQL) queries to create views. The dotted lines give the role of each element in relation to the others, while the solid lines give the role of the tool.

2   Methodology

We describe our approach mainly with respect to the GSN argument structures created using our tool AdvoCATE (although the principles can be applied more generally). AdvoCATE already offers several features: filtering and searching the argument, and showing/hiding sub-arguments relative to a node. The search mechanism allows a string search on different node fields (e.g., identifier, description, etc.), which can also be filtered by node type. However, our requirement is to develop a mechanism to query arguments in a much richer way, making use of both syntactic (i.e., structural) and semantic information. Fig. 1 shows our methodology for using the Argument Query Language (AQL) to query safety case argument structures and create views.

2.1   Semantic Enhancement

The main idea is first to semantically enrich the GSN nodes in the argument structure. Thus, in addition to the descriptive text, e.g., the actual claim for a goal node, we associate nodes with *metadata*, given as a set of *attributes*.

For example, we can use metadata to relate nodes containing informal claims, with those containing the formal equivalents. We can also use metadata to indicate an association between an instance node in an argument, and the source node in the pattern from which it was generated. Another type of metadata can be used to indicate that a node is linked to some external artifact(s). More generally, we can use metadata to give provenance information, such as representing how a node was constructed (e.g., via some formal method) or tracing information (e.g., to a system or standard).

In general, metadata are meant to reflect a variety of domain knowledge. Thus, we use different domain ontologies, which capture the relevant concepts and their interrelations in a domain, to give the semantics of the attributes. For example, from a requirements ontology, we can provide attributes to goal nodes that reflect not only concepts such as *requirement, formal requirement, safety requirement*, etc., but also relations such as *formalizes* or *is allocated to*. Then, by drawing from a system organization ontology, we can add more information about the specific system, subsystem or component to which the requirement applies. In the absence of an ontology, we can rely on terminological information, such as a glossary from a standards document, or procedural guidance documents.

2.2 Sources of Queries

We see queries and views as a means to express, respectively, specific questions relevant for argument structure creation, review, or modification, and their responses. Potential sources of queries, besides the experience of the safety engineer or the assessor, includes domain knowledge, such as that contained in regulations, standards, guidance documents, artifact documentation, documentation for processes and procedures, etc. To illustrate, we give some scenarios:

Supporting Safety Argument Development and Change: When developing a safety argument for a complex system, arguments addressing all parts of the system may not all be created at the same time. These present some simple query needs, e.g., determining the claims that remain to be supported or how/if high-risk hazards have been addressed. Similarly, a developer may want to view specific fragments, e.g., how a formal method was applied to develop a claim or how a specific pattern has been instantiated. Furthermore, when redesign/replacement of some components is required, we can use queries also to identify those argument fragments that ought to be updated to reflect the revised safety analysis, and, in turn, to understand the impact of those changes on the overall safety argument.

Addressing Traceability Concerns: In general, demonstrating traceability is a requirement during certification, e.g., as part of the software approval process [9]. An important form of traceability is to show how requirements from regulations, standards and other relevant guidance documents are linked to the appropriate evidence items. For instance, item 5.b.(5) of the safety checklist in FAA Order 8130.34B, Appendix D [10], requires describing how software requirements are validated and the means for software verification. In addition to providing descriptive text—as is the case in practice—we believe that an informative response also could include an appropriate slice or *view* of the airworthiness assurance argument structure, showing the claims relevant to software requirements, the applicable context under which validity can be claimed, the relevant assumptions and justifications, the strategies for verification and validation (e.g., formal verification, and inspection against domain knowledge, respectively), and how these have been applied to refine the claims made.

Supporting Assessment and Review: As part of the different milestones of the systems engineering process [11], engineering artifacts (as well as the safety case) are to be reviewed and accepted before development proceeds. Simple queries on the safety argument can be used to determine whether the relevant obligations have been met. For example, during a Preliminary Design Review (PDR), we can query the safety case to establish whether or not all the identified safety requirements have been allocated.

2.3   Components of Queries and Views

For this paper, we mainly focus on queries that operate on GSN arguments although, eventually, we want to expand the scope of queries to include the entire safety case.

Conceptually, queries in AQL comprise a combination of properties of both the semantic and the syntactic information in the argument structure. As described earlier (Section 2.1), metadata, i.e., attributes on nodes, provide a way to access the semantic information. To access the structure, AQL queries contain expressions referencing GSN syntax. The language (described subsequently in Section 3) itself consists of a selection of *atomic* queries that can be grouped with the usual logical connectives (and, or, xor, not), as well as the *path quantifiers* [ ] (all), and ⟨ ⟩ (some), to specify query relations. The language also contains constructs to access structure in terms of the relative arrangement of nodes, e.g., *above, below, directly above*, etc.

Taken together, we can express some relatively complex queries in the form of concepts that AdvoCATE can understand, so that an informal, natural language query in the domain can be expressed as a formal AQL query over the GSN argument structure. Here, we note that the translation of an informal query into a formal one, and the resulting view generated, depends on the purpose of the query. For instance, consider querying for an *incomplete* argument. If the purpose were simply to locate a set of undeveloped nodes, so that the safety case author(s) can further develop them, it suffices to specify a formal query whose result is exactly the set of undeveloped nodes of interest, e.g., goals nodes marked *to be developed*. Alternatively, if the purpose were to assess, say, whether or not a claim has been supported by evidence, or the extent to which it has been developed, then a view containing greater details is more useful. Then, we can specify an appropriate formal query in AQL which will result in an argument structure view containing any goal or strategy not immediately (or eventually) followed by other goals, strategies or evidence (See Section 5 for a concrete example).

The outcome of executing a query on an argument structure is an argument structure *view*. A view is a diagram showing the fragment(s) of the (source) argument that satisfy the query. In our implementation, we collapse those nodes that do not satisfy the query into *concealment nodes* ($\mathcal{C}$-nodes, for short), which we annotate with the number of hidden nodes. A $\mathcal{C}$-node can be (temporarily) expanded to show the corresponding fragment in the source argument. To reduce visual clutter, by default we only show $\mathcal{C}$-nodes that appear between two regular nodes. So, for example, if a context node does not satisfy a query, it does not appear in the view. One consequence is that if the root node does not satisfy the query, the view will consist of several unconnected fragments, though this preference can be changed.

We allow multiple views for a given argument structure, reflecting the application of different queries. The views and the queried structure are kept consistent with each other in our implementation, so that a change in any one of the views/argument structure is either propagated to the rest or, in the case of an inconsistent change (due to independent unsaved edits, say), the user is alerted.

3   Foundations

3.1   Metadata

Metadata is associated with individual nodes (rather than globally with the entire argument). Each node has a set of associated attributes, which are declared and can be parameterized over parameters of specific types. Nodes have instances of attributes with values that comply with the type of the parameter (which can itself depend on the node). In general, we draw these parameter values from a domain ontology (See Fig. 3 in Section 5, for an example). The grammar of an *attribute declaration* is:

```
attribute ::= attributeName param*
param ::= String | Int | Nat | nodeID | sameNodeTypeID | goalNodeId | strategyNodeId |
          evidenceNodeId | assumptionNodeId | contextNodeId | justificationNodeId |
          userDefinedEnum
```

The type of a parameter can either be:
- a basic type, i.e., a string (String), an integer (Int), or a natural number (Nat)
- a *node type*, which can be used as parameters in three different ways:
  - NodeID: any kind of node
  - sameNodeTypeID: the parameter must be the identifier of a node of the same type as the node with the attribute.
  - Specific node parameter types, which allow specification of a node of a given type: assumptionNodeID, contextNodeID, evidenceNodeID, goalNodeID, justificationNodeID, strategyNodeID.
- A user-defined enumeration (userDefinedEnum): for example, we can define the parameter types

```
severity ::= catastrophic | hazardous | major | minor | noSafetyEffect
likelihood ::= frequent | probable | remote | extremelyRemote |
               extremelyImprobable
```

to define the parametrized attribute risk(severity, likelihood). Then, we can give an *attribute instance* as: risk(severity(catastrophic), likelihood(extremelyImprobable)). We will just use "attribute" when it is clear from the context whether we mean attribute instance or attribute declaration. Note that we do not force the values of different enumerations to be distinct.

3.2   Syntax and Semantics

Query Syntax. Queries are defined with respect to a signature given by the declared metadata. Henceforth, we will assume that this signature is fixed, and let A range over attribute instances and N range over node identifiers. We will also use $\mathcal{F}$ to indicate a *node field* and write $\mathcal{F}$ **has** v where $\mathcal{F}$ is one of the fields id, type (t), description (d), attributes (m), status (s), and v is an appropriately typed concrete value.

The node identifier (id) and description (description) must be strings; node type is one of goal g, strategy s, evidence e, context c, assumption a, and justification j; attributes takes an attribute instance(A), and status takes *tbd* (to be developed). For the fields id and type, **has** means equality; for the field description, **has** means sub-string, and for the fields attributes and status, **has** means set membership.

Definition 1 (Pre-query). *A pre-query is a term constructed according to the following grammar:*

$Q ::= true \mid \mathcal{F}$ **has** $v \mid$ isAbove $\mid$ isBelow $\mid$ isDirectlyAbove $\mid$ isDirectlyBelow $\mid$ $Q(N) \mid$ not $Q \mid Q$ and $Q' \mid \langle Q \rangle \, Q'$

Now we define well-formedness rules on pre-queries, which will allow us to define queries. We give these as inference rules for the *arity* of a query:

$$\frac{}{\mathcal{F}\ \textbf{has}\ v : 1}\ v \text{ well-typed for } \mathcal{F}$$

$$\frac{}{\texttt{isBelow} : 2} \qquad \frac{}{\texttt{isAbove} : 2} \qquad \frac{}{\texttt{isDirectlyBelow} : 2} \qquad \frac{}{\texttt{isDirectlyAbove} : 2}$$

$$\frac{Q : 2}{Q(N) : 1} \qquad \frac{Q : n}{\text{not } Q : n} \qquad \frac{Q : n \quad Q' : n}{Q \text{ and } Q' : n} \qquad \frac{Q : 2 \quad Q' : n}{\langle Q \rangle \, Q' : n}$$

Here $Q : n$ means that query Q is well-formed and represents a property of n node arguments. An inference rule states that if the hypotheses hold (i.e., the queries above the line are well-formed with the specified arities) then the conclusion holds (i.e., the stated query below the line is well-formed with given arity).

Definition 2 (Query). *We define a* query *to be a pre-query Q such that $Q : 1$ according to the pre-query well-formedness rules.*

We do not need to supply all the parameters in an attribute instance in a query. For example, we can write attributes **has** risk(likelihood(probable)) to mean: find a node with an attribute risk whose likelihood is probable and with *any* severity. We can abbreviate this further by writing attributes **has** risk(probable), which will look for any parameter with value probable, or even attributes **has** risk with which to find nodes tagged with any risk values. We can omit the second argument of a top-level quantifier, in which case it is taken to be true. For example, a root node can be queried by not$\langle$isBelow$\rangle$, which is equivalent to not$\langle$isBelow$\rangle$*true*. A derived syntax for queries is given as:

$$
\begin{aligned}
false &= \text{not } true \\
\text{(or)} \quad Q \text{ or } Q' &= \text{not (not } Q \text{ and not } Q') \\
\text{(xor)} \quad Q \text{ xor } Q' &= (Q \text{ and } Q') \text{ or (not } Q \text{ and not } Q') \\
\text{(all)} \quad [\, Q \,] \, Q' &= \text{not } \langle \, Q \, \rangle \text{ not } Q'
\end{aligned}
$$

Semantics of Queries. In order to give semantics to queries, we first give semantics to argument structures.

Definition 3 (Safety Case Argument Structure). *A safety case argument structure is a 3-tuple* $\langle N, f, \to \rangle$ *where* N *is a set of nodes;* f_X *(where* $X \in \{t, d, m, s\}$*) gives the node fields:* type, description, attributes, status; *and* $\to$ *is the connector relation between nodes. Various restrictions[3] must be placed on* $\to$ *to ensure that an argument structure is well-formed. We have* $f_t : N \to \{s, g, e, a, j, c\}$ *gives node types,* $f_d : N \to string$ *gives node descriptions,* $f_m : N \to A^*$ *gives node instance attributes, and* $f_s : N \to \mathcal{P}(\{tbd\})$ *gives node development status.*

Note that, here, we equate nodes with their identifiers. Also, it is possible to give many variants on this definition (as we have done previously [12], [13]), depending on the information that we want to associate with the argument. Here, we include all information that is relevant to the definition of the queries. Next, we give semantics to queries, as:

$N \vDash true$

$N \vDash \text{id } \textbf{has } v \iff N = v$

$N \vDash \text{type } \textbf{has } v \iff f_t(N) = v$ $\qquad N, N' \vDash \texttt{isAbove} \iff N \to^+ N'$

$N \vDash \text{description } \textbf{has } v \iff v \text{ substring } f_d(N)$ $\qquad N, N' \vDash \texttt{isBelow} \iff N' \to^+ N$

$N \vDash \text{attributes } \textbf{has } v \iff v \in f_a(N)$ $\qquad N, N' \vDash \texttt{isDirectlyAbove} \iff N \to N'$

$N \vDash \text{status } \textbf{has } v \iff v \in f_s(N)$ $\qquad N, N' \vDash \texttt{isDirectlyBelow} \iff N' \to N$

$\qquad\qquad\qquad\qquad\qquad\qquad\qquad\qquad\qquad\quad N \vDash Q(N') \iff N, N' \vDash Q$

For compound query terms, we need to give rules for either one or two nodes. Write $\bar{N}$ to mean either N_1 or N_1, N_2. Then,

$$\bar{N} \vDash \text{not } Q \iff \bar{N} \nvDash Q$$
$$\bar{N} \vDash Q \text{ and } Q' \iff \bar{N} \vDash Q \text{ and } \bar{N} \vDash Q'$$

For quantifiers, it is simpler to give the two cases separately:

$$N \vDash \langle Q \rangle Q' \iff \exists N' \text{ such that } N, N' \vDash Q \text{ and } N' \vDash Q'$$
$$N, N' \vDash \langle Q \rangle Q' \iff \exists N'' \text{ such that } N, N'' \vDash Q \text{ and } N'', N' \vDash Q'$$

Semantics of Views. There are two (equivalent) ways to define views, depending on whether we treat concealment nodes as a special kind of node or as part of a link. Though each definition has some advantages, the simplest is to use nodes.

Definition 4 (Argument View). *An argument view is a 5-tuple* $\langle N, \mathbb{C}, f, \gamma, \to \rangle$ *where* N *is the set of argument nodes,* $\mathbb{C}$ *is the set of C-nodes,* f *gives node fields for* N, $\gamma : \mathbb{C} \to nat^+$ *gives C-node counts, and the connector relation* $\to$ *is subject to the same restrictions as in Definition 3 (that is, if* $x, x' \in N$ *and* $x \to x'$*, then there are restrictions on the types of* x, x' *to prevent illegal links). Moreover, if* $x' \in \mathbb{C}$ *then* $f_t(x) \in \{g, s\}$*; if* $x \in \mathbb{C}$*, then* x' *can have any type; we cannot have both* $x, x' \in \mathbb{C}$*.*

In practice, to reduce clutter, the tool allows additional restrictions to be placed when creating $\mathbb{C}$-nodes. For the examples in this paper (Section 5), we also require that $\forall \gamma \in \mathbb{C} . \exists n, n' \in N . n \to \gamma \to n'$. We can also relax this condition so that $\mathbb{C}$-nodes are added as root. The last condition prevents $\mathbb{C}$-nodes at the edge of the view, since they can only appear between regular nodes (as mentioned in Section 2.3). Next, we relate views to arguments.

---

[3] See [12] for details.

Definition 5 (*A*-view). *Let* $A = \langle N_A, f_A, \rightarrow_A \rangle$ *and* $V = \langle N_V, \mathbb{C}, f_V, \gamma, \rightarrow_V \rangle$ *be an argument and a view, respectively. We say that* V *is an* A-view if $N_V \subseteq N_A, N_A \cap \mathbb{C} = \emptyset, f_V = f_A \upharpoonright N_V, \rightarrow_A \upharpoonright N_V \subseteq \rightarrow_V$, *and there exist mappings* $f : N_A \rightarrow N_V \cup \mathbb{C}$ *and* $g : N_V \cup \mathbb{C} \rightarrow A$ *such that* $g; f = id$, *and* $f; g(x) \rightarrow_A^* x$.

The latter condition forces the map from a $\mathbb{C}$-node to be to the root of a concealed sub-DAG. Note that, in general, f is partial and so, therefore, is $f; g$. However, g and $g; f$ are total.

Now, we define the views which result from queries. First, we need to define those fragments of an argument which are concealed by a query. Let Q be a query and define $S_Q = \{n \in N \mid n \nvDash Q$ and $\exists n_1, n_2 . (n_1 \rightarrow n \rightarrow n_2$ and $n_1, n_2 \nvDash Q)\}$. A *path*, p, is a sequence of connected nodes. If p connects nodes n and n' we write $p : n \rightarrow^* n'$. Then, define the relation R_Q as $n \, R_Q \, n' \iff \forall p : n \rightarrow^* n' . \forall n'' \in p . n'' \nvDash Q$.

R relates nodes which are in the same concealed fragment. It is easily seen that R_Q is an equivalence relation, and so we can form the partition $S_Q \backslash R_Q$, i.e., the set of concealed fragments.

Definition 6 (*Q*-view). *Given argument* $A = \langle N, f, \rightarrow \rangle$, *and query* Q, *we define the* Q-view of A as $\langle N_v, \mathbb{C}, f_v, \gamma, \rightarrow_v \rangle$, *where the components are defined as follows:*
(a) $N_v = \{n \in N \mid n \vDash Q\}$
(b) Let $S_Q \backslash R_Q = \{H_1, \dots, H_m\}$, *and define* C *as a fresh set of elements* $\{c_1, \dots, c_m\}$.
(c) $f_v = f \upharpoonright N_v$
(d) $c(c_i) = |H_i|$
(e)

$$n \rightarrow_v n' \iff \begin{cases} n, n' \in N & and \ n \rightarrow n', or \\ n \in N, n' = c_i \in C & and \ \exists n'' \in H_i . n \rightarrow n'', or \\ n = c_i \in C, n' \in N & and \ \exists n'' \in H_i . n'' \rightarrow n' \end{cases}$$

We now state (without proof) that queries give rise to well-formed views. Recall that we assume that queries and arguments are defined over a common attribute signature.

Theorem 1. *Let* Q *and* A *be a query and argument, respectively. Then, the* Q-view of A is an A-view.

4   Implementation

We have implemented the query/view mechanism in our toolset, AdvoCATE [8]. The tool stores the views associated with a diagram as special properties of the diagram, in particular as two lists in the diagram file itself: (a) all the view names associated with the diagram, and, (b) correspondingly, the query that maps to each name. In the interface, views appear by name as sub-items in the project explorer, under the corresponding diagram, e.g., as shown in Fig. 2. The figure also shows how node attributes are displayed (in the properties panel) along with other node fields. We draw the attributes from a domain-specific grammar, an excerpt of which is given in Fig. 3.

Although not shown in Fig. 2, we have implemented some additional usability features, such as the ability to open multiple views simultaneously in separate *tabs*, i.e., multiple canvases. The end-user can save changes either to the argument structures,

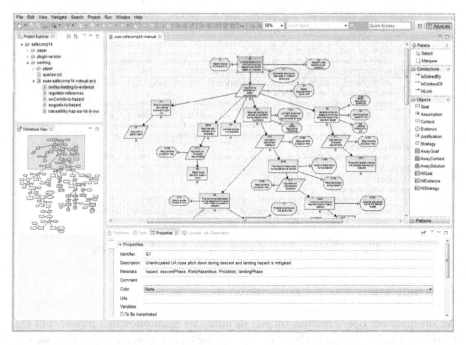

Fig. 2. Screenshot of AdvoCATE: (a) queries appear as sub-items of the argument structure file, in the project explorer panel on the left (b) the canvas is used to create GSN argument structures using the palette on the right, which provides the different GSN nodes and links (c) queries are run by entering them in the query text-box in the toolbar.

the queries, or both. Users will also be shown the current query, and can edit it further before saving. When any change is made either to the source diagram or a view, it is reflected in all views and the original diagram.

Due to space limitations, we only briefly describe the algorithm underlying the query/view mechanism. Let A be an argument structure, Q be a well-formed query, N be a node in A, and τ be a table of query results. If τ contains the result of applying Q to A then, using the function $\texttt{computeView}(A, Q)$, create a view as the conjunction of the nodes and links in τ. Then, according to the restrictions of Definition 4, create and link C-nodes to hide all nodes in A absent in τ. Otherwise use the function $\texttt{satisfiesQuery}(A, Q, N)$ on all nodes of A to locate those nodes that satisfy Q, store the result to τ, and call $\texttt{computeView}(A, Q)$ to create the view as earlier. The $\texttt{satisfiesQuery}(A, Q, N)$ function recursively evaluates the syntax tree of Q, iteratively locating the nodes in A such that the function returns $true$. We now state the correctness of the algorithm (without proof) as:

> If $\texttt{satisfiesQuery}(A, Q, N)$ returns $true$ then $N \vDash Q$ and
> If $\texttt{computeView}(A, Q) = V$ then V is the Q-view of A

Query execution is reasonably fast, taking under a second to process large diagrams containing upwards of 500 nodes.

```
requirement(id, hierarchyLevel, assuranceConcern)
formalClaim(id), informalClaim(id), hazard(id)
       id ::= int | string
       hierarchyLevel ::= highLevel | lowLevel
       assuranceConcern ::= functional | safety | reliability | availability | maintenance
requirementAppliesTo(elementLevel, elementType, element)
       elementLevel ::= system | subsystem | component | module | function | model | signal
       elementType ::= hardware | software
       element ::= aileron | elevator | flaps | propulsionBattery | avionicsBattery | actuatorBattery |
                   avionics | autopilot | FMS | AP | aileronPIDController | elevatorPIDController |
                   propulsion | engine | propeller | engineMotorController | actuator |
                   flightComputer | wing | actuatorMotorController pilotReceiver | IMU
references(variable)
       variable ::= aileronValue | pitchAttitude | flareAltitude | vRef | vNE | thrust | vS1
regulation(part)
       part ::= 14CFR23.73 | 14CFR23.75
risk(severity, likelihood)
       severity ::= catastrophic | hazardous | major | minor | noSafetyEffect
       likelihood ::= frequent | probable | remote | extremelyRemote | extremelyImprobable
isFormalizedBy(sameNodeTypeID)
```

Fig. 3. Excerpt of domain specific grammar for metadata

5 Application

We illustrate our query mechanism and its utility by application to a fragment of the
Swift UAS safety argument (See Fig. 4a for a bird's eye view): in particular, we describe some queries based on the motivating scenarios described earlier (Section 2.2)
and show the resulting views. The argument structure (in Fig. 4a) concerns, in brief,
the mitigation of a specific safety hazard—*unanticipated nose pitch down during descent and landing*—that can result in a loss of the aircraft and damage to the runway.
The argument develops the root claim of hazard mitigation into sub-claims concerning
the various contributory system functions, including software/hardware, components,
and operations, which are then linked to the evidence, e.g., available from experimental
data, procedures, and verification activities. In preparation for querying the argument,
we added metadata to the nodes using user-defined enumerations (see Section 3) and a
domain-specific grammar (Fig. 3).

Requirements address an assurance concern at a particular level of hierarchy, and can
be applied to system elements of various types. As motivated earlier, (Section 2.2), an
assessor might want to examine whether traceability exists from hazards to all relevant
system safety requirements, high-level and low-level requirements, down to software
requirements. We can specify such a traceability query in AQL in a straightforward
way, as shown in Fig. 4b. As mentioned earlier (Section 3.2), some of the parameters
of the metadata can be omitted in the query. The resulting (bird's eye) view (Fig. 4c)
contains goal nodes with metadata about the hazard and requirements to which they
are related. These goal nodes, in turn, are linked using $\mathcal{C}$-nodes. Fig. 4d shows the top
right leg of the view (Fig. 4c), showing traceability from a high-level requirement on the
avionics system, to the high-level and low-level avionics software requirements relevant
for the mitigation of the descent phase hazard.

Note that we can create the view shown in Fig. 4d by constraining the traceability
query, e.g., by including attributes about the avionics software. We can further constrain
the query to only consider hazards with a certain risk level. For example, by including

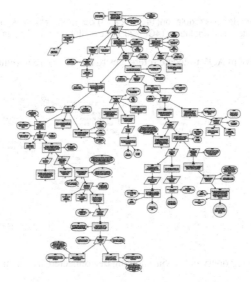

(a) Bird's eye view of a fragment of the Swift UAS safety case in GSN.

type **has** goal and (attributes **has** hazard or (attributes **has** requirement(safety) and
attributes **has** requirementAppliesTo(system)) or attributes **has** requirement(highLevel) or
attributes **has** requirement(lowLevel) or attributes **has** requirementAppliesTo(software))

(b) AQL traceability query.

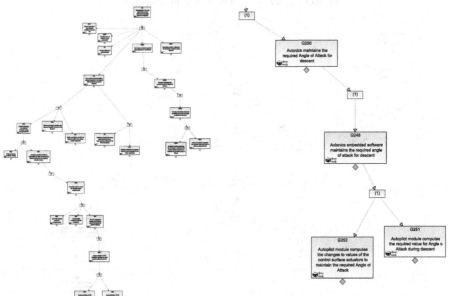

(c) Bird's eye view showing the result of a
traceability query applied to Fig. 4a.

(d) Goal and $\mathcal{C}$-nodes showing links from a
high-level requirement to software requirements for the avionics.

Fig. 4. GSN argument fragment for the Swift UAS, AQL query and the resulting view

(type **has** goal) and (attributes **has** regulation(14CFR23.73) or attributes **has** regulation(14CFR23.75))
or <isBelow>(attributes **has** regulation(14CFR23.73) or attributes **has** regulation(14CFR23.75))

(a) Query in AQL to locate references to regulatory requirements.

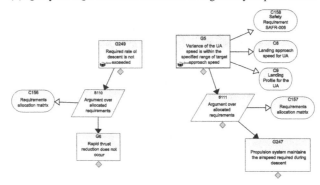

(b) View resulting from the query in Fig. 5a, showing disconnected argument structure fragments.

Fig. 5. AQL query and view showing those parts of the argument fragment of Fig. 4a referencing regulatory requirements

[isAbove] (not (type **has** goal or type **has** strategy) or <isAbove>(type **has** goal or
type **has** strategy or type **has** evidence)) and (<isAbove> type **has** evidence or type **has** evidence)

(a) AQL query using only structural references.

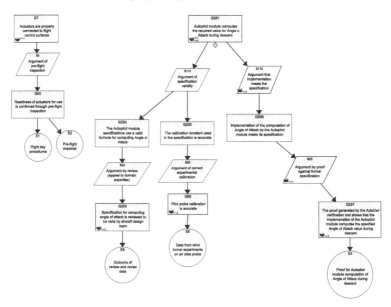

(b) View produced by applying the query in Fig. 6a to the fragment in Fig. 4a.

Fig. 6. Query and View: All nodes from which all paths lead to evidence

the AQL expression attributes **has** risk(severity(catastrophic), likelihood(remote)) in the query of Fig. 4b, we can generate a view (not shown here) of traceability to only those hazards whose likelihood of occurrence is remote, and whose severity is catastrophic.

Another query on the argument structure can be to identify those parts that address concerns from regulations, standards, and guidance documents. For example, Part 23 of the Federal Aviation Regulations (FARs) specifies requirements concerning aircraft performance during landing, e.g., approach speeds (14 CFR §23.73), the conditions to be met for accomplishing a safe landing within the required landing distance (14 CFR §23.75), etc. To formulate an appropriate query, first we locate all goal nodes with the attributes regulation(14CFR23.73) or regulation(14CFR23.75), using the grammar of Fig. 3. Then, to determine the extent to which the corresponding claims have been addressed in the argument, we locate those fragments whose roots are the located goal nodes and show the entire structure to highlight the relevant context, assumptions and justifications, if any, and the reasoning used. Fig. 5a and Fig. 5b show the relevant AQL query and its corresponding view respectively. From the latter, we can infer that there are claims in the structure that reference the regulatory requirements, but that they are yet to be fully developed. To determine the exact extent of how the regulations are met, an assessor could navigate to, and examine, the external documentation referenced from the nodes shown in the view.

Thus far, our queries have shown how we use simple combinations of structure and metadata to produce views that address domain specific scenarios: namely, establishing if and how some regulatory requirements have been addressed, and showing the traceability concerns that may be required by assurance standards. However, we can also use AQL to specify more complex queries that produce meaningful views and operate on the structure alone. One such example concerns querying for those fragments which are *completely developed*, i.e., all nodes from which all paths lead to an evidence node.

In fact, this query gives a way to determine the *internal completeness* of an argument structure from a purely structural standpoint. That is, the property that—assuming valid reasoning from premises to conclusions, and not considering the confidence needed to accept a claim/argument—there exists no claim (i.e., goal node) in the argument such that a path from it does not end in evidence. We specify this query in AQL as given in Fig. 6a, and the resulting view is shown in Fig. 6b. Thus, an argument structure that is identical to the view produced by applying this query is internally complete.

To understand this query (Fig. 6a), we include some basic notions for explanation purposes: An *end node* here is a goal or strategy with no goals or strategies beneath it, effectively making it the end of an *is supported by* chain. A *middle node* here is a node with goals or strategies beneath it; since only goals or strategies satisfy this condition, all middle nodes are goals or strategies). There are three types of nodes the query seeks to find: (i) end nodes that have some evidence node beneath them; (ii) middle nodes that only have other middle nodes and nodes of type (i) beneath them; (iii) the evidence nodes at the end of the argument. To express these three possibilities, we combine the three using the or operator, and simplify. Note that the simplification includes facts (expressed in AQL), e.g., an evidence node can never be above a goal.

Queries can also be used to identify parts of argument that, though complete, might not engender sufficient confidence. For example, goals associated with high risk may need to be supported by particular forms of evidence. We can then use an appropriate query to identify those argument fragments that do not meet these criteria.

6   Concluding Remarks

We have described a methodology and a formal foundation to query safety cases. Specifically, we have described how to enrich GSN argument structures with domain-specific metadata, and how to produce argument structure views by querying arguments using the Argument Query Language (AQL). We have implemented and tested a prototype of our query/view mechanism in our toolset, AdvoCATE. Using a fragment of the Swift UAS safety case argument structure as a driving example, we have demonstrated the creation of a simple set of domain concepts, its use in querying an argument, and how queries can produce specific perspectives on that argument.

The closest counterpart to our work proposes *multi-view safety cases* [14] and also operates on GSN argument structures. Here, a view is produced from, effectively, an *a priori* encoding of the elements of the argument that correspond to a specific, static, stakeholder viewpoint, e.g., a process view. In contrast, our notion of view is dynamic since it is determined upon evaluating the query applied to the argument structure. Queries have been used in safety-critical applications by [15], wherein *visual queries* are applied to *traceability information models* to show traceability. Our work is comparatively much broader in scope and considers a variety of queries (Section 2.2) including, and in addition to, traceability in safety assurance. For instance, a useful perspective to present during software approval would be showing, say, only the software aspects in an argument, or the software contributions to different hazards. We can specify these kinds of queries and generate the relevant views in a straightforward way.

Query languages exist for a variety of frameworks, e.g., databases, knowledge bases, ontologies, etc. For example, SQWRL [16] is an *ontology query language*, which offers richer logical expression than AQL (currently) does, but is more generic. PrQL [17] is a specialized *proof query language* with some similarities to AQL, though it targets a different domain. The data comprising a safety case, potentially, can be organized into a (relational) database and then queried. However, we are unaware of approaches/tools that either query argument structures in this manner, or are similar to ours.

We believe that our approach for querying safety cases can be useful to address stakeholder-specific concerns, and can help in argument comprehension by locating and displaying the relevant information of interest. However, we can do more to further improve the practical usefulness of our approach. For instance, currently we specify attributes through an interface in which the end-user relies on an external ontology or glossary of terms. We plan to integrate an ontology tool and *import* the relevant ontologies. In addition to enriching the underlying domain theory, we can enhance the query language in several ways: First, we can make several simple extensions to the atomic predicates on which the query language is built, e.g., distinguishing the different link types, *in context of* and *is supported by*. Next, a more significant extension would be the implementation of named queries, i.e., allowing queries (as opposed to views) to be saved to a library and referenced by name within other queries. This would greatly simplify the use of larger, more complex queries. We will also provide a range of useful library queries by default, e.g., finding undeveloped nodes. The current query/view mechanism is limited to the core GSN, and it works primarily on the argument structure. We intend to develop suitable interfaces to linked artifacts, which will allow us to query the entire assembly of artifacts comprising a safety case.

Acknowledgement. This work has been funded by the Assurance of Flight-Critical Systems element of the SSAT project in the Aviation Safety Program of NASA ARMD.

References

1. UK Ministry of Defence (MOD): The 'White Booklet': An Introduction to System Safety Management in the MOD. Issue 3 (January 2011)
2. Hawkins, R., Habli, I., Kelly, T.: Principled Construction of Software Safety Cases. In: 2013 SAFECOMP Workshops–Next Generation of System Assurance Approaches for Safety-Critical Systems (SASSUR) (September 2013)
3. Goal Structuring Notation Working Group: GSN Community Standard Version 1 (2011)
4. Denney, E., Habli, I., Pai, G.: Perspectives on Software Safety Case Development for Unmanned Aircraft. In: Proc. 42nd Annual IEEE/IFIP Intl. Conf. Dependable Systems and Networks (DSN 2012), pp. 1–8 (June 2012)
5. Bloomfield, R., Chozos, N., Embrey, D., Henderson, J., Kelly, T., Koornneef, F., Pasquini, A., Pozzi, S., Sujan, M., Cleland, G., Habli, I., Medhurst, J.: Evidence: Using Safety Cases in Industry and Healthcare. The Health Foundation (December 2012)
6. Denney, E., Pai, G., Pohl, J.: Heterogeneous Aviation Safety Cases: Integrating the Formal and the Non-formal. In: 17th IEEE Intl. Conf. Engineering of Complex Computer Systems (ICECCS), pp. 199–208 (July 2012)
7. EUROCONTROL: Preliminary Safety Case for ADS-B Airport Surface Surveillance Application. PSC ADS-B-APT (November 2011)
8. Denney, E., Pai, G., Pohl, J.: AdvoCATE: An Assurance Case Automation Toolset. In: Ortmeier, F., Daniel, P. (eds.) SAFECOMP Workshops 2012. LNCS, vol. 7613, pp. 8–21. Springer, Heidelberg (2012)
9. FAA: Software Approval Guidelines. FAA Order 8110.49 Chg 1 (September 2011)
10. U.S. Dept. of Transportation, FAA: Airworthiness Certification of Unmanned Aircraft Systems and Optionally Piloted Aircraft. FAA Order 8130.34B (November 2011)
11. Denney, E., Ippolito, C., Lee, R., Pai, G.: An Integrated Safety and Systems Engineering Methodology for Small Unmanned Aircraft Systems. In: Infotech@Aerospace. AIAA 2012-2572 (June 2012)
12. Denney, E., Pai, G.: A Formal Basis for Safety Case Patterns. In: Bitsch, F., Guiochet, J., Kaâniche, M. (eds.) SAFECOMP. LNCS, vol. 8153, pp. 21–32. Springer, Heidelberg (2013)
13. Denney, E., Pai, G., Whiteside, I.: Hierarchical Safety Cases. In: Brat, G., Rungta, N., Venet, A. (eds.) NFM 2013. LNCS, vol. 7871, pp. 478–483. Springer, Heidelberg (2013)
14. Flood, M., Habli, I.: Multi-view Safety Cases. In: 6th IET Intl. Conf. System Safety, pp. 1–6 (September 2011)
15. Maeder, P., Jones, P.L., Zhang, Y., Cleland-Huang, J.: Strategic Traceability for Safety-critical Projects. IEEE Software 30(3), 58–66 (2013)
16. O'Connor, M., Das, A.: SQWRL: A query language for OWL. In: Proc. 6th International Workshop on OWL: Experiences and Directions, OWLED 2009 (2009)
17. Aspinall, D., Denney, E., Lüth, C.: Querying proofs. In: 18th Intl. Conf. Logic for Programming Artificial Intelligence and Reasoning (2012)

Security Application of Failure Mode and Effect Analysis (FMEA)

Christoph Schmittner[1], Thomas Gruber[1], Peter Puschner[2], and Erwin Schoitsch[1]

[1] Austrian Institute of Technology, Safety & Security Department, Vienna, Austria
{christoph.schmittner.fl,thomas.gruber,
erwin.schoitsch}@ait.ac.at
[2] Vienna University of Technology, Department of Computer Engineering, Vienna, Austria
peter@vmars.tuwien.ac.at

Abstract. Increasingly complex systems lead to an interweaving of security, safety, availability and reliability concerns. Most dependability analysis techniques do not include security aspects. In order to include security, a holistic risk model for systems is needed. In our novel approach, the basic failure cause, failure mode and failure effect model known from FMEA is used as a template for a vulnerability cause-effect chain, and an FMEA analysis technique extended with security is presented. This represents a unified model for safety and security cause-effect analysis. As an example the technique is then applied to a distributed industrial measurement system.

Keywords: Safety analysis, security analysis, combined analysis, FMEA, vulnerabilities, cause effect chain for security.

1   Introduction

With interconnected and software intensive systems, availability and safety depend increasingly on security aspects. Threats to information security also threaten the availability or safety of a system [1]. Dependability of software intensive systems depends not only on the reliability of the used software but also on the security of the Information System. Information security is increasingly interwoven with all aspects of dependability [2]. Recent events like Stuxnet [1] or Duqu [2] demonstrated vulnerabilities in industrial or embedded IT-Systems. In order to remove or reduce these risks holistic analytical methods are necessary.

The Failure Mode and Effect Analysis (FMEA) is a structured technique which investigates failure modes and their effects. The aim is to identify potential weaknesses and improve reliability, availability or safety. A system or process is hierarchically decomposed into its basic elements and then the failure modes of the elements are examined for causes and effects [3]. FMEA was developed in the 1950s

---

[1] http://www.symantec.com/content/en/us/enterprise/media/security
_response/whitepapers/w32_stuxnet_dossier.pdf
[2] http://www.symantec.com/connect/w32_duqu_precursor_next_stuxnet

A. Bondavalli and F. Di Giandomenico (Eds.): SAFECOMP 2014, LNCS 8666, pp. 310–325, 2014.
© Springer International Publishing Switzerland 2014

by the US Department of Defense to improve the reliability of military equipment[4]. Originally, FMEA was aimed at the reliability or safety of hardware.

The failure modes and probabilities for hardware components are normally well known. Although failure modes of software are more complex and coupled with a certain degree of uncertainty, Reifer and others [5], [6] showed the benefits of performing a Software-FMEA (SFMEA). As explained in [7] when an SFMEA is performed early in the design phase of software, activities for verification and validation of software are easier to execute and a more focused use of development effort is possible.

This paper describes an approach for the combined analysis of safety and security. The basic FMEA concept is extended to include vulnerabilities and attacks concerning the security of a system. A unified cause and effect model allows examining the combined risks for a system. The following method for a Failure Mode, Vulnerabilities and Effects Analysis (FMVEA) enables the analysis of complex mission critical systems. Similar to a Software-FMEA the benefits are the easier verification and validation and the ability to focus the development effort on critical areas.

After an overview of the state of the art, chapter 3 describes the new method in detail. Chapter 4 tries to prove the applicability of the FMVEA based on an example. Finally, Chapter 5 discusses the limitations and gives an outlook on further work.

2   State of the Art

For safety, IEC 61508 [8] is the basic functional safety standard, which covers the complete safety life cycle. It describes techniques and procedures for analysis, realization and operation of safety critical systems. With respect to security, IEC 61508 Ed 2.0 (2010) contains only a few requirements: Security threats are to be considered during hazard analysis in the form of a security threat analysis (IEC 61508, Part 1, 7.4.2.3). The ISO/IEC 27000-series describes best-practices advice for information security management. They consider classic security-critical systems such as databases, servers and corporate networks. Nevertheless, we use the terms as they are defined in the ISO/IEC 27000-series for this publication and those from IEC 61508 for safety.

Although IEC 62443 "Network and system security for industrial-process measurement and control" [9] is partially aimed at industrial security, safety concerns are outside its scope.

Summarizing, a standards review shows that critical control systems have been treated by well-established safety-standards for many years, while most available security standards aim at business applications with few exceptions. The analyzed effects and causes are, indeed, different in safety and security. So, what is definitively missing is a standard which considers both safety and security equally. Without a combined approach, there is a risk to miss critical and undesirable events: Security vulnerabilities which potentially lead to safety critical events could be overlooked.

In [10] FMEA was used for the dependability analysis of web services. The approach was based on a high level design FMEA. We propose here to extend the functional FMEA [11] in order to base the analysis on a functional system model. This enables a model based analysis of all the functions at the considered abstraction level.

In addition, we propose a generic set of security based failure modes (named threat modes), based on [12] and explain the correlations between the threat modes and the system quality attributes [13]. Generic threat modes allow anticipating potential threats first, assess the consequences and then identify potential causes.

3   FMVEA Concept

The basic approach to carry out an FMEA is described in IEC 60812. Based on this description, the flow chart includes the following steps.

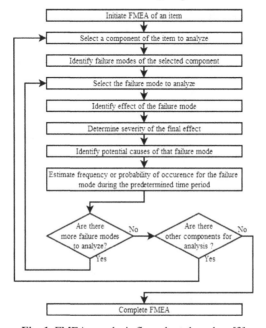

Fig. 1. FMEA - analysis flow chart, based on [3]

A system is divided into components, and failure modes for each component are identified. For each failure mode the effects, the severity of the final effect on the system and potential causes are examined. As far as possible, frequency or probability of the failure modes are estimated.

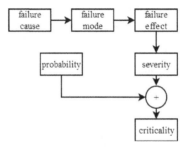

Fig. 2. FMEA - cause-effect chain

The cause-effect chain analyzed with an FMEA is shown in Figure 2. Each failure mode has a failure cause, and each failure effect is associated with a failure mode that causes the effect. A failure effect leads to an unintended scenario. The severity describes the significance of the scenario. The frequency relates to failure cause and effect, and it describes how likely the event is.

Definitions according to IEC 60812 [3]:
- **Failure cause:** why did the item fail
- **Failure mode:** manner in which an item fails
- **Failure effect:** consequence of a failure mode in terms of the operation, function or status of the item
- **Failure severity:** significance or grading of the failure mode's effect on item operation, on the item surrounding, or on the item operator; failure mode effect severity as related to the defined boundaries of the analyzed system
- **Failure criticality:** combination of the severity of an effect and the frequency of its occurrence or other attributes of a failure as a measure of the need for addressing and mitigation

To include security in the analysis, a comparable cause-effect chain is necessary. It is possible to divide security-critical events into similar steps. The suggested parts of a security cause-effect chain are the following elements.
- Vulnerabilities
- Threat Agent
- Threat Mode
- Threat Effect
- Attack Probability

3.1   Vulnerabilities

The essential precondition for a successful security breach of a system is a weak spot or vulnerability. A vulnerability is comparable to a failure cause and represents the basic prerequisite in security. ISO/IEC 27002 defines vulnerability as "a weakness of an asset or group of assets that can be exploited by a threat" [14]. For information security ISO/IEC 27005 [15] divides vulnerabilities into categories:
- Hardware vulnerabilities
- Software vulnerabilities
- Network vulnerabilities

Additional vulnerability classifications are the Microsoft Security Development Lifecycle (SDL) [16] and the CWE[3] (Common Weakness Enumeration). The CWE is a detailed and community-developed list of common software weaknesses.
Figure 3 shows an overview of a possible categorization based on ISO/IEC 27005 [15].

---

[3] http://cwe.mitre.org/data/index.html

Following a top-down approach, vulnerabilities at a lower design level get more specific. The list is non-exhaustive. For software vulnerabilities the CWE lists additional software weakness types.

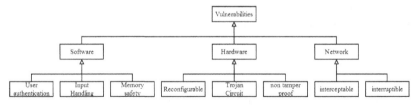

Fig. 3. Classification of vulnerabilities

Vulnerabilities can be located at network, hardware and software level. Hardware vulnerabilities are especially a challenge for security engineering if parts of the embedded systems are employed in a potentially not trustworthy environment. In addition, hardware could generally be equipped with additional malicious components [17]. Reconfigurable means a microcontroller is reprogrammable. This could be because one step in the commissioning process has not been executed. With not tamper proof hardware, an attacker could access hardware components and execute direct attacks on the hardware.

If an attacker (= *threat agent*) exploits a vulnerability, the security of the system is at risk. Vulnerabilities without a threat agent do not lead to an effect and have a negligible risk attached. A threat agent is a necessary extension for the safety cause-effect chain.

3.2   Threat Agents

Threat agents represent the active element which is trying to exploit the vulnerability. Examples for possible threat agents are hacker, computer criminals, terrorists, industrial espionage or insiders [15]. For now, inmate threat agents like viruses are not considered.

The closest corresponding element in safety would be the random event that causes an element to fail. In contrast to the random element a threat agent has a motivation and an objective. Table 1 lists different threat agents with objectives and characteristics.

Table 1. Threat agents, based on [15]

Threat agent	Objective / Aim	Characteristic
Hacker, Cracker	Challenge, Ego, Rebellion, Status, Money	Limited resources Random attacker
Computer criminal	Destruction of information, Illegal information disclosure, Monetary gain, Unauthorized data alteration	Monetarily motivated
Terrorist	Blackmail, Destruction, Exploitation, Revenge, Political Gain, Media Coverage	Ideologically motivated
Industrial espionage	Competitive advantage, Economic espionage	Purposeful attacker
Insiders	Curiosity, Ego, Intelligence, Monetary gain, Revenge, Unintentional errors and omissions	Internal knowledge Easy access

3.3   Threat Mode

Threat mode classifies the way in which vulnerabilities are exploited. Vulnerabilities can be exploited in various ways, each with different effects and prerequisites. Potential threat modes depend on the system and on the capabilities of the threat agent. Threat modes can be simple like jamming a connection or elaborate operations such as exploiting an injection flaw vulnerability, which requires access to the input system and sending an exactly formulated input signal. In general, this can be mapped to a violation of a security attribute.

The mapping of security attribute to system quality attribute varies for each individual system. Depending on the system, every threat mode could affect any dependability attribute (Reliability, Availability, Maintainability, and Safety) - or not.

A common model for the categorization of threats is STRIDE [18]. As described in Table 2, an exploited vulnerability leads to one of the following generic effects.

Table 2. Threat modes

Threat mode	Description	Violated security attribute (generic effect)
Spoofing identity	Accessing a system, disguised as another actor	Authenticity
Tampering with Data	Unauthorized modification of data	Integrity
Repudiation	Actions can be assigned to one actor	Non-repudiation
Information disclosure	Accessing restricted data	Confidentiality
Denial of Service	Restricting or preventing access to a service or function	Availability
Elevation of privilege	Actors may perform actions with a higher authority level	Authenticity

A threat mode is similar to the failure mode of safety and describes the manner in which the security fails.

For a classification of threat and failure modes the approach described in [19] could be used. Different properties of failure modes are described and sorted.

3.4   Threat Effect

Similar to the failure effect in safety the threat effect is the consequence in terms of the operation, function or status. While the threat mode characterizes the violated security attribute, the threat effect describes the violated system quality attribute [13]. Violated attributes are not limited to security. All dependability attributes may be affected. Which attribute is actually violated in a particular case depends on the system, its environment and the operational state.

3.5   Attack Probability

In order to assess the criticality of a security attack, severity and probability of the attack needs to be evaluated. While the severity can be assessed with the help of domain experts, probability is defined differently for safety and security.

For a safety based event the probability describes the probability of failure of hardware or software. For a security based element the attack probability describes the probability of the threat agent to accomplish the threat effect. This depends not only on the threat agent itself but also on system properties and the system environment. If a system is not connected to a public network and located in a restricted area, a successful attack is relatively improbable. In addition to the technical probability of an attack, each threat agent has different motivating factors and capabilities. Capabilities are an umbrella term for financial resources and knowledge or possibly other resources of the threat agent used to exploit the vulnerability. Motivation and capabilities characterize the threat agent and their *sum* constitutes the *threat properties*.

- Motivation (1 = opportunity target, 2 = mildly interested, 3 = main target)
- Capabilities   (1 = low, 2 = medium, 3 = high)

In addition to the properties of the threat agent, different system properties influence the probability of an attack. Reachability is characterized by a number between 1 and 3 and describes how easy it is to connect to the system. Examples for reachability 3 are systems which are directly connected to the internet and discoverable with tools like SHODAN[4]. If a system is not directly connected to the internet but accessible by an internet connected network, then it is assigned reachability 2. Systems with no network connection at all have reachability 1.

In addition to reachability, another factor that describes the susceptibility of a system is the unusualness of its components and architectures. It can be assumed that potential threat agents have less knowledge about unusual systems and the effort to find flaws and exploit them is higher. The *sum* of both properties characterizes the *system susceptibility*.

- Reachability (1 = no network, 2 = private network, 3 = public network)
- Unusualness (1 = restricted, 2 = commercially available, 3 = standard)

The combination of *system susceptibility* and *threat properties* for attack probability is influenced by the DREAD Risk assessment model [12] and the OWASP Likelihood assessment method. Like in the DREAD approach, we estimate the probability by summing up system susceptibility and threat property values. In combination, the four properties allow a semi-quantitative assessment of the probability.

It should be noted that the probability table lacks a calibration with the failure probability in order to introduce it in a common safety and security method.

While this approach should bring reasonable results, the results are based on an assumption about attack frequency and not on empirical data. In order to get better estimates for frequency or probability, empirical values for attack probabilities for

---

[4] SHODAN is a search engine for internet connected SCADA systems.

Table 3. Estimation table for attack probability

System Susceptibility	2	3	4	5	6
6	8	9	10	11	12
5	7	8	9	10	11
4	6	7	8	9	10
3	5	6	7	8	9
2	4	5	6	7	8
	2	3	4	5	6	Threat properties

different systems could be useful. Since security for industrial information systems is a relatively new area there is not much empirical data. Besides historical incident data, different projects try to collect information about attack probability [20]. To gather information about attack probability or frequency, honeypot systems are used. A honeypot is a closely monitored decoy system which acts as a trap for potential threats. In a research experiment from Trend Micro Inc. three different honeypot systems were used [21]. One was a simulated water supply facility with connected pumps and purification systems running on Apache web server. For the next setup an internet connected programmable logic controller (PLC) was set up to imitate a temperature controller in a factory which had temperature, fan speed, and light settings. The last Honeypot Setup was a server running PLC control software and a web server to imitate a human machine interface (HMI) connected to a PLC.

Trend Micro Inc. concentrated on planned and targeted attacks and integrated measures like firewalls in order to filter automated "drive-by" attacks. In the first 28 days of the experiment 39 attacks were reported [21]. Unfortunately no long-term study for industrial information systems is known at this time. Therefore all results should be taken with a pinch of salt. They may help in estimating the magnitude of threats but for now they shouldn't be used as valid numbers for quantitative analysis. But in the future both approaches will yield better estimations for attack probability. In any case, probability and frequency of successful attacks my change over time depending on the evolution of methods, the increase of knowledge about control and protection systems, and other causes. Therefore, security measures have a much shorter lifetime than safety measures and need unfortunately more frequent updates.

3.6   FMVEA Cause-Effect Chain

With the single components for a security cause-effect chain described in the previous sections, we are able to generate a combined cause-effect chain for safety and security. The combined approach includes safety and security causes for a negative effect on system quality attributes.

The extended flow chart for an FMVEA in Figure 5, includes security in the analysis. As described in [1] there are different ways in which security or safety properties of a system can influence security or safety risks. Therefore, while the consideration of failure or threat modes of an item is split, the analysis of effects and causes combines both viewpoints.

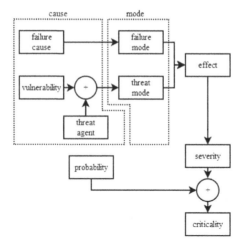

Fig. 4. FMEVA – cause-effect chain

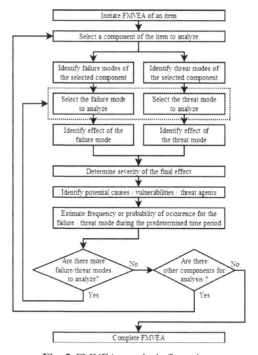

Fig. 5. FMVEA - analysis flow chart

4   Example Application of the FMVEA

As an example, an engine test stand in an industrial plant is analyzed. The engine test stand consists of one or more measurement devices with smart maintenance features. The measuring devices are configurable for different engines. The measurement and configuration data should be only locally readable and writeable. For maintenance, lifetime data (= device conditions) is stored on the measurement device. The device itself can check its conditions in order to schedule maintenance activity. The device conditions can also be checked from a remote side. In order to check the conditions remotely the measurement devices are directly connected to a public network like GSM. Mission statement for the system is: Dependable measurements of different systems

4.1   Functional Analysis

In order to get the individual components, a functional analysis [22] at system level is conducted. Useful results for the FMVEA of a functional analysis are the functional tree, the functions / device matrix and the connection matrix. The functional tree (see Figure 6) identifies the functions of the system based on the mission statement.

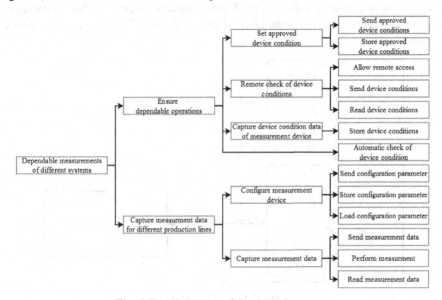

Fig. 6. Functional tree of the example system

Table 4. Functions / Device Matrix

Functions		Devices		
		Measurement Device	Local HMI	Backend System
	Perform measurement	X		
	Send measurement data	X		
	Read measurement data		X	
	Send configuration parameter		X	
	Store configuration parameter	X		
	Load configuration parameter	X		
	Send approved device conditions		X	
	Store approved device conditions	X		
	Store device condition	X		
	Allow remote access	X		
	Send device conditions	X		
	Read device conditions			X
	Automatic check of device conditions	X		

The functions / device matrix (see Table 4) maps the system functions to physical devices. In our example, the system consists of Measurement Devices, the Local HMI and the Backend System.

With the connection matrix (see Figure 7), necessary connections between devices are identified and marked with "x".

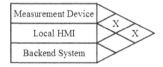

Fig. 7. Connection Matrix

The analyzed system (see Figure 8 for a system overview) has connections between Measurement Device and Local HMI and between Measurement Device and Backend System.

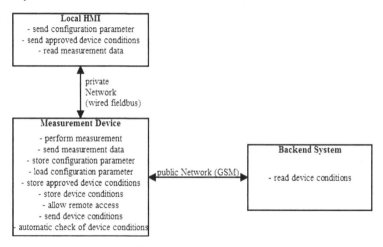

Fig. 8. System overview

4.2   Failure and Vulnerability Analysis

The system is analyzed according to the flowchart of Figure 5. The first chosen component is the measurement device. In order to identify potential threat modes the generic threat modes from STRIDE [18] are used. Applying the general concept of "spoofing of identity" to the Measurement Devices, a potential threat mode is that an attacker masks himself as the measurement device and communicates with other devices.

FMVEA Table. Table 5 shows a short excerpt from the FMVEA table for the described system.

Table 5. FMVEA example

	ID	Vulnerability	Threat mode	Threat effect	System status	System effect	Severity	System susceptibility	Threat properties	Attack probability
measurement device	1	No device verification, man in the middle attack with physical access to measurement device or connection	Attacker is pretending to be the measurement device	send false measurement data	Normal operation	System is no longer reliable	Critical	4	Insider: 4	8
									Hacker: 3	7
	2	GSM connection, Base station emulation, man in the middle attack	Attacker is pretending to be the measurement device	send false device condition data	Remote query of device status	System is no longer available (unnecessary maintenance)	Marginal	5	Insider: 4	9
									Hacker: 3	8
	3	GSM connection, Base station emulation, man in the middle attack	Attacker is pretending to be the measurement device	intercept user credentials	Remote query of device status	System integrity is hurt	Insignificant	5	Insider: 4	9
									Hacker: 3	8
	4	No device verification, man in the middle attack with physical access to measurement device or connection	Attacker is pretending to be the measurement device	Intercept configuration changes	Configuration change	System is unreliable and potentially unsafe	Catastrophic	4	Insider: 4	8
									Hacker: 3	7

In the following section, the elements of the table are explained in detail. If an ID is used it refers to the ID column.

Threat Mode:

- The Attacker is pretending to be the measurement device. Spoofing of identity attacks only work at connected devices and for functions with a communication aspect. Potential effects are submitting wrong measurement data, submitting wrong device condition data, intercepting user credentials or blocking out configuration changes.

Threat Effects:

1. The attacker is able to send false measurement data to the Local HMI. This leads to wrong measurements and an unreliable system.

2. While the Backend System executes a remote query of the device conditions, the attacker is able to send wrong device conditions. If the sent device conditions are worse than reality, unnecessary maintenance is

caused. If the sent device conditions are better than reality, a defect of a Measurement Device may remain undetected.

3. While the backend system tries to login on the Measurement Device an attacker disguised as the Measurement Device is able to intercept the login credentials. This may cause no direct severe consequences but it hurts system integrity and enables a malicious user to access the measurement device.

4. The attacker intercepts configuration data and acknowledges the configuration change to the Local HMI. If multiple measurement devices are employed for one test stand different configurations could lead to inconsistent and incompatible demands

Severity:

For the severity assessment, the classification from IEC 61812 was used. This classification does not include privacy as a factor, only consequences for the dependability are considered.

1. Wrong measurement data means that the reliability of the whole measurement system is endangered. The attacker has the choice to send positive data for bad devices or negative data for good devices. This could lead to an increased rate of misproduction or to an increased liability for defective products. (Severity = critical)

2. Submitting of wrong device condition data. While wrong device condition data does not directly influence the measurement data, the attacker could use it to trigger or delay maintenance. A prematurely triggered maintenance reduces the availability of the whole system. While an early maintenance leads to production downtime, it does not endanger the quality of the products. (Severity = marginal)

3. Intercepted login credentials could be used as a first step enabling further attacks. But they do not cause immediate danger to dependability attributes. (Severity = insignificant)

4. Different configuration on measurement devices could lead to a potentially dangerous situation[5]. Incompatible demands and commands on the engine under test could potentially destroy the engine and the test stand. (Severity = catastrophic)

Vulnerabilities:

Different vulnerabilities can give an attacker the opportunity to masquerade as a Measurement Device. In order to pose for the Backend System, an attacker could exploit vulnerabilities in the connection between these devices and conduct a man-in-the-middle attack.

---

[5] The engine test stand is able to test lubrication in curves. For this the engine is tilted. If a measurement device performs other measuring cycles at this time the engine and the test stand could be destroyed.

1&2. The attacker could exploit flaws in the GSM connection and intercept the GSM connection with his own fake base station [23] (= "International Mobile Subscriber Identity (IMSI) catcher"). After this, any communication between Backend System and Measurement Device will be routed via his system.

3&4. In order to pretend to be the Measurement Device in a connection with the Local HMI physical access to the device or the connection is necessary. This reduces potential threat agents to insiders or intruding attackers. Then the attacker could integrate his own device in the communication or intercept and replay commands. Most field buses have negligible security features or none at all; if an attacker achieves physical access to it, this part of the system is endangered. Possible solutions would be a change to a protocol with integrated security features or a physical protection of the connection.

Probability:
Attack probability depends not only on the attacked system element but also on the attacker. In order to quantify threat properties two different threat agents are described:

- Insider: Inside attacks are among to the most dangerous attacks. While they may not have hacking experience they have knowledge of the system and easy access to critical elements of a system. In addition they are highly determined and focused on their target.
  - o Motivation (3 = main target)
  - o Capabilities (1 = low)
  - o Threat Properties: 4

- Hacker: Hacker describes a person who seeks and exploits weaknesses in different information systems. While they are motivated by a multitude of factors and mostly don't aim to cause direct harm their action may have negative consequences. They have good technological knowledge and other resources useful for an attack.
  - o Motivation (1 = opportunity target)
  - o Capabilities (2 = medium)
  - o Threat Properties: 3

For a spoofing threat mode the attacker needs to target a connection. In case of the Measurement Device a threat agent could either aim at the GSM connection between Measurement Device and Backend System or at the internal connection between Measurement Device and Local HMI.

- GSM connection: While a GSM connection is not that common for non-commercial applications components are commercially available. As a wireless connection a GSM connection is publicly accessible.
  - o Reachability of the system (3 = public network)
  - o Unusualness (2 = commercially available)
  - o System Susceptibility: 5

- Internal connection: internal connections are not publicly accessible and best described as a private network. Most fieldbus systems are not common for non-commercial applications but components are commercially available.
  - o Reachability of the system (2 = private network)
  - o Unusualness (2 = commercially available)
  - o System Susceptibility: 4

5   Limitations and Further Work

Similar to the SFMEA a FMVEA is best suited for a qualitative high level analysis of a system in the early design phases. A general limitation of the failure mode and effects analysis is the restriction to analyze only single causes of an effect. Because of this some multi-stage attacks could be overlooked. This concern could be particularly relevant for security event chains, if several systems have to be compromised in order to reach a target system. Recent developments in combining FTA with Attack-Trees for a combined analysis could support a FMVEA in considering all security risks [24].

Further research is also needed to achieve a reliable assessment of the risk related to security concerns. Especially proven data for attack probability or frequency is needed. This would allow a calibration of the criticality of security threats in order to obtain results comparable with safety criticality. The semi-quantitative approach which distinguishes four factors for probability, split into system and attacker properties which influence attack probability is only a first approach to tackle this challenge. The attacker properties also only works for human threat agents, approaches to include inmate threat agents need further research.

Acknowledgment. The work presented in this paper has been supported by the European Commission through the FP7 Joint Technology Initiatives (Call ARTEMIS-2012-1, Project Arrowhead, Grant Agreement Number 332987).

References

1. Dong-bo Pan, F.L.: Influence between Safety and Security. In: 2nd IEEE Conference on Industrial Electronics and Applications, ICIEA 2007, pp. 1323–1325 (2007)
2. Lautieri, S.: De-risking safety [military safety systems]. Computing and Control Engineering 17, 38–41 (2006)
3. IEC 60812: Analysis Techniques for System Reliability – Procedure for Failure Mode and Effects Analysis (FMEA). International Electrotechnical Commission
4. MIL-P-1629: Procedures for Performing a failure mode, effects and Criticality analysis. Department of Defense (US)
5. Reifer, D.J.: Software Failure Modes and Effects Analysis. IEEE Transactions on Reliability 28(3), 247–249 (1979)
6. Jacob, N.J.S., Stadler, J.: Software Failure Modes and Effects Analysis. In: 2013 Proceedings-Annual Reliability and Maintainability Symposium (RAMS), pp. 1–5 (2013)
7. Haapanen Pentti, H.A.: Failure Mode and Effects Analysis of Software-Based Automation Systems. STUK-Y TO-TR-19 0, vol. 2, p. 2 (August 2002)

8. IEC 61508, Functional Safety of Electrical/Electronic/Programmable Electronic Safety-related Systems (E/E/PE, or E/E/PES). International Electrotechnical Commission (2010)
9. IEC 62443: Industrial communication networks - Network and system security. International Electrotechnical Commission
10. Gorbenko, A., Kharchenko, V., Tarasyuk, O., Furmanov, A.: F(I)MEA-technique of web services analysis and dependability ensuring. In: Butler, M., Jones, C.B., Romanovsky, A., Troubitsyna, E. (eds.) Rigorous Development of Complex Fault-Tolerant Systems. LNCS, vol. 4157, pp. 153–167. Springer, Heidelberg (2006)
11. Haapanen, P., Helminen, A.: Failure mode and effects analysis of software-based automation systems. In: Radiation and Nuclear Safety Authority, Helsinki, Finland (2002)
12. Frank Swiderski, W.S.: Threat Modeling. Microsoft Press (2004)
13. Laprie, J.-C.: Dependable Computing: Concepts, Limits, Challenges. Digest of Papers FTCS-15, 2–11 (1985)
14. ISO/IEC:27002: Information technology - security techniques - Code of practice for information security management. International Organization for Standardization (ISO), International Electrotechnical Commission (IEC)
15. ISO/IEC 27005, Information technology — Security techniques — Information security risk management. International Organization for Standardization (ISO), International Electrotechnical Commission, IEC (2008)
16. Microsoft, "Security Development Lifecycle," Microsoft (2010)
17. Tehranipoor, M., Koushanfar, F.: A survey of hardware Trojan taxonomy and detection (2009)
18. Shostack., A., Lambert., S., Ostwald., T., Hernan, S.: Uncover Security Design Flaws Using The STRIDE Approach. MSDN Magazine (2006)
19. Powell, D., Stroud, R., et al.: Conceptual model and architecture of MAFTIA. Technical Report Series-University of Newcastle Upon Tyne Computing Science (2003)
20. Eric Byres, J.L.: The Myths and Facts behind Cyber Security Risks for Industrial Control Systems. British Columbia Institute of Technology (2004)
21. Wilhoit, K.: Who's Really Attacking Your ICS Equipment. Trend Micro Incorporated (2013)
22. Viola, N., Corpino, S., Stesina, F., Fioriti, M.: Functional Analysis in Systems Engineering: methodology and applications (2012)
23. Meyer, U., Wetzel, S.: On the impact of GSM encryption and man-in-the-middle attacks on the security of interoperating GSM/UMTS networks. In: 15th IEEE International Symposium on Personal, Indoor and Mobile Radio Communications, PIMRC 2004, vol. 4, pp. 2876–2883 (2004)
24. Steiner, M., Liggesmeyer, P.: Combination of Safety and Security Analysis - Finding Security Problems That Threaten The Safety of a System. In: SAFECOMP 2013 - Workshop DECS (ERCIM/EWICS Workshop on Dependable Embedded and Cyber-physical Systems) of the 32nd International Conference on Computer Safety, Reliability and Security (2013)

Safety and Security Interactions Modeling Using the BDMP Formalism: Case Study of a Pipeline

Siwar Kriaa[1,2], Marc Bouissou[1,2], Frederic Colin[1],
Yoran Halgand[1], and Ludovic Pietre-Cambacedes[1]

[1] Electricité de France (EDF) R&D
[2] Ecole Centrale Paris
{siwar.kriaa,frederic-ep.colin,yoran.halgand,
ludovic.pietre-cambacedes}@edf.fr, marc.bouissou@ecp.fr

Abstract. The digitalization of industrial control systems (ICS) raises several security threats that can endanger the safety of the critical infrastructures supervised by such systems. This paper presents an analysis method that enables the identification and ranking of risks leading to a safety issue, regardless of the origin of those risks: accidental or due to malevolence. This method relies on a modeling formalism called BDMP (Boolean logic Driven Markov Processes) that was initially created for safety studies, and then adapted to security. The use of the method is first illustrated on a simple case to show how it can be used to make decisions in a situation where security requirements are in conflict with safety requirements. Then it is applied to a realistic industrial system: a pipeline and its instrumentation and control system in order to highlight possible interactions between safety and security.

Keywords: Safety, security, interdependencies, modeling, industrial control systems.

1 Introduction

Modern industrial control systems are becoming increasingly complex and interconnected due to the integration of new information and communication technologies. The remote supervision and control of infrastructures means that these control systems are increasingly connected to external networks. Moreover, the migration towards standard communication protocols such as TCP/IP and the use of off the shelf components enables cost reduction, faster deployment and provides more flexibility. This radical transformation of control systems however introduces many security-related vulnerabilities such as software design flaws or vulnerabilities in publicly available protocols; that may endanger the overall infrastructure safety.

Safety and security risks converge when industrial infrastructures are supervised and controlled by digital control systems such as SCADA systems. It is consequently important to consider possible interdependencies between safety and security for a complete risk assessment and management. Typically we are interested in demonstrating how security issues impact safety and vice versa.

A. Bondavalli and F. Di Giandomenico (Eds.): SAFECOMP 2014, LNCS 8666, pp. 326–341, 2014.
© Springer International Publishing Switzerland 2014

In this paper, we propose to model safety and security interdependencies for an industrial case study using the Boolean logic Driven Markov Processes (BDMP) formalism. The approach used in this paper was first introduced in [12] where it was illustrated on a pedagogical use case. In this paper we apply it on a realistic industrial case study taking into account the system architecture. We discuss in Section 2 the convergence of security and safety issues in industrial control systems and their possible interdependencies. We give in Section 3 an overview of the BDMP formalism and the associated KB3 platform. We explain in Section 4 the benefits of BDMP on a simple example where safety and security are in contradiction. We provide in Section 5 the description of a pipeline case study architecture, the associated BDMP model and give qualitative and quantitative results obtained from it. Section 6 concludes the paper and introduces future work.

2 Safety and Security Interdependencies in ICS

2.1 Scope and Definitions

Safety and security can have different meanings according to the context and the technical communities; for instance safety is not defined in the same manner in the aerospace and nuclear communities. Consequently, it is important to clarify the signification of these terms in each context to avoid ambiguities. The SEMA referential proposed in [16] enables to frame the use of the terms "safety" and "security" based on two distinctions: System vs. Environment (S-E) and Malicious vs. Accidental (M-A). The first distinction is based on the origin of the threat or event leading to the considered risk and what it impacts (whether risk originates in the system and impacts the environment or vice-versa). The second distinction defines the nature of the threat or event giving birth to the considered risk, whether it is malicious or accidental. A system to system dimension is added to complete the coverage. In the frame of this paper, security is related to risks originating from or exacerbated by malicious intent, independently from the nature of the related consequence, whereas safety addresses accidental ones, i.e. without malicious intent, but with potential impacts on the system environment.

2.2 Related Work

In the literature, many authors raise awareness about the new security risks introduced by digitalized control systems and their potential impact on critical infrastructures safety in different industrial areas: aerospace [1], automotive [7], rail [17], building [10], energy [3]. These risks are also considered in emerging and dedicated industrial standards, like the IEC 64443 international standards series.

Historically separated, safety and security have long been treated by two different communities and with different methodologies. The need for a common framework integrating both safety and security issues is today becoming urgent with the increasing number of cyber-attacks targeting critical infrastructures. A common framework was addressed by Eames and Moffet in 1999 [4]. Much research has recently been carried-out triggering multiple cross-fertilizations between the two domains [13] but also several new approaches that propose to combine safety and security analysis in risk assessment [10,9,18,12,6].

2.3   Types of Safety and Security Interdependencies

In the literature some papers [4,10] outline possible interactions between safety and security requirements that can be either synergies or conflicts. In [12], Pietre-Cambacedes identifies four kinds of interdependencies:

- Conditional dependency: fulfillment of security requirements conditions safety or vice-versa;
- Mutual reinforcement: safety requirements or measures contribute to security, or vice-versa. Such situations enable resources optimization and cost reduction;
- Antagonism: safety and security requirements or measures lead, when considered together, to conflicting situations (cf. example in Section 4.1);
- Independence: no interaction.

These four kinds of relationship will be the basis of our study in the sequel.

3   Presentation of the BDMP Formalism and the KB3 Modeling Platform

The BDMP formalism enables graphical modeling of safety [2] and security [11,14,15,8]. BDMP models integrating both aspects are introduced in [12]. Visually similar to fault trees (or attack trees), BDMP provide good readability and a hierarchical representation. BDMP model the different combinations of events (leaves of the tree) that lead to the top event (system failure/damage). Additionally BDMP enable dynamical modeling with a special type of link called a "trigger". Each basic event of a BDMP is associated with two distinct Markov processes corresponding to two possible modes of the basic event. The mode chosen for a given leaf at a given instant depends on the realization of other leaves, which is modeled with triggers (see example in Section 4.1). BDMP have interesting mathematical properties enabling an efficient processing for BDMP that specify Markov processes with very large state spaces [2]. The relevance of using Markov processes for security modeling is discussed in [11].

The KB3 platform [14] enables to input graphically BDMP models and generates textual models (in the Figaro modeling language) describing them. These latter are used as input to the KB3 quantification tools (FigSeq and Yams) in order to compute the probability of the top event and the different possible scenarios leading to it, sorted by decreasing contribution to the top event probability.

Table 1. Basic BDMP leaves for safety modeling

Representation	Modeled behavior
	This leaf is used to model a failure in operation, when the modeled component is active. Failure occurs after a time exponentially distributed (parameter λ) and can also be repaired in a time exponentially distributed (parameter μ).
	This leaf is used to model a failure on demand, likely to arise instantaneously when the leaf changes of mode (activated or not), with a probability γ. Failure can be repaired in a time exponentially distributed (parameter μ).

Table 2. Basic BDMP leaves for security modeling

Representation	Modeled behavior
	The "Attacker Action" (AA) leaf models an attacker's step towards the realization of his/her objective. In Idle mode, the action has not yet been tried. Active mode corresponds to attempts with a time to success exponentially distributed with a parameter λ. The Mean Time To Success (MTTS) for this action is equal to $1/\lambda$.
	"Instantaneous Security Event" (ISE) leaf models a security event that can happen instantaneously with a probability γ when the leaf switches from the Idle mode to the Active mode.

BDMP are used in the process of risk evaluation. Thanks to extensions described in [15], BDMP also allow detection and reaction modeling. We illustrate is Section 5 this ability and its utility to optimize the choice of countermeasures against attacks.

The details of the formal definition of BDMP are given in [15]. For reference, we show in Tab. 1 and Tab. 2 the main leaves used to build the BDMP models in the following and the behavior they model.

Besides the classical links used to connect a gate to its sons (represented as solid black lines), BDMP contain two special kinds of links described in Tab. 3.

BDMP have advantages both for building models and processing them. They are hierarchical, which means that in order to build a BDMP, the analyst starts from a high level of abstraction and progressively refines into detail levels. Abstraction is a fundamental mechanism used by the human mind for dealing with complexity. At each step in the reasoning (i.e. at each construction of a gate), the number of manipulated elements is small enough to reduce the possibility of errors. This process is also traceable, which implies that a model can easily be reviewed and checked, looking for potential incompleteness.

Table 3. Special links used in BDMP models

Representation	Modeled behavior
– – – – ➤	Defines the dynamic aspect of BDMP. The element pointed by the trigger link is not activated until the realization of the origin gate/leaf of the trigger. When this element becomes activated, it transmits the activation signal it receives from its parents to the sub-tree targeted by the trigger.
– – – – – ➤	Creates a constraint in the order of realization of instantaneous events (on-demand failure leaves), in the case where they are required simultaneously.

The processing of BDMP is facilitated by the concept of "relevant events". The transition from false to true of a leaf (due to accidental failure or attack success) is said to be relevant if it changes the distribution of the instant where the top event will be realized. BDMP use a trimming mechanism of irrelevant events that considerably reduces the number of sequences explored by FigSeq and makes the explored sequences more interesting qualitatively (all the events listed in sequences are relevant). This concept and its advantages are described in details in the seminal paper on BDMP [2].

4   Illustration of Safety and Security Interdependencies

We propose in this section to show the importance of considering together security and safety aspects for an accurate risk evaluation and for decision-making in system design or exploitation.

4.1   Example of an Antagonism

We consider a person being at home and choosing whether to keep the house door locked or unlocked. When considering fire hazard and for safety reasons the door must be kept unlocked in order to facilitate evacuation. However, when considering potential attacks and for security reasons the door must be kept locked. This example is similar to the case of the exit door addressed by the literature in [19,4,5].

The undesirable event of our use case is some form of harm to the person, called later *person integrity affected*. We start our study by making a pure safety analysis considering only accidental events. The person can be harmed if a fire is accidentally initiated in the house and it is impossible for him to escape as the door is initially locked and the person cannot open it (lock blocked, keys not found). The BDMP given in Fig. 1 models this scenario. Here the *door locked* leaf corresponds to an instantaneous event which can happen with a probability of 0.5. The two triggers define the dependencies between the events associated to the leaves. When the *fire* leaf becomes true it creates, thanks to the first trigger, a mode change for the leaf *door locked*. Consequently, the latter can either stay false or switch to the true value (with probability of 0.5 for each alternative). If the *door locked* leaf becomes true it creates in turn a mode change for the leaf *door impossible to open*. According to the same mechanism, this leaf can instantly either remain false or take the value true. With this model, it is possible to see that the top event can never happen if the door is unlocked (i.e. when *door locked* takes the value false).

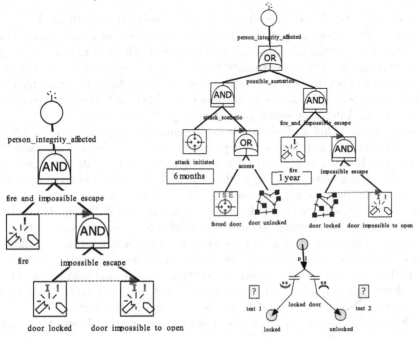

Fig. 1. BDMP modeling only safety hazards

Fig. 2. BDMP modeling safety and security hazards

We consider in a second stage security-related events that may lead to the same undesirable event: a burglar can attack the person in the house to get the combination of a safe. The burglar can enter the house directly if the door is unlocked or he can force it if it is locked. We give in Fig. 2 the BDMP model covering both safety and security hazards. The Petri net models the fact that the door can be initially locked or unlocked with a probability of 0.5 for each alternative. Initially, a token is placed in p1. This token enables to activate at t=0 the transition *locked door* and at t > 0, the token is definitively either in place *locked* or in place *unlocked*. The Petri leaf *door locked* (resp. *door unlocked*) is true when there is a token in the *locked* (resp. *unlocked*) place (this is ensured through a non-graphical link between Petri leaves and the places).

Using the FigSeq tool we calculate for one month of mission time, the events realization probabilities (Pr) based on an estimation of the probabilistic param-

Table 4. Scenarios probabilities when the door is locked/unlocked

	Pr(attack scenario)	Pr(fire and impossible escape)	Pr(person integrity affected)
Locked	7.06e-02	7.85e-04	7.14e-02
Unlocked	7.06e-01	0	7.06e-01

eters of each BDMP leaf (fire estimated once a year, attack estimated once per 6 months, Pr(*forced door*)=0.1 and Pr(*door impossible to open*)=0.01). These parameters were chosen arbitrarily. The purpose of this example is not to give realistic estimates, but rather to show the reasoning. Results show that the probability of affecting the person integrity increases from 4.17e-4 when considering only safety hazards to 0.388 when considering additionally the attack scenario.

We give in Tab. 4 the probability of respectively the attack scenario, the accidental scenario (*fire and impossible escape*) and the top event (*person integrity affected*) in cases when the door is kept locked and when it is kept unlocked. The antagonism between safety and security is quantitatively verified: the probability of the attack scenario is lower when the door is locked while the accidental scenario is not possible when the door is unlocked. However, we can see that the top event probability is clearly higher when the door is unlocked. The optimal decision under the assumptions made here (this includes four parameters: the frequency of fire and attacks, and the probabilities of a burglar forcing the door and of the house occupant not being able to evacuate if needed) is to lock the door. If the parameters were radically different (house occupant is an old and blind heavy smoker, living in a very secure district, next to a police station), the quantification of the same model could lead to unlock the door.

Although elementary, this example shows the importance of considering safety and security together in the risk evaluation phase in order to identify possible conflicts between the two disciplines. Using BDMP we can not only identify the conflicts between safety and security measures, but also help choosing the most appropriate combination of security and safety measures for minimizing the global risk.

4.2   Example of Synergetic Interdependencies

We give in Section 5 a detailed case study inspired from the industrial domain. We do the same kind of analysis on this complex system in order to demonstrate possible synergies between safety and security measures.

5   Case Study

5.1   System Architecture Description

The system considered in the sequel is a hypothetical cyber-physical system used to transport a polluting substance. It is composed of a pipeline equipped with pumps used to force the stream and valves used to allow or block the stream. Throughout the pipeline sensors measure the pressure and flow inside each section of the pipeline. Each piece of equipment (pump or valve) is controlled by a Remote Terminal Unit (RTU) that communicates with a remote Control Center (CC). The tasks of the RTU are to:

- Collect data from sensors used to measure the pressure and the flow in the vicinity of each pump and valve;
- Control the operation/speed of pumps and the opening/closing of valves;
- Send data and alarm signals to the CC and receive instructions from it;
- Exchange with neighboring RTUs pressure measures and shutdown signals.

Safety requires RTUs to verify that the pressure in the pipeline does not exceed a maximum value P_{max}. Each RTU also calculates the pressure difference between the neighboring RTU and its own sensors: $\Delta P = |P_n - P_{n-1}|$. If ΔP exceeds a threshold ΔP_{max}, the RTU sends an alarm signal to the CC, which sends back an order to all RTUs to stop pumps and close valves. In addition the RTU sends a shutdown signal to its neighboring RTUs. The pressure difference threshold is generally reached when the pipeline is broken; this implies that the pressure measured before the break is too high compared to the pressure measured after the break, which makes the pressure difference large. A safety requirement enables each RTU to stop the pump or close the valve it controls when ΔP_{max} is reached or when it receives a shutdown order from other RTU without waiting for CC instructions. This action is called later the "Reflex Action" and provides redundancy with CC instructions, with a higher priority. The architecture of the case study is given in Fig. 3. We assume RTUs are locally installed on pumps and valves and communicate with them via a wired link. Sensors which are relatively distant and scattered all through the pipeline use a wireless link to communicate with RTUs. Supposing that the pipeline is hundreds of kilometers long and that it is a hundred kilometers distant from the CC, we assume that communication is ensured by a GSM network. The industrial protocols used are Modbus/TCP for RTU-CC communication, Modbus/RTU for inter-RTUs communication and WirelessHART for sensor-RTU communication. These assumptions will be used later to estimate security events parameters.

5.2   System Modeling

The BDMP supporting a risk analysis of this system is given in Fig. 5. It models the different scenarios that lead to pollution of the environment (the top event). There are three types of possible scenarios: attack scenarios, accidental scenarios or hybrid scenarios. The first type of scenarios is a successful attack initiated by a malicious person, the second type is based on mere accidental events like failures of the system's components and the third type is a combination of attacks and components failures. This latter type best characterizes the possible interactions between safety and security events.

As explained in Section 3, BDMP use hierarchical reasoning in order to cover all the possible scenarios. The top event: pollution can be realized if and only

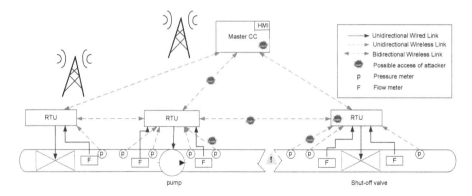

Fig. 3. Architecture of the case study

if the pipeline breaks and the protection system fails to react. The protection system refers to the detection of the pipeline break by RTUs and the system shutdown either thanks to the reflex action or by orders sent by the CC. The protection system can fail to react for two different reasons: either it was deactivated before the break by an attacker, or it accidentally does not work.

This reasoning corresponds to the top level of the BDMP. The gate named *attack protection syst then pipeline break* is a "PAND" gate, which becomes true only if its left input is true before the right input becomes true. If an attack is perpetrated after the pipeline break, this will not worsen the situation.

The Attack Scenario: We suppose that attacks for such an industrial infrastructure follow a Poisson process with an occurrence rate of once every 3 years. We assume that in the case of this pipeline, such a value can be defined based on the organization security historical data and on intelligence reports. The attack scenario starts by deactivating the protection system before provoking the pipeline breach by using the water-hammer phenomenon (closing suddenly a valve downstream when high velocity associated with a high pressure is propagating in the pipeline which causes a shock). In the attack preparation phase the attacker starts by getting access to the SCADA system: either by taking control over the CC (physically or remotely) or accessing physically to the RTU or creeping into the network via the communication link (between the RTU and the CC or between the sensors and the RTU). Secondly, the attacker must understand the system operation in order to be able to deactivate the protection system. Depending on what the attacker has gained access to, he will act differently in order to deactivate the protection. The attack steps in this phase will be quasi instantaneous (ISE security leaves) as the attacker has previously understood the system operation and is able to manipulate it. In order to deactivate the reflex action of RTUs the attacker can simply jam the communication between the RTUs so that the pipeline breach cannot be detected. The house event *No reflex action* models the existence or the non-existence of the reflex action as a safety measure implemented locally in the system; this leaf is set either to true or to false prior to any quantification. After preparing for his attack, the attacker is ready to break the pipeline with a water-hammer by provoking a high pumping pressure in the pipeline and closing suddenly the valve downstream which causes a pressure surge able to create a breach at the weakest point in the pipeline.

The Accidental Scenario: In this case pollution is caused if the pipeline breaks accidentally then the protection system fails to react. The protection failure is realized in two cases: no instructions given by the RTU or the on-demand failure of the equipments (valves and pumps) to react properly. The first case is realized if the RTU fails or if it doesn't react which implies that it receives no instruction from CC and it does not activate its reflex action. Safety leaves of the BDMP detail the accidental events leading to such scenarios.

The Hybrid Scenario: This scenario is built up from both accidental and malicious events. We can imagine that the attacker can remotely deactivate the protection system then give up the attack because he does not succeed in creating the water hammer. Then he can just wait until the pipeline breaks accidentally instead of trying another attack. This scenario has a very low probability and supposes that the protection system deactivation is not detected until the pipeline breaks.

5.3   Qualitative and Quantitative Analysis

To make the quantification, we associate the model leaves with parameters based on the estimation of the MTTS for security events, the MTTF for safety events and the probability for instantaneous events (see Tab. 1 and Tab. 2). These parameters are estimated by security and safety experts based on the assumptions we made on the protocols and the network (see Section 5.1). We also suppose that the attacker has a minimum knowledge of SCADA systems and protocols without necessarily being an insider. These parameters are marked on the model in Fig. 5 with comment boxes.

Results given below were obtained with FigSeq, as explained in Section 4.1. Based on the given parameters the pollution probability is estimated to about 2e-2 for a mission time of one year. We can see that attack scenarios are situated at the top of the list of scenarios. The most probable attack scenario given in Tab. 5 is the one in which the attacker gets access to the RTU, takes control over the equipments and sends false data to the CC and to the neighboring RTUs.

We give in Tab. 6 the probability of the most probable attack sequences according to the type of access. We infer from results that the RTU is the most critical and vulnerable component in our case study. Being left on the pipeline with little physical protection it is easy to attack. These results are of course based on the estimations we give to parameters, for instance we supposed that sensors communicate with RTUs using the WirelessHART protocol which is a secured protocol using authentication and encryption. The attacker must first find a vulnerability before gaining access to the communication link. On the other hand, the Modbus/TCP protocol used for RTUs and CC communication is not secured and data can be clearly read once the attacker accesses the GSM network.

Table 5. Most probable attack scenario from the BDMP model

Transitions		MT Proba	Contrib.
Name	Rate		
failF(attack occurence)	2.28e-5		
aa success(access to RTU)	0.0208		
aa success(understand syst operation)	0.0208	1.31e-2	0.67
ise nd real(falsify data sent to CC)	0.6		
ise nd real(falsify data sent to other RTUs)	0.6		
ise nd real(falsify instructions sent to equipments)	0.7		
ise nd real(high pumping pressure activation)	0.7		
ise nd real(closing valve)	0.7		

Table 6. Probability of attack sequences according to the type of access

Type of access	RTU	CC	CL(RTU & CC)	CL(sensors & RTU))
Pr(pollution)	1.31e-2	2.92e-3	7.85e-04	1.62e-4

The first hybrid scenario given in Tab. 7 has a probability of 4.03e-4, in which the attacker deactivates the protection system then gives up the attack before the pipeline breaks accidentally.

The first accidental scenario given in Tab. 8 appears with a probability of 1.98e-5 and consists of accidental break of the pipeline and failure of the sensors to communicate correct measures to RTUs. Redundancy among sensors and the elimination of single points of failure could be considered to prevent such accidental scenarios. Results demonstrate that the hybrid scenario is more probable than the accidental scenario. Security events accelerate very much the realization of the undesired event (pollution).

5.4 Safety and Security Interdependencies

We propose in this section to highlight the possible interdependencies between safety and security in the use case, and to illustrate how the model can be used to choose appropriate detection and reaction measures.

Mutual Reinforcement: The reflex action is a safety module implemented locally at each RTU in order to act in case of accidental pipeline break. In order to assess its influence on the system we calculate the pollution probability with and without reflex action (*No reflex action* leaf activated/deactivated). Results demonstrate that the pollution probability increases by 13 % if no reflex action is implemented at the RTUs (1.95e-2 with reflex action to 2.2e-2 without reflex action). The reflex action represents an additional barrier for the attacker to overcome. If the attacker causes the pipeline breach without deactivating the reflex action this latter would react to prevent pollution as the breach would be

Table 7. The most probable hybrid scenario

Transitions		MT Proba	Contrib.
Name	Rate		
failF(attack occurence)	2.28e-5		
aa success(access to RTU)	0.0208		
aa success(understand syst operation)	0.0208	4.03e-4	0.026
ise nd real(falsify data sent to CC)	0.6		
ise nd real(falsify data sent to other RTUs)	0.6		
ise nd real(falsify instructions sent to equipments)	0.7		
no realization(high pumping pressure activation)	0.3		
failF(pipe break accidentally)	1.14e-5		
failF(pipe break accidentally)	1.14e-5		

Table 8. Most probable accidental scenario

Transitions		MT Proba	Contrib.
Name	Rate		
failF(pipe break accidentally)	1.14e-5		
good(CC RTU communication lost)	0.99954	1.98e-5	1.01e-3
good(Control Center)	0.999886		
good(RTU)	0.999862		
good(faulty operator)	0.99977		
failI(faulty sensor measure)	0.00023		
good(inter RTU communication lost)	0.9993		

detected by RTUs. We can infer consequently that this safety measure reinforces the system security.

Conditional Dependency: This kind of interdependency is the most common and implies that the safety level is dependent on the security level. This is more straightforward as, generally, the attackers' goal is to cause safety accidents through compromising the system security. This interaction is illustrated in the two following situations:

- As modeled in Fig. 5 the attacker can access the system via the wireless communication link between sensors and RTUs which is more difficult when the communication is secured. In this case the attacker can manipulate data sent by the sensors to RTUs in order to deactivate the reflex action. The attacker can even exploit the normal functioning of the reflex action to cause the pipeline breach; typically send low pressure measures to the RTU controlling the pump to activate high pumping speed and then when high pressure is reached the attacker can send false low pressure measures to the RTU controlling the valve downstream. This RTU will calculate a high ΔP (high P_{n-1} received from the previous RTU and low P_n given by the attacker) and close the valve leading to a water-hammer. We remind that the reflex action is considered to have a higher priority as a safety module over CC instructions as this latter might detect inconsistencies in the RTUs measures.

– Strengthening the system security by adding detection and defense measures enhances the system safety as it contributes to the reduction of pollution probability. It is possible to include detection aspects in the BDMP model. The general idea is that each attack step can be detected at various moments: when it begins, during its progress, when it succeeds, or after completion. Whenever detection occurs, this changes all success rates or probabilities for attack steps which are still to be completed. The only thing the analyst has to do to take detection into account in the BDMP model is to change a global option in the model and add in each security leaf the detection rate and the realization rate after detection. This does not require any change in the BDMP structure. These detection parameters are taken into account in the quantitative processing. This increases considerably the number of sequences to explore, because each scenario of the model without detection can lead to many variants with detection occurring at various stages.

In order to evaluate the efficacy of detection we have done a sensitivity analysis; the results obtained are given in Fig. 4. We first assess the pollution probability evolution in two extreme cases: without any attack and with attacks but without any detection mechanism. Then we take into account detection and response measures and compare two detection strategies. We can model in the BDMP many detection strategies and various responses for each of them; we have chosen a simple scenario in order to be able to explain it concisely. We suppose that in the so-called "good detection" strategy, the RTU attack is detected at the instant where it succeeds with a probability γ ($\gamma \in [0.5 , 0.9]$). No other detection mechanism is implemented. The reaction is the fact that the subsequent attack step becomes impossible: the attack is completely blocked. To obtain the "bad detection" strategy, one simply has to replace "RTU" by "communication link between sensors and RTUs"' in the previous description. We have chosen here to place detection measures at the beginning of the attack on the components that are most and least likely to be attacked (cf. Tab. 6).

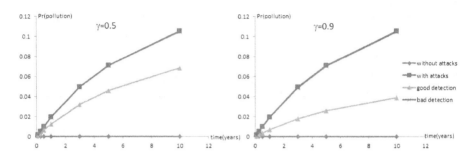

Fig. 4. Comparison of various detection strategies

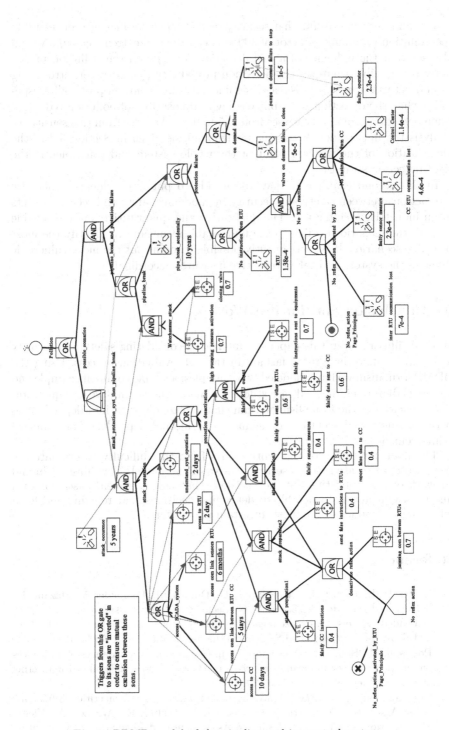

Fig. 5. BDMP model of the pipeline and its control system

We can infer from results that security related scenarios increase considerably the pollution probability (factor of 400 between the two extreme cases). We can also see that the influence of a bad detection strategy on the pollution probability is negligible whatever the detection probability (γ). However introducing a good detection strategy decreases significantly the pollution probability especially when the detection probability is high (almost 43% of pollution reduction when detection probability passes from 0.5 to 0.9). We infer from this sensitivity analysis the importance of the qualitative analysis given in Section 5.3 in the identification of the weakest point of the whole system and consequently the right detection strategy.

In this second example we have been able to put into evidence synergetic interactions between safety and security by modeling safety and security events in an industrial architecture. The qualitative and quantitative analyzes enable to rank the scenarios leading to the undesirable event and to identify the most probable scenarios. It is consequently possible to point out the most vulnerable items in the system and take preventive measures accordingly.

6   Conclusion and Future Work

We have illustrated in this paper the interest of considering safety and security aspects in a more integrated fashion in the risk evaluation process. Using the BDMP formalism we have modeled two examples: a simple common example and a more elaborated industrial case study. Thanks to the qualitative and quantitative capacities of the formalism one can characterize different interdependencies between safety and security: antagonism, conditional dependency and mutual reinforcement.

The main limitation of this work comes from the difficulty to evaluate the parameters associated to the security leaves of the model. Therefore we intend to work on the robustness of the decisions that can be taken, based on such analyzes. Our aim it to be able to determine decisions that remain valid for a wide range of values of the most uncertain parameters.

References

1. Bieber, P., Blanquart, J.P., Descargues, G., Dulucq, M., Fourastier, Y., Hazane, E., Julien, M., Leonardon, L., Sarouille, G.: Security and safety assurance for aerospace embedded systems. In: Proceedings of the 6th International Conference on Embedded Real Time Software and Systems, Toulouse, France, pp. 1–10 (2012)
2. Bouissou, M., Bon, J.-L.: A new formalism that combines advantages of fault-trees and markov models: Boolean logic driven markov processes. Reliability Engineering & System Safety 82(2), 149–163 (2003)
3. Chiaradonna, S., Di Giandomenico, F., Lollini, P.: Case study on critical infrastructures: Assessment of electric power systems. In: Wolter, K., Avritzer, A., Vieira, M., van Moorsel, A. (eds.) Resilience Assessment and Evaluation of Computing Systems, pp. 365–390. Springer, Heidelberg (2012)

 4. Eames, D.P., Moffett, J.D.: The integration of safety and security requirements. In: Felici, M., Kanoun, K., Pasquini, A. (eds.) SAFECOMP 1999. LNCS, vol. 1698, pp. 468–480. Springer, Heidelberg (1999)
 5. Hunter, B.: Integrating safety and security into the system lifecycle. In: Improving Systems and Software Engineering Conference (ISSEC), Canberr, Australia, p. 147 (August 2009)
 6. Kornecki, A., Subramanian, N., Zalewski, J.: Studying interrelationships of safety and security for software assurance in cyber-physical systems: Approach based on bayesian belief networks. In: 2013 Federated Conference on Computer Science and Information Systems (FedCSIS), pp. 1393–1399 (2013)
 7. Koscher, K., Czeskis, A., Roesner, F., Patel, S., Kohno, T., Checkoway, S., McCoy, D., Kantor, B., Anderson, D., Shacham, H., Savage, S.: Experimental security analysis of a modern automobile. In: 2010 IEEE Symposium on Security and Privacy (SP), pp. 447–462 (2010)
 8. Kriaa, S., Bouissou, M., Pietre-Cambacedes, L.: Modeling the stuxnet attack with BDMP: towards more formal risk assessments. In: 2012 7th International Conference on Risk and Security of Internet and Systems (CRiSIS), pp. 1–8 (2012)
 9. Nai Fovino, I., Masera, M., De Cian, A.: Integrating cyber attacks within fault trees. Reliability Engineering & System Safety 94(9), 1394–1402 (2009)
10. Novak, T., Gerstinger, A.: Safety- and security-critical services in building automation and control systems. IEEE Transactions on Industrial Electronics 57(11), 3614–3621 (2010)
11. Pietre-Cambacedes, L., Bouissou, M.: Beyond attack trees: Dynamic security modeling with boolean logic driven markov processes (BDMP). In: Dependable Computing Conference (EDCC), 2010 European, pp. 199–208 (2010)
12. Pietre-Cambacedes, L., Bouissou, M.: Modeling safety and security interdependencies with BDMP (boolean logic driven markov processes). In: IEEE International Conference on Systems Man and Cybernetics (SMC), pp. 2852–2861 (2010)
13. Pietre-Cambacedes, L., Bouissou, M.: Cross-fertilization between safety and security engineering. Reliability Engineering & System Safety 110, 110–126 (2013)
14. Pietre-Cambacedes, L., Deflesselle, Y., Bouissou, M.: Security modeling with BDMP: from theory to implementation. In: 2011 Conference on Network and Information Systems Security (SAR-SSI), pp. 1–8 (2011)
15. Pietre-Cambacedes, L., Bouissou, M.: Attack and defense dynamic modeling with BDMP (extended version). Tech. rep., Technical Report, Telecom ParisTech (2010)
16. Pietre-Cambacedes, L., Chaudet, C.: The SEMA referential framework: Avoiding ambiguities in the terms "security" and "safety". International Journal of Critical Infrastructure Protection 3(2), 55–66 (2010)
17. Smith, J., Russell, S., Looi, M.: Security as a safety issue in rail communications. In: Proceedings of the 8th Australian Workshop on Safety Critical Systems and Software, SCS 2003, vol. 33, pp. 79–88. Australian Computer Society, Inc., Australia (2003)
18. Steiner, M., Liggesmeyer, P.: Combination of safety and security analysis-finding security problems that threaten the safety of a system. In: Proceedings of Workshop DECS (ERCIM/EWICS Workshop on Dependable Embedded and Cyber-physical Systems) of the 32nd International Conference on Computer Safety, Reliability and Security (2013)
19. Sun, M., Mohan, S., Sha, L., Gunter, C.: Addressing safety and security contradictions in cyber-physical systems. In: 1st Workshop on Future Directions in Cyber-Physical Systems Security (CPSS 2009), Newark, United States (2009)

A Pragmatic Approach towards Safe and Secure Medical Device Integration

Christoph Woskowski

Zühlke Engineering GmbH
Landshuter Allee 12
80637 München, Germany
christoph.woskowski@zuehlke.com

Abstract. Compared to other safety-related domains, harmonizing efforts regarding electronic device integration and interaction – in terms of real-time and remote control – are conducted less ambitious in the medical device sector. There are a couple of reasons for this restrained progress. Traditionally, medical devices are either both small-sized and self-sufficient or they are highly integrated parts of a complete setup provided by one vendor. Especially when equipping critical care facilities such as intensive care units, producer and brand diversity is low, whereas the pressure of competition is high. The results are proprietary communication and control solutions when connecting devices in order to interact. On the other hand, any modern hospital heavily relies on highly available critical medical devices providing and sharing data but also on confidentiality and integrity of vitally important information.

This paper discusses a pragmatic risk-based approach to handle integration problems facing the current situation described above, while focusing on future development challenges. The background of this paper is a project for defining a safe and secure integration interface that – open to integration partners – enables to monitor and remote-control a critical medical device.

Keywords: medical device integration, remote control, safety-critical, cybersecurity, risk-based approach.

1   Introduction

Who bears the risk of connecting medical devices with each other or with other hospital IT?

In an increasingly connected environment, underdeveloped harmonization regarding medical device interaction and integration leads to incompatibilities as well as to increased safety and security risks. Those risks become evident at boundaries between two or more devices from different vendors to be integrated. Because of the unavailability of an obligatory standard – IEC 80001-1 [1] is not harmonized – the responsibilities are not sufficiently defined. There are commonly accepted standardized protocols and interchange formats like DICOM [2]. But those are only applicable for special niches like storing and transmitting information in medical imaging.

A. Bondavalli and F. Di Giandomenico (Eds.):   SAFECOMP 2014, LNCS 8666, pp. 342–353, 2014.
© Springer International Publishing Switzerland 2014

However, it is not possible to prevent electronic devices containing a communication or connectivity option from getting directly or indirectly connected to an IP-based network. Off-the-shelf solutions are available for most interfaces and protocols, enabling conversion to Ethernet, WiFi or GSM. Many of those adapters even are equipped with a – very often vulnerable – web server, making any attached device available and thus attackable via the internet. Any present-day vendor producing critical electronic devices would be well advised to consider this possibility.

Of course in today's critical care units and other vital parts of a modern hospital, there are already a lot of devices that innately are equipped with Ethernet or wireless interfaces (WiFi, Bluetooth, GSM etc.) and by those means are connected to protected parts – so called VLANs – of the hospital IT network. Version 3.0 of the IEC 60601-1 standard (IEC 60601-1:2005) [3] requires critical medical networks to have no physical connection with other parts of the hospital network. This apparently has changed, since the newest version 3.1 of IEC 60601-1 (IEC 60601-1:2005 + Cor.:2006 + Cor.:2007 + A1:2012) [4] does not contain this passage anymore. Actually, there can be no guarantee, since there is no assurance of physical disconnection – not in case of an intended wired-only solution and even more so in the wireless case. Still many vendors developing today's critical care systems seem to be unaware of the fact, that internal or external proprietary communication protocols and interfaces might get exposed and be accessible from outside a considered closed system. It is not even necessary to think in terms of hackers or attackers. Just unintended "flooding" of a critical considered-private communication channel, for example caused by a misconfigured Ethernet switch or a private device carelessly brought into the network might have an impact on availability and integrity of vital data and services – with potentially fatal consequences.

Against this background the paper proposes a pragmatic, risk-based approach towards safe and secure critical medical device interfaces:

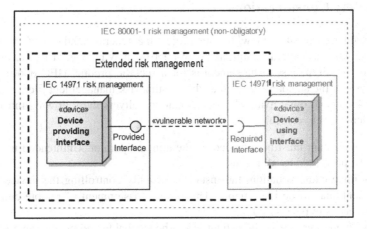

Fig. 1. Proposed extended risk management

Since device manufacturers have to take increased responsibility for the interoperability and external interfaces of their critical products, they might do so by extending the required IEC 14971 - compliant risk management [5] beyond device boundaries. The extended risk management covers interface safety, interface usage and network security aspects as well as definition and application of appropriate risk mitigation techniques (see **Fig. 1**).

2   Initial Situation

The critical medical equipment considered here, is a successful product in the intensive care market and predominantly being sold as stand-alone device. It is capable of moving automatically in preprogrammed ways into predefined positions. The human operator is able to operate the device using the control panel mounted on the device's casing as well as via cable remote control and wireless remote control.

Alternatively, the device can be part of a larger system. As a deeply integrated component, it is then controlled by an external control unit and being moved together and in coordination with other intensive care equipment. In this case, the whole system of systems is being sold as one product of an integrator or of a different medical device vendor. The only role left for the original producer of the critical component is to be junior integration partner and Original Equipment Manufacturer (OEM) respectively.

Considering this, the producer and vendor of the moveable medical device decided to develop and provide a generic integration interface – open to all integration partners. Thus, besides continuing the OEM business, this enable the producer to present the own brand as well as the own product as equal partner in one-to-one integration solutions.

3   Safety Considerations

From a regulatory point of view, for this project the general standard IEC 60601-1 is applicable, whereas general requirements of 60601-1 may be overwritten or bypassed by specific requirements in the standards for a specific product (IEC 60601-2-XX). The analysis of the standards as well as the existing risk management file (as required by IEC 14971) and other available documentation delivers the following functions to be considered safety-critical:

- Every movement must be intended by the human operator. Unintended movement has to be prevented by all means.
- In any imaginable situation, the instance currently controlling the device and its movements has to be identifiable. Thus a clear assignment of remote controlling devices needs to be ensured.
- In case of an emergency, the patient has to be reachable and positionable for treatment. Thus even in a single-fault condition it has to be possible to return the device into an emergency position.

The safety concept of the stand-alone variant of the critical medical device already takes those safety-critical functions into account. Via the control panel mounted on the device's casing – exhibiting highest control priority and diverse power and communication sources – the human operator is always able to stop and overrule any movement. Additionally, the operator can always return the device into a position, which enables emergency treatment of the intensive care patient. Several implemented measures make sure, that the system in itself is single fault proof against unwanted movement. Every remote control is clearly assigned to the device it controls by applying a pairing procedure. A range- and direction-restricting mechanism ensures line-of-sight between the human operator using a remote control and the moveable intensive care equipment.

With respect to the whole system safety, the integration interface to be developed must not undermine the safety concept stated above. Although a separate risk management file will be generated for the integration interface in order to provide necessary input for the risk management process of an integration partner (as required by IEC 60601-1 and IEC 80001-1), there is no separation of risk management of the critical device and its external interface. Quite contrary, the interface has to rely on and support the already implemented risk measures as well as to use concepts similar to the proven solutions. Since a new interface always means to open at least parts of a system and in case of remote control even to give up and lose some internal control, there is always the risk of reducing the overall system safety and security. Managing and mitigating those risks therefore has to be an essential part of the project at hand.

4   Security Considerations

Down to the present day the medical device sector lacks in specifications and legally binding standards on how to address the security question in the medical device development process. This is especially a problem for design and implementation of security-aware communication interfaces and protocols for critical medical equipment. After all, the Medical Device Directive [6] (MDD, Directive 93/42/EEC) at least demands that medical device manufacturers have to show that the applied solutions take "account of the generally acknowledged state of the art".

But what is state of the art? As a general rule – besides the directly applicable medical standards – it is the state of the scientific and technical knowledge. This explicitly includes draft versions, not yet harmonized standards and guidelines by the authorities – especially if already applied by comparable products. Referring to its own guidelines, the American Food and Drug Administration (FDA), which is also in authority for the medical device sector, states that: "Although guidance documents do not legally bind FDA, they represent the agency's current thinking. Therefore, FDA employees may depart from guidance documents only with appropriate justification and supervisory concurrence." [7] In order to find some guidance and hints on how to address security in the project at hand – considering its objective to develop a generic and open integration interface for a critical medical device – the following documents and statements have been considered relevant:

- *Draft ISO 80001-1:2009, Introduction:* "The manufacturer of a medical device intended to be incorporated into an IT-network might need to provide information about the medical device that is necessary to allow the responsible organization to manage risk according to this standard. [...] risk management should be applied to address the following key properties appropriate for the IT-network incorporating a medical device: [...] – data and system security." [1]
- *Draft ISO 80001-1:2009, chapter 3.5:* "For a medical device whose intended use includes connection to an IT-network, the medical device manufacturer shall provide [...] the technical specifications of the network connection of the medical device including security specifications" [1]
- *FDA draft guidance (Nonbinding Recommendations) "Content of Premarket Submissions for Management of Cybersecurity in Medical Devices", chapter 4:* "Ensure secure data transfer to and from the device, and when appropriate, use accepted methods for encryption" [8]

The above mentioned draft guidance released in June 2013 by the FDA, also demands that medical device manufacturers should define and document their cybersecurity risk analysis and management plan as part of the required risk analysis. Although the IEC 14971 risk management process never is mentioned explicitly, the idea of extending the required analysis towards security-induced hazardous situations obviously would satisfy the intention of the FDA guidance.

5   Non-functional Requirements

Non-functional requirements generally have the greatest impact on architecture and design of a system or a sub-component like an external interface. During the requirements elicitation phase those anchor points are collected and documented with adequate care. The following listing displays the "guardrail" of the integration interface architecture and thus also influences the available options for risk mitigation, as stated later on:

- **Safety:** The interface must fulfill the general (IEC 60601-1) and product specific (IEC 60601-2-XX) safety requirements: prevent unwanted movement, ensure clear assignment of remote controlling devices and enable emergency positioning for patient treatment.
- **Correctness:** The interface should handle the possibility of multiple simultaneous and concurrent attempts to control the (movement of) the critical device.
- **Reliability:** The interface should provide either real-time control of the devices' movements or it should fail gracefully without affecting the rest of the system.
- **Usability:** Design and documentation of the interface should enable fast implementation of integration solutions containing the critical moveable device.
- **Efficiency / Scalability:** The communication protocol should support narrow-band serial connections, unreliable wireless connections as well as broadband Ethernet.
- **Maintainability:** In order to facilitate integration and support, the communication protocol should have a human readable and comprehensible format.

- **Portability:** Since parts of the communication protocol will have to be implemented on client side, too, standard solutions, platform independent languages and libraries shall be used.
- **Security:** A pragmatic risk-based approach has to ensure that the implemented measures for mitigating security risks are as comprehensive and effective as possible but only as complex, limiting and restrictive as necessary.

6   Adapted Risk Analysis

Any risk-based approach has to start with identifying the potential risks a critical system may be posing to its environment and especially to human beings. In the medical device sector, like in other safety-related domains, the identification and analysis regarding risks is a task for domain experts. These specialists can rely on their expertise, their experience as well as on available standards and guidelines. It is advantageous though, to additionally consult safety experts from other domains, but also security experts, especially if security aspects have not been addressed before.

Following the adapted IEC 14971 workflow describing risk management activities [**Fig. 2**], intended use and safety-critical functions of a medical device are confronted with one or more foreseeable hazards (potential sources of harm) as well as one or more corresponding hazardous situations (circumstances of exposure to hazards).

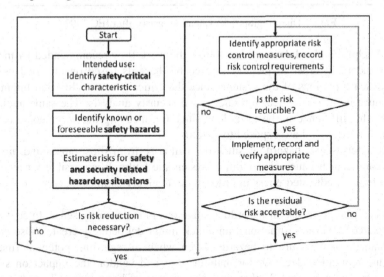

Fig. 2. Detail of the adapted IEC 14971 workflow (changes in **bold**)

The risks regarding a hazardous situation are finally expressed by the two components, severity and probability of occurrence of harm (injury or damage to the health of people, damage to property / environment). If this combination and thus the risks are unacceptable, then risk mitigation is required. Afterwards, severity and probability are estimated again in order to evaluate whether after applying mitigating measures risks are acceptable or not.

In most cases it is not possible to exactly measure the risk or its components. Instead qualitative severity levels (negligible, minor, serious, critical and catastrophic) and semi-quantitative probability levels (frequent, probable, occasional, remote and improbable) are used [**Fig. 3**]. It is the task of the domain experts to assign the appropriate attributes based on their knowledge and experience. Especially considering security risks, this is a very difficult task, since not only reliable statistical numbers are missing but also because of lack of experience.

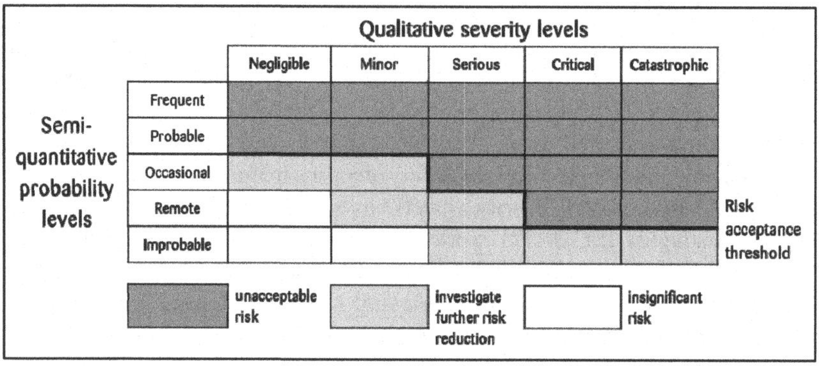

		Qualitative severity levels				
		Negligible	Minor	Serious	Critical	Catastrophic
Semi-quantitative probability levels	Frequent					
	Probable					
	Occasional					
	Remote					
	Improbable					

Risk acceptance threshold

	unacceptable risk		investigate further risk reduction		insignificant risk

Fig. 3. Three-region risk evaluation matrix after IEC 14971

It is still helpful and valid though, to follow the work flow recommended by the IEC 14971 standard in order to identify foreseeable hazards based on intended use and safety-critical functions of the system, since the critical functionality that might possibly induce harm is identical for safety- and security analysis. The same applies to hazards. The difference is the hazardous situation, meaning the way people and the environment in general are exposed to hazards.

In the safety sense, hazardous situations can arise from slips, lapses and mistakes or they can occur because of random or systematic faults. It is possible for an expert to try at least an educated guess in order to qualitatively estimate severity and probability.

This is different in case of hazardous situations in the security sense. In contrast to safety-related hazardous situations, an attack might deliberately create those critical circumstances of exposure to hazards. Even when disregarding potential financial losses and reputation decrease for manufacturer and vendor, the impact on system safety cannot be neglected. In that case, the severity of harm to people and environment might be no different from a comparable safety-related incident but the probability of occurrence definitely is not the same. The probability of an unprotected or vulnerable system connected to the internet being scanned or attacked is one [9]. As already explained in the introduction, even though a critical medical system should not be connected to the internet, this is in practice hard to prevent.

Thus for the project at hand, the probability of occurrence of harm for a security-related hazardous situation – before mitigation – is considered at least medium level (occasional). This means, mitigation is required for all security-induced hazardous situations with serious, critical or catastrophic severity of harm.

7   Risk Mitigation Example

The following example illustrates the proceeding of risk analysis based on the adapted IEC 14971 workflow [**Fig. 2**]. The example starts with the identification of one intended use, specifically a single safety-critical function: the prevention of unwanted movement, or – formulated in the positive sense – the maintenance of the intended and adjusted position. The corresponding hazard is the leaving of this intended and adjusted position by means of an unwanted movement.

Safety-Related Hazardous Situation. The occurrence of an unwanted movement trigger is a hazardous situation now briefly considered solely from a safety standpoint.

There are a number of corresponding circumstances imaginable – starting from operating error, over electromagnetic impact to effects of an implementation bug. Although the probability of occurrence of harm may be considered occasional or even remote – the exact values are not relevant for this example – the consequences of uncontrolled movement in an intensive care environment may range from permanent impairment or life-threatening injury of any attendant human being to the worst case of patient death. The corresponding severity level is "critical" or even "catastrophic". This indicates an unacceptable risk, so applying mitigating measures is mandatory. The following exemplary measures are already implemented by the critical device itself and thus only mentioned briefly:

- No movement can be started by a single trigger. In order to start motor activity, two independent triggers (electrical signals, protocol messages etc.) are necessary.
- A human operator has to authorize every movement before it starts and continuously as long as the movement lasts.
- Any movement trigger must be reactivated repeatedly – re-send the message or pulse the signal - in a tight interval in order to continue motor activity (keep-alive).

Quality assurance has to evaluate whether the measures taken are effective in order to mitigate risks or not.

Security-Related Hazardous Situation. The mitigation strategy for security risks in this example is more complex and requires balancing of seemingly conflicting demands and requirements. In order to demonstrate this, the following security-related hazardous situation, which is very similar to the safety-induced situation above, is used: movement triggers – unwanted by the human operator in authority – are deliberately injected into a valid connection.

Several kinds of attacks could realize the injection of a critical protocol message, among them the well-known man-in-the-middle attack and the replay attack.

The former is necessary in order to tap or hijack a valid connection or session and the latter enables to capture and resend valid protocol messages – with potentially catastrophic outcome (severity).

Since all security-induced hazardous situations have been assigned a probability of occurrence of "occasional" (see chapter Risk Analysis) the resulting risk is unacceptable and requires mitigation.

So how does a possible mitigation strategy look like? Considering both mentioned attacks man-in-the-middle and replay, it is noteworthy, that replay is not possible without tapping and hijacking the connection first. One part of the risk-mitigation strategy would be to hinder capturing of a session or connection. There is no way to completely eliminate the possibility of a man-in-the-middle attack though, since it is part of the interface's function to facilitate an Ethernet connection. Ethernet inherently allows traffic-monitoring for any connected participant and even re-routing of network traffic.

One obvious solution for protecting communication over an insecure or vulnerable channel against eavesdropping or capturing would be encryption. The FDA even encourages encrypting data transfer to and from a medical device [8].

Encrypted communication though contradicts with the maintainability requirement of a human readable and comprehensible protocol format. Additionally, it does not solve the problem of establishing communication with the correct partner in the first place. And finally, it is not necessary to hide the communication contents, since no patient health information deserving protection will be transmitted.

Actually the first part of this security risk mitigation strategy only has to make sure, that communication solely is established and maintained with the correct partner and that any protocol message can be unambiguously correlated to its source. In the security domain it is best practice to use standard- and proven solutions to common problems. The proven solution for the current problem is standard authentication.

Authentication is the process of one communication partner proving its identity to the other one, in this case of the controlling system to the one to be controlled. There are different ways for proving an identity to a remote instance. Although a hard-coded identifier might suffice in order to authenticate the external system claiming control of the critical moveable device, there are some downsides:

- How to transfer a secret ID using a human readable protocol?
- How to add new or remove invalid external systems to / from the list of accepted and well-known devices (scalability)?
- How to ensure line-of-sight of controlling system and controlled device (as claimed by the critical devices' safety concept)?

There are also already proven solutions for these problems. A common HTTP scheme based on a Hash Message Authentication Code (HMAC, RFC 2104) [10] may be used for authentication.

Instead of a hard-coded identifier, a so called "shared secret" enables to prove the identity of the requesting device. Like for example in a pairing process of Bluetooth devices or when using a security token for logging into a company network, a periodically generated PIN is displayed on one device to be entered manually at the other device.

This shared secret (the PIN) is then used to calculate the HMAC for each message to be sent. This process based on a hash algorithm is comparable to calculating a checksum that includes both message and secret key. As a side effect, using HMAC also enables to detect manipulation of the message content. Since the output of the HMAC algorithm in this case fulfills the same function as a signature, the whole process of calculating and adding a HMAC to a message might be seen as "signing" the message.

The HMAC solution enables authentication even for a human-readable message format, is scalable using a generated shared secret and enforces a line-of-sight at least during connection establishment (reading and manually entering the PIN code). Thus it fulfills the first part of the risk-mitigation strategy – it complicates capturing of a session or connection and thus the so-called man-in-the-middle attack. It is not able to eliminate the possibility though, since brute force or social engineering methods might still enable to determine the shared secret. In the end, the mitigating measure makes it hard to generate a valid protocol message from scratch in order to inject it into an existing connection.

A replay attack is still possible though, without limitation. An attacker with access to the corresponding network is able to capture a valid and correctly signed movement command and to inject copies of it (replay) into the same ongoing communication.

A proven solution for hindering replay attacks is called "salting". An ever-changing factor like a timer, a continuous index or counter (the "salt") added to the secret key (PIN) used by the HMAC algorithm, makes every signature quasi-unique. Even for an identical message contents the calculated HMAC – and thus the "signature" of the message – differs and thus enables to detect and handle untimely or copied messages.

Thus the final mitigation strategy in this example has three major components:

- A shared secret enables to prove and validate the identity of an external system.
- A signature-like mechanism (HMAC) ensures authenticity of received messages.
- "Salting" of the generated signature enables the detection of copied messages.

This example solution only uses proven and standard mechanisms as advocated by security best practices.

8   Related Work

There are already a number of approaches towards medical device integration and interoperability. Starting an integration project, available standardized solutions of course would be the first choice for implementation. Because of their different focus on mere imaging and medical data exchange, some standards like DICOM [2] and HL7 [11] are not suitable for remote and real-time control of critical systems, though. Arney et al. [12] propose an Open Source middleware solution – following ASTM F2761-09(2013) [13] and ISO/IEEE 11073 [14] design and architecture principles – for solving interoperability problems of critical medical devices. The ISO/IEEE 11073 medical device communication standards directly address interoperability problems. Because of an inherent complexity, lack of easily adaptable reference implementations and strong references to out-of-date technologies (infrared wireless) most vendors did not adopt the ISO/IEEE 11073 standards so far [15]. The "Design Pillars for Successful Interoperability" presented by Arney et al. [12] on the other hand strengthen the argument for establishing a standardized solution.

Other generic solutions – such as the application of SOA-principles (Service Oriented Architecture) for medical device integration [15, 16] – as well are costly to implement and hard to establish as a standard by a single vendor. It is possible though, to adopt parts of the underlying standard technology; for example XML as messaging format.

Kühn et al. [17] suggest a risk based approach for bridging the gap between the responsibilities of different medical device vendors according to IEC 14971 in case of an integrated solution. In compliance with (to be harmonized) IEC 80001-1 the integrator / clinic operator performs a gap analysis based on the risk management files of the manufacturers. The deployment of the above proposed extended risk management [**Fig. 1**] by all involved vendors would help to minimize the gap a priori.

9   Conclusion

According to IEC 60601-1 and IEC 80001-1 it is the responsibility of the medical device manufacturer to provide information and input to the integrator in order to facilitate the overall risk analysis, which is required when integrating a critical medical device into a larger system of systems. Only delegating or forwarding the integration risks though puts a heavy burden on the partner who is responsible for the integration. If additional risk mitigating measures are required and to be implemented by the integration partner, the costs might outweigh the benefits or it might not even be possible to implement required measures outside of the critical device.

The presented example shows that it is beneficial for a medical device manufacturer to think in a risk-based way about interoperability and integration during device development or alternatively in a separate device integration interface project. Measures that can be applied during development and within extended boundaries and responsibilities of the device and its external interfaces may reduce risks and thus costs for an integrator. Although some measures (like HMAC-based authentication) will have to be implemented by the connected systems too, the usage of proven and standard solutions and libraries reduces the effort considerably.

The example also shows that it is possible to take a risk-based approach towards security, especially if security vulnerabilities also pose a safety risk for patient and personnel. In this sense, the described solution already complies with a draft version of an FDA guideline, presumably to be accepted in the near future.

Although many of the presented technical aspects are indeed very specific and form in a sense a proprietary solution – developed and maintained by one vendor –, the pragmatic approach of extending risk management beyond the currently required boundaries are a generic concept. Also, for many safety-related products it might be beneficial to consider security vulnerabilities to be a safety threat that can be explicitly addressed by the overall risk management process.

References

1. IEC 80001-1 Ed. 1.0, Application of Risk Management for IT-Networks incorporating Medical Devices - Part 1: Roles, responsibilities and activities. IEC Geneva (2010)
2. Digital Imaging and Communications in Medicine (DICOM), Part 1: Introduction and Overview, National Electrical Manufacturers Association (2011)
3. IEC 60601-1:2005 Ed. 3.0, Medical electrical equipment - Part 1: General requirements for basic safety and essential performance, IEC Geneva (2005)
4. IEC 60601-1:2005 + Cor. :2006 + Cor. :2007 + A1:2012 Ed. 3.1, Medical electrical equipment - Part 1: General requirements for basic safety and essential performance, IEC Geneva (2012)
5. IEC 14971 Ed. 2.0, Medical Devices: Application of Risk Management to Medical Devices, IEC Geneva (2007)
6. Council Directive 93/42/EEC of 14 June 1993 concerning medical devices, Official Journal of the European Communities 1993., L169
7. Code of Federal Regulations (CFR) Title 21, § 10.115 (d) (3), U.S. Office of the Federal Register (2000)
8. FDA draft guidance "Content of Premarket Submissions for Management of Cybersecurity in Medical Devices", U.S. Food and Drug Administration (2013)
9. Zeng, Y., Coffey, D., Viega, J.: How Vulnerable are Unprotected Machines on the Internet?, Passive and Active Measurement (PAM) Proceedings (2014)
10. Krawczyk, H., Bellare, M., R. Canetti, HMAC: Keyed-Hashing for Message Authentication, RFC 2104 (1997)
11. Hettinger, B. J., Brazile, R. P., Health Level Seven (HL7): standard for healthcare electronic data transmissions. Comput. Nurs. 12(1): 13–16 (1994)
12. Arney D., Plourde J., Schrenker R.,Mattegunta P., Whitehead S.F., Goldman J.M., Design Pillars for Medical Cyber-Physical System Middleware, In Medical Cyber Physical Systems Workshop, MCPS (2014)
13. ASTM F2761-09(2013). Medical Devices and Medical Systems – Essential safety requirements for equipment comprising the patient-centric integrated clinical environment (ICE) – Part 1: General requirements and conceptual model. http://www.astm.org/Standards/F2761.htm
14. ISO/IEEE 11073, Health informatics - Medical / health device communication standards, ISO Geneva (2006)
15. Pöhlsen S., Entwicklung einer Service-orientierten Architektur zur vernetzten Kommunikation zwischen medizinischen Geräten, Systemen und Applikationen, Dissertation, Universität zu Lübeck (2010)
16. Mauro C., Serviceorientierte Integration medizinischer Geräte, Dissertation, Technische Universität München (2012)
17. Kühn F., Leucker M., Mildner A., OR.NET – Approaches for Risk Analysis and Measures of Dynamically Interconnected Medical Devices, In Medical Cyber Physical Systems Workshop, MCPS (2014)

Author Index